DATE DUE

JUL 1 8 2012		

D1242175

NOV

Swaggart

Ann Rowe Seaman

Swaggart

THE
UNAUTHORIZED
BIOGRAPHY
OF AN
AMERICAN
EVANGELIST

CONTINUUM • NEW YORK

1999

The Continuum Publishing Company
370 Lexington Avenue, New York, NY 10017

Printed in the United States of America

Library of Congress Cataloging in Publication Data

Seaman, Ann Rowe.
    Swaggart : the unauthorized biography of an American evangelist /
Ann Rowe Seaman.
        p.   cm.
    Includes bibliographical references and index.
    ISBN 0-8264-1117-7
    1. Swaggart, Jimmy.   2. Evangelists—United States Biography.
I. Title.
BV3785.S84S43   1999
269'.2'092—dc21
    [B]   99-32595
                                                                   CIP

To Gary, Barron, Julia, Cynthia, and Augie

Contents

Metairie, Louisiana, Fall 1987

On October 17, 1987, on a dreary strip of unplanned growth to the west of New Orleans, a man wearing jeans and a baseball cap crossed a motel parking lot paved with white gravel. He walked up to a tan late-model Lincoln Town Car and stooped down near the right front tire. He looked around, unscrewed the valve cap, bent the stem, and let the air hiss out. His shoes crunched hastily back through the gravel toward Room 12.

The parking lot belonged to the Travel Inn Motel. It sat on Airline Highway, in an area of railroad tracks and gray, vague buildings that seemed to have no fronts, a place of smokestacks, loading docks, and chain-link fences.

A message to travelers was painted on a wooden fence made of buckled white horizontal boards that spilled into the overgrown bar ditch. "Single room $18. Nice clean rooms. Day rate $10 and up." Another sign, in the window of the drive-up lobby kiosk, was more revealing:

"Positively no refunds," it said, "after 15 minutes."

The building was painted raw umber. Decaying plastic tub chairs sat outside the rooms on the cracked sidewalk—in case a guest wanted to sit in the sweltering heat and take in the sight of the parking lot dotted with mostly old, faded American cars.

Guests, always women, often chose to do so. They sat with their backs to the wall, under window panes held in place by flaking grout. The women eyed the cars that nosed into the parking lot and looked at the drivers; they cut deals with eye contact. The Travel Inn was a pragmatic place.

No one was sitting outside at mid-afternoon on Saturday, October 17, but in Room 7, Debra Arlene Murphree peeked through her curtains. Debra, a stocky, pale woman of 27 with black hair, high cheekbones, and thinly plucked eyebrows, saw the man trot away from the Lincoln Town Car and into Room 12. She knew him. He was one of her customers. He was a part-time sheriff's deputy.

She turned to another customer now sitting in the plastic padded armchair next to the other window, facing the ill-fitting green curtain that slopped over the moldy air conditioner in the window across the room. A TV was mounted near the ceiling, and the bed was utilitarian: a foam mattress and box springs on a metal frame. They had not gotten down to business yet, but the table was where he usually sat, his feet planted on the orange shag carpet. Like most of her clients, he had only a first name: Billy.

Seeing the deputy had bothered her.

"I don't like the way this looks," she said.

She got no flak from Billy. He was always nervous about the law, and invariably asked whether "the cops [are] bad" when he arrived to see her.

She let the curtain fall back into place. She had been arrested twice on prostitution charges in the past few weeks. Room 7 was her regular place and the cops knew it; she had photos of her children—aged 10, 8, and 7—on the dresser and kept personal items in the room.

Billy rose to his feet, scooped up the $20 bill he had laid on the table, and asked if she could walk down and meet him at Popeye's. The fast food place was a couple of blocks down Airline Highway.

"Wait a minute, stay put," she said.

She wanted to make an appearance at the door to assure any watching vice officer that there was nothing going on in the room. She stepped into the open doorway, wearing white jeans, a sleeveless blouse, and sandals, and looked out casually. She was very feminine, with a little gap between her front teeth and a softly Southern accent. She had two small, crude tattoos, one on each arm, and an engaging little sneery grin. She understood that men wanted to do things nice women wouldn't do with them, and that grin made it okay. She was a quiet girl who knew how to keep her mouth shut.

A light blue car drove past, turned, and came back.

Billy came up behind her and stood for a moment, looking around. He was one of her cheaper clients, but then he seldom took more than 15 or 20 minutes of her time. He hadn't even asked for intercourse, except once—which was the main reason she put up with his miserly fee. His habit was to ask her to pose in positions he found exciting; he never paid her more than $20 for this.

He was a gentleman among her customers. She liked him: "He never tried to hurt me or got loud." He was real polite and nice, always used a soft voice.

He'd asked her to have sex with another woman in front of him. That was fairly common. If he asked for oral sex, he used a condom. He was very concerned about AIDS. When he was done, he would pull up his pants and leave, dropping his money on the formica table. For the year he had been visiting her, he had never tipped her.

He stepped around her and walked to the tan Lincoln.

♦   ♦   ♦

October in Baton Rouge was crisp and sunny, with a hard blue sky and a nice breeze off the Mississippi River. Every Sunday people nudged down Bluebonnet Road by the thousands, stacking up in the special turn lanes installed to accommodate traffic at Jimmy Swaggart's overflowing Family Worship Center. He was always expected to preach a powerful sermon, and he never disappointed.

On one side of Bluebonnet Road was the bulk of the ministry Jimmy and Frances Swaggart had built up over 30 years: the big, sand-colored World Ministry Center, flanked by the flags of some of the 195 countries reached by Jimmy's telecast, and its constellation of multi-million-dollar facilities—the Family Christian Academy, the Morris Plotts Gymnasium where the award-winning basketball team of the Jimmy Swaggart Bible College played, the state-of the-art building where videotapes were edited and dubbed in a score of languages for distribution throughout the world, and the buildings that housed the huge mailing operation, the crusade team's mobile production equipment and its five 18-wheelers, the telethon operation, the travel operation, the maintenance operation, and, of course, the 7,500-seat Family Worship Center.

The Jimmy Swaggart Ministries also included a Christian elementary and high school, and an enormous mail order facility that did so much business the ministry had its own zip code. The Family Worship Center, completed in 1984, was already being planned to accommodate 2,500 more visitors. Jimmy's organization was a major employer in the city of Baton Rouge, with a payroll of over 1,500. It issued more building permits than the state of Louisiana. It took in $500,000 a day.

Two pedestrian walkways crossed to the other side of busy Bluebonnet Road, where two residence halls for the Bible college rose twelve stories each—the Minnie Bell Swaggart Hall, named after his late mother, and the D. Mark Buntain Hall, named after an admired missionary to India—plus the classrooms, fitness center, and administration building. Another new multi-story dorm was going up next to the administration building.

A strip of retail—housing the Delchamps food store, a drugstore, and shops for flowers, cards, books, haircuts, and coffee—was located next to the dorms on Bluebonnet and fed off of the clean-cut Bible college students. Like most commercial strips, it was low on architectural imagination, a scar on the fecund bayou setting behind it of tall pines and understory woods where creeks flowed and frogs sang out. But it was thriving.

The Jimmy Swaggart Ministries, 35 years ago a teenager's daydream in a dreary sharecropper village 90 miles up the Mississippi River, was in 1986 a reality, spreading physically over some of Baton Rouge's prettiest real estate and electronically over the entire planet.

In the past five years, his ministry had exploded with popularity. Called by God on the sidewalk in front of his hometown movie theater when he was eight years old, Jimmy Swaggart had, by October 1987, become one of the most popular video preachers in the world.

Born in tiny Ferriday, Louisiana, he went on the air in 1973 in Baton Rouge, when he was 38 years old, tall and solid, good-looking and full of sauce. Like the other video preachers, he stood behind a pulpit. But he did not stay behind it, puling and beseeching. His microphone was not fixed on the pulpit or pinned to his lapel. It stayed in his hand, big and phallic, eight or nine inches long, with a fat bulb on the end. He used it instinctively, clutching it sometimes with both hands, squeezing it, sometimes waving it, sometimes holding it daintily between two fingers, the pinkie crooked, when he made biting comments about wimpy, vain, blow-dried preachers who thought they could somehow get around God's wrath with their carry-on about psychology and prosperity.

In the middle of a sentence, he would whirl and stride to the piano, slip onto the bench, and begin running his thick fingers delicately up and down the keys, honky-tonk style.

This was Jimmy Lee Swaggart, prowling across the stage, shouting, whimpering, strutting, whispering, whipping out his handkerchief and mopping his face, then slapping it downward as he leaned forward from the waist, legs stiff, heels together like a Russian officer bowing to the Czar, to bear down on his audience. Soon you could catch him in Houston, Dallas, almost anywhere in the South.

By the end of 1987 his television audience was estimated by Arbitron to be more than 2.1 million per week in the U.S. His message reached millions of other souls in 143 countries. The only ministers within striking distance of his success were venerable Tulsa faith healer Oral Roberts and possibility-thinker Robert Schuller in Orange County, California.

His crusades were packed even in Catholic countries, into whose economies he pumped millions of dollars with church schools and outreach programs. He visited heads of state and dabbled in politics. Standing with Chile's president in January 1987, he denounced the former government and mentioned his friendship with President Ronald Reagan; he prayed with El Salvador's president the same month.

Jimmy had recently returned from a triumphant crusade tour in Monrovia, Liberia. He was also fresh off a write-up in the October 1987 issue of *Current Biography,* in which he was depicted as a leader, a straight shooter. Considering the mistrust by many of the burgeoning political clout of the Christian right, Jimmy came across as a statesman with credibility.

Part of that credibility came from his fearlessness in the pulpit, noted in *Current Biography:* he took on Catholics and Jews, New Age theology, Christian-Theme-Park theology, Feel-Good theology, Prosperity theology. In the fire-breathing tradition of the 19th-century circuit riders from which his denomination had sprung, he gave special attention to adultery and all its trappings, such as dancing and rock music. "It's my business," he said, "to make you kind of hot where you're sitting . . . It's my business to keep you up at night, to make you toss and tumble, unable to sleep."

He seemed piercingly aware that sex had been the downfall of many great men of God.

Current Biography called him "one of the most influential Christian exponents of right-wing populism in America" and the most-watched television evangelist in the US. It noted he was the only celebrity televangelist to yet endorse a candidate in the 1988 presidential race (Pat Robertson) and that he had met not only with President Reagan, but with Vice-President George Bush. It spoke of his disciplinarian father, his childhood inklings of greatness, his Faulknerian clan, his hardships, and the stubborn healing persistence in his life of music.

Inevitably, it compared him to his first cousin, rock pioneer Jerry Lee Lewis, noting like many others the seesaw of fortune the two seemed to ride: bad luck for one seemed to presage a burst of fortune for the other.

◆   ◆   ◆

The Family Worship Center was an eight-sided building made to evoke a revival tent, with a simple, dramatic cross soaring from its roof. Around it was a huge parking lot, dotted with tree-and-shrub islands. In the middle, fenced off by chain link, was a shred of the creek they had paved over to make the parking lot. The main entrance off Bluebonnet Road, World Ministry Avenue, was neatly groomed and planted with azaleas and other flowering shrubs.

People parked their cars, pulling starched and scrubbed children out behind them. Young couples arrived, the women rouged and hair-sprayed and scented and pantyhosed, with tinkling bracelets and Bibles with lace or denim covers, the men necktied and contained inside colorless suits. As with most churches, there appeared to be few men who came to the Family Worship Center without women, but there were plenty of women without men.

They streamed up the six sets of broad, shallow steps through three massive double glass doors, into the foyer that ringed the Family Worship Center's sanctuary like a doughnut. At every outside door were large, heavy doormats, colored wine-red with white doves outlined on them.

On the two 30-foot-high walls flanking the foyer entry hung Florentined aluminum continents ten feet high, with rashes of small knobs and red buttons showing where the Jimmy Swaggart Ministries had Bible colleges and ministries, and television downlinks or stations over the world. Underneath the maps was a long string of photo panels, lit from behind, of poor people with third-world faces.

At Christmas, a huge tree was erected in the foyer, covered with ornaments from all over the world. The bookstore was stocked with Bibles, textbooks, social commentaries, audio and video tapes, booklets, the ministry's magazine, the *Evangelist,* bookmarks, mugs, refrigerator magnets.

The sanctuary filled rapidly, the balconies packed. Filtered light streamed in from panels high in the ceiling, illuminating the large raised platform where Jimmy would pace, jabbing the air with his finger. At stage right was a brace of chairs known as the Amen Corner. Visiting clergy and church bigwigs sat there, joined by Jimmy's wife Frances and 33-year-old son, Donnie.

The atmosphere on Sunday was like a concert hall. A gray cyclorama flanked the stage, giving the feeling of a great castle with heavy drapes on the walls to keep out the chill. Musicians peeked out from behind it. People greeted each other and marked their seats with Bibles while they looked for friends.

Suddenly, the curtain lifted in swags, letting out rousing music and a view of the band and choir, stretched across the entire back wall of the stage: horns, guitars, drums, 120 or more jiving blue-robed singers, a bank of microphones for the lead singers, and Jimmy's big Steinway grand off to the left. A man came forward, seized a mike, and began singing without preamble, the first of a host of church favorites such as "Leaning on the Everlasting Arms," in barely-disguised boogie. Everyone sang and clapped along, smiling. The service in this church didn't "begin"; it was launched.

The Amen Corner filled with beaming men in handsome suits, who sang and pumped their bodies to the music and waved to friends. People stood up, clapped to the beat, sang out strongly and with a sense of ownership of the music and the church. Men sang with emotion, many of them as talented as the song leader. At the Family Worship Center, the music belonged to the people. But there was barely a whisper of difference between it and that devil's music played by Jimmy's cousins Jerry Lee Lewis and country crooner Mickey Gilley.

Song after song filled the sanctuary. People started raising their palms upward toward the stage in attitudes of praise and reverence. Joy bubbled onto their faces and they began to enter light trances. Some held their hands up, as if they were toddlers wanting God to pick them up. Others sang with their eyes shut tight, releasing, lyric by lyric, the filthy, burr-clogged beasts of failure and despair they had dragged into the Family Worship Center to leave at the altar.

"Glory! Glory!" they yelled, "Praise God! Praise Jesus!" Perspiration began to gleam on faces as people moved out into the aisles to dance in the spirit.

Over the choir could suddenly be heard a distinctive, velvety baritone. The excitement elevated. Jimmy and Frances had slipped into the Amen Corner, where he had picked up the mike waiting on his chair.

Frances, a pretty, dark-haired girl when she and Jimmy had married as young teenagers, was now ash-blond. She had taken her time becoming a blonde, and done it with tact and restraint; no one swayed Frances Swaggart or stampeded her into anything. Her hair floated around a round, foxlike face with quick brown eyes.

It was probably Frances who was responsible for Jimmy's tasteful suits; on television debating with Ted Koppel, or praying with heads of banana republics, or facing an 80,000-person SRO crowd in some far-flung amphitheater or soccer stadium, he never came across as gaudy and attention-starved like some other televangelists. He wore nice suits or well-integrated outfits: powder-blue pants and matching tie, white shirt, navy suede blazer.

The musicians bore only vestigial traces of the entertainment world, where they had gotten their experience. A harmonica player who had the sweetness of a child under his hard-bitten face wore red and black snakeskin boots and a big Texas-shaped ring; a choir director's conservative suit terminated in saddle oxfords.

The only member of the troupe, in fact, who really had permission to echo Nashville—hot pink and aqua, snakeskin, fur—was Frances. She would be seen wearing Gypsy-looking dresses with scooped necklines and large shoulder pads. Her skirts were often filmy chiffon, perhaps with a silver lamé scarf tied tight over her hips. She liked swaying, rustling, mystery clothing, the kind that releases scents when its wearer shifts in her chair. With an instinct for finishing touches, she favored jewelry and showy pumps.

She never entered the bimbo territory that other televangelist wives such as Tammy Faye Bakker and Jan Crouch staked out with their lurid clothing and makeup. Still, when Frances walked onstage and sat among the men in their conservative suits, it was as if a parrot had flown in and perched in the Amen Corner.

Jimmy glanced at the audience to see if they were ready for more. They were. He jumped up and strode across the stage, expertly dodging the mike cord.

"Come on!" he yelled. "Sing it, Church!" People grinned conspiratorially at each other and laughed. They jived, stomped, and clapped.

Jimmy gestured to a trumpet player, who came up, pointed his horn in the air and did a slow, sweet, bluesy, sensuous solo. The harmonica weaved in and out, gravelly and wicked here and there, and the audience swooned and giggled. Jimmy had actually created a church where people could be "in The World but not of it." As if to rub The World's nose in this, Jimmy went to the pulpit and said, "My, my, my! Nashville and Las Vegas have nothing over that!" And then gestured to the band to kick in again. He was giving his conservative hellfire church permission to flaunt the music of flesh, of New Orleans, of mixed drinks with paper umbrellas, rich food and wild dancing. The grins were especially big in the Amen Corner.

Jimmy knew his business: the half-hour of music put people into a trance. They were dancing in the aisles, flailing and hyperventilating with glazed, excited eyes. A fat young man with an Elvis face and a bad-boy haircut, with sharp gray slacks and a pink sport coat and tie made hard downward slapping motions with both hands, and then broke into a wild jig in the aisle, jabbing his toes into the carpet with blinding speed.

A slim young black man danced gracefully down to the dais and all around it, followed by a heavy man dressed in a snappy business suit, with a bald head and a paunch, the image of Bull Conner, jitterbugging with his palms upward in the supplication position. A black woman jumped stiff-legged like an African deer. A fat woman came reeling out from her pew, with bare feet, flopping her body and banging into the backs of the pews. Those near her waited for her to spin out onto the floor, but she never did. Her eyes were open but unseeing.

This sort of thing never got on Jimmy's television shows. His church was one where ecstasy was the objective—people surrendered to a state of possession called the "infilling" of the Holy Ghost, or the Holy Spirit—but he didn't want to seem on the Holy Roller fringe to his large viewing audience. His television formula was mainstream: all the good stuff—joy, forgiveness, some brimstone, music, tears, fashion, a big peer group that was, in this generation, richer and more acceptable than the poor, alienated, fat generation that preceded it—and none of the bad. No Jim Jones, dead in the Guyana jungle, no messiah complex, no presidential aspirations.

Jimmy finally silenced the choir and musicians and made a few announcements, giving people time to calm down a little. He told a few humorous stories, and Frances came up and gave testimony about the ministry, as was their routine. One day, for example, she called a deaf Native American woman up to the front and introduced her. From the ministry hotline she had learned that the woman was saved when her 14-year-old son was signing a Jimmy Swaggart telecast to her, and the son was saved, too, in the process. It was Frances' idea to bring them forward and hug them in front of the congregation.

After announcements, Jimmy began to preach. He always worked hard at it, pouring himself into it. He made his hand into a pistol and pointed it at people; he threw his arms back and pushed his chest out like a toad. He held his hand up like a claw at the audience, his voice a bull-bellow. He used no notes.

They understood him. They felt grateful. They murmured, Praise Jesus, Glo-ray, Glo-ray to God, Praise God. They closed their eyes and tears squeezed out. He was truly lifting something from them, some lie or misunderstanding. They may not remember exactly what they had learned, or even be able later to quote what the anecdote was, but they would remember the release, the sweet warming relaxant of truth that allowed them to forgive something suddenly in that moment.

"Brother Swaggart preached a fine sermon today," they would say.

He'd lift the Bible high in one hand, the mike in the other, and shout: "That's the reason the devil wants us off this television!" He knew his audience wanted the enemy named: the devil. They wanted it externalized; they wanted to believe that the devil got into them from the outside. Somehow, through their weak flesh, he got in and tricked them. He did this daily. Daily. It happened to everyone, so don't feel bad about it, but come to church and give the devil two black eyes. It's hard to do it driving in your car, or at work, because you're on the devil's turf then, you're in The World. But in church, at the Family Worship Center, the devil is exposed—by Brother Swaggart— and we can kick his ass.

When Jimmy cocked his body like a bantam, chin out pugnaciously, the audience howled with delight. When he began to whisper into the mike, the women shifted on the pews and crossed their legs. His voice was sexy and he knew it. The men sat entranced. He was making love to their wives without dishonoring anyone, and it was all perfectly okay.

When he'd say, "You're not getting it, are you?" they knew it was nearly over. He was pretending to be exasperated with them, and they knew that soon he would uncork some final verbal feat. "Come on!" they would shout.

Once, he yelled, "I'm sick of filthy, depraved, long-haired, smelly, stinky, beer-guzzling, coke-snortin', marijuana-smokin' freaks!" Another time, in a milder mood, he announced an "old-fashioned, heartfelt, Holy Ghost, heaven-sent, Devil-chasin', sin-killin', true-blue, red-hot, blood-bought, God-given, Jesus-lovin', hand-clappin' camp meetin'!"

People would leap to their feet, and the sanctuary would be filled with shouts and raised palms. They would leave their pews and mill in the aisles. It would be time for the offering and then for the altar call, when people went down to the platform to give themselves to Jesus.

The altar call was like a muffled feeding frenzy. The music was gentle, slow, and sweet, as hundreds of people crowded forward to be touched. The elders from the Amen Corner pushed through the crowd, laying on hands and murmuring. The people were fastened onto the octagonal platform. Elders' faces clenched as they concentrated, babbling low, eyes closed, hands on people's heads or shoulders.

Donnie and Frances and Jimmy would also come forward and place hands on the tops of the supplicants' heads or the backs of their necks. They would hug them and pray hard as their charges fell back and cried, their defenses peeled down to the wishbone. Jimmy would intercede for them in the first person. "I can't handle it alone," he would say emotionally to God. "I just can't handle my life any more, I can't do it."

He used the tones and gestures of the old-time preacher, tapping into the feeling-clean memories, the memories of dress-up clothes and a Sunday roast.

As the service wound down, people milled around the stage, looking happy and relieved. Although they called it "being filled," it had the gutted, vacant look of emotional exhaustion. Eyes and noses were red, there was sparse singing and clapping. People hung on for awhile, chatting. The stage lights went down, the crowd thinned. Jimmy and Frances hurried off through a special door. Shortly the Family Worship Center was dark and quiet and empty.

◆   ◆   ◆

Nineteen eighty-seven had been filled with notoriety for religious leaders and in particular for Jimmy. The Christian right was gaining such political viability that the agendas of its leaders—ministers like Jerry Falwell, Billy Graham, and Pat Robertson—were being openly courted by Republicans and openly challenged by Democrats. Falwell's Moral Majority, founded in the 1970s, had become a robust eminence in Republican platforms. Vice President George Bush addressed the 1987 annual convention of the National Religious Broadcasters in Washington, D.C. Pat Robertson, head of the 33-million-subscriber Christian Broadcasting Network, planned to run for the GOP nomination for president.

Jimmy's denomination, the Assemblies of God, had outstripped the growth rate of every mainline religious group in the U.S. over the last decade. It was the tenth largest Protestant body in the U.S., and the largest Pentecostal body in the world. There were more than two million Assembly of God adherents in the U.S. and 14 million more worldwide.

On March 18 that year, Reverend Jim Bakker resigned as head of the PTL television ministry in a sexual and financial scandal that had been simmering for years. PTL (for Praise The Lord or People That Love) was the booming, loose-cannon ministry in Charlotte, North Carolina headed by the boyish, diminutive Bakker and his heavily made-up wife, Tammy Faye. Bakker resigned when the *Charlotte Observer* revealed his 1980 affair with a church secretary, Jessica Hahn, and told of hush money paid her from PTL's coffers.

The public became enthralled with the baby-faced Bakker, who was accused of bilking followers and using their donations not just for hush money, but for outrageous luxuries and perks. Television news ratings were astronomical whenever any aspect of the Bakker story was covered, largely because of Tammy Faye. Tammy's grotesque makeup, garish Nashville-style outfits, heaps of tasteless jewelry, low-cut necklines, wigs, breast implants, onscreen airing of marital problems, and confessed enslavement to a "shopping demon" made irresistible video for a nation still wedded to the image of a preacher's wife as someone with decent hemlines and sensible shoes.

Jimmy Swaggart had played a key role in Bakker's resignation. Bakker accused him of trying to gouge him out so he could get his hands on Heritage USA, PTL's $172-million Christian theme park and hotel complex in Ft. Mill,

South Carolina. But that was not true. Heritage USA was losing money; Jimmy had other reasons for his enmity with Jim Bakker.

Now broadcasters like Ted Koppel from ABC-TV's "Nightline" were looking to Jimmy for intelligent perspectives. He was articulate and candid about the religious community's problems. Newscaster Dan Rather called him "the most effective speaker in the country." Jimmy Swaggart came across as a statesman whose credibility could help straighten the listing ship of the Christian right.

But the PTL affair had exhausted Jimmy and brought uncertain gains. His national prominence brought out local media adversaries: a Baton Rouge television station, WBRZ, cobbled together a documentary rehashing past problems of his ministry. The *New Orleans Times-Picayune,* unable to resist the peg to Jim and Tammy Bakker, also Assemblies of God Pentecostals, followed suit. His non-profit tax status was being challenged, and a House subcommittee heard testimony accusing preachers like Jimmy, Robertson, Falwell, and others of breaking federal tax laws, evading local laws requiring permits for solicitation over television, and violating FCC licensing requirements. He was the target of numerous lawsuits, ranging from cities claiming he owed taxes on sale of religious merchandise to an action that he had damaged someone by using their dead relative's personal story in a sermon.

Twelve major Jimmy Swaggart Crusades—massive gatherings of the faithful that went on for days—had been scheduled for 1987, most of them abroad. He traveled with 82 tons of equipment and an enormous crusade team, and attended to musical rehearsals, meetings with government functionaries and heads of state, coordination with Assemblies of God missionaries, visits to projects his ministry was funding, and preparation of messages. He had been a featured speaker at the National Religious Broadcasters' meeting in February 1987, and was constantly tugged by visitors, formal dinners, and the affairs of his 800,000-circulation *Evangelist* magazine, his 1,450-student Jimmy Swaggart Bible College, and his highly popular "camp meetings" in Baton Rouge—five-day services which attracted thousands of visitors from all over the U.S. Even independent Frances complained, "We never have any time alone any more. All you do is pray."

◆ ◆ ◆

Billy walked to the tan Lincoln in the parking lot at the Travel Inn, opened the door, and slid onto the seat. He started the engine, and began backing out when he realized he had a flat tire. He pulled back in, in front of Room 6. As he changed the tire, Debra sat on the curb next to a small rectangle of sour dirt with a weak Spanish dagger plant poking out of it. If he was stopped, she fretted, it might go badly. Lots of girls had been busted this week. As he worked, perspiring in his sweat suit and headband, she entreated him not to tell the cops anything.

He hoisted the spare onto the nuts and started tightening them. Debra glanced around. Across the highway was a billboard that showed an open Bible. In large letters was a verse from the book of John: "Unless a man is born again, he cannot see the kingdom of God! Your eternity is at stake!"

Her eyes roved, rested on the window of Room 12, and froze. In the window was a telephoto lens, draped with a black cloth.

Debra ran back into her room and watched through a crack in the door as a blue car pulled into the lot. A man got out. Debra didn't recognize him.

The man barked a name as he approached the Lincoln. Billy didn't look up. Before she closed the door of her room, she heard the stranger say to Billy, "What do you think you're doing?"

2

Rebuke before All

The man was tall and handsome, a skilled orator who wore tinted aviator glasses. He was Marvin Gorman, a prominent Assemblies of God minister and an old friend of beleaguered PTL leader Jim Bakker. Gorman had had a church in New Orleans since 1965.

Up until 15 months ago, Gorman had been an upcoming competitor for the 13 million Americans that were regular viewers of religious shows, and for the donor pool that varied between one and two billion dollars per year.

He had been a rising star, with a big local congregation and regular appearances on Jim and Tammy Bakker's popular show on PTL. His own daily talk show, "Marvin Gorman Live," was broadcast over PTL and on 37 independent stations. He had two stations of his own, was buying a third, and had just secured a satellite uplink. He was a national Assemblies of God Executive Presbyter, a leader who helped set national church policy, and he had once been a front-runner for the top position, General Superintendent.

But things had changed abruptly for Marvin Gorman 15 months ago, on July 15, 1986. He had been summoned to a meeting of the brethren, to discuss charges he had committed adultery. In front of several church officials, he reluctantly admitted that, in 1978, he had counseled a suicidal parishioner. Solace had turned erotic, but guilt overcame him before any sex act took place, and he left, he said. He told the woman's husband of the incident and asked forgiveness.

One of the men, the most prominent one, opened a Bible to the First Book of Timothy, Chapter 5, Verse 20: "Them that sin rebuke before all, that others may also fear."

That meant his colleagues were going to be hard on him. After an extremely tense discussion, Gorman agreed to step down from his New Orleans pulpit for rehabilitation. But he asked that the "rebuking before all" be kept quiet until after a $16 million loan agreement for a new church and two new TV stations closed tomorrow.

His accusers refused, saying it would be dishonest. Marvin Gorman was ruined. The next day, he resigned as pastor of the church he had built up over 21 years. Over the next months, as he tried to rally support for his remaining television ministry, he kept hearing ever-escalating stories about adulterous affairs he had presumably had. His $16 million loan went away. Soon he was defrocked and in bankruptcy, with $3.5 million in debts.

In March of 1987, he filed a $90 million lawsuit against the people at that July 15, 1986 meeting, claiming they had slandered him and destroyed his ministry out of jealousy and greed.

Now one of them was sitting inside Marvin's blue car in front of the Travel Inn, crying. "I'm sorry I've hurt you," he said, "and I'm gonna make it right."

The two men agreed to talk further.

At the Sheraton Hotel in Kenner, Louisiana, the next day, Marvin Gorman showed mercy. He had no wish to get even; he just wanted to build his church back up. He secured a promise of apology to start the process of his reinstatement; everyone cried and hugged, and his guests left.

But Gorman wondered how good his hole card was. Who in the national church hierarchy, headquartered in Springfield, Missouri, would believe he had caught such a prominent brother with a prostitute, and heard him confess in the car to having solicited them many times?

Even if they did, they might cover it up. He had seen what happened with his friend Jim Bakker. The presbyters had taken an outrageously long time to even consider disciplining him. Even with the *Charlotte Observer* hounding them and the rumors about Bakker—homosexual acts with his aides, embezzlement of church monies, bribes and hush money paid to keep the lid on what Jessica Hahn called his sexual assault of her—of the utmost gravity to church doctrine, it seemed they had turned a deaf ear because Jim and Tammy Bakker were stars.

No, it was doubtful Gorman would have a warm welcome in Springfield.

Not without the photos, anyway. They had come back perfect. He wondered if his fallen brother would have to learn about them the hard way.

Frances

In the fall of 1986, Frances Swaggart gave a rare interview. Frances had little regard for the media and tightly controlled everything that went out about the ministry or her family. As a consequence, she was little pictured except in broad strokes: steel magnolia, iron-willed, fiercely protective of Jimmy, important role in running the ministry. Her motivations and personality were, in one sense, open for all to see: she lived for God. In another sense, they were obscure: no one knew what had most formed her. Her childhood with an alcoholic father? Pentecostalism? Jimmy? Teen motherhood?

In a 1986 interview with *Baton Rouge Magazine*, she came across as a pretty Southern belle, at ease in her showcase home, playing with the three grandkids and their puppy, Rocky Lee Swaggart, and working in the ministry office, every inch the executive. She was the epitome of style and taste, relaxed in the kitchen whipping up some treat in slacks or a spring frock, tailored dresses and pearls at the office, always feminine.

She was only 15, young and pretty, when she married Jimmy. Thirty-four years later, she was a tough CEO who went after Jimmy's detractors with a deadeye for the jugular.

"Frances is full boss now," a relative of Jimmy's said with some envy. Indeed, Frances accompanied Jimmy everywhere important. She was with him at all his crusades. Her relatives were sprinkled in jobs throughout the ministry. She supported Jimmy's strenuous objections to Jim Bakker's focus on entertainment instead of on spreading the Gospel. She was with him in the summer of 1986, when he was asked to fly to Assemblies headquarters in Springfield to discuss some of his more vitriolic telecasts. She was sued in 1987 for allegedly trying to sabotage one of his competitors.

She did the hiring and firing at the ministry, dealt with mail complaints, pleas, testimonials. She did all the troubleshooting. She ran the place like a Fortune 500 company and was so strong in her sense of service to God that the *Baton Rouge Magazine* interviewer found himself monitoring his voice and words. She was a good cook, a loving grandmother, a jogger, a woman of discipline.

One could see how much Jimmy admired her. It was hard to talk about her, he told one reporter, and he said the same thing a year later, when Frances allowed herself to be interviewed for a book called *Christian Wives*. Both of them said they were very compatible, enjoyed each other's company, loved each other, had a strong marriage, had no family problems, enjoyed their grandchildren.

Frances' admiration and faith sustained Jimmy and propelled him steadily upward over the years. He spent hours in his study every day, praying, working on his messages, and studying. Asked if she felt neglected because of this, Frances said no; she respected him for it.

Jimmy said Frances was a very understanding wife. "If I have to go somewhere without her," he said, "it's like part of me is missing."

About him, she said, "I personally think he's a prophet, I'll be honest with you."

4

In the Beginning

"Old man Lewis was a little old runt, wasn't as big as your fist," said one of his grandsons. But the runt would cast a long shadow into the future of his clan.

A photo of Leroy Milton Lewis, Jimmy Swaggart's great-grandfather, early in the century shows a slit-eyed, bewhiskered man, wearing battered work boots and rough pants but a gentleman's coat and hat. Sitting outside in a wooden rocker, he peers at the camera with an enigmatic expression, as if he's deciding whether to recite you a poem or cut your throat. Lee Lewis was given much but lacked character. This quality was called by his progeny the "Lewis weakness," a weakness for whores when he had a wife of virtue and spirit, a weakness for whiskey and escape. But also a weakness for poetry, and for music.

At 31, Lee married a young cousin barely out of puberty—his first cousin—just like his grandson Jerry Lee would do 70 years later, and shock the popular music world. Lee invited his voluptuous 13-year-old cousin Arilla Hampton to one of those country dances that lasted several days, where men sneaked off between reels and drained whiskey jugs back in the trees.

He compromised her in some way, and leveraged it into marriage, convincing her that her reputation was on the line.

"In them days," said one of their daughters, "girls couldn't stand to have nothing talked about them . . . Mama told me, 'I didn't love your daddy, I just married him to keep people from talking about me.' "

They were wed on January 28, 1888. It may have started out a loveless marriage, but 11 children sealed it, and out of the strength of that first-cousin, child-bride union came a streak of incredible talent, grit, success, and tragedy. One of those 11 children would be the father of Jerry Lee Lewis, the pioneer rock pianist who, along with Elvis Presley, Carl Perkins, Chuck Berry, and a handful of others, changed the face of popular music in the world.

Another offspring, Irene, would be the mother of Mickey Gilley, the country singer who led the citybilly craze of the early 1980s and saw the film hit

Urban Cowboy memorialize the subculture that grew up around his booming Gilley's Club in Pasadena, Texas.

And Ada, hardheaded, determined fourth child of her parents' troubled marriage, would be the grandmother of Jimmy Swaggart.

At 18, Ada was spirited and strong-willed. She had already had a brief marriage and divorce—a downright scandal in those days—and she drank and took up cigarettes, marks of a rebellious woman. But 21-year-old Willie Harry Swaggart, called W. H., was equal to her. He was tall and beefy, unlike her father. His size and steady gaze seemed to mark him as everything her father wasn't. He had been born to farming and worked hard.

Jimmy's grandparents said their vows at the courthouse in Monroe, Louisiana, on February 25, 1914; neither of them had more than a passing acquaintance with a church.

A few weeks after their marriage, a religious group formed in Hot Springs, Arkansas, only a couple hundred miles up the road. It took the name Assemblies of God. Some 70 years later, it would be the fastest-growing denomination in the world, and much of that growth would be attributable to Ada Swaggart's handiwork—her beloved grandson, Jimmy.

Cloven Tongues Like As of Fire

The 20th century plopped in with some baggage. Urban social problems—child labor, prison conditions, corrupt and unfeeling judiciaries, the bleakness of city and factory life—were laying the foundation for a religious split that would last the rest of the century.

A new liberal "social gospel" set the mainstream churches the task of curing society's new ills, but they clashed with conservative Protestants who were at the forefront of a premillenialist movement aimed against the migration of Catholics and Jews to the U.S. in the late 19th century. Early in the new century, two California oil millionaires published the first parts of a 12-volume work called The Fundamentals. The Fundamentals held that (1) Jesus Christ is deity; (2) there was a virgin birth and a resurrection of Jesus; (3) there will be a Second Coming of Jesus; and (4) the Bible is without error. The new fundamentalist movement drew people seeking a safe haven from the chaos of their rapidly urbanizing and modernizing country.

Fundamentalists were suspicious of education and of modern scientific thought, especially the evolutionist theories of Charles Darwin. The major universities, founded by moral Puritan fathers on strictly religious principles, were now accused of being the political tools of liberal social engineers pushing the social gospel.

It was New Year's Day in 1901 when something happened at the Bethel Bible School, a mansion bought from a ruined real estate magnate on ten acres of fruit orchard on the outskirts of Topeka, Kansas. Holiness preacher Charles Fox Parham had opened the school in October of 1900 with a philosophy: no curriculum except the Bible; no faculty except the Holy Ghost; no course of study except as the director felt moved by the Holy Ghost to assign. The Holiness movement was a widespread rural trend begun a few decades earlier, with roots deep in frontier and even colonial America.

For several years, Parham had been reading about an old phenomenon, glossolalia—speaking in tongues. Considered by Christians to be evidence of blessing by the Holy Ghost, or the Holy Spirit, this intensely emotional experience of ecstatic, unintelligible speech had a long tradition in Europe, especially in France and England. But its Christian tradition was sporadic; it had been discredited as Satanic for at least 900 years by the Catholic church. Psychologically, it is often connected with powerlessness, surfacing historically in times of severe religious persecution or decline, or economic privation. It is egocentric, meaningful only to the utterer, though it requires a listener. It was seen occasionally in the U.S., but was considered something only fringe groups did.

But Charles Fox Parham was hoping glossolalia might make a legitimate comeback as a tool of worldwide evangelism. He believed that tongues speech was always in known languages, as was implied in the New Testament book of Luke, and believed its real fate was a sort of linguistic spontaneous combustion that would do away with grueling, time-consuming language study for foreign missionaries.

The book of Acts 2:1–4 tells about tongues: on the day of Pentecost, the Jewish spring harvest festival, Jesus' disciples were all gathered, when "suddenly there came a sound from heaven as of a rushing mighty wind, and it filled all the house where they were sitting. And there appeared unto them cloven tongues like as of fire, and it sat upon each of them. And they were all filled with the Holy Ghost, and began to speak with other tongues, as the Spirit gave them utterance."

Parham decided that the school would pray all night on New Year's Eve, 1900, for glossolalia.

All over Topeka, churches held watch-night services. By sunrise, no manifestation of the Holy Spirit had occurred at the Bethel Bible School, but the students continued to pray. At the evening service, a 30-year-old student named Agnes Ozman asked headmaster Parham to lay his hands on her as she prayed with escalating energy. As they both concentrated hard, she broke out into a chattering vocalization—tongues.

Parham later claimed it was Chinese, and that Ozman was unable to speak English for three days afterward. He claimed that when she tried to write down her experience, it came out in Chinese characters. Ozman's account differed, but her teacher's more spectacular version—which also included a halo around her head and face—was the one that survived in the popular story mill.

Over the next few days, one after another of the students began speaking in tongues. They later described the phenomenon as being filled with overflowing joy and laughter too deep to be expressed, of beginning to praise God, but feeling words inadequate to express their euphoria. One woman described her tongue thickening, said she was unable to think any more—and said her mouth became "filled with words I didn't understand. I tried not to laugh for I feared to grieve the Spirit. I tried to praise Him in English, but could not, so I just let the praise come as it would in the new language . . ."

Word of this marvel spread, and in a few days a dozen ministers appeared at the ongoing Bethel services. They, too, were possessed of tongues, speaking and singing, it was reported, in six languages. Finally, Parham himself, kneeling behind a table, started praising God in what was reported as Swedish.

The new followers would be called Pentecostals in honor of their imitation of the events at the Jewish harvest festival of Pentecost in the book of Acts.

The local paper, perhaps casting about for tales of miracles to usher in the new century, covered the strange spectacle. Then, according to some Pentecostal historians, the school was beset by linguists, native speakers of the purported languages, and government interpreters. Reportedly, they verified that at least 20 certifiable languages were spoken flawlessly. Parham's zeal for world missionary seemed launched.

Before the summer was out, however, the school went broke and closed. The mansion immediately reincarnated as a night club, and then burned to the ground in December of 1901. A planned coast-to-coast evangelical tour made one stop, Kansas City, before breaking down under ridicule from the press. Even one of Parham's own students told reporters, "I believe the whole of them are crazy. . . . They were racing about the room talking and gesticulating and using this strange and senseless language which they claim is the word from the Most High."

But if the Pentecostal movement seemed dead in its cradle, it wasn't. Four years later, in 1905, Parham surfaced in Houston and opened a second Bible college. Again, his adherents spoke in tongues. One of them was a gifted black minister named William J. Seymour.

Thus began a bizarre convergence of ideologies: Houston's local segregation laws meant Seymour had to sit behind a curtain when he attended Bible school classes for whites. But at worship services, blacks were welcome, and Seymour was even invited to preach. In fact, Parham was grooming him to preach among "those of his own color" when Seymour—who had not yet experienced glossolalia himself—was invited to co-pastor a Holiness church in the fastest-growing city in the nation: Los Angeles.

Seymour journeyed to Los Angeles in January 1906, earning rancor along the way from a helper who denounced him as a "very untidy" man who took the cake for all the "religious fakes and tramps" she had met. At his first sermon, he exhorted the congregation to seek the gift of tongues—to them, a radical, maybe Satanic manifestation—and was padlocked out of the church.

He was taken in by a family living on Bonnie Brae Street, where he held rowdy meetings that attracted working-class blacks and whites. In April, he and seven others finally received the gift of tongues, and word spread. He found an old livery stable—used and then abandoned as the African Methodist Episcopal church—at 312 Azusa Street, and moved his growing meetings there. They went on day and night, nonstop.

"New Sect of Fanatics is Breaking Loose," bannered the *Los Angeles Times* on April 18, 1906. The next day the new Pentecostals were displaced on the front page by the San Francisco earthquake, which they saw as God's judgment on journalistic scoffers. They predicted a similar fate for Los Angeles, and made it known that the Azusa Street mission was open to anyone seeking salvation before the new quake shook some of the sprawling town's 228,000 citizens to death.

This time it worked: Seymour's tongues speech and ecstatic, excited preaching launched the biggest revival in U.S. history. It went on day and night for over three years and attracted pilgrims from across the country. Its fame spread to other countries. Meetings went from ten in the morning until predawn.

Charles Fox Parham, Seymour's mentor, became bitter over the direction of Seymour's success, calling the Azusa Street mission a place where "negroisms" were passed off as manifestations of the Holy Spirit. Ironically, he came to echo his own secular critics in calling for "decency and order" in the services instead of "consum[ing] ourselves in riotous sensations of the flesh and a sensual working up of feeling" and in "chattering, jabbering, wind-sucking and jerking fits"—the sort of frenzy that spawned the disdainful term Holy Roller. Parham was to be profoundly disillusioned at the direction tongues speech would take, for never did his hoped-for language explosion take place. He still hotly condemned any non-human-language glossolalia—which is what most tongues speech would turn out to be. Eventually, the only people who would be able to understand Pentecostal tongues would be other Pentecostals.

Parham's movement might have taken a wrong turn at Azusa Street in his opinion, but the interracial element worked in Los Angeles. It became a quality marking Pentecostalism from the beginning (though Seymour later refused to allow whites to be officers of his mission). The crossing of racial lines was only one of the qualities that marked Pentecostalism as an outlaw movement.

In a few generations, the same crossover, in the same religious milieu, would produce rock and roll.

THE ASSEMBLIES OF God was a quarrelsome young faction that came directly out of the Azusa St. revival in Los Angeles. Pentecostals were fearful that too much organization would interfere with the moving of the Holy Spirit through their congregations, and they clashed over matters of sanctification, baptism, and other doctrine. But they were also afraid of passing up God's mandate to spread the Gospel all over the world. The fundamentalist message was falling on fertile ground, and the fledgling denomination came together in April 1914 from 17 states, plus Egypt and South Africa, in Hot Springs' drafty Grand Opera House, which operated a saloon on the first floor. Upstairs, they settled their differences enough to organize a General Council and set an agenda.

Ferriday

D uring Ada Lewis' childhood in the tiny farming community of Snake Ridge, Louisiana, the family became acquainted with the Gillys, a farming clan who had come from New Orleans when their own family fortunes nearly evaporated. Jhatme Fillmore Gilly and his wife Mollie Leopard had 13 children, and four of their sons would marry Lewis girls. A Lewis son would also marry a Gilley daughter (the surname acquired an *e* in the next generation).

But the new families found farming at Snake Ridge hard. The cotton and beans, beets, corn, and rye they planted were constantly sabotaged by freezes, floods, and boll weevils. The clan began to cast its eyes 40 miles south, to the promising village of Ferriday. There, farmland was richer, and new timber and government industries were moving in.

In 1924, one of Ada's sisters packed up and left Snake Ridge for Ferriday, followed shortly by another sister and then a brother. In 1930, Ada and W. H. Swaggart moved there. By this time they had two teenagers—Arilla, named after her grandmother Lewis, and Willie Leon, a hot fiddle player nicknamed Sun, who would become the father of Jimmy Swaggart.

Ferriday, Louisiana was laid out in 1903 as a railroad stop in Concordia Parish, and incorporated in 1906. It was originally part of the Helena Plantation, the 4,000-acre dowry of a girl named Helen Smith when she married William Ferriday in 1827.

When the first of the Lewis-Swaggart-Gilley families arrived in the late 1920s, Ferriday was still a rough, muddy outpost. Stock ran loose in the streets, their droppings making a steamy barnyard stench during the hot, rainy summers. There was no electricity in the town, but some stores and rural homes had artificial gas for lights. It was a wild town, measled with moonshine stills and slot machines.

But life abounded. The growing season spanned two-thirds of the year and fed families. Something was always blooming—azaleas or camellias or the big-leafed magnolias. Vines crawled on everything: clematis, honeysuckle, jasmine and passionflowers, drunk on plentiful rainfall, ran like wild children through the shabby little river towns, bringing grace to the dank cabins of Negroes and sharecroppers and the ordinary poor.

Concordia Parish had both fertile cotton land and primeval forests of giant hardwoods, but water ruled its nature. Bounded by rivers and riddled with swamps and bayous, the parish flooded somewhere every time it rained. Huge cypress trunks, torn from their roots, would gush out of the woods and hurtle down the swollen waterways, to be seized, sawed up, and sold by itinerant lumberers who had no land but lived on houseboats. During flood time people took refuge in attics and barn lofts as their fields went under; when the sky cleared, they floated down the streets of town in rowboats and fished for perch from their front porches. The dirt roads in and out of Ferriday were almost impassable during rainy season and most went unpaved until 1942, when Jimmy was seven; the main street through town, Fourth Street, wasn't fully paved until 1951, when he was 16. Jimmy was one of many children who caught malaria which, along with yellow fever, erupted during flood times.

In 1927 the levee that contained a contorted loop of the Mississippi River burst near Ferriday and the river crashed through the countryside, sweeping everything before it. President Hoover rushed to the area with the Red Cross and wept as he watched a black family cling to their cabin while it ripped down the river. Crops were ruined and school was out for months. The flood made it clear that bond money had to be gathered to address the problem of wild water. One public bridge, road, or levee project could feed hundreds of families for months or years. Jimmy's grandfather, W.H. Swaggart, was employed at it, as were Mickey Gilley's father and other members of the clan.

JIMMY'S GRANDPARENTS, Ada and W. H., arrived with their two teen-agers in the middle of a malaria epidemic and a heat wave so intense it even decimated the boll weevil population. W.H. was an expert trapper and hunter, and he could make almost enough off the local raccoons, skunk, possum, rabbit, and mink in two months to get the family through the winter. There were also sawmills, the paper mill, the pecan harvest, and the big cotton farms, always in need of laborers to plant, cultivate, and harvest. W.H. also farmed on shares, growing mostly cotton and corn. But farming wasn't for him; what really put food on the table was his bootleg whiskey.

"They'd come and carry him off," said his daughter Arilla, Jimmy's aunt. "Mama would take us to visit him in the parish jail—he'd be in there about four or five months. That's why we stayed out of trouble. My father sold whiskey all my life, and he drank it all my life."

W.H. was a smoldering, authoritarian man with a strong work ethic. But he was a trying husband. Besides being regularly arrested for moonshining, he resisted the blandishments of church when Ada later began attending, and like Lee Lewis, he was a carouser. His infidelities began early.

Though Ada was a drinker herself and W. H.'s bootlegging kept bread on the table, the country's attitudes toward drink were hardening, and it categorized her family as low-class. By the time Ada was married, the Temperance Movement, broad in the previous century, had focused itself more sensibly on alcohol, and the U.S. Congress had begun passing the laws that in 1920 led to the 18th Amendment—Prohibition.

Ada craved respectability, and the way to get it was through the church. Over the years, W.H. provided the grist for her spiritual mill, and it would be Ada who would influence her grandson Jimmy to become a minister, Ada who would inspire his blowtorch preaching style, and Ada who would provide the boogie-woogie piano genes.

But it took 25 years of grinding for her epiphany to take place.

◆　◆　◆

A few years before Ada and W.H. arrived in Ferriday, Jimmy's maternal grandfather, sharecropper William Herron, moved his mentally ill wife and his hard-working brood of seven to Ferriday from the Crowville-Winnsboro area.

One of the Herron girls, Minnie Bell, was 13. Plenty of boys liked to watch her walking barefooted and bare-legged down the dusty country lane to sell a few eggs or buy a tin of coffee at the store. She was a woman-child with only the dimmest idea of what she was provoking in men, but her affections were already being sought by numerous boys—including Ada's brother Robert Jay Lewis. Boys hung around the Herrons' small house a few miles west of town on Highway 15, where Minnie Bell, next-to-youngest of seven, cooked, laundered and cleaned for herself, her parents, and one brother left at home. She tended the vegetable garden, worked in the fields, and managed to go to school.

By age 15, she was a beauty, with green eyes and wavy brown hair parted on the side like a little girl's, clear skin, and full, white teeth. Unlike her sisters, who had thin lips, Minnie Bell had a pretty mouth with a perfect cupid's bow. She played guitar and sang in a clear contralto.

Sun Swaggart, 17, joined the competition for her. He was, in the loosest sense, her nephew, since her sister Mamie was married to his uncle, Elmo Lewis, brother of his mother Ada. Sun had charms: he played a hot fiddle and was in demand for parties around the area. And he was ambitious; even at 17, he felt he could do better for Minnie Bell than the hard life she'd had so far—certainly better than his Uncle Elmo had done for Mamie—because Sun wanted to be a lawyer. Watching his trapper father deal with the fur buyers at nearby Vidalia, he loved how, after the deals were cut, the talk would always turn to courthouse matters; Vidalia was the Concordia Parish seat. Sun listened, fascinated, to their analyses of the law, and how well or poorly the attorneys had presented their cases. He had wanted to be a lawyer since the age of ten, he told Minnie Bell.

The dream persisted even though he dropped out of the ninth grade to work full time. In 1932, the year he turned 17, five thousand banks closed, and one out of four American workers was unemployed. Roosevelt's New Deal had generated the "tree army"—the Civilian Conservation Corps—and Sun, W.H., and many other cousins and relatives got work with the C.C.C. digging stumps, planting trees, draining swamps, and building roads for a dollar a day. Even though Ada was unhappy that Sun quit, it was hard to justify sitting in a schoolroom all day in the middle of a worldwide depression when there was work to be had.

Gradually Sun edged out Minnie Bell's other suitors, but the road was not smooth. He found that his beloved had a temper that rivaled his own—Sun could be bitter and humorless and was quick to anger—and they often fought. In 1933, when she was 16 and he 18, they split up. Sun had plenty of choices. He was tall, with light auburn hair and heavy-lidded, intense blue eyes. He was training to be a light heavyweight boxer, and it gave him a grace he kept all his life; agile and polished, Sun was known as a smart fighter. The husky sweetness of his voice, singing or talking, could turn the head of any female, and even though his grammar reflected his limited schooling and rough life, he was well-spoken. He had a natural, God-given authority.

He ignored Minnie Bell for two months, but kept finding himself thinking about the little house on Highway 15. Finally he drove W.H.'s old truck down there and parked where he couldn't be seen. There she was, alone, chopping cotton in the little patch behind the house. She was 17, and still unclaimed. He watched. And made up his mind.

Soon she put down her hoe and walked to the house for coffee break, a farming ritual that was seldom breached. While she was inside, Sun slipped out of the truck and took over her hoe. When she came back out a half hour later, her work was almost finished.

She put her hands on her hips. Sun wiped the sweat off his forehead and invited her to come watch him box a big farm boy who had been training in the C.C.C. camp. A number of people had money on Sun despite his smaller size.

She and his sister Arilla went together, and Arilla recalled the first few minutes of the fight: "That boy hit Sun with the first lick . . . When he hit him the second lick, his head flew toward us and landed right in front of us and his head shot partway off the edge of the mat. We went to screaming; we thought he was dead." The match was over.

In February of 1934, Minnie Bell suddenly agreed to marry him. Neither of them could have cared less that they were related by marriage. If their marriage could be seen to make their children their own first cousins, each other's first cousins, their parents' first and second cousins, their parents' niece and nephew, their grandfather Swaggart's first cousins and him his own uncle, Sun his own uncle, and Sun his Uncle Elmo's brother-in-law, they didn't care.

It was a good omen that they had the same birthday, February 15. On February 13, 1934, in the teeth of the Great Depression and two days shy of his 19th and her 17th birthday, Sun and Minnie Bell were married at the home of a local preacher. Sun gave up boxing. They settled into quarrelsome, unhappy days.

Stars Are Born

It was just after New Year's in 1935. Senator Huey Long, populist hero of Louisiana who had brought so many jobs to the state, had eight months to live before an assassin's bullet would cut him down in the corridor of the capitol at Baton Rouge.

The families of Ferriday were caught in a great bitter cold wave that killed the rising hopes of the fruit trees and drove their sap back down toward their roots. It got down to five degrees. The fragile new snap beans, kohlrabi, and broccoli were gone. Oats were already up and waving in the wind when the killer frost came; even the onions and shallots froze. They looked at the damage and knew they would have to replant.

The cold wave persisted nearly two weeks into the new year; on January 8, it spread a few hundred miles from Ferriday to a shack in East Tupelo, Mississippi, where firstborn twin boys were delivered of a young, poor mother. The first one was pulled out dead. His mother cried, and named him Jessie Garon Presley, after his paternal grandfather. The other one lived; she named him Elvis Aron.

The rest of January 1935 was marked by cold, gray skies and hardly any sunshine. On Turtle Lake, three miles west of Ferriday off the Jonesville Road, hidden on an island where they were sure no one would happen on it, was a whiskey still. Manned by Lewis family members, it was bankrolled and supervised by Lee Calhoun, husband of another Herron sister, Stella.

Calhoun, so tightfisted he wore a rope for a belt and a sock on his head most of the time instead of his good hat, was a natural entrepreneur who still showed strong traces of the Louisiana frontier he'd grown up on. He drove a truck with no door and operated on the margins of legality with horse and cattle deals, cotton land and other "dirt," bootleg whiskey, auto parts, sometime oil wells, and many other enterprises. He owned a dozen low-rent shacks in the black part of Ferriday—called Chocolate Quarters or Bucktown by whites—along with a handful of small, humble homes he rented or sold to the parade of needy relatives he acquired when he married wild young Stella

Herron, 23 years his junior, and took in her child by a cad who had reportedly vanished on learning she was pregnant.

Today, in late morning, Lee Calhoun was there to check things over. They
had just begun to get a good brew, and their product was in demand. Prohibition had been overturned in 1933, but the tax on legal alcohol encouraged
entrepreneurship. Calhoun rode on horseback from his cabin nearby through
the woods behind the lake. He tied his horse and whistled. After a while, he
saw Elmo Lewis nudging the punt silently through the water. Lee climbed in
and they nosed back out into the current.

Young Sun Swaggart and his father, W.H., were tapping the brew. The
men moved around, talking, rubbing their cold hands under the flame that
fed the mash. The crackle of flame and snap of twig floated in the soggy air.
They failed to notice the faint rustlings coming at them from all sides. Suddenly they were surrounded by shouting revenuers.

Someone had snitched; there were plenty of enemies of drink about, not
to mention Lee Calhoun's many business adversaries.

The men were rounded up; on the mainland they were cuffed and loaded
into the back of a cattle truck. As the truck pulled out onto the dirt road
leading to the Jonesville Road, the driver saw a girl trotting heavily toward
them with a panic-stricken face. The handcuffed men began shouting and
waving to her.

The driver stopped and got out. He could see she was pretty, with her
green eyes and red lipstick. She was just a girl, and far into pregnancy. When
he asked whose wife she was, Sun jumped off the truck and stepped forward.
Minnie Bell began to cry. The driver stepped over and unlocked Sun's cuffs.
"Get her out of here," he said, looking at the weeping girl.

By that afternoon, the Calhoun house, on a levee off the Jonesville Road,
was full of people. Fifty or more family members milled around with officers
of the law, trying to negotiate. Lee Calhoun, whom certain law enforcement
people owed favors, made the best arrangements he could.

Stella, Minnie Bell, and Mamie stayed in the background. When the dust
settled, W.H. Swaggart, Elmo Lewis, and a handful of other relatives were
carted off to New Orleans to prison. To no one's surprise, Lee Calhoun was
let off on a technicality. The three Herron sisters heaved a sigh of relief. They
looked to Lee, the economic linchpin of the clan, for protection.

IT RAINED MOST of February, and the huge, unconscious Mississippi,
wall-eyed and tossing, was swollen with rain. Ferriday was surrounded by
rivers; down Highway 84 toward Jonesville, the Ouachita and Tensas Rivers
merged with the Black at Wildsville.

At least the weather had warmed up and the crops were thriving. By the
first week in March, the early corn was standing tall in the fields. Strawberries

that had made it through the January cold snap were nearly ready to pick. It was rainy and windy, but many days the temperature was in the 50s.

Minnie Bell, her belly enormous, was due in a week. She and Sun had moved in with the Calhouns for the birth. The Calhoun home was always open to kin in need. The Herron sisters rallied around Minnie Bell; the back bedroom was prepared for childbirth.

On the night of March 14, 1935, Minnie Bell went into labor. Her sisters and her mother-in-law Ada Swaggart scurried back and forth between Stella's kitchen and the back bedroom while Sun and Lee Calhoun hung around in Lee's little office in a front room of the house. An hour and a half after midnight, Sun heard a tiny, quivering cry. A month ago he had turned 20. Now he was a father.

They named the baby Jimmy Lee. Jimmy because Minnie Bell liked it, and Lee after Lee Calhoun.

Six months later, on September 29, Mamie Lewis, her husband Elmo newly home from jail, began her own labor. The summer cotton harvest was churning through the gins, and the corn and sweet potatoes were just being harvested. It had been raining; it was the coldest day that month, and the smell of fall cut the air as Mamie's ordeal began in the Calhouns' back bedroom.

There were some ominous signs. The baby was coming breech, but the town doctor was drunk and could not be roused. Elmo made a dangerous delivery, pulling the child out by its feet. Whether the baby suffered brain damage from oxygen deprivation is still under debate in the family. It was later reported that a strange dog appeared and howled outside the bedroom window during the birth. The family scoffs at that, but no one denies the intuitive aptness of it, for this baby was Jerry Lee Lewis, the Killer, who would take the sacred music of his church into the blasphemous world, and give it libido, and pay for it with a life of unbroken tragedy.

Five months later, on March 9, 1936, Irene Lewis Gilley, Elmo and Ada's sister, hurried aboard the ferry to cross the rain-swollen Mississippi River to Charity Hospital in Natchez. There she gave birth to a change-of-life son she labeled George in the hospital, but whom she renamed Mickey Leroy when she got back home to Ferriday. He was a pampered little boy who would grow up to be an enduring country-western musician, good-natured, generous, and beloved of his fans. Little George-cum-Mickey Leroy Gilley would turn out to be one of urban country music's major anchors.

The Church That Darwin Built

J immy was born only a decade after the notorious Scopes "monkey trial" had heated the simmering confrontation between Christian fundamentalism and the press to a boil. Many American writers—H.L. Mencken, Sinclair Lewis, Erskine Caldwell, John Steinbeck—already saw American democracy as an anti-intellectual glorification of the ordinary that was particularly lethal when infused with the kind of fundamentalist orthodoxy that viewed education as dangerous. It bloomed in laws like the one John T. Scopes challenged in Tennessee—the law against teaching evolution in public school.

When Scopes, prosecuted by prominent fundamentalist Christian Democrat William Jennings Bryan, was found guilty, press-pulpit battle lines hardened. Mencken, covering the trial for the *Baltimore Sun,* described with scornful wit the carnival of fundamentalists, wearing sandwich signs, "bellowing apocalyptic hymns," and carrying placards that labeled Scopes' attorney, Clarence Darrow, a beast with seven heads. Two years later, Sinclair Lewis' *Elmer Gantry* was published, the story of a venal traveling preacher that formed the prototype for the liberal view of the American evangelist. A year after that, in 1928, Christian fundamentalists helped defeat Al Smith's presidential campaign.

Secular radio shows like "Amos 'n' Andy" and Fred Allen were being challenged by religious broadcasts. Bishop Fulton Sheen's "Catholic Hour" in New York was a competitive commercial broadcast that paid for itself; Father Charles Coughlin's conservative radio diatribes made him such a potent political force that his church finally silenced him. The Federal Radio Commission, the precursor to the Federal Communications Commission, started refusing to grant licenses to religious broadcasters, calling them "propaganda stations."

Pentecostal evangelist Aimee Semple McPherson broadcast from the powerful radio station in her spectacular Angelus Temple in Los Angeles. Her constantly rumored "indiscreet" behavior helped keep her on the front pages of the *Los Angeles Times,* and in 1926 she was tried for perjury over a wild story that she was kidnapped. Her followers didn't seem to care; her case was dismissed and her ministry continued.

The Assemblies of God, founded the year Ada and W.H. Swaggart married, was a Pentecostal denomination like McPherson's. By the time Jimmy was a year old, in 1936, it was the largest, with 150,000 members across the country.

This most American of denominations was a Holy Roller church, traditional fodder for secular journalists. The epithet came from two seminal events that the faithful experience: getting saved, and getting filled with the Holy Ghost, in that order. The first, which means surrendering one's life to Christ, is an intense and emotional moment of breakdown, when all posturing, all holding back, and all constructs of the ego—status, self-image, self-control—dissolve. It is an ecstatic unburdening, a release and a rapture. You might fall to the ground and praise God and weep, for in that moment, every single misstep, every unkindness, every crime, large and small, is wiped away. The adjective used overwhelmingly to describe it is "clean."

The second experience is an escalation of the first: one gets filled with the Holy Spirit of God, or the Holy Ghost. This event is considered a great gift and means that one is actually possessed by God in that moment. It brings with it status, since not everyone is given the gift, and it is assumed that those who are are in some way pure or chosen. Its chief symptom is speaking in tongues—glossolalia—though it might also result in falling to the ground, rolling, running, or dancing. It is taken extremely seriously by Pentecostals, so that a person thus anointed is expected to stay close to the church for life.

◆　◆　◆

Ferriday had no Pentecostal church, so some of its citizens were dubious when, in the spring of 1936, a 17-year-old Assemblies of God Pentecostal girl, Leona Sumrall, arrived in town, convinced that God wanted her to start a church there. Inspired by an affectionate older brother, a preacher who had been saved out of sin and miraculously rescued from tuberculosis, plain-faced Leona stalked the town until she had milked from its pillars some chairs and plank seating, a platform, an old loaner piano, a couple of temporary rooms for herself and her mother (remembered by residents only as Mother Sumrall), and groceries to keep them going long enough to launch an outdoor youth revival.

Leona got permission to hold her shindig in a tent on a vacant lot on Texas Avenue, just down the street from the Billups gas station. Lee Calhoun saw them there one day, breaking off the dry waist-high weeds and pulling them out to clear the lot.

"My husband was kinda nosy," said Stella Calhoun. "When they told him they were called [to bring a church to Ferriday], he said, 'Well, who is heppin' you ladies?'" The only answer they had was "the Lord."

They told him they could only manage a tent right now, but someday there would be a church building. Touched, Lee promised, "Well, stay in there awhile, but I'm going to have you a church built, if y'all gonna build one here, I'll build it fer ye. And y'all can pay me when you git credit."

"Seeing those women, out there by themselves, out here away from their home, . . . seeing them willing to do such as that, you see, well, it kina got aholt of him," said Sun. "[Calhoun] was very hard, cursed all the time, but yet he did have a good heart." Indeed, tightfisted Lee was good to the poor.

"Lee Calhoun would tear up those deeds to houses [in Bucktown]," Jerry Lee remembered. He went with his uncle once to drop off sacks of groceries to a black family that owed Calhoun money. Calhoun had his nephew go up to the porch to make the delivery, and when he returned, hissed, "Boy, you ever tell anybody I did that, I'll kill you!"

Lee put his kin to work however he could, preferring to pay in some way other than cash. "He had a big peach orchard at Turtle Lake," said a relative. "We'd help him can the peaches, and he'd give us a big party with a Negro band." Elmo and Mamie Lewis got free rent at another Calhoun shack—cold, with a dirt floor—for "holding" a piece of land while Calhoun fought the couple in court who said he'd cheated them out of it.

Sun was the manager of the Billups station down the street from where Leona and her mother were clearing weeds for the revival tent. He and Minnie Bell lived in a little shack behind the station with their toddler, Jimmy, and they watched as Leona worked on the lot. One afternoon he saw a large truck pull up, and volunteers unloaded benches and a piano. Leona and Mother Sumrall went from door to door, inviting the townspeople to services that night.

Sun was not religious, nor was his young wife. Neither of them had ever been inside a church except for a couple of funerals Minnie Bell attended as a child. Neither owned a Bible. In fact, when they weren't fighting—both of them suffered from hot tempers and what they called "nerves"—he and Minnie Bell sang and played for the secular world, at dances and parties in the area. That night, Sun saw some of his relatives walking into the tent, and heard rousing music—piano, guitar, banjo, violin, tambourine, harmonica.

The music went on day and night. After a couple of nights, Sun took up his fiddle and he and Minnie Bell walked down with the baby and slipped onto a pew. Very shortly they realized it was a Holy Roller church. They were repelled; people fell to the floor or hopped around, flailing their arms and letting their heads loll backwards while their eyes rolled up.

They only went to the services a couple of times, and it was of no particular interest to them when a pack of drunken local bullies followed Leona back to her room and threatened to run her out of town during the first week of her revival. (She faced them down and they retreated.) Like many Holy Roller revivals, the Sumralls' efforts were beset with saboteurs and scoffers.

Eventually, a local businessman took pity on the women and gave them a little lot on Texas Avenue, near the edge of town. It took them a few years to get a small Assembly of God church built, with Lee Calhoun's help, before they moved on, but there is no record that the Swaggarts, Lewises, or Gilleys did anything much about going to church while their children were toddlers. Sun himself felt in no need of it.

"Fact is," he said at 75, still a restless man, ruddy and fit, with a gusty laugh, "I never did hardly go to church when I was a young man a day of my life . . . I was quite hard. I prided myself in what I didn't do! I couldn't take much pride in what I did do."

His mother Ada, struggling with W.H.'s infidelity, their poverty, and her own drinking and smoking, and worried about Sun and Minnie Bell's fights in front of young Jimmy, had been dabbling in Christian Science, the movement founded in 1875 in Massachusetts by Mary Baker Eddy that stressed miraculous healing. Christian Science taught that matter was illusory, that Christ and God were to be seen not as human manifestations but as impersonal principles, that God would never assume human form. The Bible was treated as merely a source of information about these matters—a rather unreliable one, in fact.

"My mother [Ada] gave us—don't steal, don't take anything that don't belong to you, don't lie, don't take God's name in vain . . . she instilled that." She had managed to scare Sun away from smoking, and he felt self-righteous, even smug, when members of the little Sumrall church smoked, drank, or cursed, which most of them did in their daily lives.

Mamie and Elmo joined the church within the next year or two, and though Sun and Minnie Bell attended because they enjoyed playing music there, four years passed without finding them much closer to God than they'd been the night they first wandered down to the tent service.

However, Lee Calhoun's leadership in financing the church was the sort of thing that brought reputation and status, two commodities the families yearned for. As was the pattern among the competitive Herron sisters, Stella led by influencing Calhoun to front some money; Mamie immediately associated herself with the Assemblies of God church once it was funded, and Minnie Bell would eventually become one of the church's pillars. Mamie could not make herself be consistent, could not lose herself in the commitment to the church, but Minnie Bell could and would.

After his own conversion years later—which would take a turn that would humiliate Jimmy—Sun maintained that it didn't matter what got you into church, whether it was to keep up with the Calhouns or have a social tree to climb. As long as you got there.

A Goodbye, and a New Bargain

In the early spring of 1938, when Jerry Lee was two, Elmo Lewis and Lee Calhoun were again caught making illegal whiskey. Elmo was sentenced to five years in Angola prison, 60 miles down the Mississippi River.

This was crushing to Mamie. They were already poor, and now the bread-winner, such as he was, was gone. She threatened to leave Elmo, and from prison he had no way to win her back.

He had been making the brew with Lee Calhoun, and even though Lee had the cash to bribe his way out of jail, he decided to let the state of Louisiana pay his rent for a few months. Mamie took eight-year-old Elmo Jr. and three-year-old Jerry Lee and moved into the Calhouns' rambling house, which had been moved from Turtle Lake to 8th Street and Louisiana Avenue in Ferriday and enlarged with several add-on rooms.

Though Stella was the family's benefactor, spreading Lee's largesse to her two younger sisters and other relatives, she also never let them forget it. She couldn't help reminding her siblings who was paying for a kid's new shoes, or whose land they were sharecropping, or whose shack they were renting for peanuts. Over the years, Elmo constantly suspected he was being exploited by his benefactor-in-law.

"We'd see [Aunt Stella] coming," said Mamie's daughter Frankie of later years, when the Lewises lived in the remote shack on Black River that they rented from the Calhouns as their sharecroppers—a shack with no indoor heat, plumbing, closets, or interior doors.

"We'd see the dust from her car. Mother would run and hide and grab all her things—if she'd bought anything new at town—and put it under the bed, because she knew Aunt Stella would kick us out. Daddy would say, 'Here she comes, Mamie! Bull-of-the-Woods!'" Bull of the Woods was a popular chewing tobacco.

But Stella could hardly be blamed for her heavy hand. She had grown up "working like a mule"; as a child, she worked as hard for her size as a grown man, hauling water to the fields at age six and taking care of Mamie, four, and their baby brother. When Mamie turned six, Stella turned the baby over to her, and moved into long days chopping and hoeing cotton, pulling corn, digging potatoes, or fielding whatever crop was in—and helping with the new baby, Minnie Bell.

For some of her sisters, it was little different than in childhood. Sharecropping was a subsistence living; the families kept bees and chickens, and sister Viola fended off destitution in a two-room cabin near Bayou Macon, trading molasses, made on a crude cane mill turned by a mule, for flour or meal that came in cloth sacks, which were sewed into clothing when empty. They heated with iron cookstoves and fireplaces, hung their clothes on 16-penny nails, carried water in from an outdoor pump, and were often only one or two pans of cornbread ahead of malnutrition.

Stella owed Lee everything. She was afraid of wasting his money. Though she and Mamie were very close in age and attitudes and had a natural alliance, and Stella loved Mamie's two sons, especially Jerry Lee, she had raised Mamie and knew she had a predatory streak. Mamie loved her kids and could be loads of fun, but she seemed to have a deep conviction that she was owed something. So Stella kept the hammer down on her.

But the sisters became close during their husbands' absence. Having the men off in jail took the edge off their competitiveness, and they spent their days amicably, looking after their children and seeing to Lee's fields and rental properties.

Jimmy spent time at the Calhoun house, playing with Jerry Lee and with Stella's daughter Maudine. Sun was possessive of Jimmy and Minnie Bell, and jealous of her sisters. But Minnie Bell visited the Calhoun house often. She and Stella tried to encourage Mamie to stay married to Elmo.

Minnie Bell knew how the Lewis men could get you to believe in them— hadn't Sun promised her he was going into law? And here he was, gathering nuts and chopping cotton and hunting meat for the table just like the rest of them. But she would never reveal her doubts about Sun to her sisters. That would give them an edge, and they already had an alliance. Minnie Bell was still the baby sister.

And even if Sun had not made his mark in law, he was high-minded compared to both Elmo and Lee Calhoun. He had a sense of class, of how to do things right. He was picky about who his son visited, and he and Minnie Bell didn't let Jimmy run wild like the two Lewis boys, Jerry Lee and Junior. Sun wouldn't even let Jimmy visit his maternal grandmother, Theresa Herron, because of her mental disturbance.

Theresa had once been a laughing, fun-loving woman who adored dancing and taught it to her daughters, but she became demented, launching herself into screaming rages, throwing objects at her children and grandchildren, breaking windows, bellowing and chasing after the school bus, throwing rocks. She would run out the door, sometimes undressed, at any time of the day or night. Often she had to be chased by one son-in-law or another and brought back and subdued. Her illness had disrupted her family beyond retrieving. It drove her husband out of the house to live in a little shack in the back yard. She was unable to take care of herself, and was passed around among her married children for years.

Her husband, William Herron, added to his wife's suffering by becoming the lover of Eva Lewis Gilley, Ada's married sister. The affair would last many years, and though it might have been understandable, the lovers could hardly have been more callous. They made no secret of their affair, Eva driving up boldly in a Cadillac and honking for William while Theresa screamed and cried inside, begging him not to leave.

While Calhoun and Elmo were in prison, the sisters talked about what a divorce would do to Mamie's boys, especially Junior. The eight-year-old adored his father, which was one of the few things that could stanch Mamie's resentment of Elmo. Junior wrote Elmo in prison.

June 14, 1938

Dear daddy, how are you felling I am all right. I am staying all night with Maudine to night I am growing every day. Maudine's helping me to right the letter. The boys and I had a good time at school. i am 8 years old I will soon be 9. daddy I still love you so much that i dont no what to do. Your lovely Son Junior

Lee Calhoun came home in July 1938, and the tension between the sisters returned. Mamie moved out, into another Calhoun-owned cottage down 8th Street. One August day, Junior and little Maudine Calhoun, also eight, were playing. They spotted a mule-drawn wagon, driven by an elderly black man, laboring slowly up the highway toward the little store half a mile away. They jumped onto the wagon's tongue.

The driver jiggled the reins, and the two mules plodded faster. Junior was not afraid to jump off while it was moving, but Maudine was. Sissy! Junior leapt off and taunted her.

The next moment, a car hit him.

"Killed him dead," said Stella. "Mamie like to went crazy. . . . several of them around here tried to get her to, you know, sue the man. No, dear, she wouldn't do it for nothing in the world. He wouldn't've killed that child if he could help his self."

Years later, when her remaining son was famous and her financial security assured, Mamie received a letter from the man who had killed Junior. He had been tormented all these years, he confessed, because he had been drunk that day. And he had continued to drink and drive for many years afterwards. He was in Alcoholics Anonymous now, and was apologizing to everyone he had hurt because of alcohol. Could she ever find it in her heart to forgive him?

Mamie thought of that dismal time, of her husband in prison, of her plans to leave him. There had been many, many drunken scenes with Elmo after that. Severe troubles with Jerry, the two daughters she would soon give birth to, her grandchildren, nephews, nieces, and others had filled the decades following Junior's death. Emergency numbers had made their way into her address book in the years after Jerry made it big—numbers of psychiatrists and crisis staff who could be reached at home during the terrible hours between midnight and dawn. Mamie thought fleetingly of her brown-eyed third-grader who could sing any tune perfectly after hearing it once. She crumpled up the letter and threw it in the trash.

Junior was given a pauper's burial on August 6, 1938, with only a rock placed on his grave in the Hewitt Cemetery at Snake Ridge. Elmo was brought in handcuffs, and taken back to prison as soon as the little wooden box was lowered into the ground.

The two-year-old whose hand Mamie held in the cemetery that day would shoulder the burden of her losses. From that moment, she began to count on him. Little Jerry Lee would be the one male who would not let her down.

Very soon, a parallel disaster would visit Jimmy's family. Through tragedy and death, Jerry and Jimmy would become their mothers' Golden Boys, the chief tools of their competition and of their quest for meaning in life.

MAMIE SCRAPED TOGETHER some money after Junior died and bought a life insurance policy for Jerry, worth barely enough to give him a decent burial. The policy cost only two dollars a year, but it purchased a little peace of mind for her.

One day, several months after Junior's funeral, Elmo appeared at the door. He had run away from prison. Angry as Mamie had been at him all this time, she fell into his arms and wept.

Gradually, they eased back into marriage, but there was a new bargain between them now. Somewhere, Junior's death had to be reckoned. Surely Elmo must bear some of the guilt. Mamie arrived at his liability: if he had made a better living instead of moving his family from job to job, living with a mattress in the car in case they had to leave in the middle of the night, he wouldn't have gone to prison, and Junior might have been with him somewhere—hunting or plowing, instead of playing on the highway.

Sensing the power of her new allegiance, Elmo turned his gaze in its direction, and contemplated his only son. Blond, jug-eared, pasty-skinned, grubby, and willful, the child was suddenly fiercely precious. Elmo could feel an almost physical need to be first in the boy's affections, partly to console himself for the contempt he felt from Mamie, and partly from a visceral male compact with his son against the power of the female.

Jerry became the center of a power struggle he would never fathom. He was indulged by Mamie, not disciplined, told he was perfect. Yet he was yelled at, cursed, slapped, and whipped if he did something to enrage Mamie personally or embarrass her. Mamie's refusal to discipline him after Junior died was presented as love, and accepted as such by the rest of the family, though Elmo dimly guessed how destructive it was of Jerry and fought a losing battle with Mamie over it.

Jerry became the family's white blood cell colony, fighting the poisons of rage and blame that flamed up in the crises of 1938. To him fell the role of healing the calamities that rained on the family that year, before he was three years old. It was a role whose pressures took a devastating toll. Jimmy would soon fall into a similar role.

10

Another Goodbye

Minnie Bell was pregnant again. The baby was due at the end of 1940, and as soon as it was born, Sun wanted to get out of Ferriday. He was ready to make something of himself.

His sights were set on Texas, where his sister Arilla lived with her husband, Frank Slampa. Frank, a rigger, had gotten work building a levee on the Rio Grande River in the border town of Rio Hondo. Sun planned to get work on the levee.

It had been a good year for furs and pecans, so there was money to get them there. Sun's real goal was to get into produce—the Rio Grande Valley was covered with farms. Minnie Bell could do some picking, too, when the baby was big enough. If things went right, within a couple of years Sun would have a truck or two, then a fleet. He planned to be hauling produce all over Texas and Louisiana.

In December, Minnie Bell gave birth to a beautiful son with a full head of black hair. She named him Donnie. Within weeks, on a bitter winter morning, she and Sun loaded their pickup, covered the load with a tarp, and climbed into the cab with four-year-old Jimmy on the seat between them and the new infant on Minnie Bell's lap. In the back of the truck was a load of frozen meat Sun planned to sell in Texas.

They drove, quarreling, through freezing rain across Louisiana, heading south for the Gulf of Mexico, stopping by the side of the road to nap. Minnie Bell nursed Donnie and sang hymns she'd learned at the Assembly of God revival meetings, until they rolled into the sunshine of the coastal bend of the Gulf of Mexico.

It was muggy and warm. The landscape turned deserty, dotted with stunted mesquites, but the cultivated fields were something to see. In the hard, bright sunlight, they drove past farm after fertile farm: tomatoes, squash, beans, cantaloupe, cucumbers, peas, eggplant, broccoli. Orchards filled with oranges, lemons, grapefruit, and avocado rotated with walnut, pecan, and date groves.

They reached Rio Hondo. Sun and Minnie Bell had never seen palm trees, and Rio Hondo had groves of them, waving in the Gulf breeze. It was beautiful, like a promise all but kept. Seeing the plentiful produce and feeling the sultry air in the middle of winter, Sun's heart filled with hope. He was going to make it here. Compared to cold, muddy Ferriday, this was paradise.

The Slampas and their two daughters were living in a rented house. They were glad to see the Swaggarts; Arilla and Minnie Bell had missed their friendship, and Jimmy was glad to get out of the truck after the long trip.

They rented one of the rickety little tourist courts where migrant workers packed into the little one- and two-room cabins and where prostitutes might hang out in the smelly rooms dominated by a sagging double bed with a cheap chenille spread, a couple of sticks of furniture, and a linoleum floor worn through to the boards. Nine or ten of the little buildings typically were arranged around a sandy courtyard, empty except for a cluster of mesquites, or a bed of Spanish daggers contained in a rock circle. Stickers, goatheads, and weeds spread across the gravelly soil. Trucks and cars were parked at the cabins, each of which had a stoop and a front door.

The first disaster was the meat. The ice melted rapidly in the warm climate, and it all spoiled. Sun was devastated. He was so sure he was going to make money on it, and instead he'd lost a chunk of his precious investment stash.

Not long afterward, Minnie Bell, weakened from childbirth and the long trip, developed an excruciating pain in her ear. Sun had to pay for a doctor, who said it was an abscess and should be lanced at the hospital. The Swaggarts kept the problem at bay with warm oil and compresses, but Minnie Bell came down with a bad cold. Soon the whole family had it.

A Mrs. Robbins, who lived in the cabin behind them with her husband and grown son, nursed the family. But Minnie Bell got sicker, and again the doctor visited. This time he was worried; both Minnie Bell and the baby were burning with fever. After examining them, he said it was pneumonia. They needed to be hospitalized immediately.

Sun took them, and returned sourly to the tourist court with Jimmy. Now every penny would go for doctors, the hospital, and medicine. A great bitterness rose in him.

Then Jimmy gave the telltale cough. More doctors, more medicine: Sun felt it all draining away, every dream, every bit of hard work, every penny he had scrounged.

As he stood in the drugstore in Rio Hondo, waiting for a prescription, something happened inside him. He may have snapped, or it may have been the onset of his own bout with pneumonia. Years later, Sun would describe it as the voice of God addressing him.

"The druggist had gone into the back, when I heard a voice . . . Said 'Sun, your son's going to die.' And that was said three times. I looked around, and I didn't see nobody. There wasn't nobody in the store.

"I thought then that crying was for the ladies, 'cause they was weaker than the strong men, and ladies would weep, but . . . a man, they didn't. That was my idea. And so I was trying to straighten up when I saw the druggist come back. But y'know, you can't hide it, you can't hide it. And he said, 'Mr. Swaggart,' says, 'you don't have a thing to worry about. You have the best doctor in all this country."

A few days later, Donnie died. He was not quite three months old.

With Minnie Bell still in the hospital, Sun took Jimmy, now also fully sick, and traveled to the cemetery. Like Junior Lewis, Donnie was given a pauper's burial, and with the help of his kin and the Robbinses, Sun put the tiny casket into an unmarked grave. Confused and guilty, afraid he had brought about his son's death, Sun wept.

11

Guilt

The broken little family dragged back to Ferriday to accept the charity, once again, of Lee Calhoun. They moved into a little house Calhoun had built on Tyler Road, next door to Mamie and Elmo. Once there, they fought without letup.

The only breeze of mercy on Sun was that it was fate that had derailed his plans this time, not a decision to quit school or get married, or getting his wife pregnant. Still, things got much worse after they returned.

Jimmy and his cousins were used to family warfare. Both of Jimmy's sets of grandparents fought, and Mickey's mother Irene, Ada's sister, had as difficult a marriage to womanizer Arthur Gilley as Ada had with W.H. Swaggart. Irene once smashed the windows of Arthur's car after he was seen driving a girlfriend through town in it; another time she went looking for him, found him at a bar with one of his girlfriends, and aimed her little pistol at the woman, firing past her ear.

Elmo and Mamie warred after Elmo returned home from prison. There was the demented violence of grandmother Herron, and "Papa" Herron, her husband, sometimes seemed not much different than his wife. Once he jumped up in front of several grandchildren and shot a pet cat that was meowing while he was trying to nap. Another time, he was twirling a lock of Jerry's hair and the child told him to stop. His grandfather hit him so hard it knocked him across the porch.

But Sun and Minnie Bell's fights after they lost Donnie frightened Jimmy and cut him to the quick. They were constantly screaming at each other, he said. He would remember all his life how it crushed him to hear his mother sobbing behind the closed door of the bedroom after a quarrel with Sun: "It hurt my heart." Once, Jimmy wrote, they argued about what Minnie Bell would cook for dinner, and she got so mad she threw the pot of food—blackeyed peas—out the door. "There was no other food in the house," said Jimmy, and Mamie and Elmo quietly picked up the peas. "That night . . . no one spoke at the table."

Years later, knowing he had been a harsh man, Sun would take on a staggering load of guilt, saying that the Rio Hondo disaster was his fault, including Donnie's death, because he had been running from God. "I knew in my heart that I was the one who had caused God to take my child."

But Sun was also stung by the failure of his plan to put together a fleet of trucks and make it big in the produce business. He knew his wife, plus everyone back home, had been watching to see if he could carry that off. His inability to do so truly was a stroke of terrible luck, but it still felt like failure. Sun would find great comfort in the notion that it was God who had blocked his plans in Texas. God, he decided later, had big plans for little Jimmy and needed the child to be raised back home, in the church. Since Sun ignored all the signs, God had no choice but to knock him upside the head by spoiling his meat, stonewalling his job, gutting his plans, and finally, killing his baby.

That reasoning represents a terrible collaboration of cruelties: guilt so severe and self-love so meager that Sun would accept the blame for illness and death; and expectations of himself so bullying that he was convinced he could have prevented Donnie's death if he'd just gone to church. This inflated burden of individual importance—which draws its power from self-loathing, yet is the only source of relief from that self-loathing—formed the basis not only for Sun's later epiphany but for many of the miracles and mysteries of the Pentecostal church.

At first, though, Minnie Bell could not help blaming Sun for the baby's death just as Mamie had blamed Elmo for Junior's. She was trying to view Sun's stinginess as thrift, but when the baby died, her mind sought answers. What if Sun had gotten her and Donnie to the hospital sooner? Had he resisted until it was too late? Knots of resentment and guilt formed between them. The guilt and blame would do a toxic work before the church finally gave them a way to get Sun off the hook.

Young Jimmy was absorbing the guilt with acute sensitivity. Even though he was barely five, he knew his parents' fights had to do with Donnie and the run-down little tourist court in Texas. He wanted so badly to fix that.

Later in his life, he would symbolically go back down that road to find the crumbling motel where he saw everything: hope and despair, guilt, love, poverty, charity, sickness, and the monumental failure of the flesh, as Donnie perished and whores plied their trade and Sun's truckload of meat spoiled in the heat. As an adult, he would go back again and again, and try to find all the pieces: first Donnie, and the lost money, and then the secret of the kindness of Mr. and Mrs. Robbins, strangers who had taken care of the young family for no reason other than that they wanted to help. Lastly, he would try to rescue the flesh.

Belonging

After Donnie's death, Minnie Bell started taking a deeper interest in church. She couldn't forget the Robbinses. What they did was close to the real promise she sensed in the Scriptures, not this ridiculous holy rolling stuff. True, getting filled with the Holy Ghost and dancing in the spirit and all that seemed to take people out of themselves. But surely there was more to spiritual life than just relief from pain for a few hours a week—and then only if the Spirit saw fit to fill you.

You might go to church and pray hard and live an exemplary life all week long and the Spirit would pass you over week after week, sometimes for years. It happened to Stella and Lee all the time. You never knew why, what you were doing wrong, or how you could improve your chances of getting the Holy Spirit.

Supposedly, being ignored by God this way was some test of faith, but shouldn't there be some connection between a person's acts and her rewards? These thoughts simmered in the back of her mind, and left her confused. This was doubting, and doubting in the Pentecostal belief system was a failing. You were supposed to have faith.

Mamie had also found a sisterhood in the Pentecostal practice, and church became a comfort to her after Junior's death. But she had some problems, too. She could never understand, for example, why her going to the Arcade Theater on Louisiana Avenue to see *The Mark of Zorro* caused God such agonies of sorrow. She didn't dare discuss such questions with anyone, though—except Stella. Then she might get a scornful cackle and an earful about some church types being so stiff you couldn't pull a needle out of their rear end with a tractor.

Sun and Minnie Bell fell into the habit of going to the little Assembly of God church on Texas Avenue after they returned from Rio Hondo. The little one-room building looked like an ordinary house except for the double front door with glass panes in the shape of crosses. Inside were plain wooden pews and a plain pulpit. But it became a refuge. The church genuinely needed them to make music on Sundays, and that was satisfying. Sun played violin and Minnie Bell was song leader.

The Assembly of God was made up of their relatives and people like them, an intimate club of townspeople who knew what it was like to be on the outside looking in. Though the holy-roller demonstrativeness was repugnant to Minnie Bell and Sun, they came to look forward to the fellowship.

But they still wouldn't go forward to be saved—much less get into that Holy Ghost business. After what they'd been through, some of the church members wondered why. "I guess the people thought that . . . if we didn't give up our hearts to the Lord [after losing Donnie], then we couldn't be reached," remembered Sun. "Because of the way it happened with us and yet we wouldn't come to God. Y'know, you hear that expression, aw, they'll never get saved, y'know. I think that had something to do with [what happened] later on."

◆ ◆ ◆

The summer of 1940, after Sun and Minnie Bell returned from Texas, Sun's mother Ada had an experience that changed the course of her life—and Jimmy's.

At 45, Ada was in a spiritual crisis. W.H. got a real job—as night marshal of Ferriday—but he started using his patrol car to squire women around after dark. "Pa Swaggart," as he was known to the locals, preferred women from Bucktown, and relatives whispered that he had a second house there. By the time of his death in 1971 at the age of 78, W.H. was rumored to have fathered at least four black children in Ferriday. His relationship with Ada remained stormy until her death.

"Once," said an in-law, "Ada laid in wait behind the front door for Pa to come home from Bucktown. She had a high-heeled shoe, and when he came in, she jumped him with that shoe and beat him black and blue." Another time, he ran into the back of a log truck in his patrol car, and called a cousin to come pick him up and take him to the hospital. With him was his very young black mistress. They were both hurt, but W.H. didn't want an ambulance. Losing his job would be a disaster; it was steady income and it brought a measure of respectability to his long-suffering wife. He clung to it for nearly ten years.

Ada wanted to make things better, but everywhere she looked she saw love and goodness wasted. Her brother Elmo was in and out of prison and had seen his oldest son killed by a drunk driver. Her other siblings and their children were struggling with all the old demons: lust, alcohol, meanness, poverty. She saw music, which she recognized as something with a sacred nature, get dragged to drunken gatherings and hammered into obscenity. She had seen too many mornings when her first thought on awakening was that something bad had happened the night before—and flooding memory never failed to confirm it. Even her attempts to be a good Christian seemed cursed: when Donnie and Minnie Bell got sick, a prayer vigil had been organized at Ada and W.H.'s house, but Leona Sumrall had arrived to find everyone drunk.

Now her grandbaby, beautiful little Donnie, was dead.

And Jimmy, who gazed up at his philandering grandfather's police badge with awe, was clearly wounded. He was just a baby of five, but his gray-blue eyes were full of pain. More, they were filled with a terrible compassion for his warring parents.

For some time, she had been dabbling in religion. She had tried Christian Science because it seemed willing to reconcile itself to humans' weaknesses, but the transformation she sought seemed as far away as ever. There was no emotion there, nothing that resonated with her life experience. Christian Science taught that God never had and never would come in human form, because God was a set of principles, not a man or an incarnation.

The Pentecostal practice, on the other hand, understood what her life had already taught her. It gave her not principles, but concrete things: a messiah, apostles, an ancient book of mysteries, and a God who wasn't afraid to point the finger at you but who showed you how to make up for your sins and how to forgive others for theirs against you. She was interested.

She began attending the Assembly of God church off and on, going for the companionship and music but steadily absorbing the message. "Jesus is gonna heal you," they repeated, "if you'll just turn your life over to him." There was nothing else in her life, no person, no prospects, nothing on the horizon that promised anything close to this wholeness.

Ada had also heard incredible stories of what the power of the Holy Ghost did for people who got it. It was like getting laughing-loving drunk with no hangover and no guilt or shame and a high that lasted for days and set you on the right course. It was what drew people to the camp meeting revivals in sweltering heat and freezing rain. Without it, you couldn't be a true disciple.

That summer of 1940, she visited her younger brother John Lewis and his wife Lottie (another Gilley) at Snake Ridge for a Pentecostal revival. At a field near the joining of two flat, broiling-hot country roads, a stream of cars and pickups converged. Dust rose, mingling with waves of heat that danced on the blacktop. Next to a field where new cotton had sent up a six-inch mat of green leaves was a fallow pasture where people were headed. Stands of trees—hackberry, black locust, catalpa, ash, maple—clustered here and there in the fields carved out of the surrounding woods. In the distance rose the crooked brow of Snake Ridge, and beyond it the thick line of trees that ran along Bayou Lafourche.

Set up near a stand of trees in the field was a large revival tent with its sides rolled up and cars parked helter-skelter around it. It was made of canvas and was supported by a large wooden center pole. At the head was a dais, a piano, the choir's chairs, the pulpit. Wooden chairs faced the dais in rows, and signs tacked to the support poles said things like, "Praise the Lord" and "Christ is the Answer."

People arrived tired from the heat, but as they sat, hands folded over purses or Bibles, eyes closed, lassitude ebbed. There was a warm camaraderie; people waved to Ada and John and Lottie when they arrived. Friends reached up to clasp a hand or pat an arm as they made their way to their seats. Babies slept on blankets on the grass, watched by older siblings, or napped on the seats of the cars, with doors open to the warm air.

It was pleasant to see and be seen in your best—the women in flowing dresses with clusters of silk flowers at their throats, wearing gloves and rib-boned hats, and the men in clean white shirts, snap-brim hats, and ties. Seeing men and women all carrying the same Bible, all equals in the same search for something higher, gave a beautiful sense of belonging. They might be poor and marginal in the outside world; their disappointments and betrayals might be white-trash ones of alcohol or gambling or infidelity, but under the revival tent, it was all leveled by God's love. Everything was forgiven.

The tent filled with the twangy sounds of singing. Then came the preaching; when it warmed up and got exciting, calls of Praise Jesus! and Amen! and Glo-ray! would ring out. Men and women sat in fervent prayer or stood and raised their palms to the sky.

The services, with singing, preaching, and prayer, lasted for days, breaking only for people to make camp and picnic.

And then, suddenly, while she stood during an afternoon break, praying, Ada felt the Holy Ghost hit her. She dropped to the grass. She heard her voice rattling out language, but it had no meaning. Waves of emotion and utter joy engulfed her. She lay on the ground with her hands in the air in an attitude of praise. John and Lottie stood next to her and gave thanks to God.

13

Softening

W hen Ada returned from Snake Ridge, she looked at her only grandson differently. The cute five-year-old had too much of the look of the Depression about him. Ada knew that it came not from physical but from emotional want. If his parents could get saved—and experience the Holy Ghost—that look would largely change.

So Ada proselytized and exhorted her children. She was at them day and night to give up their lives to Jesus, and get the Holy Ghost. Sun resented it. He felt she was hinting that he was responsible for Donnie's death because he had been running from God. That made him guilty and defensive. Then he was made aware of something called a rebelling spirit—and the clear implication was that he had it. That infuriated him. He had worked hard to get to Rio Hondo, and by the way, he'd gotten pneumonia, too. He hadn't gotten any attention, what with Minnie Bell and the kids, but by God, he had it, too. Probably worse than the baby, the doctor said.

His mother seemed to think that just because he'd had that premonition about the baby in the drugstore in Rio Hondo, God was stalking him or something. But why would God be singling him out? He went to church. He didn't smoke and chase women. Why didn't she go pick on some of those tobacco-stained old hypocrites who got drunk every Saturday night and then got down on their knees every Sunday? The bottom line for Sun was, he could just tell it was going to mess up some of his new plans for making money.

But six months after he and Minnie Bell had returned to Ferriday from Rio Hondo, the church's pastor, Tom Holcomb, had an experience that affected Sun and Minnie Bell deeply and softened them up for Ada's pressure.

Sun remembered: "Tom and Bessie [Holcomb] had a beautiful baby. And the baby got sick and died, just like that. And it kinda happened kinda like ours. They was from Texas, away from home in Louisiana . . . it was us in reverse." They were never able to have another child.

What amazed Sun was how the Holcombs handled it. They didn't suffer from guilt. There was no assumption that God was punishing one of them.

There was no blaming, no defending, no victims, no judging, no fights. They just grieved together and then tried to heal.

It also touched Sun that Pastor Tom Holcomb, whose brother was a professional singer and who himself sang in a strong, beautiful tenor, was donating his services at the little church; it had no money to support him. He worked full-time in Texas and drove with his wife to Ferriday on the weekends to offer his love and talent to 20 or 30 faithful people. It was the same kind of mystery as the Robbinses.

Sun began to wonder if Ada might be right about a couple of things. But he was certainly not going to let her know that.

"Ninety-nine Cents out of Every Dollar"

n the summer of 1941, President Roosevelt froze all Japanese assets in the United States. War was in the air.

Jimmy, bright and ahead of his group, started second grade in September. On Sundays he went to church with his grandmother or his feuding parents. In his free time he and the other boys played war with sticks for guns and cloth Bull- O'-the-Woods tobacco pouches filled with powdery dirt for grenades and bombs. Slingshots loaded with acorns made good weapons if you were careful not to overdo the drawback and put somebody's eye out.

The boys were excited about war. The adults said it would end the Depression, and the radio was full of war news—in between the kids' beloved "Gangbusters" and "Jack Armstrong, the All-American Boy." At the Arcade movie theater, newsreels showed black-and-white footage of Nazi troops invading the U.S.S.R., and of President Roosevelt meeting with Winston Churchill. The funny papers carried "Private Snafu."

Jimmy had a special standing among the boys because of his grandfather's important-looking badge and cap. It had a whiff of military authority for the band of six- and seven-year-old cousins who played war among the trees, bushes, and water-filled ditches in their little sprinkle of houses out near the Jonesville Highway. They also tried to claim a "distant cousin" connection with a Ferriday hero, aviator Claire Chennault, who was going around the country with President Roosevelt's blessing soliciting volunteer pilots from the army, navy, and marine corps to go rid China of Japanese invaders.

Sun and Minnie Bell's fights made home an unhappy place, and Jimmy stayed away as much as he could. There was an ever-building score to settle with his father as soon as Jimmy got big enough, for the days when Minnie Bell retreated, sobbing, into the bedroom.

There was one distraction that year, though: Minnie Bell became pregnant a third time. In the fall of 1941, less than two years after Donnie died, she gave birth to a daughter she named Jeanette.

Sun's fix on life continued to crystallize into one concern: making money. He was of thrifty German extraction, and added to that was a profound family loss that haunted his life. Sun's grandfather, Richard Edward Swaggart, was just a toddler when he and his brother were sent to live with other family members so their mother could marry another man. Shunted from pillar to post, Richard Swaggart craved something that meant status in the South, and that no faithless human could ravage: land. In land rested a family's worth. If you had land, there was a chance to climb upward. By contrast, a white sharecropper was hardly higher than a slave.

Richard Swaggart worked himself and his children nearly to death to build up a farm outside Monroe. Then, in 1911, at 60, he died of influenza. His wife soon followed, leaving four barely-grown children—one of them Jimmy's grandfather, W.H. Within a year, the farm was lost—acquired, says the family, by lawyers.

W.H.'s story echoed through Sun's growing-up years, charged with acrimony, tragedy, and sorrow. The demoralizing loss flavored the Swaggarts' lives right into Jimmy's generation, for Sun fixed his sights on restoring his family's lost status. It was part of what had made him want to be a lawyer, and it gave him a pathological fix on money.

"Sun Swaggart gets 99 cents out of every dollar," his relatives said. He was always looking for ways to make money, and hoarding it became an obsession. He would show up at Irene Gilley's house nearly every day for a cup of tea or coffee, often at mealtime. "Aunt Reenie," as she was known, was a good cook, and manners required that you always offered food to a visitor, even a penny-pinching nephew. But reciprocity was hard to come by. Once Aunt Reenie dropped in on Sun and his third wife, Dorothy. They sat for awhile chatting, and no one offered Irene refreshments. Finally she asked for a cup of tea. Sure, Sun said, if she would give them some money, Dorothy would go out and buy some tea bags.

"We'd help him go around buying furs," said Cecil Beatty, a cousin Jimmy's age. "He kinda got big with it . . . we'd load them on the truck. I used to pick cotton with Jerry Lee and Jimmy, too. Out on Highway 15, for Uncle Sun."

But Sun paid poorly, barely giving the kids enough money after a day's labor to see a movie. He kept his money in a sack hidden in the bedroom.

"If you'd ever go and eat dinner at his house? He'd always act like he hated to see you eat. He'd watch you the whole time," said one of Jimmy's cousins.

Jimmy was an industrious child, but the clan tsk-ed because Sun made him buy his own clothes. Minnie Bell's sisters and other family members whispered about it.

"Sun's a money lover," said Cecil Beatty. "If you worked for Sun Swaggart and you made fifty cents a day, you were doin' good. What he cared about was makin' money. And right up to this hour, this second, he's the same as he's always been.''

Minnie Bell gritted her teeth under the disapproval, but she never defended Jimmy against Sun. Even her sister Viola Beatty, with her sharecropper husband in their two-room shack at neighboring Swampers, Louisiana, managed to buy their five children one set of school clothes a year. But everything Jimmy was given or denied was pitilessly traced back to some chore he had done or not done. Nothing was free—he learned that early.

"It wasn't fair to do Jimmy that way," his cousin David Beatty overheard his parents say more than once. "He was their child, and they should have bought him the clothes . . . Uncle Sun was real mean to Jimmy in a lot of respects."

Sun demanded obedience, and Jimmy didn't dare talk back to him, or he would find himself sprawled on the floor. As a cousin put it years later, "What our parents called discipline would be called child abuse today."

She remembered a threat Sun would hiss at Jimmy, nieces, and nephews, or Jimmy's playmates when he got mad: "I'm gonna get in my car and run you over."

"If [Jimmy] challenged his father," she said, "Uncle Sun would . . . just deck him."

"Jimmy was scared to death of his daddy," another cousin said. "He couldn't run with the crowd. Uncle Sun wouldn't let him."

"When Jerry Lee and Mickey and Cecil and Wayne and all that bunch was running around, the only one that wouldn't bum around with them was Jimmy Swaggart," said a longtime family acquaintance, Frank Rickard. "Jimmy Swaggart was tucked up under his mama's tail."

The anger Jimmy had to repress tumored into bouts with depression later in life. These bouts became complex, and became entangled with sexual desire. He would call them "demon oppression" and "attacks of Satan."

Texas Redux

On Sunday morning, December 7, 1941, about the time Jimmy and his parents usually walked down the gravel road to church, dawn was breaking on the Hawaiian Islands. In the early morning light, two successive waves of Japanese bombers, fighters, and torpedo planes—more than 350 of them—struck the U.S. Pacific Fleet at Pearl Harbor. They crippled ships and aircraft and killed several thousand troops and civilians. The next day, the U.S. declared war.

Jimmy and his playmates were thrilled and scared. President Roosevelt went on the radio, and families everywhere sat, riveted, while he asked them to defend their country. Immediately, turmoil was everywhere. The U.S. had a War Department which only functioned during time of armed conflict. The army was made up of volunteers, and recruitment parades sprouted in every town. Jimmy's cousin Paul Beatty joined, and soon gave his young life. But his pension would rescue the remaining Beattys—Minnie Bell's sister Viola and her brood—from near-starvation.

Sun, like most men with families, didn't volunteer. But word quickly spread in Ferriday that a defense plant in Texas was hiring thousands of laborers at good wages. Sun made an immediate decision to go. It was another shot at a grubstake, maybe enough to get a start buying land and rental houses like Lee Calhoun. It seemed like Texas was going to give Sun a second chance.

Once again, Sun, Minnie Bell, and Jimmy got into the family truck with a new baby and headed for Texas in winter. They headed due west this time, and the weather was not mild as in Rio Hondo. It was more like Ferriday: freezing rain or cold, sunny days. The defense plant was in the pretty river town of Temple, in the central Texas hill country.

Sun got a job. The Depression ended as the country cranked up for war. New marvels and luxuries started appearing, including a new invention that was the talk of the 1941 World's Fair in New York—television. Louisiana was still seven years away from its first television station, WDSU in New

Orleans. To the slew of Swaggart-Lewis-Gilley cousins growing up in the town, a world that included television seemed light-years away. No one dreamed that among the grubby, laughing boys playing in Ferriday's ditches was one who would make the medium obey him as though he were a world-class ringmaster.

Sun and Minnie Bell's sojourn in Temple turned out similar to their Texas experience two years before. The job dried up after a few months, and they returned to Ferriday. Their experience had been chaotic, as the little Texas town filled with workers and couldn't handle the influx (Jimmy remembered students sitting on the floor because there weren't enough desks at school).

This time, however, they returned with money in their pockets and both children in good health. They came back in early spring and moved back to Tyler Road. Sun began tracking the doings of politicians to decide how to invest.

16

The First Surrender

S even years after Huey Long's assassination, Louisiana's government was still utterly his creation, likened by some to a sheikdom. Politicians knew they had to promise Huey Long-type civic projects to get elected, and deliver some roads and bridges to stay in office—and Sun knew from Lee Calhoun that you had to watch what the politicians did and then try to get into their slipstream. Not long after he and Minnie Bell returned from Temple, he heard rumors that a new highway was going to be put in on Tyler Road. He bought 10 acres there as an investment.

He had other schemes, too, but now that the Depression was over, there were new, unexpectedly subtle pressures regarding money. Yes, the wartime economy opened up opportunities to make money that had never been there for people like Sun, but if you failed, you could no longer blame hard economic times.

The church offered a complicated refuge from this. It seemed to say, "We'll take you just like you are, God doesn't care if you make it big and become the next Lee Calhoun or not." But there were subtexts: "It's okay to fail—we even expect you to." And, "Promise not to go putting on airs and acting like you're better than we are."

There was still bitterness between Sun and Minnie Bell about Donnie, too. Later Sun would identify this discomfort as what naturally happens when someone is "running from God," but he was hardly doing that. He was a better churchgoer than most men. The fact was, he and Minnie Bell couldn't help wanting a reason for the death. But they'd grown up in families where any request for an explanation was seen as blaming. It wasn't that Sun was running from God, and therefore God was chasing him down with a hide whip, but rather that his unhealed family problems were bearing down on him, and God was the only hope of relief from them.

One night, not long after they had returned from Temple, Sun and Minnie Bell took Jimmy and went to hear a visiting evangelist at the church. The man was a curiosity: he had been raised a Catholic, but his whole family became Pentecostal after his mother's cancer vanished when she visited a famous Pentecostal healer.

That night at the services, Sun, softened up by the loss of Donnie, his frustrated lawyer plans, the fights at home, the fears he might not make a bang-up financial success even in good times, his mother Ada's pressure to get saved, and the exemplary way the Holcombs had handled their baby's death, went down at the altar call and surrendered.

He would never forget the peace he felt when he asked Jesus to save him. When she saw him, Minnie Bell went down and surrendered, too.

Ada was ecstatic as a broker closing a big deal. This was the first step toward getting the Holy Ghost, that overflowing joy she wanted for her kids more than anything else.

His parents' constant fighting, said Jimmy later, let up after that. But he was still scared to death of his father. Sun's discipline and bullying of Jimmy didn't change. And though things seemed better after his parents were saved, part of their power struggle would turn out to have simply been driven underground.

In Sunday school, Jimmy read Bible stories. His favorite was David and Goliath, he wrote years later. He loved to sit and imagine he was David. Haul back the sling, whirl it fiercely, and expertly loose the heavy stone at just the right spot and moment to smash that hateful giant right between his mean blue eyes.

17

Taboo

Ada, tall and likeable, had a handsome, bony face and wavy hair going to gray. She was articulate, a quick and efficient woman. Though she bore down hard on her son and his wife about getting the Holy Ghost now that they were saved, her new sobriety did not quell her natural humor. When she smiled, it was total; she had no prim or withering or faint or ironic smiles. Her loud, warm laugh would fill a room with her enormous sense of fun.

Dour Sun had not inherited this from his mother. But Jimmy had, and it drew him to Ada's doorstep—as a baby, he had nicknamed her Nannie—almost every day.

Many times Jimmy had heard her describe Snake Ridge, and the tiny farming community where she had grown up with her ten siblings, and the revival tent there where she had gotten the Holy Ghost. Jimmy would walk to town to her house on Mississippi Avenue, where she would sit him down at the foot of her chair and tell him about it: the nonstop services, the music, the constant praying, and her hunger for something transforming in her life.

When she got to the part about going over to pray under a grove of trees with her brother, Jimmy tensed, because he knew what was about to come. As Nannie described what happened under the trees, how the Holy Ghost had swept down like a ball of fire and cracked her open, leaving her talking in a language she had never heard before, Jimmy watched expectantly. Sure enough, Nannie's posture would change, and one or two of the words of an ordinary sentence would shoot out of her mouth instead of being spoken. Her speech became staccato, possessed. Soon a gush of bubbly sounds, unintelligible, would come streaming out of her mouth, rising and falling.

Jimmy would sit, chills running over him, watching as his grandmother was transformed, until finally the stream of words trickled to a stop and she was still. She would smile at her grandson.

Jimmy would cry. But he would want to hear the story again. It was sensational—and it had the aura of taboo. Even though his parents had been saved, he knew how they felt about the Holy Roller stuff. They still scorned that Holy Ghost business. And he knew the people of the town laughed at it and scorned the Holy Rollers for it, too.

Sun cracked down on Jimmy's visits to Nannie. "She's gone crazy over religion, she's gone foolish over it," he fumed. "From now on, you stay away from there, boy!" All he had to do was lay his hand on his belt buckle.

The Holy Ghost seemed like grownups' business, and there was some relief that his father was protecting him from it. There was some pride that Sun and Minnie Bell were too dignified for it. But on the other hand, anything the adults were that touchy about must be important. Jimmy was a curious, smart kid. He started sneaking over to Ada's house to hear the story and watch her go into possession. The more Sun raved about her fanaticism, the more urgently Jimmy felt the need to hear the story again.

It was perhaps his earliest exercise in what would later emerge as a pattern: performing ably for those who paid his freight, but slipping off to seek other aspects of himself in forbidden places. The more taboo the aspect, the more interested he became in it.

It was only a matter of time until he pondered the unthinkable: what would happen if *he* got the Holy Ghost?

Revival

L ouisiana Avenue, Highway 84 (and also called the Jonesville Road), was
the "Mason-Dixon Line" through Ferriday. South of it was Bucktown.
North was the tiny grid of streets that contained the neat, tree-lined
homes of merchants and schoolteachers and professional people. West,
toward Jonesville, the town petered out after five blocks into a racial no-
man's-land of small and humble cottages, some without electricity or indoor
plumbing. This was where Jimmy's clan lived, in an area where blacks and
whites mingled, living like an old married couple who get along because they
know each other's sore spots.

On Texas Avenue sat the little white box with a sign identifying it as the
Ferriday Assembly of God Church. There were vacant lots all around it and
one across the street from it, and a sluggish, tree-choked finger of bayou
behind it. A stone's throw away, across Louisiana Avenue on unpaved Tyler
Road, lived Jimmy and his family.

From the front porch of his family's little cypress-wood cottage, Jimmy
could sit with his chin in his hands and see across the highway to the church.
Though he was only seven, he had finished second grade in May, a couple of
months after the family had returned from Temple, Texas. He was happy in
the familiar world of barefoot summers, swimming in Lake Concordia or
Lake St. John, playing with his cousins—and, now more than ever, going to
church.

In the late afternoon, when the sky would often become overcast, lifting
the choking summer heat, the members of the congregation could be heard
across the highway, preparing for another night of revival. Jimmy could visu-
alize the wooden pews, the platform that served as an altar, the pulpit, the
piano.

Revival, with guest preachers and visitors from other towns, usually went
on for two weeks or more, depending on the moving of the Holy Ghost. The
bigger revivals took place outside of town under large, open-sided tents like
the one Ada had visited, but smaller ones were held at church. The women

wore summer skirts, and the children often went barefoot. Extra chairs were set out, and the doors and windows to the little white building would be left open to catch what breeze there was. Bugs would fly in, attracted to the light. A visiting preacher might bring a pile of bandanna prayer cloths, used for the laying on of hands, for wiping sweat off the hardworking preachers and musicians, and for covering up women's legs when they slipped to the ground in ecstasy and their dresses hiked up.

The tambourines, violins, guitar, piano, and singing that came out of the little building made revival irresistible. There was the hand-clapping kind of song that made people who believed worldly dancing was a thing of the devil stomp and jitterbug and run through the aisles and shout and fall down on the floor. There was the hymn kind, that made them sway, and lift their palms to the ceiling and weep. And there were songs that nobody realized actually had nothing of the sacred in them, like "Jesus on the Main Line (Call Him Up and Tell Him What You Want)" that made the Son of God into something like Santa's chief elf.

Led by the preacher, people prayed for each other, cast out sickness and evil, confessed their sins, and bore witness to what God had done in their lives. There was preaching, with the people fanning themselves, and children napping or elbowing each other furtively, bored stiff. And at afternoon services, there were big picnics, called "dinner on the ground," of fried chicken and corn on the cob and stewed tomatoes and okra and cake.

Revival was a holiday from tedium, hard work, and money worries. It brought truce to hard-warring families like Jimmy's. Music was the key: it brought out joy and celebration in the adults and pushed away the troubles for awhile. Sun and Minnie Bell usually performed at church functions, and Jimmy was proud of them. Sun would take up his violin and play behind Minnie Bell, who, Sun boasted only after her death, could put anyone in a state of worship with her beautiful singing.

When the second altar call was given by the preacher, people would stream down to the altar and "tarry for the baptism" of the Holy Ghost just like the disciples did at Pentecost. It could whip through a church or revival tent or living room prayer meeting—like a great ball of fire, they called it—igniting people and making them dance, fall, or speak in tongues. Just as dramatic were the prophecies, cases of spirit possession in which someone would loudly "give utterance," speaking in the first person as if God himself were talking.

Or the Holy Ghost could just idle through the sanctuary, hardly causing a ripple despite the hard work of the preacher and the musicians to woo it into the nest of needy sinners. If this happened at a revival, disappointed eyes would be turned on the preacher. Everyone knew he had tried his best, but there was a sense that he had failed to lead people into the correct state of worship for the Holy Ghost to enter. This was one reason revival took a while; it was hard to get to the correct state. Of course, once you did, and momentum was gained, it might happen every night. Then no one wanted the revival to end. But some evenings just ended blandly, with no anointing.

In some of the bigger revivals, if the Spirit was really moving through, people might howl like they were burning, especially if anyone was laying hands on them: that was demons coming out. Adults—men with tattoos and women in their Sunday best—would cry, their chins trembling. Preachers would rip the bandanna prayer cloths into shreds, and wrap them around people's necks or lay them across their foreheads, yelling, "I wanna feel God come through my hands and HEAL ya, thankyou Jesus, can God deliver a drunk? Yes he can! Hallelujah, brother, I see the Lord all over you, let Him touch you tonight, oh, God is so REAL tonight, hallelujah, help me prove God for these blessings, that pain and sorrow will leave ya!"

Women would come to the altar with chattering teeth and trembly arms, fry cooks with their hair nets on and grandmas with bifocals. Let God use you, the preacher would yell. Men strained with their eyes closed; women would stagger and sink to the floor as the kids stared; sometimes an older woman would hurt a hip or something and not even realize it.

Ada got the Holy Ghost easily, and uninhibitedly danced and shouted "in the Spirit" at church. She might get the Spirit when she was out in the yard, or in public in front of people who weren't Pentecostal, and break into tongues. Jimmy's parents hated that. She was making a spectacle of herself.

" 'Say, you need the *Holyghost!*' " Sun would mock his mother.

Plenty of the very folks who got carried away with that *holyghost* in church, Sun snorted, went right back to smoking, drinking, cussing, and lying during the week. And had that *holyghost* kept her husband away from whiskey and other women? No—even though she pressured W.H. into attending church with her, he still had his little gals all over town.

Frankly, Sun thought, he had done quite a bit better with Jimmy and Jeanette than his own parents had done. He wasn't always getting arrested in the middle of the night for whiskey, like W.H. had. He had some investments, some land now. He was getting ready to build himself a house on his ten acres. And he'd been saved; he was living for God and taking his kids to church—that was far more than his parents had done when he was growing up. He'd even given up playing music for the World—he no longer brought out his violin for dances and parties. No, Ada's mission was burning so hot in her because of *her* past life, not because he was doing anything wrong. Between her and Theresa Herron, it looked like the kids weren't going to have a normal grandmother.

Minnie Bell had spoken to their preacher about whether a person had to jump up and run around and cry and shout in tongues and fall on the ground like Ada to prove they were really saved.

"No," he had said, and she felt vindicated. But, he had explained, there were certain gifts of the Spirit that only people who were saved could manifest, and one of them was speaking in tongues.

That showed you were not only saved, but that you were filled with the Holy Spirit in the same way the apostles had been on the day of Pentecost in Jerusalem, as told in the Book of Acts. When a sound of rushing wind entered the room, he explained, all of the apostles saw the same vision, cloven tongues, and they began to speak in languages they had never learned. A crowd gathered. Jerusalem had a large international community, and there were two reactions: one group was astounded to hear the language of its various homelands—Parthian, Elamite, Libyan, Roman, Hebrew, Cretan, Arabic. Aren't all these men Galileans, they asked? How can we hear every man in our own tongue, wherein we were born?

The second group said what Sun and Minnie Bell and the non-Pentecostals of Ferriday were inclined to think: "these men are full of new wine." No one in the Swaggart family was a stranger to that phenomenon.

There was no way a person could speak in tongues, though, the preacher told Minnie Bell, without being filled with the Holy Ghost. Faking that—no one would dare. It would be an appalling sacrilege. God would not forgive that.

Well, Minnie Bell wondered, could you be filled and still not speak in tongues and fall down and holler? Brother Culbreth smiled kindly at such questions. His experience was that when people were infilled with the Holy Ghost, they knew it, and if they wanted to lie down on the floor and praise the Lord at the top of their voices, 20 mules couldn't stop them. And they didn't give two hoots in a haystack what anybody thought about them.

Well, Minnie Bell vowed, you wouldn't find her doing it. And she and Sun also vowed that Ada would not pressure Jimmy to do it. It was one of the things that held them all together, this bond against Nannie's fanaticism that Jimmy secretly breached whenever he dared.

♦   ♦   ♦

Over the next year, Ada intensified her crusade. Under her forbidden tutelage, Jimmy began to see the Holy Ghost as a vaccine against suffering. Ada seemed to be promising that somehow he, the church, and perhaps his parents' music could be welded into a giant poultice that would heal his family once and for all.

But first he had to get the Holy Ghost. By the tender age of eight, he had gone forward in church so many times, asking to be filled, that when nothing happened, he wrote later, he felt himself "growing desperate."

"I don't think the world could ever understand," he told his congregation years later, "my need to get the Holy Ghost." Indeed, Jimmy himself would never really penetrate the psychological complexity of what it meant to him as a child, with the pressure he was under. But in the 1980s, as his huge ministry toppled, he would return again and again in his sermons to images of the weed-choked Ferriday of his childhood, where Nannie's plain frame house sat down the road, baking in the summer sun. "I prayed all the time when I was eight or nine," he bellowed at his flock one day, as if in pain. "We weren't into weenie roasts, we weren't interested in television. We went to prayer meetings. That sounds boring? Not OUR prayer meetings!"

Ada began to give him lessons in how to pray for the Holy Ghost. "Believe BIG!" she would tell him. "Don't you pray a PUNY prayer! God is a BIG God!"

The Theater of Salvation

War news was everywhere in the summer of 1942; the adults talked about it constantly. Jimmy played with his cousins—Paul's brother David Beatty, who was Jimmy's age, Jerry Lee, Sullivan Herron, and Mickey Gilley in the bar ditches on the flat, weed-choked roads and in the vacant lots and woods around their houses. The boys tied sticks together crosswise and flew them through the air. They made whistling Doppler sounds of plane engines and bombs dropping, eerily accurate from the newsreels they saw at the Arcade Theater.

They played along Tyler Road, near Jimmy's house, on 8th Street, and on Mississippi Avenue near Ada's house. They pushed rock tanks along muddy roads somewhere on the Russian front as the summer heat rose in waves off the earth. They divided into teams, fought, took prisoners. They played soldier, and sprawled dead on the ground. There were no curbs along Ferriday's unpaved streets, and water from frequent rains ran in the ditches and stagnated in the heat. The boys caught frogs, fished in the bayous, pretended to shoot Indians and criminals with their long stick-rifles of elm or cypress or hackberry. Often Jimmy had to leave to do chores. Jerry and Mickey seldom did, and Jerry ran wilder than any of the other boys.

Besides war, the boys talked about church, and competed over the subject of whose parents were saved and whose were not. Jimmy's, Jerry's, and Mickey's mothers were all saved, but the status of their fathers varied, with Sun the most virtuous, since he had been saved—had given his life to Jesus. They worried about how the devil can get in you; the adults had said that famous faith healer A.A. Allen made a snake come out of a kid's throat at a brush arbor revival. Jimmy was important because his dad played violin and his mother was a song leader at church. And his grandfather was still night marshal. But he was still scornful of the Holy Ghost, though he secretly prayed for it, and the others listened to him.

"Jimmy!" When Sun's voice cut through their play, Jimmy would drop his toy and leap up. As he tore off toward his house, the other boys paused, ready to scatter. They were afraid of his father, too.

Subtle power struggles developed: in church, Jimmy would sit next to his father and begin praying like the adults, murmuring or whispering aloud in the Pentecostal style. Gradually, he would increase the volume, until Sun would punch him; he would quiet down, and later his father would fret that he was "putting on" in church—a kind of mild blasphemy that Sun disdained.

Unaware of any aggression toward his father, Jimmy felt he was simply doing what the adults said was important.

Since she had surrendered her life to Jesus, Minnie Bell had been pressuring Jimmy to get saved, too. She drilled it into him that it would mean a lot of sacrifices.

She had given up movies not long after she was saved, because they were of the devil. There was a sadness about that, because Minnie Bell adored movies. They broadened her world, they gave her an escape, they comforted and informed her. But she didn't stop Jimmy from going. It had to be his choice to stop. However, she made sure he never felt good about going.

One Saturday afternoon at the Arcade Theater in Ferriday's one-block downtown, Jimmy wrote, he stood in a line of kids. It was 2:30; the matinee was a western. The tickets cost 10 cents. The ticket window wasn't open yet.

Just as with Sun at the drugstore in Rio Hondo, a voice came to Jimmy.

"Do not go into this place," Jimmy reported the voice saying. It said it wanted to set him apart "as a chosen vessel to be used in My service."

That very day, Minnie Bell had told him he shouldn't be going to the matinee. And that was what troubled him as the line inched forward. He really shouldn't be here. He should not go into the dark, barely-cool theater filled with excited kids and their sweaty summer smell, and the sounds of Charms lollipops being sucked and roasted peanuts cracked apart while the kids waited for the theater to darken for the newsreel.

As he stood among the other children, the difference between himself and them felt acute. David Beatty's dad sometimes sold peanuts outside the theater for extra cash; that seemed to broadcast the cousins' poverty to the other kids. Those kids went to churches on the other side of Ferriday, bigger and nicer churches than Jimmy's. He was one of those Holy Roller kids, and he knew it. But their parents didn't have the same determination to seek God as his relatives did. And he knew it was easier for a camel to go through the eye of a needle than for a rich man to get into heaven.

He left the ticket line and spent his movie money at Vogt's Drugstore, on a triple-decker ice cream cone, and felt, he wrote later, "as if a thousand pounds had been lifted off my shoulders."

Minnie Bell asked why he was back home so early.

Jimmy sat at the table. "I didn't go," he said. With an instinct for drama, he said no more.

"Why?" His mother finally asked. She had stopped wearing makeup since she was saved, and she never wore jewelry or hair ornaments any more. Her clothes were plain and decent. She did not have a fat, tired look like her sister Mamie, nor Aunt Stella's hard-bitten look. Her face was sweet. She kept the house clean. She cooked, washed, farmed, did her duties uncomplainingly, gave her time to the church, was kind and sweet to others. She simply refused to fight with Sun any more, and the family had begun to see her as saintly.

"I gave my heart to the Lord," he said. "I'm not going to the movies any more."

Her eyes filled with tears.

THAT VOICE at the theater, Jimmy later said, marked the day he was saved. No one is alive who knows if the story is true; his mother was long dead by the time the tale came out, and the event happened on a Saturday when none of his many cousins showed up for the matinee—a rare Saturday indeed. Like many of Jimmy's key childhood reminiscences having to do with his Call to the ministry, this incident had no witnesses. God spoke to him in a Biblical dialect, eschewing contractions and using words like "vessel"—like, in fact, something that might happen in a movie.

He has never seemed to think it revealing that he was saved at a theater of performing arts, rather than in church, at the altar. Did he never notice over the years how the church and the movie house were both theaters, one secular and one religious, how they competed with each other as temples, one sacred and one profane, and how they looked almost the same—seats facing a stage where a compelling story is being told? And did he never ask himself, in the years after his great release that day in front of the secular theater, why and how he came to be carrying a thousand-pound weight on his eight-year-old shoulders in the first place?

But whether his story is precisely accurate or not, whether he was "saved" in the right order—before he got the Holy Ghost, in the Pentecostal praxis—and had to make a small adjustment in his story after he became famous, it makes no difference. His cousins confirmed that he did have the character at age eight to give up movies, and the moment he did was the moment a power-less child discovered the key to power. Not only was he saved, he had cracked the code. He had found something that would bring his parents together, that would set him apart competitively from the other cousins, who would never be able to equal this sacrifice, and that would make his mother happier than Sun could make her. It would undo some of the times of hearing her sob behind her closed bedroom door.

He hungrily moved forward to bigger and better audiences, more and more scrutiny and notice. But he never liked writers or reporters to probe for any truth except the one he wanted told.

Defection

One Saturday morning in the summer of 1943, Jimmy was playing in the street a few blocks from the church on Texas Avenue. A prayer meeting was in progress there for the anointing on another revival. Jimmy and several other little boys were engrossed in their play when a loud cry split the blue sky above their heads. They dropped their sticks and looked around, all except Jimmy. Even before the scream began repeating itself, he was swept with dismay. The voice was coming from the church, and it was his mother's.

His whole body went hot with shame, and his face burned up to his scalp. When the other kids dropped their game and headed for the church, he slipped off and ran home across rocks and stickers. It was as if Mama had broken a family pact, one of the few that held them together. It was one thing for Jimmy to sneak off and visit Nannie and watch her forbidden actions, but officially, he, Daddy and Mama were far above that kind of thing.

Now it was as if Mama were one of those women who fell to the floor with her skirt up, for the whole world to see. She had crossed over to Nannie's side, leaving Jimmy unsure of where he stood. The big worry was how Daddy would take it. Were they headed for the old days of fighting and screaming again?

He arrived home to find his maternal grandfather, Papa Herron, looking for the midmorning cup of coffee he was in the habit of taking at his daughter's house. From the sorrows of alcohol, stomach problems, and women, Papa Herron's temper was not long, and he was working himself into a black snit. Before long Sun's pickup whipped into the yard and Jimmy's parents got out. His mother's face was alight, and she was bursting with the sounds of Nannie's unintelligible language. Papa Herron got a couple of words into a tirade before he noticed his daughter's extraordinary state. She leaped up onto the porch, took her father in her arms, and whirled him around.

It turned out that most of the congregation had been overcome with the Holy Spirit that morning. A visiting evangelist, brother J.M. Cason, had preached a sermon filled with the kind of emotional praising and weeping that used to disgust Sun and Minnie Bell. Who would have thought that nearly everyone in the church would be seized? Mamie, Ada, Mickey's mother Irene—they ran, they shouted, they fell, and they spoke in tongues.

Soon Jimmy found out that Sun was not one of them, though he seemed pleased with his wife's euphoria.

Jimmy watched his father closely over the next weeks. Sun got very quiet about the anointing of the Holy Ghost, and quit criticizing "holy rolling." He also quieted down about Jimmy visiting Nannie.

It was not lost on Jimmy that his father could not get the Spirit to enter him. Sun prayed for it, he went down and lowered his head on the altar or lay on the floor. It was he who had led Minnie Bell to salvation, and she received the gift of the Holy Ghost easily now. The Bible said that the man should be the spiritual leader of his family. But he never came up spouting in tongues.

One night in late August of 1943, the Swaggarts left the house after supper was washed up to walk the quarter-mile to church. The dirt road still felt warm from the sun. It was a long block to the rocky gravel of the Jonesville Highway, and then a block of dirt road again over to Texas Avenue. The lights and music were already piercing the evening.

In Jimmy's mind, almost at the surface of consciousness, a battle was about to be decided. Sometimes it wasn't clear whom he should try to please at church: Nannie, Mama, Daddy, or God. But since his mother had gotten the Holy Ghost, he really wanted it badly, with as much passion as he had mistrusted it before.

It was rapidly becoming a matter of status in the family, for attitudes were shifting to a consensus that a person had to be quite pure for this sort of witnessing, and you had to have it to truly be a peer in the church. Not being able to get the Holy Ghost was now beginning to seem more like you were marked—as either possessed of a rebellious spirit, like Sun later said he was, or so deeply sunk in some private sin that God just couldn't get through.

Minnie Bell had been so proud when Jimmy gave up movies. It had brought him much favorable attention and envy.

She would be even more proud if Jimmy could just get the Holy Ghost. Especially if he could be the first among the cousins—maybe even before Sun. Aunt Mamie had been able to speak in tongues several times, but neither Elmo nor Jerry Lee could. Neither could Aunt Stella or Uncle Lee Calhoun, though they had put up the money for the church and attended regularly. They routinely went and knelt during altar calls, but never did either of them fall to the floor in surrender to the Lord, and never did they come up bubbling in tongues. Lee remained what everyone called a "hard sinner," gambling, smoking, cursing, and engaging in things outside the law.

To outstrip adults like Daddy, Uncle Lee and Uncle Elmo. . . . He had prayed and concentrated hard, but nothing happened. The services tonight would be the last revival before school started.

After the singing had stirred people, the visiting preacher, Sister Thelma Wiggins, gave a fiery sermon. The regular preacher, Brother Henry Culbreth, started a hymn, and all around Jimmy people sang with their eyes shut or their hands lifted into the air. Some sat with hands on the pew in front of them, fingers laced together, elbows on their knees and forehead resting on their hands. People murmured softly in prayer, crooning "hallelujah, glo-ray," over and over. Jeeeeee-zuss, the adults whispered and moaned all around Jimmy. Jeeee-zuss.

The Spirit seemed to be stirring in the room. The level of excitement edged upward. This was the time when the preacher might start a chant of exhortation: "Come on! Step OUT! Step out, in the name of the Lord, hallelujah Jesus! Ever one of you has got trouble and sorrow, now I wantcha to start PRAISIN' the Lord! Why doncha lift up your HANDS and call upon his name, praise him tonight, thankya Jesus, oh, hallelujah, thankyou-Jesus!" The worshippers would hear an endless mantra about how they didn't have to go to hell, didn't have to go to the Lake of Fire.

All around Jimmy, the adults were raising their hands upward and murmuring or shouting "Yes, yes! Amen! Thankyou-Jesus!" They moved into the aisle and down toward the altar. Jimmy was on his knees near the piano. A shaft of brightness seemed to find him.

He felt something happening inside him. The Holy Spirit!

The church elders laid their hands on people's heads, necks, and shoulders, and prayed hard for the spirit to move. "God be on this young man and loosen his tongue. As the Holy Spirit is in here right now, blessed Jesus, let it speak through this servant. Oh, thank you, God, thank you, Heavenly Father!"

Sun, having knelt and prayed, but without result as usual, was almost back to his seat. As he turned to step into the row, he saw Brother Culbreth motioning to him. Sun went back to the altar, wading into the sounds of tongues—"Ah-menee-bed-enemee-bou-dee-fou-mou-dali-eye-hun-dai!"

Brother Culbreth whispered to him.

"He's prayed through."

He pointed down at Jimmy, kneeling on the platform.

Sun heard his boy talking rapidly, his eyes shut tight. He had heard tongues many times before, but never before or after did he remember it sounding like this. The sounds coming from Jimmy's mouth were beautiful, splendidly fluent, and people were looking at him. Sun felt a strange urge to kneel in front of his son. He didn't know why, but he felt like getting as close to the child as he physically could. He knelt, but kept a few feet's distance so as not to disturb the flow.

Jimmy spoke with confidence. His head bowed, Sun peeked at his son. The boy was totally assured. He spoke on and on, not in a loud voice, but with a strange authority. Sun noticed that the church had quietened and some worshippers were standing around the altar watching. Jimmy's little-boy voice, eerily commanding, rose above the other murmurs in the room, and then ceased.

"Praise Jesus!" whispered the preacher. Jimmy opened his eyes. He was flooded with a feeling of peace and security he had never felt before in his short life.

SUCH A POWERFUL blessing of the Holy Ghost was, of course, very well received by Jimmy's parents and the members of the church. He got much positive attention and approval. For several days after the experience, he refused to speak in English, being overcome by tongues almost every waking moment.

A couple of days after his breakthrough, Minnie Bell sent Jimmy to the post office to buy a stamp. When he got there, he was seized with another spell of the Holy Ghost, and he made the clerk (who was not Pentecostal) nervous and a little impatient by repeatedly asking for the stamp in tongues. Finally he had to leave without it, and when he arrived home, he was not punished for failing to do the errand.

Nowadays, this tale is recited in Jimmy's writings and sermons with much head-shaking insider amusement at people like the clerk, who will never "get it" about the Holy Ghost. It always brings knowing laughter and amens from the audience.

However, for the eight-year-old Jimmy, the post office stunt was cheeky, the kind of bold move that would carry him far in the evangelical field. He was running his new-found status up the flagpole to see if it would bring him approbation in the larger world as it had in his extended family. When he got rebuffed, he was tasting the sort of consequences that would separate him all his life from the American mainstream and cement him firmly to his own kind.

Significantly, it wasn't long after Jimmy's sensational experience that Sun got the Holy Spirit himself.

Then Jimmy pulled another coup.

The Blockbuster

It was late morning in the summer of 1944. The fields of Concordia Parish still had their freshly-turned spring scent although the seed of new cotton had already sprouted. In back-yard gardens and truck patches, potatoes, beans, alfalfa, and corn had willowed into adolescence. The smell of living earth floated on the air and hung over the town.

Jimmy, age nine, walked along the Jonesville Road in the heat. His cornsilk hair hung in uneven bangs above his eyes. They were beautiful eyes, blue like his father's, and mercurial.

He had just finished fourth grade, although he was barely nine. He was far smarter than his parents realized. Though they were proud he had learned to read quickly and liked books, they had no idea how much he took in.

He was on the way to his great-aunt Irene Gilley's house. Again, there was a revival going on, and every day one of the faithful like Aunt Reenie would hold a prayer meeting for its success.

Jimmy reached the Gilleys' little two-story rented house on a commercial strip of Mississippi Avenue in Ferriday's tiny downtown. The lower floor of the house was a pool hall run by a local merchant. The Gilleys lived above it, in a one-bedroom flat for which they paid $35 a month. The whole family— now just Mickey and his parents, since his older three siblings had grown up and left home—resided in the living room because Irene rented out the bedroom to overnight tenants to make ends meet. Mickey slept on a mattress of unmilled cotton; baths were sometimes with water from a rain barrel.

His father, Arthur Gilley, was a good-looking, genial man who worked at various enterprises, from driving a taxi and operating a pool hall to working for Standard Oil to, finally, running the Bonnie Belle and other little bars around Ferriday and up the highway toward Vidalia. But he was a womanizer, and that got expensive. So he was not inclined to tell Irene much about his income, except how little there was of it.

Ada—Jimmy's Nannie—was there in her sister Irene's living room, already praying in the heat. She and Irene had become regular "prayer warriors" at the church, holding special daily meetings to invoke God's blessing on everything from revivals to marriages to children and crops.

Irene kept her old ice box, cooled with block ice, in the living room, where her derelict tenants couldn't get at it. Several kids were perched around, leaning back against it and sitting on the furniture and the floor. Everyone was praying, and the praying did not stop when Aunt Reenie silently motioned Jimmy into the room. Later, she would wish she had noticed more about him that day, whether he looked different.

BACK DOWN THE mile that Jimmy had walked, Sun Swaggart straightened up from his planting and wiped his forehead. It was dead quiet in the ten-acre field behind his house, except for bird-cry. Inca doves, robins, and redwing blackbirds flitted through the woods at the edge of the field. He looked back across the field toward the little house, about a quarter mile away. It sat close on the Tyler Road.

Ferriday had changed little since his parents had arrived in 1930, in the lap of the Depression. He had been only 15. Now he was 29, a fine-looking man, though hardened by disappointment. He still played his fiddle, but now only at church. He was still full of schemes for making his fortune and getting out of Ferriday, but they were receding. He had forged a vexatious marriage with a pretty, headstrong girl, and they had fought without letup. But the Lord was healing that. Slowly, the Lord was healing that.

He looked down. The row was almost finished on the little knoll where he was standing. He began planting the fall okra.

He was covering a hole when, for the second time in less than five years, he heard a voice speak clearly inside his head.

"Your son is saying the things that will come to pass."

His first instinct, he later said, was to get away from the little knoll. He walked over to the far side of the field and puttered there about half an hour before returning to the okra patch. As soon as he stepped up the gentle grade to the spot where he had been, it happened again. This time he listened.

"Your son is saying the things that will come to pass," the voice said twice more.

Sun stood still.

From the house, he heard an excited call. There was Minnie Bell, running across the field toward him, waving her hands excitedly. Trotting behind her was his father, W.H. Breathless, they stopped in front of him.

"Jimmy's prophesying!" Minnie Bell said.

"I know," he replied. He explained the voice.

She stared at him. He wasn't sure what she was thinking. Maybe she thought he was trying to upstage the boy.

◆   ◆   ◆

In Irene Gilley's living room, Jimmy had been saying there would be a terrible disaster. He spoke in two other languages besides English, and it didn't sound like tongues speech. After speaking, he sat quietly, looking down at the floor.

The next day, it was decided that the morning prayer meeting should be held at church, because there were suddenly twice as many people interested in the services, and Irene's house was too small. Curiosity was high; had God really spoken through the Swaggart child? That was German he was speaking, wasn't it? Sounded like German. The other one sounded like Japanese.

People stood on the front stoop of the church and on the lawn of tough, weedy pinwheel grass and stared in the Swaggarts' direction as they approached. Some of them had looks of wonder and pride, some of envy, others of skepticism. Ada, of course, was proud. By the time the prayer meeting started, the church was full. It was Jimmy's second real audience.

Again that day, and for the next three days, during sessions of intense, sweaty mass praying, Jimmy moved into the state he later described as "standing outside my body. . . . I didn't know what was happening. . . . then I began to describe exactly what I saw."

What he saw became something of a secret. Sun was not allowed to talk about it after Jimmy became famous; Frances didn't like him to. But family members remembered, and Jimmy himself reported some of it: he saw "a powerful bomb destroying an entire city . . . tall buildings crumbling . . . people screaming." Others say he predicted a tsunami or flood over Ferriday.

The prophecies always happened at altar call, when everyone was praying. "His voice would *sound*," Sun said later. "Not loud, but it would carry, you see. Supernatural. And everybody in that building heard it, and in just a few seconds' time. And then there was nothing but quietness, and him speaking. In these different languages. And then giving the interpretation of it."

On the fourth day, Jimmy was Front Page in his big extended family, and even Lee Calhoun, who went to church to please Stella but never showed up at the prayer meetings, came. Sun felt excitement when Lee sat down. He called him "Mr. Calhoun" out of deference to Lee's wealth and stature, even though their wives were sisters. Lee listened at altar call as Jimmy spoke in a language that sounded like German. There was an interpretation. Lee turned and whispered something to the man beside him.

After the service, Sun went to the other man.

"What'd Mr. Calhoun say?" he asked.

"Well, he said he knew that child couldn't [fake] that. And he said, 'you know, that child spoke wisely!' " Sun felt pride welling up in him. Further, the friend told him, Calhoun had said that he didn't believe that "it's just for right now"—he believed Jimmy was predicting something that would happen in the future. But the main thing was, Calhoun had said he knew there was no way it could be faked. Calhoun was a shrewd man, hard to fool.

The prophecies went on for one more day. "Nine *messages*," Sun said, "was given in the course of five days. . . . Some things would be cleared up . . . someone would say to me, 'I just don't know about that.' And then it would be cleared up the next message, and then they would look over at me and smile."

"When he talked," said Jimmy's Aunt Arilla, "it sounded like a language, and it was different from ordinary speaking in tongues. But you couldn't tell if it was Japanese, or German. He said there wouldn't be anything left in Ferriday, not even an ant. Some people believed it was prophecy, and some said it didn't amount to anything."

There were many skeptics, but the people who were present agreed on one thing: the messages were amazingly specific. They described the exact dimensions of the bombs. They described a great flood over Ferriday, and they told exactly how wide and how deep the water would be. One of the bombs had a name.

"He said, 'Great Britain has invented the ten ton bomb. And they have called it the Blockbuster,' " said a family member.

"That was 1944 too, see. He told what it weighed, the name of it, what the name of the nation was that invented it, everything. See, right at that time, Hitler was wreaking havoc on the high seas concerning our troops. With his submarines. And we couldn't do anything about it. So we was losin' the war, cause he was stoppin' our ships, tore em up."

One morning several months after the prophecies, that same relative picked up a copy of the *Monroe Morning World*. In the big type reserved for historic news, said the relative, it told about a "ten-ton bomb that Great Britain invented." The bomb was called Blockbuster.

But the news media had reported on several bombs labeled "blockbuster" over the past two years. Maybe it never occurred to Sun and Minnie Bell that Jimmy read the papers, too. Or maybe Jimmy was breaking his vow now and again, and sneaking in to see the newsreels at the Arcade.

However, Jimmy had also predicted a massive bomb, bigger than the Blockbuster, and this one had not been made public in the papers or newsreels yet.

Rivals

Paths of ambition converged in the family, and camps formed. Jimmy's prophecies gave Minnie Bell's and Ada's stature in the church another big boost, and he became their project. Mamie also examined her children—she had given birth to daughter Frankie in 1943—for godly qualities that might be developed, and she and sister Stella cultivated Jerry, who was turning out to have a talent for music.

These groupings were natural; Minnie Bell was much like her sister Viola, who was 13 years her elder and a sweet mother figure, "normal as apple pie," according to a niece. Now Ada, 22 years older, was the same mother figure to Minnie Bell.

Stella and Mamie were less than two years apart in age and were close in temperament. Both had been wild girls, and both had malignant tempers but could turn on considerable charm. Both were fun-loving and congenial when it suited them, and they cared deeply about their children. Both had a fierce bond with Jerry.

There was plenty of other familial rivalry, both active and vestigial, in the Jimmy-and-Jerry camps, too. Ada and Elmo were siblings; Elmo and Sun uncle and nephew, married to two of the five Herron sisters and competing to please them. There was pressure to measure up to Lee Calhoun.

These rivalries affected marital relationships as well as natal ones, with parents vying with each other for their children's affections or for control or influence over them. It is widely written, for example, that 1943 was the year that eight-year-old Jerry Lee marched up to his Aunt Stella's new piano, picked out a song on the black keys, and uncorked the flow of genius that helped define a new genre of music that would sweep the world.

Stella did buy a piano about that time, and made it available for Jerry to play, and Jerry did have a lot of talent. But it was really Junior's death that set him on the path. Ever since Junior's death, Jerry had felt the slippage between his parents, and knew that, like Jimmy, he was both their battlefield and the ground for their truces. By the time both boys were eight, it was clear to them that their fathers had failed their mothers—Jerry's because he drank and didn't make a good living, and Jimmy's because he was mean-sprited and stingy.

"I loved my daddy so much," Jerry said at 57. "But my daddy was a good-for-nothing, he was a weak man. The Lewises were no good, they weren't worth a plugged nickel. They would just set up there and get drunk and let the women handle it, the women and children. They wouldn't help the women and children."

When Mamie was mad at Elmo, she'd say to Jerry, "I'd give anything in the world if I could change your name from Lewis to Herron."

Jerry was made to go to revivals and listen to terrifying sermons where sweaty, wall-eyed preachers yelled, "You want to escape the *Lake of Fire*, don't you? Yes, of course you do! Because there won't be any mercy for you *there!*"—but then Mamie let her likeable boy run wild, right toward the Lake of Fire—lying, stealing, failing in school, disobeying rules, not having chores like the other kids, running around all over town to places the other kids were forbidden to visit—which compounded his guilt and fear of God's wrath a thousandfold. She insured his affection and loyalty and then turned the job of disciplining him over to the vengeful God of the Pentecostal church. She called him "Son" all the time, according to his favorite ex-wife. She didn't call him Jerry, because she wanted to keep before him that sacred, fearful, emotionally incestuous role he must play: her possession.

What happened when Jerry sat down at Stella's piano at age eight was that the weight of his parents' focus on him—their competitiveness, anger, love and ambition, cherishing, competence and incompetence, all of their meta-morphosed grief—plus a genetic load of talent magnified by generations of cousin unions—spotted an outlet. When he began to play, the relief of losing himself was no doubt great.

Jimmy was set on a similar path, by a similar circumstance, a year after Jerry was. The death of Donnie, and the need to heal his parents, the pressure from Nannie and Minnie Bell to excel in the church, the need to best his father and make his mother proud, and the same genetic load of talent, also found an outlet.

"I'VE ALWAYS SAID that the big difference in Jerry and Jimmy was their mothers," said Myra Lewis Williams, Jerry's cousin and third wife, the notorious "child bride" who derailed his career at its height and who, according to many, was the only woman he ever really loved. "These kids were raised with this, 'women are sacred, just a little below an angel.' Almost as if she was a religious figure. I'm not going to say it was unnatural, but it was odd, very odd. They will never utter a word against their mother."

However, "Aunt Minnie Bell was an angel. And you can see the difference in the directions the two of them took."

Jimmy set himself apart from his cousins, as a prodigy should. He made an altar out of an old log in the woods behind his house, and prayed there daily and noisily. Sometimes he prayed so ostentatiously that people grinned. Sun knew there was much sincerity in Jimmy, but there was much performance, too, and sometimes he bordered on disrespect. It was not something one should object to or try to control too much, however, because by definition prayer was between God and Jimmy.

The two boys went to school and played together constantly, but their lives were a contrast. At seven, Jerry had been sent to live with Stella and Lee while his parents went on the road looking for defense work like Sun and Minnie Bell had. Resources were lavished on Jerry: new clothes, a room of his own, an allowance, medical care, access to a piano. The stigma attached to the movies made no impression on him. Nor did he feel constrained to pray hours a day to impress the adults, nor build a makeshift altar, nor go to almost daily prayer meetings.

Jimmy's environment was one of fierce female virtue and determination. His days were consumed by church, Sunday school, revivals, camp meetings, prayer meetings. Years later he would say he didn't know what a thermometer looked like as a kid, because when he got sick, Minnie Bell would pray about it, and then tell him he was healed and to go out and play.

Jimmy distinguished himself in his piety from all his cousins, but especially from Jerry. He didn't have access to Aunt Stella's purse, but he had developed a rich reading life, and he gave more than one teacher hope that a little Holy Roller kid could make it out of Ferriday.

In the spring before the prophecies, Jerry Lee failed third grade, while Jimmy, already a year ahead though only six months older, passed fourth grade handily. Jimmy found his cousin crying in the schoolyard on the afternoon report cards were handed out, afraid to take his crop of Fs home to Elmo. Jimmy took him back inside the building to talk to Mrs. West, Jerry's teacher. He explained that Jerry would be beaten and maybe killed. Though that last was pouring it on, the teacher had seen enough rough families in Ferriday to know that a lot of what passed for discipline was actually battering. She rewrote the grades so Jerry barely passed.

Jimmy was also better behaved than Jerry. Even though he was "kind of touchy; he'd pop you one," according to Mickey, you could deal with Jimmy. Jerry fought and quarreled more, was undisciplined, didn't have as many chores or curfews as the other kids. That made him more popular, but clearly Jimmy's camp, run by Ada and Minnie Bell, was laying up treasures in heaven, while the Stella-Mamie-Jerry camp was going for the earthly rewards.

This was exemplified in the stubborn spiritual problem that kept Stella and Lee Calhoun from assuming the unchallenged leadership that Stella had hoped for when Lee helped build the church—their inability to get the anointing of the Holy Ghost. You had to be pure of heart for it to happen to you, and many of the congregation had managed to get pure enough at least once. But not Stella and Lee.

It was a mystery. It seemed that even the first step toward the anointing—giving their lives to Jesus and getting saved—would be a threat to their hard-won financial status, for it would mean no more moonshining, loansharking, cattle rustling, buying political favors, or slumlording, for starters. And true, Stella liked to smoke and drink, dance, gamble, and hear a good off-color joke; but hadn't she earned every bit of fun that came her way? She tried to watch her mouth, but damned if she was going to buy that you were chalking up time in hell if you hit your thumb with a hammer and let something slip. If not for their ways of livelihood, there wouldn't even be an Assembly of God church in Ferriday in the first place.

And Stella was a good person; she helped others and was generous to a fault. Wasn't that what God asked of his people, not that they go down and howl and wallow on the ground in front of everybody? She seldom expressed such things, and she did worry about her spiritual condition. She really didn't have anything to replace religion with, so she did the best she could, going to church often. She and Lee set a good example, always going down at altar call and kneeling in prayer. No one could say they weren't good church people.

Stella listened in silence to her kin talk about the sweetness of it, the peace, the feeling of having no more burdens. Minnie Bell, Mamie, their Herron sisters-in-law, their Lewis in-laws Irene and Ada—all the women in Stella's circle, almost—had been saved and then received the all-important gifts of the spirit. True to the Word, the Lord seemed to be making an example of Lee and Stella: one had to choose between the status that comes from wealth and that which comes from renunciation. It was a sad, but to some family members secretly rather satisfying, underscoring of God's position on rich people and camels.

Last Chance

On July 6, 1945, a huge cloud lifted itself above the desert in the no-man's land near Alamogordo, New Mexico. Robert Oppenheimer, director of the Manhattan Project, watched his handiwork and quoted the Bhagavad Gita: "I am become death, the shatterer of worlds."

In Ferriday, Jimmy and Jerry, Mickey, David Beatty, and the other boys played on the 3,667 feet of the new Vidalia-Natchez bridge across the Mississippi River. They were unaware of the atomic bomb or the Bhagavad Gita, and had only a vague sense of the place called New Mexico.

"Who could even think of a weapon in that day comparable to the atomic bomb?" Sun Swaggart would reply 45 years later when asked about Jimmy's Blockbuster prophecies and his warning of an unnamed bomb, bigger than the Blockbuster. "It's unbelievable, you understand . . . Y'see, it was considered a fairy tale in those days. How could anything like that be?"

A year had passed since the prophecies. In a haunting photo of Jimmy during that year, his eyes held some awareness that soon there would be no turning back for him—his life would never really be his own and he looked like he already knew it.

But in the early summer of 1945, before Hiroshima and Nagasaki, there was a chance. David Beatty remembered some of their boyhood stunts: lying flat on their backs in a little boat, they'd force the boat through a narrow pipe that funneled water under Highway 84 by pushing against the slippery inside wall with their palms, their faces inches from the pipe's curved surface. "We coulda got stuck—we COULDN'T have . . . pushed the boat out with our hands, slippin' on the mud or whatever in there . . . my stomach does flip-flops thinkin' about it. And we did it. A LOT of times."

"I guess [Jimmy] was the toughest of all three of us," Mickey said. "Nobody picked on him. He had the reputation for being a fighter. I guess it doesn't take very many times of not backing down from a fight to get that reputation. Anyway, people left him alone. He wanted to be a boxer [like Sun]."

They played in Lake St. John, though they'd had no swimming lessons. Jerry Lee couldn't swim at all. Once, cousin Cecil Beatty saved Jerry's life. "[Jerry] suddenly slipped off the bank into the deep part. I got him by the hair. Pulled him in by his long, wavy hair!"

They played a game called "conquered-unconquered," where the boys vied to do something dangerous, sometimes jumping off a building, sometimes running along the tops of boxcars behind the train depot and jumping from one car to the next as fast as they could, including the slippery cylindrical ones. If it got too easy, they'd jump across to another set of cars on the next track and then back. They did the same on buildings downtown, jumping from one roof to the next. "You had to close your eyes and jump," remembered Gerald Lewis, another cousin.

Mickey was genial, prodigiously strong, and good at sports. He and Gerald were close. Once when Mickey spent the night, Gerald's parents clucked how he had misbehaved, and if Irene didn't get control of him, he was going to grow up to be a real bad boy. "I'm just as bad as he is!" Gerald blurted.

Mamie didn't want to know all the things Jerry was up to. After taking out burial insurance on all her children after Junior's death, Mamie felt that whatever Jerry did, at least she would never bury another child with only a rock for a headstone.

Once Mickey and Jimmy were along when Jerry walked the rail on the Mississippi River bridge, hundreds of feet above the water. "You're conquered!" he yelled triumphantly as he jumped down. "I sure am!" agreed Mickey, aghast.

One of the forbidden things Jerry did was sneak over to Haney's Big House, the rambling black dance hall on Highway 84 on the way to Vidalia. He'd watch the musicians, the drinking, and the wicked dancing. He wasn't exactly permitted to do these things; it was that, by the age of 10, he feared no authority except Mamie, and her punishment didn't stick because she didn't really mean it.

Jimmy was growing up pretty much like the other boys except for his exile from the movie theater. But in August 1945, when atomic bombs were dropped on Hiroshima and Nagasaki, his prophecies were resurrected for discussion. What had been a good hunch on the part of a bright kid with an instinct for drama started to gather some of the weight of myth, at least among his champions. "Nobody thought the prophecies were childish any more," he wrote years later.

Then, astoundingly, the year the war ended, Jimmy's flood prediction came about. The Mississippi River flooded its worst since the devastating inundation of 1927. Ferriday had to be evacuated to the levee at Lake Concordia, and the Swaggarts, along with scores of other families, lived for weeks in a tent city.

The water poured through the Swaggarts' little house on Tyler Road. But since it was made of cypress, it didn't split and loosen after the water receded, and they were able to move back in with minimal repairs. Once again, people remembered that Jimmy had prophesied Ferriday under water. The "'45 Backwater," as Sun called the flood, didn't put Ferriday as deep as the ocean, but people noticed three things: that a big flood had been predicted by Jimmy; that it happened at around the same time as the huge bomb Jimmy had predicted; and that the Swaggarts' house was spared complete destruction.

With encouragement from these events and some willing adults around him, it was easy for Jimmy to start believing he had actually predicted the atomic bomb. He knew in his heart what had happened to him as he gave the prophecies, and when he had spoken in tongues to the postmaster the year before that. Certainly it was sincere. But were the prophecies really from God? Or was there a subtle line that got crossed, from being willing to be used by God to actually *willing* a thing to happen? He had concentrated hard and prayed for God to use him, until it came about. What if it was of Satan, the Great Deceiver? Could he insinuate himself into a prayer and trick you into thinking God had answered it?

"When a person prophesies," according to Pentecostal scholar Cecil M. Robeck, "people don't ask if it's true, because they're afraid they'll be judging God. At the time Jimmy did this as a child, people would have been open toward it, and accepted it. This is typical of Pentecostals: God can speak through someone who is open, willing to be used as a vessel of God, a passive vehicle. Jimmy's description of what happened showed him being passive. What's different is the source of the utterance."

No one could ever be sure that source wasn't Satan. Discernment of the source was itself a gift of the spirit, but was it possible to be fooled, or fool others, when you were "in the spirit?" Maybe. According to Robeck, "The Pentecostals would express it like this: everything God has, Satan tries to counterfeit."

And by Jimmy's time, Christianity had so demonized the underworld that the shaman, whose role is to make forays there and come back with knowledge and help for others, had long been denied acknowledgement.

Mickey didn't remember the prophecies the way some family members did.

" 'Ferriday is gonna be as deep as the ocean.' What a bunch of bullshit! [Jimmy] had everybody shook up, saying they were gonna bomb Ferriday and it would be as deep as the ocean, as wide as whatever, you know, he had all the dimensions and everything. You know how Jimmy—have you ever watched him preach? Jimmy is a master storyteller. He'll have you crying like a baby."

WITH THE SPOTLIGHT on him again as a prodigy, the curtain closed between Jimmy and the other kids. While still touchy and hot-tempered like Sun, he started taking on some of the saintly attributes of his mother.

"He's a precious person," said Jerry's sister Frankie Terrell. "He was always so special. If I accidentally—always when I would get tickled I would . . . get myself wet. And Jimmy would never laugh. He would always shame the other boys, the other cousins, he would say, 'Look, she couldn't help doing that.' I just loved him to death."

But there was a downside she remembered, too: "I've never felt [that Jimmy] was a human being. No one felt comfortable around Jimmy Lee . . . everybody was so hush-hush, nobody would say, utter 'dern' or 'damn' or anything. And everybody would put on the biggest act . . ."

The revelation of the atomic bomb the summer he was ten sealed his fate. Frankie Terrell said, "We respect people that are, as they say, anointed. An anointed minister, we respect them. . . . there's some things you don't fool around with. You just don't fool around with God, or His people . . . so [the family] just always overemphasized on Jimmy, and his mother, and his grandmother . . . they preached to that child constantly, he never—he just didn't get to do all the things other boys did."

If the adults said he was anointed, he'd better not argue. The God that "chose" him might not take kindly to that.

"You didn't live the life you were given," Mickey said. "You lived the life the church told you to. We were taught that our way was the only way to get to heaven. Women couldn't wear jewelry, they couldn't cut their hair, they couldn't color their hair, they couldn't wear short sleeves. You were not allowed to do anything that the church didn't teach; you'd die and go to hell."

Christianity rejected the body and focused on the problem of pleasure. In the Pentecostal faith, the fear that pleasure takes one away from God had metastasized to banish a wide spectrum of pleasures, from adornment and hairstyle to spirits and tobacco, from dance, literature and film to, most vociferously, sex.

"It was ridiculous," said Mickey. "Why would God care if you got someone to trim your hair like you wanted it? Why would God care? And if you were a parent, and your kid was bad, would you send your kid to the inferno they told us about? What parent would send his kid to hell? It was child abuse! Yes, I bought into it, I was just a kid, and I say it was child abuse!

"Some of the things they would come up with, they were very harsh, trying to keep the kids in line. . . . I was taught that, one drink of beer and BOING! Down to hell you go. I remember being a child and crying in my bed, begging God, 'I don't wanna burn forever and ever!' I was scarred by religion."

The apparent supernatural power of prayer, and the implied ability of God to turn it against him if he got too rebellious, was always before Jimmy, as well as the other boys. Irene and Ada would get together and pray that something bad would happen to the bar that Mickey's father owned in Ferriday. It burned down, and then nothing would grow on that lot, according to family tradition. Another tradition holds that Irene and Ada prayed fervently for an old woman who lived in a shack in Irene's back yard, who was terminally ill with a wasting disease. She outlived both of them. Jimmy himself claimed to have been healed by prayer, of an unnamed childhood malady that caused him to faint and vomit.

Being bright, he became adroit at mixing the adults' agendas with his own. His uncle John Lewis remembered with amusement how Jimmy maneuvered Ada into helping him avoid his chores.

"One day, Jimmy was supposed to be planting something—Sun had sent him out to plant. He planted two-three rows, and then, he told us later, he got 'burdened.' He just couldn't work any more. He felt a great weight on him. He left and went to Nannie's and told her he needed her to pray for him, because he felt a heavy burden on him that was keeping him from doing his chores. . . . Well, Sun noticed Jimmy was a little long in coming back to the house. So he went out, and found the planting hadn't been done. When Jimmy got back, he said, 'You ever do that again, and I'm really gonna lay it on you!' "

Later, in his sermons, Jimmy would imply that his church life had been intense and thrilling, that it banished boredom, rebellion, and the lures of The World. He prayed all the time when he was a kid of eight or nine, he said, and he wasn't "playing church" like the other kids. "I meant business!"

But the truth was that he sometimes sneaked out of the sermon, according to his cousin David Beatty. By the time of the atomic bomb, with no "manifestations" for over a year, he no doubt felt much like David: "I hated all of it. Why did they have five stanzas in every song? And why'd they have to sing 'em TWICE? God-a-mercy, cut me some slack! I was bored outta my skull. Jimmy, Jerry, Mickey and all of us cut our names in the pews in the back. We'd be bored to death during Sunday School."

As a preacher, Jimmy would seldom, if ever, celebrate the boredom and the sneaking out, the rebellions and the attempts to contact a more ordinary, unremarkable ten-year-old boy inside himself during that year of respite. He would no longer own that little boy, whose ordinariness threatened to upend a big emotional investment by the adults.

HE LATER RECALLED that it was at age 10 or 11, about the time Hiroshima and Nagasaki were bombed, when he first felt the "oppression" that would torment him his whole life. Standing next to a fence, he felt a "terrible foreboding" come over him. He had a vision. A globe of the world was spinning above his head. A voice said, "You will not do it. You will not do it. I will stop you." The voice sounded threatening, taunting. In retrospect, he decided this was Satan demanding of God that he have an equal shot at this child God had called to evangelize the world. He decided this was the only explanation for why he felt torn apart by this oppression from that time on.

But there were other kinds of oppression looming. By 10 or 11 he had already developed a secret interest in the forbidden. Sex was certainly in that category. Later that secret interest would not be silent, and it sought an arena that would tolerate—and integrate—Jimmy's carnal self.

Many Are Called

"So the last shall be first, and the first last: for many be called, but few chosen."

—Matthew 20:16

T he war was over. Gas rationing ended. Cotton prices rose, pleasing the farmers of Concordia Parish. You could buy just about everything again except sugar. People felt confident enough to start families: Mickey's sister married; his brother Aubrey had recently married Lola Herron, Minnie Bell's niece. After the war, Elmo was finally able to buy his first little house. But he immediately put his family under intense financial strain by mortgaging the house and taking the money to Monroe to buy a Starck upright piano for Jerry Lee. The piano would eventually go to the Smithsonian Institution, but when Elmo bought it, it sent a message to Lee and Stella and the rest of the watching family that Elmo had some pride, that he didn't have to be dependent on Lee Calhoun for everything. But it didn't last; he was soon financially entwined with Lee again.

The boom in radio sales before the war had resulted in a great homogenization of American music, which had, at least commercially, been defined since before the turn of the century by people who lived in cities—jazz, "sacred" tunes, and semi-classical music. Country or rural music of the sort sung by the cousins and their families was seldom heard on the radio before the war. Then a musicians' strike gave hillbilly music a chance, and a new market was discovered.

Jerry's father played the guitar and sang Woody Guthrie songs. In churches throughout the South, white folks' vale-of-tears wailing mixed with blood-thumping black blues. Church music was pious but earthy, and among the Pentecostals, it was always a tool of the emotions, never of the cerebellum.

Being a Pentecostal meant breaking the rules of sacred music the way it was played in the mainstream churches: slow, formal, and reverent. The Pentecostals played tunes, not hymns. Many of their songs (like many hymns, in fact) were adapted out of the dance hall, sung with religious lyrics but retaining a distinctly worldly backbeat. The Pentecostals *owned* their music; it was everyone's, and it was an integral part of the all-important tongues speech. You could not get to that state of ecstasy without music, and they used the instruments they had at hand. Thus the Pentecostals introduced dance-band instruments like tambourines, fiddles, drums, mandolins, guitars, and triangles to their meetings.

Jerry played with his daddy's guitar, he hummed without thinking about it. He took the guitar to school and played it during recess. Music seeped into and out of the boys. Mickey asked for a guitar, and his mother bought him one. Sun's sister Arilla acquired a piano, and invited Jerry and Jimmy in to play often.

Shortly after he made the prophecies, Jimmy had begun to beg God for the gift of music, promising he would never play in a night club and would "always use the talent for your glory." He was especially impressed by Brother Cecil Janway, a visiting preacher who played and sang skillfully. He watched closely, and after the services, he made some of the chords he had seen Brother Janway make. Soon he was amazing his parents with his skill.

Jerry played at Stella's house. He imitated at first, but then he made the music his; new energy seemed to come out of him.

But there were several memorable influences on the boys. Besides Brother Janway, there was a local black handyman called Old Sam. Whenever he was working nearby, the kids would beg him to come to the nearest house that had a piano and play. With a skillful left hand, he added a rolling beat to popular tunes that was much more exciting than anything the boys had heard in church, on the radio, or in music lessons. They learned to imitate him, cultivating a sound that would mutate into a revolution and last for generations.

Sun and Minnie Bell amassed enough money to get a piano and give Jimmy lessons. He was too advanced, hated the boring plunking, and quit after four lessons. Jerry was also given lessons, but quit after the teacher slapped his face for cursing. Shortly after that, he was sent to Pine Bluff, Arkansas to visit Mamie's sister Fannie Glasscock. He came back in six weeks with more piano skills than the stodgy teacher could have drilled into him in a lifetime. His cousin Carl Glasscock had taught him the honky-tonk-style that was irreverently called Holy Ghost Boogie.

Mickey's mother bought a piano, too; the first tune he learned to play was the "Missouri Waltz." But when Jerry came over, Mickey would pay close attention, especially to Jerry's adaptation of Old Sam's "walking" left hand. He and Jerry and the other boys played all the time, becoming obsessed. "That piano's takin' over!" Irene would complain—though the boys could keep on her good side by playing beloved hymns such as "I'll Fly Away," "Keep on the Firing Line," and "The Old Rugged Cross."

CHARISMATIC CHRISTIANITY boomed after the war. The three largest Pentecostal sects that emerged were the Assemblies of God, the Church of God, and the Pentecostal Holiness Church. The Assemblies was the largest of these. Pentecostals were more affluent now, and had stopped fighting over every little doctrinal twist. They had finally been admitted in 1943 to the National Association of Evangelicals, the successor of a major fundamentalist group that had rejected them during the Depression. They formed their first major association; eight large sects comprised the Pentecostal Fellowship of North America.

A new healing revival began churning through the small towns and industrial communities of the South and Midwest. In the South, the woods and roads were full of traveling evangelical healers.

Sun Swaggart started to get interested in it. Sun had been doing a little preaching, and met many who joined the movement. From these small independent Pentecostal ministries came a generation of preachers who shook off their hometown shackles and became powers in the larger world—with the help of radio and, later, television. The postwar faith-healing revivalists were precursors of the televangelism phenomenon where Jimmy was to make his mark.

Americans were fascinated with the faith healers, partly because the war and the bomb had left them with anxiety, and partly because some of the healers were lurid and sensational. Faith healing had enjoyed a long tradition in the church, including prayers for the sick and belief in divine intervention in human affairs; to become a Catholic priest, in fact, one still has to prepare to cast out demons. In the 20th century this healing torch seemed to have been passed to the evangelicals.

Their rapturous revivals could go on for weeks. Not since the days of the circuit riders on the frontier had so many people been so encouraged in release of all kinds, from weeping, falling on the ground, leaping, running, and dancing in states of transport, to public confession of their sins, lapses, and shames.

In April of 1946, when Jimmy was 11, an astounding 25,000 people journeyed from 28 states and Mexico to Jonesboro, Arkansas, about a day's drive from Ferriday, to listen to the preaching of Pentecostal mystic William M. Branham, a modest man who was not gaudy and sensational, but rather had such a luminous presence that the mere sight of him could bring people to tears. After he left Jonesboro he was followed by a permanent entourage of campers who couldn't let go of the ecstasy and the sense that they were in the presence of God around him.

These evangelists—men like Branham, Oral Roberts, Jack Coe, A.A. Allen, O.L. Jaggers, Raymond T. Richey, and others—had certain things in common. Almost without exception, the successful ones came from poor families and had tales of tragedy, humiliation, and suffering, especially during the Depression. Many had come from harsh homes where their fathers or stepfathers had beaten them; some had run away.

All suffered intense discouragement, going to bed hungry, preaching in the freezing rain to a handful of people in some tiny church or mission for only a few dollars, not knowing where their wives and children would be sleeping from night to night. Rural poverty was the thread on which these men were strung like God's baubles, and most ended up grateful for their hardship, feeling it had taught them something invaluable. It was hard to knock them over with disappointment and failure.

Most of them had some element of intense religiosity in their background. When the father was an alcoholic brute, the mother was most likely to be deeply religious. Most felt some miracle had occurred in their lives—a divine healing, a visitation from God or an angel, or a rescue from alcoholism or a dark path. Almost all felt a "call" to preach and heard the voice of God definitely say something like, "son, I've called you to preach the Gospel throughout the world" or "Go into every land and heal the sick."

Many used music to control the mood of the services, which generally lasted four or five hours. Most had total confidence in their charisma, and many claimed healing power in specific places, like their right or left hand. All had some sign of the anointing: a voice, a vision, an angel or spirit. They were accustomed to hard work, and thought nothing of spending hours and hours onstage, clapping, singing, praying hard, laying on hands, shouting, exhorting the crippled to walk and the blind to see.

In 1947, the revival really erupted. Suddenly, prayer for the sick and gatherings of vast crowds for healing and renewal were happening all over the world, set off by the American movement. "A generation grew up," said Pentecostal historian David Harrell, "that would never forget the ecstatic years from 1947 to 1952, years filled with long nights of tense anticipation, a hypnotic yearning for the Holy Spirit, and stunning miracles for the believers performed by God's anointed revivalists."

Sun was captivated. When Jimmy was about 12 or 13, Sun and Minnie Bell started traveling to small towns around the area to help set up churches and organize congregations. Sun was a scalding, hellfire preacher, but the main draw was the music they made, with seven-year-old Jeanette on squeezebox and Jimmy on piano when they could get him to go.

For every healer that made a national reputation, there were hundreds like Sun, caught up in the great fever, loving the travel, feeding off the expectation and excitement of the crowd, however small, and making his (or her—there were many women evangelists) unique contribution to the postwar movement.

The movement's enemies were the failures to heal, the ridiculing by the press of their claims, the disapproval of other denominational leaders, and the growing attention of the government—which was interested in subjects like IRS audits, mail fraud, and operating businesses without a license. The evangelists were harassed by local law enforcement as well as the press, because the services were weird and noisy, besides cutting into the local churches' collection plates. More than once, the ropes securing Sun's tent were cut down in the night. The evangelists, their lives ironically much like musicians', met at all-night cafes in the wee hours after services and talked and fretted over these problems until dawn.

Their excesses were picked up eagerly by the news media. A.A. Allen was a truly gifted healer who lost his bearings trying to hold onto his fading fame. As the healing revival came to its close, Allen claimed regularly to raise the dead and heal incurable diseases. His testimonial claims included a woman who had swallowed an open safety pin and felt it rise into her mouth when Allen preached; a man who "passed" six cancers into a jar; a woman who lost 200 pounds on "God's reducing plan"—in front of the congregation; a hermaphrodite who was changed into a male at a service, his large breasts disappearing on the spot. Allen got into legal and logistical trouble with his resurrection claims when people started mailing dead bodies to his Arizona headquarters to be "raised."

By 1956, the media's accusations of hucksterism marked the decline of the revival: one evangelist claimed he had 17 witnesses to the resurrection of a woman who had been dead half an hour. Another claimed he could see out of his glass eye. During one period, someone noticed that evangelists had claimed three million converts in Jamaica, when there were only a million and a half people on the island.

And there was the repulsive element of healing. Evangelist LeRoy Jenkins' newsletter description was typical: a sick woman "spit up a bloody cancer which had long roots on it . . . it almost choked her to death while it was coming up." One supplicant claimed to have been healed of blood clots, mastoid trouble, sciatica, body pains, throat trouble, bloody sores inside his nose, astigmatism in both eyes, nervous tic, kidney trouble, sinus, gastritis, athlete's foot, rectal trouble, an ankle injury, and "tired shoulders."

The evangelists' problems were compounded when the services started to attract people who were unstable to start with. These types were especially attracted by the exorcisms, because they believed they were possessed by demons, including those of sickness, lies, drinking, fornication, spending, divorce, insanity—even Hitler demons surfaced after the war.

It was easy for this to get out of hand, because what these people often wanted more than to be exorcised was to be able to act out their sickness in an accepting environment. It was subtle—the way Satan is reputed to be subtle, in fact—the Great Deceiver turning a healing into a rout because the evangelist dare not be so heartless as to throw such disruptive people out—if he could even discern whether they wanted healing or just to satanically loose demons onto the service and discredit it.

Many Pentecostal preachers were known for loving luxury—an understandable weakness for men raised in poverty, but devastating to their secular and mainstream religious credibility. Fancy cars and mansions were always the subject of scandal. Another staple was the air of sexual license that hung over revivals. There were, as in frontier times, always whispers of people getting aroused by the singing and emotion and going off into the woods; the 19th-century wisecrack that "more souls were begat than saved" at revivals was resurrected for the new evangelical surge.

When they were criticized, the ministers called it an attack of Satan, who was trying to destroy the movement of the Gospel in the world.

The serious healers, like William Branham, tried to grapple with some of the paradoxes found in all kinds of healing, but were ridiculed for it because they were operating on intuition instead of from medical knowledge. When they offered insightful reasons why healings didn't last or didn't take—such as that, once the healed person gets back to his real life and allows unbelief to creep back in, he loses his connection with God and his power to heal himself; or that the very work of healing meant taking sickness into account as part of the healing, as a divine manifestation of what is wrong—they were scoffed at for making excuses.

The more responsible preachers knew that the power of suggestion and the prayers of other people were strong factors in healing. Other factors were the willingness of people to be healed; how high their expectations were that it would happen; the group concentration in prayer that amounted to powerful mass meditation; the importance of attending every service so as to get immersed in the hypnotic broth; the willingness to convince oneself that this was God's will; the conscious surrender of your ego to the group, and the belief in their goodwill for you; allowing yourself to get excited by the music and by the emotional testimonies of others who had been delivered; and the willingness to prepare yourself for healing before the meetings—by reading specific chapters in the Bible, praying, reading accounts of Jesus' healings, and consciously empathizing with those he healed.

After all this preparation, if you were willing to believe in the anointing of the evangelist and willing to enter a state of arousal, it really might be that the only other thing you needed was for that sweaty shaman to lay his hands on you, and you really might be able to jump up out of your wheelchair, even if only for a minute or two.

But the healers were not sophisticated or educated men. They could not intellectually defend these ineffable factors, especially when their less scrupulous or ill-guided brethren were making a mockery of them. And the skeptics would never voluntarily consider the role of psychosomatic healing or psychology in the revival—that sells no newspapers.

The skeptics seldom complained that the staid and respectable Catholic faith was also rife with miracles, oracles, healing waters, stigmata, visions, and goddess worship. None of them guffawed at the notion that those "props" all had genuine meaning for Catholics, and a viable place in that religious system. It was the circus atmosphere cultivated by the huckster evangelists that made their movement into a bull's-eye.

One preacher stated it as well as it could be said by an evangelist: doctors cannot heal, he said. They keep people alive, and he was glad they existed, but they can't heal anyone. That was true, of course—all any doctor could ever do was manipulate factors that interfered with the body healing itself— and the serious evangelists all admitted they couldn't heal. But they didn't hear doctors admitting that, nor reporters balancing their stories with it.

Finally, instead of just sticking to the notion that faith is the prime ingredient of healing, and faith is a mystery; that salvation is always the unembodied goal, some healers fell into the trap of trying to provide physical proof to the skeptics. Even though a few evangelists successfully awed medical experts with confirmed before-and-after displays of healing, that effort was a mostly unmitigated disaster.

When Jimmy was 12, William Branham visited Shreveport, Louisiana, near the Texas border. His revival was a fantastic success and the word spread; in the fall of that year, he attracted 70,000 to a meeting in Vancouver. His sponsor in Shreveport was Jack Moore, a building contractor. Moore's daughter described watching Branham arrive at their house: "Could I ever forget the first time I saw him—that Sunday afternoon in 1947 when a little '38 Ford turned in our driveway, and a slight, tired man with the deep eyes of a mystic got out and looked around. As I watched from the window, I began to weep for no apparent reason, except that my heart seemed to break."

Running from God

Though he and Minnie Bell were pursuing itinerant preaching around Ferriday, Sun made a small incursion into the merchant class that was much more comforting to Jimmy as he entered adolescence. Sun's new grocery, run by W.H. (who was no longer a lawman) when Sun and Minnie Bell were out of town evangelizing, gave Jimmy a secular foothold in the town. He was tired of being a little Pentecostal prodigy.

Jimmy was growing up, and it was becoming harder and harder to get him to go to church regularly. He was the only one of his crowd who was still making even a half-hearted effort to obey. It wasn't just that his cousins were less pious; it was that the old strictures were breaking down. High school and college were now within reach for a generation of poor kids whose family tradition had been to drop out by age 15. More of these kids stayed in school longer. Better-educated Pentecostal teens became embarrassed by their parents' lack of sophistication, and resentful that they still clung to the church's strictures when there was no material reason for it any more. The Pentecostal cult of poverty, a boon when making a lot of money had seemed impossible anyway—was no longer as relevant to their lives.

Jimmy hadn't been to a movie in five years, an extraordinary show of discipline. His cousins and playmates still went regularly to the Saturday matinees. No one really seemed to take religion seriously any more; many of his friends and cousins had quit attending church altogether. Jimmy's status as a pious outsider was now a lonely, empty role that brought no satisfaction.

One day, shortly after he had turned 13, he screwed up the courage to ask his parents if they thought it would be okay for him to go to the matinee. They were lying on the bed after lunch, and they just stared at him.

He asked again, but still his parents did not answer. Finally they both started to cry. Neither of them said a word to him.

He went on to the movies, but he left halfway through, literally sick with guilt.

Naturally, he accepted all the blame for this, later citing it as an example of how pure his parents were, while he, a child of 13, was "running from the call." He never questioned whether his parents were being extraordinarily manipulative.

Not long after that, a school medical screening showed a rapid heartbeat, and the doctor advised him not to take up any school sport. He was 14, and shattered. His body was maturing, and he was becoming a tall, good-looking boy. As he had dreamed of being David and killing Goliath in Sunday school, Jimmy dreamed of besting his father at boxing.

"Uncle Sun never forgot those [boxing] days," said Jimmy's cousin Gerald Lewis, who also had a rapid heartbeat that kept him out of sports. Sun "had whipped everyone in Ferriday" before he was beaten by the boy from the C.C.C. Camp who weighed 260 pounds and had been formally trained. Sun weighed 165 and was self-taught.

"My goal was to become the heavyweight champion of the world," Jimmy wrote. "I wanted to be strong and powerful."

Now that dream was gone. Bitterly disappointed, Jimmy poured out his heart to his mother. Minnie Bell was set on Jimmy keeping his position as the family's anointed one. Instead of comforting her son, she suggested that God was behind the rapid heartbeat, because Jimmy was "going the wrong way."

But Jimmy continued to pull away from his role as the little family avatar. Since his belief system meant he was constantly in the wrong anyway, he began to sneak out at night with Jerry and steal things. At first it was a lark—as Mickey said, "They just did it for mischief. To see if they could get away with it, . . . like you go out on Halloween night and tear it up." But it didn't stay that way for long.

Jerry's stealing was from the first unchildlike and bold. He wasn't just cutting up, toiletpapering houses and moving garbage cans down the block. He and Jimmy, along with several other boys, were stealing things they could sell. They stole hubcaps and took batteries out of cars; Jerry was caught stealing a gun, and was suspected of stealing a motorbike. They broke into warehouses and stores and stole jewelry and watches from places like Rexall Drug and the newly opened Hollis Jewelry on Louisiana Avenue. Jimmy stole from his father's money bag hidden in the bedroom, according to a cousin who got blamed for it.

For kids who had trouble staying in school, this was not a particularly rare deviation; the question was whether they would get straightened out or get in with the wrong crowd. Most of them did straighten out once girls came into their lives. Jimmy did a lot of it out of boredom, but he was also trying to work through his father's miserliness. He was trying to confront the urgency to get wealth that had become a festering mystique in his life. It had to be penetrated.

The boys' early adolescence coincided with the completion of the Mississippi River bridge linking them to Natchez, Mississippi—which immediately widened their world exponentially. In Stella's car, Jerry and his friends spent more and more time exploring the underbelly of Natchez and the little outlying juke joints—the Hilltop Inn, the Swan Club—on Highway 61, which ran from New Orleans through Mississippi, up to Memphis and beyond.

The same Puritanical seizure that had led to Prohibition brought about the suppression of red light districts, "with the ironical result," wrote historian J.W. Cash, "that the majority of Southern hotels immediately turned into brothels." Natchez' most famous establishment was at 516 North Rankin, near the railroad track. This was the house of Miss Nellie Jackson, the great Madam of Natchez who was murdered in 1990 at the age of 87 by the jilted boyfriend of one of her girls. He knocked on her door, threw kerosene on her when she answered, and then followed it with a match. The fire flashed back onto the killer, igniting the kerosene can and burning him to death as well. There were other whorehouses in Natchez; one of Jimmy's relatives is reputed to have worked at one briefly in her youth. Nellie Jackson herself presented a Gilley in-law with a wedding gift in the 1940s.

It was a time when pornography, crude but effective, beckoned—for boys, a viable substitute for Bucktown or the expensive and wicked Nellie Jackson's. The mimeographed texts that were passed around until they were ragged usually consisted of a man taking a girl off into the woods and having one sexual adventure after another with her, such as the girl eating cherries one by one off his erect penis; when she got to the last cherry, he added the "cream." Even a story that dumb was wildly arousing to boys who would desperately love to have sex with a female.

Visual pornography took several forms. The poor man's version consisted of doctored-up Sears catalogues—the lingerie section, with nipples and pubic hair added. There were decks of playing cards featuring oral sex and a variety of positions, spiced up with whips, lace, and feathers.

There was also the classical source—*National Geographic,* with its photos of bare-breasted "natives"—and nudist magazines from Sweden; and there were the "eight-pagers" or "Tijuana Bibles," little booklets of drawings of popular cartoon characters engaged in various sex acts—Maggie and Jiggs, Little Orphan Annie and Daddy Warbucks, Lil' Abner and Daisy Mae, Nancy and Sluggo (and Aunt Fritzi), Archie and Veronica.

Legitimate places to actually learn about sex were virtually nonexistent. Parents spoke in disapproving code and kids guessed among themselves at the meanings.

With money he made from working in his father's grocery, Jimmy began to spend his time at Red's Pool Hall in Ferriday with one of his Beatty cousins (who in later years would use Jimmy's influence to help soften a prison sentence). The rest of the time he practiced piano with Jerry Lee. By age 13, Jimmy and Jerry were piano prodigies, in great demand to play at area churches. But when they started putting the rhythm they'd learned from Old

Sam into songs like "Just a Little Talk With Jesus," they got into trouble. The congregation liked it, but the preacher heard something wicked in it and made them stop.

Sun needed a piano player to attract people to his services. But Jimmy had no desire to make the dreary trips with his parents and his little sister, sitting in the back of a car, looking out the window at the gray winter sky and trees dripping with rain, on the way to set up some tent warmed with kerosene heaters. Just to harangue a few rednecks in some little dead-end community into getting the Holy Ghost? It wasn't like good-looking girls flocked to these things. And he couldn't play piano in any way that had any fun to it, like he'd learned from Old Sam. He had to play like an old cripple, so it wouldn't raise his father's hackles.

By the time Jimmy was 12 or 13, Sun and Minnie Bell had begun to leave him behind. They arranged for him to have some meals at his aunt Eva Gilley's Cozy Cafe on Louisiana Avenue. "I'd try to come home every seven or eight days and spend a day or so," said Sun of those years, but the fact was that Jimmy was left alone much during his adolescence. Ferriday was still a rough place, and without parental supervision, dirty pictures were the least of the trouble for Jimmy to stumble into.

"There was slot machines everywhere in Ferriday in them days," said Jimmy's cousin Cecil Beatty, brother of David. "It was wide open. You could do anything you wanted as long as you had the money to get out of it. There was bodies in the alleys. You better come in before dark. We had to when we were kids."

Once the boys were hanging around the barber shop on Louisiana Avenue, eavesdropping on an argument the barber was having with one of his customers in the chair. Suddenly the disagreement took an ugly turn, and the barber tried to stab his patron. The man leapt up and ran out the door, but the barber chased him down the street and killed him.

Jimmy's grandfather was no longer night marshal, and not all his relatives were great Christian examples. There was his aunt Eva's (sister of Nannie and Aunt Reenie) long-running sexual relationship with his grandfather Herron, and Eva's cafe, where he took meals, had slot machines where even children could gamble—Gerald Lewis once saw a young boy win a large heap of coins there—and though it was a modest place, she somehow had a Cadillac and her husband Harvey seemed to have plenty of money and wore a diamond ring.

It was rumored that Harvey Gilley, who died in 1951, was secretly poisoned or otherwise helped along toward death by Eva, who reportedly pulled the rings off his still-warm fingers before the police were called to keep them from being stolen by Ferriday's finest or the funeral parlor folks. Even in their sixties, Eva and her sister Jane (grandmother of Jerry Lee's beloved wife Myra) would go over to Natchez and hit the clubs. Jerry's sister Linda remembered, "They used to embarrass the hell out of me! I'd go out to a night-club and be sitting there and they'd come in, and they'd be drinking and they'd have young men with them. . . . [they'd be] dressed like real young girls . . . They were rockin'!"

"I wouldn't want this attributed to me," said a family member, "but Jimmy and Jerry went to one of those houses of ill repute [in Natchez] when they were about 13 or 14." Whether the boys did anything or just got cooed over by the women was not known.

Jimmy was also gambling, which was wrong but whose sting he mitigated by refraining from grosser sins like smoking and drinking. As his trips with his evangelist parents got rarer, Jimmy felt ever more tormented by his bad behavior. Minnie Bell was in the habit of coming into his darkened room on her return from a trip in the wee hours and standing over his bed, praying audibly for him as he feigned sleep. After she left, he often cried himself to sleep. The constant diet of guilt worked away at him, and he tested everything on which it was founded. But he only succeeded in creating more guilt.

In writing years later about his sin of going to a movie again at age 13, he said, "I was afraid to ask God to forgive me, for that would mean confessing something was wrong in my life."

Whether or not that was a veiled reference to things worse than movies—like pornography—it revealed a mechanism of the Pentecostal worldview: if you felt bad about something you did, it must be because *you* were in the wrong. Questioning the thing that made you feel bad was out of bounds. Forbidden to love the body, required to treat it as a betrayer, a Pentecostal boy still had to find outlets for sexual arousal. Most of them felt guilty and drifted away from the church that made their God-given urges such a stench in God's nostrils.

Jimmy drifted away, but he was set up to come back. His parents and grandmother had cultivated a habit of isolation in him by insisting that he set himself apart from his peers at a young age. He had a way of dealing with pornography, masturbation, and the guilt they caused—splitting them off and giving them a room of their own in his head. He'd had a secret life for years, starting with his forbidden trips to Nannie's and his nighttime thefts with Jerry Lee. Now he was an unsupervised young teen in a rough, raw town. Everything was in place for the development of a self-feeding obsession with sex.

The Anointing of Satan

Nineteen forty-seven, the year Jimmy and Jerry turned 12, "Louisiana Hayride" debuted on KWKH radio in Shreveport, and both boys loved it. Jerry especially loved Hank Williams' voice, and was greatly influenced by him. Their parents liked the program, too, despite their church's admonitions against playing music for The World. Williams was wildly popular, and not even the pious in the church complained that the tune of his worldly "Honky Tonk Angels" closely resembled their beloved hymn "Great Speckled Bird."

It was a time when radio and television stations, looking for programming, sponsored local talent shows. Communities picked up on this and started holding events at school auditoriums and parks. Jimmy and Jerry entered one little contest after another, usually playing double pianos. There were always rumors of "talent scouts" in the audience for shows like the Hayride and the "Grand Ole Opry."

At the talent shows, they could freely play Old Sam's rhythms and those Jerry had picked up at Haney's Big House on Highway 84. Since they had been playing piano, the boys—but mostly Jerry—had been sneaking down to Haney's at night from time to time, sometimes accompanied by other cousins, to watch the goings-on there.

"Haney's [Big House] was a huge colored dance hall, the biggest one in this part of the country," said Frank Rickard, a family friend. "And Jerry Lee and them would just slip out there and go look in the windows and watch 'em play."

The large frame establishment owned by Big Will Haney sat at the edge of town, on a little bayou that ran under Highway 84. Black musicians traveled there from all over the South, the best blues players in the world—though the world neither knew nor cared—following the crops for work, and they stopped awhile at Haney's to sing and play piano and guitar, to dance and get "tore down" and then vomit up the night's crimes out back, under tough hackberry trees pulled at by equally tough grapevines.

As often as he dared, Jimmy sneaked out with Jerry Lee to peek through the windows at Haney's to see the dancing that got raunchy with the night and the drinking, and hear nasty jokes and music with bawdy lyrics. Haney's, usually packed, never closed.

The only white people allowed in Haney's were Natchez disc jockeys, who had to stay at their own table next to the stage. Young men like Muddy Waters, who had picked cotton outside of Natchez, and newcomers whose names were not known yet—Ray Charles, B.B. King, Bobby Bland—were regulars at Haney's along with ancient blues wizards, unknown stylists.

"We'd go down there," Jerry recalled for biographer Nick Tosches, ". . . and sell newspapers and shine shoes and everything, and we'd keep on doin' it until nobody was lookin,' and then we'd work our way through the door, y'know. And them cats is so drunk they couldn't walk . . . Man, these old black cats come through in them old buses, feet stickin' out the windows, eatin' sardines. But I tell you, they could really play some music—that's a guaranteed fact."

Before long, Jerry didn't bother to sneak into Haney's any more—he openly sat in on the piano. There was no controlling him, anyway. He was often the only white person in the place. Jimmy didn't dare try such a thing. His father would probably kick him out of the house.

But there were other places to hear the music. "It wasn't just Haney's Big House," said Rickard. "There was Good Time Charlie's, and the Money Wasters' Club . . . these were all black places. Good people." Rickard wore an orange checked vest into one of the clubs. "Charlie said to me, said, 'Look, Mr. Frank, how much is them vest?' I said, 'well, I paid 20 dollars.' 'How much would 50 of them be?' And I went down and got a fella in business in New Orleans to make him 50 vests for eight dollars apiece. And he had Money Wasters—MW—put on 'em."

Jimmy and Jerry won so many talent contests that they were refused entry to any more. Jimmy was bothered by his promise to God to never use his skills to play for The World, but the adulation and attention were too much to resist. David Beatty remembered the thrill of their first talent show in 1949. He, Jimmy, Jerry Lee, and Mickey, all 14, played at Ferriday High School.

David was on electric guitar. "We were doing 'Wine, Wine [Wine Spodie-odie]'. . . . When I got to the chorus . . . It was just the boogie, what we called the boogie . . . And them kids, girls, I never will forget all that screaming, they went crazy. They was screaming and carrying on, and we won the talent show hands down . . . it was just exhilarating."

Jimmy and Jerry moved on, competing against adults who played professionally for dances and in clubs.

Around Jimmy's 15th birthday, they entered a talent show in Jonesville, about 30 miles west of Ferriday. There were 35 contestants, and Jerry and Jimmy performed separately. Jimmy was up first, and this time the thrill was serious. The audience was filled with adults. These were his *elders*. He played "Wine Spodie-odie" like he'd never played before, like he was possessed, and the crowd cheered and whistled and stomped. It went through him like a current. This was the anointing of The World he had been warned of so many times, and he could see why it was such a big deal.

Jerry won first place. In the car on the way home with the jubilant Lewises (Jimmy's parents would never have driven him to such an event), Jimmy was depressed. He later said it was because he knew he'd broken his promise to God, and that he knew the anointing he'd felt was from Satan. But Jerry had also bested him, and he had to endure the ride home with Elmo and Mamie stroking Jerry's wavy blond ego.

This contest was a turning point in his life. He had been a medium for something new and powerful, a sexually explosive music that he already knew was wrong because his minister wouldn't let him play it in church and because he saw how familiarly it curled and mingled in the thighs and throats of the women and men at Haney's Big House and the other black clubs.

Jimmy had already done some time as a medium—in the church on Texas Avenue and in prayer meetings. He understood how you have to surrender yourself and let the power come over you. But this power was far scarier than the Holy Ghost.

Not long after the boys' triumph at the high school talent show, Jerry Lee was offered a job playing at the Wagon Wheel in Natchez, and he took it with his parents' blessing, though he was not yet 15 and it was illegal, because it paid far better than sharecropping.

Jimmy worked in his father's store, making $4 a day. He spent his free time trying to multiply it. He gambled and shot pool and rolled dice and felt guilty about it, but money, his father's nemesis, was an ever-beckoning temptress.

One day a Natchez club owner came into the store and offered him an illegal job like Jerry's—$16 to play a couple of hours on Saturday nights. Jimmy wanted that job. But it was his luck that W.H, his grandfather, was standing there, fussing over the shelves with a cocked ear. If he even hinted that he might cut such a deal, it would get back to Ada immediately, and then to his Mama. Upset, he refused the offer.

Narrow the Path

"Narrow is the way, which leadeth unto life, and few there be that find it."

—Matthew 7:14

In ninth grade, Jimmy and David Beatty both failed algebra. They were passed on to the tenth grade, but had to stay in ninth grade homeroom, which was humiliating. After that, school steadily lost its hold on Jimmy, and in the tenth grade, he quit.

David's alienation was much like Jimmy's. "I didn't care about anything, and nobody in my family had an education anyway. A couple of my brothers had made it to the seventh grade, but I was big-time, I was almost in tenth grade. My parents were almost illiterate. There was no way Mama [Minnie Bell's sister Viola] could intelligently communicate with me about anything."

David's description of his state as a teenager mirrors what Jimmy says about himself at that time. "My self-esteem was very low. I felt like nothing, like nobody," said David. He was ashamed of his father's work—sharecropping and whatever he could pick up—just as Jimmy was of Sun's traveling evangelism. "My daddy was mean, too [like Sun]," said David. "But [he] . . . made me go to church."

David knew his father would kick him out of the house if he didn't go. But he and Jimmy had both stopped praying for salvation or the Holy Ghost.

"I never went to the altar, I wouldn't go. I would go on Wednesday night, to prayer meeting with Mother, and it was deadly dull. . . . I hated all of it." Like Jerry and Jimmy, he started stealing.

Jimmy's stealing was more serious than David's, and it was making him miserable, but he kept doing it. In his writings, he refers to his teenaged stealing as a game, but it was less a game than an obsession with money and stature that echoed his father's. By the time he was 16 or 17, he had a cache of stolen goods that he was too scared to sell.

Then David was caught stealing. The guilt was unbearable. "At night, we all got on our knees around the couch, and Mama and Daddy would pray. Mama . . . would start with Will, then Paul, James and Cecil." When she got to David, "Invariably, Mama would cry, and it was like a branding iron on me."

One Wednesday night at prayer service, David was saved.

"It was very emotional, a real eerie thing like Mama's praying. I felt extremely convicted of being wrong. I wasn't a Christian, I never went down to the altar . . . a lot of things like that. So I voluntarily went down. I felt a big burden lifted off of me."

The church was providing relief from pressure that it itself largely imposed. The "big burden" that was lifted was the guilt incurred both for wrong actions and for neutral ones that were demonized, such as wearing jewelry or playing cards or seeing a movie. The more behaviors people could be persuaded were bad, the more power the church had to negotiate forgiveness of the inevitable transgressions, and thus the more it could recruit people's energies and resources—ideally, to the service of God, but the church usually settled for tithes.

The guilts laid on Jimmy, David, and their companions were well-meant controls, but they weren't quite fair. First, the boys' mentors had all grown up without church, drinking, smoking, and gambling, and had found deliverance in God from sin and vicious fighting. For them, the Bible was the Good News it was cracked up to be, because they had been to hell and come back. But Jimmy and David and Mickey and the other cousins hadn't. They had never failed enough to need that kind of ecstatic deliverance. For them, the Bible's message was pretty much Bad News—they couldn't do anything fun without going to hell. Unlike their parents, they could never blunder into sex or liquor or movies or worldly music with any innocence, and then learn their lesson and straighten up.

Shortly after he was saved, David felt the anointing of the Holy Ghost one night, and was overcome. He began speaking in tongues. "[It] was just an exhilarated, emotional, feeling. Joy, happiness . . . I was laying flat on my back! I just remember the waves, seems like the waves of glory. . . . Before, you feel like nothing. After you accept Jesus, you feel like SOMEBODY."

Jimmy was never caught stealing, so his return to church was delayed. But the things he stole gave him no pleasure. He couldn't even use them to express the giving nature that had made him a willing healer of his family as a child.

"He took me out," remembered David, "and showed me he had a bucket buried in an old mill of a place, and he took me out there and opened it up and just poured out every kind of diamond bracelets, and watches of every sort and description. I pulled out one and put it on my arm like that, and said, 'Boy, that's beautiful.' And he said, 'Man, you can have it.' And I said, 'No, Jimmy, I couldn't do that, man . . . I'd never be able to wear that. I'd feel guilty about it.'

"It seemed to stun him. I guess he wanted me to okay what he had done. I don't know what he ever done with all that bucket of jewels."

He didn't dare wear or use any of them, because his dad would know the minute he saw it on him. Jimmy probably thought it was because Sun was a man of God now, and Jimmy the fallen one; but that power differential was just added to the authoritarian muscle of Sun the father and boxer who had cowed Jimmy his whole life. Besides, Pentecostals weren't supposed to love things like gold watches.

He got scared when he and Jerry stole a battery and the police came to arrest them both. Jerry made up a yarn about how an old black man had given them the battery and asked them to sell it, figuring white boys would get a better price for it, and offering them a cut. Jimmy corroborated the story and they got off.

But one day Jimmy got news that seemed to be direct punishment for the stealing.

Sun's grocery store was doing fine, and Jimmy was happy with the family's improved financial situation, as well as with the pocket money he was making there. He was just beginning, at 16, to enjoy his emergence from his Pentecostal cocoon.

One day, Sun called the family into the living room and announced he was selling his part of the business—and their home as well. He had decided to go into the ministry full time. He was going to build a church of his own. Minnie Bell was 100 percent behind him.

Jimmy was horrified. He argued, but it was hopeless.

It went back to the unfinished lawyer business. Sun couldn't shake that plan, and finally, he saw how to assimilate it. There was a profession that fit many of the psychological, emotional, and social needs of the lawyer plan. It was a job that brought respect, and it was a booming field—but it wasn't held against you if you made no money at it. It required no formal education.

"In the ministry," he decided, "actually, you do become a lawyer. You have one client. His name is Jesus. And you're pleadin' his case. . . . And the people out there's the jury, y'see, they're decidin'. The way you present it, how it's presented and all, the effect it has on them—it's just like an attorney."

He tested this idea against some of the disasters of his life, and it held firm. To explain Donnie's death, he figured God was preparing him for this role as evangelical lawyer—and Jimmy for his role as evangelist. "God was breaking me," he said. "I was PROUD . . . [But] I was holding my whole family back."

And then the unarguable justification for all choices: "I think things turned out, not like I planned, but like God planned." This ability to transform any misstep into an expression of God's will can also turn despair into wisdom and growth, and death into life—long enough, at least, to get you through the week until the next church meeting.

The talent for intelligent rationalizing is a Lewis strength, the sort of functional self-deception that in fact characterizes survivors. It was the same instinct that spawned enough family mythologies for Jimmy and two of his cousins to believe in the possibility of their own greatness.

Sun sold his home, set up a tent in tiny, dreary Wisner, 30 miles away, and insisted that Jimmy play piano to help draw crowds. Jimmy deeply resented this, but after a lifetime of being the peacemaker, he found outright refusal too stressful.

"Jimmy was mad at his father for becoming a preacher just when the family was beginning to make a little money," said his cousin Gerald Lewis, "so he . . . would refuse to play. If he did play, he . . . would mess it up and Uncle Sun would accuse him of not playing it right. Jimmy would play dumb . . . and Sun would whack him on the side of his head with his [violin] bow and never miss a lick."

With both Jimmy's and Jerry's musical help, Sun raised enough money to build a church building in the fall of 1951.

For almost two years, Jerry Lee had been making money playing illegally in bars. He became the regular pianist at the roughest club in Natchez, the Blue Cat. The Blue Cat and the Canasta Club squatted with a handful of other dilapidated buildings under the brow of the high river bank at a spot called Natchez-Under-the-Hill.

Sometimes when closing time neared and things were apt to get bloody, Elmo and Mamie would drive to Under-the-Hill and sit in the parked car with a loaded pistol and wait for Jerry to get off. Jerry's sisters played in the dark on the bank of the swift-flowing river while the unbridled sounds of bar matters floated out over the water, punctuated by Jerry's equally unbridled piano.

As usual, he was in a psychological bind. The money he made in this raunchy place meant a lot to his impoverished family, living in a shack out on Black River. Mamie and Elmo were proud of him. Yet, in competition with Minnie Bell and the Swaggarts, Mamie kept him under pressure to go to church and get the Holy Ghost, which reportedly had not happened to him yet. She apparently didn't get the huge emotional contradiction in urging a 15-year-old boy to play the devil's music and then urging him to go to a church where they told him he'd burn in hell for it.

Ever since that anointing by the devil, Jimmy had been scared to break his promise not to use music for The World. But he and Jerry still endlessly plotted their escape from Ferriday. Jerry seemed capable of doing it with music, and as usual he was getting family help. Elmo encouraged his son and drove him around the countryside, hauling the piano on a flatbed truck so Jerry could draw crowds in nearby towns.

Jimmy's decision not to play in bars meant that the roads out of Ferriday were closing off. The only one really left was the ministry, which was pursued down the little cow paths and back roads that led to places like Frogmore and Jonesville and Waterproof—nowhere. Jimmy didn't want to preach in the bleak villages back in the bayous like his father. He didn't want to preach at all. He didn't want to be cut off from The World.

The memories of being saved at eight, of being the first and youngest cousin to speak in tongues, of speaking the messages of prophecy that the Lord had given him at the age of nine, of being Nannie's favorite and of praying at the log altar in back of his house, were no longer sustaining him. He was hot-tempered, moody, and angry.

Girls

On February 21, 1952, Jerry married Dorothy Barton, a preacher's daughter, in Ferriday. He was 16, she 17. Lee Calhoun, ever mindful of how badly a boy needs what a boy needs at 16, helped grease the skids past the legal nuisances of two underage kids who could wait no longer. Lee got the license, and then he and Stella provided a ramshackle but free apartment in Ferriday for the newlyweds' honeymoon.

Jimmy, stuck with his pool cue, his stolen gewgaws, his movies and forbidden books, and his misery at betraying Ada and Minnie Bell with his worsening morals, went through his days depressed. He wasn't inclined to experiment with girls, though of course women and sex were of immense interest.

"The Herrons are pretty well known in the family," said David Beatty, "the men folks have a very active sex life. ALL of us. None of us are once-a-month lovers." But Herron-blooded Jimmy did not date. For his sexual guilt and his running from God, he felt singularly unlovable. And he really had no peers; it was too late for him to ever have the life of horny teenage cutups like Jerry and his friends.

There were also a hundred things to be scared of about sex: that he could get a disease, that he could get someone pregnant—as Jerry was soon to do to someone not his current wife. That was considered disgraceful. In the 1980s, when someone innocently asked Jimmy how old his wife was when they married, a voice from 1952 answered: "She was 15—and not pregnant."

It was virtually impossible for these boys to see a woman as a person. Women had too much power. Despite the heavy religious trips laid on them that most of their urges would take them to hell, their treacherous organs cried out for females. The boys saw the power that fallen women had over their fathers and grandfathers, and the violence, grief, and trouble it caused in their homes.

Thus women were in two categories: the good woman, who protected the genetic investment, and the slut, who was a commodity like booze and ciga-

rettes. Sexual desire was a gnawing daily torture, both physically and morally. If you got a girl to pet or have sex, was she a slut? If you married her
first, wouldn't she be a good woman and then wouldn't sex be more or less
out of the question? The beloved women in his life were prayer warriors,
brides of Christ, not sex objects. They simply had to endure the sexual duties
outlined for women in the Scriptures.

Mickey, talking of his marital troubles, showed classic male resignation to
these complicated dynamics. "God put a man on the earth for one reason,
and that's to chase a woman," he said. You just get used to the trouble and
the guilt and the caring and the problems. And how could you not admire
them, women? The problem boiled down to how to keep the volcano from
erupting when you came in at 3 a.m. to your good woman.

For Jimmy to try to puzzle it out would mean deconstructing the whole
mystique of his Pentecostal teachings, as well as exploring his scary psychological landscape. And that was one place the devil was surely lurking, for
not far behind would be questioning his religious faith itself, and that was the
scariest sin of all. Doubting God essentially led straight to unbridled sinning.

It was way too risky; if *faith itself* slipped away . . . no, best to just split
off the sexual desire into known territory: look at pictures, dream of visiting
Miss Nellie Jackson's. Sex was a failing all men had, there was a huge brotherhood of failure there.

JERRY, HIS NEW wife, and David Beatty were all going off to Bible school
in Waxahachie, Texas, in September of 1952—Jerry and Dorothy on the Calhouns' nickel, of course. This was to be Stella and Mamie's last attempt to
push Jerry toward a life in the church.

David was saving his wages to attend a well-known Bible college in Missouri. Minnie Bell and Ada tried to keep before Jimmy the old image that he
was chosen of God. It was extremely painful, watching his two cousins move
into his spot.

Sun and Minnie Bell decided to move to Wisner to be closer to Sun's
church just when Jimmy was trying to get up the nerve and resources to fly
out of Ferriday. But the same conflicts that kept him leafing through Jerry's
deck of "baseball" cards instead of chasing girls also kept him from executing
his plans for escape. Part of him hoped he would be miraculously delivered
from his promise to God and be able to play music for money, that maybe
he and Jerry would get a respectable gig playing gospel for the "Louisiana
Hayride."

He didn't have the confidence to make things happen himself, and anyway,
he'd been taught that that was God's job—and he was running from God. So
he froze: as he said years later, he wouldn't be good, but he couldn't be all
bad, either.

In fact, this tendency to paralysis would plague him his whole life. But one day in the summer of 1952, a thunderbolt hit that would unfreeze him, then and repeatedly over the next five decades and more.

The thunderbolt was Frances Anderson, a dark-eyed 14-year-old from Wisner. Shortly before his parents decided to move there, he became aware that the pretty girl had joined the choir at Sun's church. As soon as he saw her, his resistance to his parents' move to Wisner evaporated.

Frances was a poor kid, living on a small farm outside town with a hard-drinking sharecropper father who also drove a taxi, a hardworking mother, and three siblings—two sisters and an older brother. Their mother washed and ironed other people's clothes and scrubbed floors to make money. She kept the kids clean, and made sure they went to school, rising before dawn to fix the family's breakfast. Then she went out and worked in the fields. They had no electricity, no indoor plumbing. They kept out the wind by nailing cardboard on the walls. A lot of times they only had cornbread for dinner.

Sun held a tent revival just down the road from their farm, and Frances walked down there to hear him and Jerry play. She was knocked out, and joined the choir at his father's church. When he saw her, some invisible cosmic tumbler turned and a lock clicked smoothly into place. It was like something in him had been scanning the horizon for what it sought, and when he saw it, he recognized it immediately.

And it came in a non-threatening package. Frances was a girl, not a woman. His mother and Ada were women; Miss Nellie Jackson's "girls" were women. Frances was fresh and pretty, a whiff of the little sister. And she came from a family poorer and less prestigious than his, so he could hold his head up about that, and enjoy her looking up to him.

Frances' family attended church sporadically. They didn't go to any particular church; sometimes they'd get on a Baptist church bus and go to Sunday school when they were older. If it seemed strange that their daughter would have given directionless, Holy Roller Jimmy Lee Swaggart the time of day, it was only because they didn't understand the power of his music.

Jimmy's boogie touch on the piano, even gelded to get past Sun, melted girls and women alike, just as his father's violin had done a generation earlier. He began to see that even in church there was a whiff of that devil's anointing when he'd played the music that would be called rock and roll, when people had leapt to their feet, stomping, clapping, screaming and whistling, and chills had run up his spine.

Once he had set his mind on Frances, he aimed that power at her. "He had a touch and a feel to his music that was very moving," Frances said primly years later, declining to reveal the heat she must have felt flowing to and from the good-looking Swaggart boy. "If he was playing a fast song, it was impossible to keep from clapping your hands; if he was playing a slow piece, it would move you to tears. . . . On his own, with his music and his ability, Jimmy could have had a terrific lifestyle."

He suddenly saw his attractive qualities, though Frances' brother Bob thought he was plug-ugly at first—"rawboned, skinny—he was the daddy of ugly." He started combing his hair and bathing and dressing carefully. Maybe he didn't have thick, wavy locks like Jerry Lee, but he was better-looking than Jerry, who never lost his pinched, country-boy mien. And he'd tasted the world's approbation for his piano skills.

There was barely any courtship; their dates consisted of sitting in church together. Neither of them had ever dated anyone else. Frances turned 15 in August, and they married on October 10, 1952, three months after they'd met—against her parents' wishes and without their consent.

Into the Fire

Jimmy watched as Oral Roberts turned every cliché about dirt-poor, hick Pentecostals on its ear. He was a phenomenon, attracting dazzling numbers of followers and great financial success. He was proving that a man could make a very good business out of all this. You didn't have to be poor to be Pentecostal any more. In 1951 he bought a huge tent that seated 7,500, launching the "tent wars," each evangelist claiming to have the biggest. Roberts would bivouac in a newly harvested field, his many-peaked oblong canvas blanketing a huge area. Dirt roads running to the location were lined with cars parked pell-mell as people climbed out and streamed under the rolled-up sides like ants into a honey pot.

The setting for the postwar religious harvest was grimmer than the fragrant, woodsy camp meetings of the 19th-century forest glades. Invariably, these field sites had no shade, and the cars baked all day in the savage heat while people stirred the air around them with fans. The smell of dry, dusty fields outside, shorn of their treasure, floated into nostrils and made babies sneeze.

But people flocked in, oblivious to the heat and dust. Soon the top evangelists' tents were bigger than the Ringling Brothers' Big Top.

Faith and miracles were quantified like tent sizes: Roberts boasted that he prayed for 50,000 sick, saved 7,000, or had 13,500 altar calls. He allegedly preached to a million and a half people during 1952, the year Jimmy married, and held 11 tent campaigns; of these he recorded 66,000 who came into the healing line and "38,457 conversions."

A.A. Allen calculated that on one tour, "the souls that were saved . . . cost only twenty-five cents each, or FOUR FOR A DOLLAR!" He compared this to another evangelist whose cost was $2 per saved soul.

One year, Roberts organized Christian businessmen to underwrite his goal of winning a million souls within the next three years. Then God told him to get out there and save a million more a year for ten years.

Jimmy, 17, took all this in as he moved miserably through his first days as a husband in the late winter of 1952. People like Oral Roberts might be cleaning up, but clearly Sun wasn't. And Jimmy and Frances were crowded in with Sun and Minnie Bell and Jeanette because Jimmy had no real job—just pick-up day labor around Ferriday—and no place to go.

He had Frances, but he'd gone from the frying pan into the fire. Once again he was trapped—this time in Wisner, which was even worse than Ferriday. He still didn't want to go to his father's services, and feel like he was the target of all that castigation and judgment in those sermons. He didn't want to see his mother's martyred face—even if he was imagining it—when he resisted going. Why did everything come back down on *him?* Why did *he* have to be the pivot-point of their respectability, so if he did one little selfish or bad thing, it made them look bad and hurt their ministry?

And now that he had Frances, he didn't want to play piano at the church. The only thing that had made it bearable was showing off for her. But when nice ladies who were pillars of the church along with Nannie, Minnie Bell, and Aunt Reenie kept asking him to play, what was he going to do, humiliate his mother and grandmother by saying no?

As usual, Jerry always seemed to have more options. When he married Dorothy, he had been set up in his own apartment by the Calhouns. Then they had bankrolled him to go to Texas to Bible school, taking his bride with him. He could screw around in Bible school and mess around on his wife; in Jimmy's most corrosive, self-pitying black moods, it might have even crossed his mind that Jerry had gotten a respectable preacher's daughter, too—not the daughter of an alcoholic sharecropper.

Jimmy's support base wouldn't even scratch up the money to send him to Bible school, and wasn't he supposed to be the one with the call? What was the Scripture? "To whom much is given, much is asked"—? It was working cockeyed in Jimmy's life. Everything was given to Jerry, and everything asked of Jimmy.

Surely he was the worst kind of fraud as he dragged himself to church with Frances but secretly kept rejecting the call they all said was on him. His temper and moods grew blacker, and he had trouble controlling them.

It helped when he got a job oiling a dragline, gritty work that left him tired, sweaty, and filthy at the end of the day. And it seemed God's judgment when Dorothy quietly returned from Texas alone to her parents' home in Sterlington, shattered because Jerry stayed out all night doing God-knows-what.

But Jimmy was filled with fear that he would lose his job because he was underage. A life immersed in the Pentecostal mindset had taught him that for every triumph the world might bestow, there was an anti-triumph right around the corner, a big bill with unholy interest sitting on it. So if he didn't lose the job because he was too young, then he'd lose it because he'd been "running," and God would snatch it back. Therefore, he yielded to another instinct that had been inculcated in him: cut a deal.

"If you'll let me keep this job," he prayed to God, "I'll come back to you."

In later years, his intense, intimate dialogues with God would take on the air of a father and son working out the affairs of the family business—and eventually the tone of partners in a joint venture. In this case, Jimmy was naively giving God a great bargain, because Jimmy's part—"coming back" to God—was a monumental sacrifice. It meant no less than laying down his life, and he knew it. He took such a commitment extremely seriously. It meant the possibility of a dreary, boring life of humility and false cheeriness and by the time he was 40, walking around like an old snapping turtle, with dandruff on his collar.

He'd been in plenty of humble little preachers' homes: photos of the grand-kids in dimestore frames on the worn-out upright someone gave the preacher and never let him forget it. Sallow lace antimacassars covering the shiny hand-grease stains on the arms of the two "good" living room chairs. The formica kitchen table with chrome legs in the scrubbed kitchen, the hand-me-down silver that tasted like metal, and the breadbox with primitive daisies painted on it by the "artistic" church pillar who sold crafts out of her home—that wasn't the life Jimmy had in mind. But what if God had it in mind for him?

He was restless and full of ambition. He had talent and he knew it, knew he was smarter than those broken-down old potato-faced hick preachers who, sweet as they were, couldn't do anything but drone on in the pulpit about how, here's what you have to do, you should do good deeds, it's not enough to just go to church, and by the way, you ole sinner, aren't you ashamed for being such a sorry so-and-so? but God loves ya anyway blah blah blah and the deadly dull prayer meetings where surly, slack-jawed teens were dragged in by worried moms who were in effect begging God the Father to take over raising their louts.

So it was a great offer, and sure enough, God snapped it up. The boss came and told Jimmy he could keep working. And then, after a couple of days of being good, Jimmy, being 17, again started turning to the pleasures he'd cultivated.

Two weeks later, his boss fired him after all. He said it was the age thing, but Jimmy knew better. He'd broken the deal, and God had seen right into his head. The only shred left of the non-transparent Jimmy was the secret one.

Once again he was back to day-labor, hauling gravel, chopping cotton, or whatever else he could scare up.

Seize the Moment

Americans had great faith in the atom; nuclear energy was going to replace fossil fuels and water power. But even though 85 per cent of Americans had approved of the decision to bomb Japan in 1945, the weapon cast a clammy shadow into the next decade. As President Eisenhower later said, living with the bomb made "a life of perpetual fear and tension; a burden of arms draining the wealth and the labor of all peoples."

During the postwar years, the surge of interest in religion and philosophy was related to the threat of nuclear war and had a distinctly evangelistic tone. A decades-long fascination with Eastern philosophy and religious thought bloomed in the uneasiness. Khalil Gibran's *The Prophet* became popular in America, followed by Theosophy, Gurdjieff groups, and Transcendental Meditation. Prosperity thinking flowered with the success of Norman Vincent Peale's *The Power of Positive Thinking* the year Jimmy and Frances married. Jews for Jesus, Synanon, Edgar Cayce study groups, the Inner Peace Movement, Scientology could all be seen as evangelistic trajectories coming out of fear of atomic annihilation. Franklin Hall's 1946 publication *Atomic Power with God through Prayer and Fasting* launched a fad that lasted for years, and his techniques were said to lead to miracles. Indeed, miracles would mark the postwar era for the Pentecostals, and spur Jimmy Swaggart to go out on the road, evangelizing.

Shortly after Eisenhower's landslide election, Jerry came home from Texas, kicked out of Southwestern Bible Institute in Waxahachie after only three months. He wasn't contrite. He had a story: he'd quit because they wouldn't let him play piano. Actually, he'd played a sacred hymn honky-tonk style in chapel, run around like a tomcat at night, gotten involved with a female student, and declined to crack a book. But that story didn't out until much later, and in the meantime he managed to actually make a brief triumph of his return, ballooning his few fortnights at the institute into an "education," being invited to preach a couple of times, and leveraging what little he could remember of theology into "memorable" sermons.

It was outrageous that he should get rewarded *again* while Jimmy chopped cotton in the sun and felt like *he* was the disgrace, though he'd done nothing wrong and cost no one any money.

AFTER CHRISTMAS, Frances and Jimmy went to hear a special guest preacher at Sun's church, Brother Vincent Roccaforte. This was the pastor who had brought Sun and Minnie Bell to the altar when Jimmy was seven. Something came over Jimmy when he saw this man who had set Sun on a path that had brought both blessings and teeth-gritting trials.

As Jimmy and Frances sat in church, eyes were on the young couple, wondering if history would repeat itself and Jimmy would re-enact his father's capitulation before Brother Roccaforte. Jimmy had always had a keen sense of what was expected of him. The act of going down there to the altar, the next generation to be rescued out of pride and stubbornness by Brother Roccaforte, had a powerful dramatic pull, and he sat considering.

As soon as the initial glory faded and this little revival was over, people would go back to their lives, off to work and sleep and drink and fight at their kitchen tables. What difference would it make in the world whether a 17-year-old kid went to some jerkwater church in Wisner or not? His unhappy vacation from his calling was the only privacy he'd had in his life since his parents and Ada had started grooming him for the ministry. This return to God would mean a return to the judgment and expectations of all those watching eyes. He'd have to account for every minute.

His four years of drifting from the church hadn't brought him many rewards. In fact, it was all slipping away. Jerry had stolen the show after coming back from Waxahachie; he'd never gotten the Holy Ghost in his life, and here he was preaching. Jimmy had never preached. David Beatty had finished high school and was working at the Billups gas station on Fourth Street in Ferriday for fifty cents an hour, saving to enter Bible college in Springfield, Missouri in January. Jimmy had seemed paralyzed, watching David eclipse him.

Jimmy had proven over and over to be extraordinarily sensitive to opportunities to heighten what would otherwise be a routine episode, and infuse it with meaning. He sat, listening to Brother Roccaforte and quickly totting up what he'd have to pay in personal freedom if he seized the limelight this night and went down to the altar. No pool, no movies, no latitude in his schemes for making money, lots and lots of church . . . as he calculated, pressure built. Timing was everything; if he didn't make the decision quickly, the moment would be gone.

He jumped up and went down to the altar.

Once Jimmy made a decision, he poured himself into the moment. This was a pattern that would stay with him over the years, albeit Frances would constantly have to overcome his pessimistic nature and his tormenting doubts when he wasn't actually immersed in the dramatic moment. This night, he knelt and sincerely, passionately begged God's forgiveness for his four years of rebellion.

As he prayed, he forgot about the eyes on him and felt something come over him he'd almost forgotten existed: relief. Guilt and confusion began to shrink away. His mother strode back and forth on the platform, arms raised, praising and thanking God in front of her peers for the return of her son. His father came down and knelt in quiet gratitude, completing the tableau for those who had seen its original enactment 10 years before. The pain of causing his parents pain evaporated from Jimmy's heart. His burdens lifted, and his eyes filled with tears.

Frances watched the scene, understanding more than she had yesterday about the symbolism and emotions that bound these people. So this was how it was to be? She was not dismayed. Her great gift, that would set her apart from other women, was her ability to manage with what she had instead of trying to change it. She went down to be saved, too.

She wasn't going to openly take Jimmy away from his mother and grandmother and mold him into her idea of what he should be. Like most girls, she probably did want to do that, but she was smarter than most girls. Her style would be to extract the best from Jimmy by mastering the rules he had to live by. She would mold him, all right—by transforming those rules.

Back in the Fold

Word flew in the family that Jimmy had come back to God. Nannie hurried to Wisner to provide what only she could: a seal on the psychological flesh of the little entity who had almost slipped through her fingers. "I knew it!" she happily crowed to Jimmy at the next service.

He and Frances moved back to Ferriday. There was a revival at a little Assembly of God church across the river, in Natchez, and he was well aware that, since he had been saved, Nannie and Minnie Bell had recruited friends to pray for him to get the Holy Ghost again. Every night he went to the altar with the same hunger and expectation he'd had when he was eight. And the same thing happened: nothing.

Frances, who hadn't even been raised Pentecostal, had no such problem. Night after night she was filled with glory and spoke in tongues, while he prayed until he sweated.

The meetings ended. He and Frances started attending new ones in Ferriday. This time, church members invited him to their homes and held special prayer meetings just for him, to ask that he be filled with the Holy Spirit. And he discovered people were not only praying for him, now they were fasting as well. But the services went on and on, and he left every one without getting the blessing. Frances was doing her part, setting the example, encouraging him, and showing faith. But nothing happened.

Finally, people started looking hard at him. "What's wrong with you?" they asked.

Of course, Nannie's reputation was on the line, and his parents'. If God continued to spurn Jimmy, would someone sooner or later figure it was because of his secret life?

Jimmy decided to open up to the only person he trusted with even a glimpse of his hidden self: Nannie. He started telling her about some of his thievery, making sure it was not of recent vintage and that they were the episodes with Jerry Lee, not his solitary robberies of only a few months back.

He had a need to confess to a man, too, and wondered if he should tell the police. Nannie nixed that, saying to just stand on the promise and keep asking.

Then Jimmy's sweet, alcohol-loving uncle John Lewis, Nannie's brother, sat down with him one night and told him he wasn't alone—Uncle John had had the same problem with the Holy Ghost. It was clear to the family that Elmo had always had it, and the Calhouns—lots of people had trouble. Uncle John advised him to just relax, and believe what the Bible said, that the Word was for him, no matter how long it took. He made Jimmy feel he wasn't doing so badly after all, and that there was no hurry.

Uncle John was the right man to give the boy this message, for his lifelong battle with the jug eased Jimmy's guilt about his adolescent crimes. In condemning his split-off self, Jimmy tended to forget that God loves sinners.

The kindness of his uncle acted on him like a balm. The very next night at church, as Jimmy lay on his back in front of the altar, concentrating hard, surrounded by family, Frances, and church stalwarts who chanted, prayed, and sang, he felt a great flood break loose inside him. His lips moved, and the current bubbled out in the unknown tongue he'd been seeking.

He jumped to his feet and shouted in tongues, and there was great rejoicing in the church.

He called Minnie Bell the minute he got back to Nannie's house. She was overjoyed, and told him that the night before, she'd dreamed he died.

JIMMY HAD equilibrium again. He began hanging out with serious people like David Beatty. Though David was still working full-time at the gas station, he wanted to try his hand at the scary, exciting act of preaching. He and Jimmy decided to try it together, like two six-year-olds jumping into the deep end holding hands.

They borrowed Sun's truck, loaded an old piano on it, and drove to Clayton, where David preached from the pickup bed.

They were completely ignored. "There wasn't but about one store and a bar in Clayton," said David. "And I was preachin', we had a little ol' microphone 'bout this big, and there wasn't *one soul* stopped and looked in our direction . . . we started back to Ferrity for him to preach, I told him, I said, 'Probably somebody heard, had their window up, and the Gospel got to them.'"

When they got to Ferriday, it was Jimmy's turn. The same thing happened. After he'd finished and they were driving away, he accused David of hiding behind the piano because he was so embarrassed. He would always characterize this period of his career as marked with "derision and ridicule." But with the instinct for symbolic action that would surface throughout his life, he decided to preach at Mangham, Louisiana, Sun's home town near Snake

Ridge. If he could make good there, or at least avoid derision and ridicule, it would prove something.

He asked Frances to go with him, worked up some songs, and carefully prepared his sermon, taking a cue from a device Jerry Lee had used with much success on his return from Waxahachie. Jerry had said you could tell the devil was in a man's house because you could see his tail stickin' up outta the roof—looked just like a TV antenna!

Jimmy's idea was more subtle and intelligent. At 18, he already sensed that he should start out talking about something topical, not God or Jesus. He styled his sermon "judgment on America," and, beginning with Hitler's invasion of Poland, planned to show how America had been drawn into deep sin after the war.

His little entourage rolled into Mangham on Saturday morning, deliberately picked because that was the day people came into town to buy groceries and do business. He set up outside the market, and launched into the format he would keep for decades: first, good, well-rehearsed, familiar music, and then a message that related to people's lives.

The actual sermon took only ten minutes and left him trembling. But a handful of people lingered for the whole show, and a kindhearted cop told him afterward that he had "the fire."

It was the first time Frances had seen him get strokes from strangers. It reinforced her conviction that she really was dealing with something bigger than Ferriday. It would be moments like this, when she stood aside and watched people stop to listen to Jimmy, that gave her not only the cues she needed to do her job, but the satisfaction of knowing that this handsome, charismatic lad was hers.

THE LITTLE "YES" in Sun's hometown made Jimmy bold enough to preach closer to home. Every weekend he hit the little communities near Ferriday—Clayton, Gilbert, Sicily Island—sometimes from a flatbed truck rigged with a mike and speakers. Frances was at his side in a freshly starched and ironed dress and flats, handing tracts to people—with headlines like "Don't Wait for the Hearse to Take You to Church" and "Movies Are Still Bad"—with her girlish smile.

The weekend trips were something to look forward to, even when the response was discouraging. Performing was becoming a refuge for Jimmy. His cousins admired and praised him, and he got better. The combination of travel and preaching started to work on him. He was becoming addicted.

Jimmy landed a part-time job with the Northeast Louisiana Soil Conservation Department, and he supplemented that with odd jobs. Sun cut him in on some small construction jobs he was doing in the area, and loaned him his truck for services. He and Frances saved every penny.

Jerry, guided by his appetites, had met high-school junior Jane Mitcham and dumped Dorothy. Over was the short-lived incarnation of Jerry Lee, Prophet of God.

About this time, 300 miles up the Mississippi River, an adorable second-grader and her parents moved into a little white frame house on June Road in Memphis. The child's father, J.W. Brown, was Jimmy's and Jerry's cousin, the son of Ada and Elmo's sister Jane. At seven, the little girl had lived more than half of the only childhood she would ever have—for she was Myra Gale Brown, who at 13 would become the notorious child bride of her first cousin once removed, Jerry Lee Lewis.

Out of Nothing

\ \ "Before Elvis there was nothing." That was John Lennon's summation. Into that nothingness, shortly after the Fourth of July, 1954, Elvis Presley's voice wafted from Memphis station WHBQ in a tune called "That's All Right."

But it wasn't really nothingness. Before Elvis nudged the mingling country, rhythm and blues, and gospel idioms into the new genre called rockabilly, there were the radio barn dances and the hillbilly music circuit, the latter not unlike the revival circuit. It started with small, local jamborees held outdoors or at some small fairground on Saturday night and broadcast on tiny backwoods radio stations. It was a major venue for aspiring young musicians like Jimmy and Jerry.

The local jamborees graduated to large regional shows organized in cities and broadcast over much bigger areas. Dallas boasted the "Big D Jamboree" and Los Angeles the "Town Hall Party," but the most important of these regional events was by far the "Louisiana Hayride" out of Shreveport. The Hayride was the only real competitor to the most prestigious country music show in the U.S.: the "Grand Ole Opry." Known as the "cradle of the stars," the Hayride had launched many Opry stars.

The Opry was known briefly as the "WSM Barn Dance" after it was begun in Nashville in 1925 as a hillbilly radio show. Its immediate success with string bands like the Gully Jumpers, the Fruit Jar Drinkers, and Dr. Bate and the Possum Hunters spawned regional and local imitators. The nearest one to Ferriday was a shindig called the "Ouachita Valley Jamboree," out of Monroe. A clean-cut, moral-looking Jerry was featured in 1952, playing gospel piano.

The hope of everyone who performed at the Ouachita Valley Jamboree was to get a spot on the Hayride, get an audience in the Texas-Louisiana-Arkansas triangle, and then launch to the Opry to make a national reputation. Jimmy had promised the Lord he'd never play piano in a nightclub, but gospel events like the Jamboree and the Hayride sponsored weren't in that category.

In the fall of 1954, Jimmy and Jerry heard that Elvis Presley had signed on with the "Louisiana Hayride." He was their age, 19, and he wasn't doing anything they couldn't do in their sleep, they felt. The Hayride signed him on for a year.

All around them, music like they could play was exploding over the airwaves. Bill Haley released "Rock Around the Clock" in 1954 to great popularity after spending several lackluster years leading a country band. Guys that had regularly oozed in and out of Haney's were suddenly drawing devotees from urban pop-music lovers who hadn't heard anything as exciting and fused since jazz.

Forces the boys had cut their teeth on, forbidden things that were very close to their experience, were just beginning to catch on in the national psyche. For there was something hidden and dirty about the term "rock and roll," something sacrilegious. To a Presbyterian kid from California, it might be a neutral term; Elvis' "Good Rockin' Tonight" was just a song about dancing or music or something. But to a Southern kid, even one not a Holy Roller, good rockin' tonight had a smirk behind it; it meant the bed is going to shake back and forth tonight, or the car up that dirt road nudged into the trees. And people will roll over and over in ecstasy.

The term rock and roll, supposedly coined by Cleveland disc jockey Alan Freed a couple of years before, was nothing new to the boys' ferreting subconsciouses. What was new was that they were hearing it accepted, even admired, for the first time. Their kind was coming into its own.

Jerry had made no promise to God such as Jimmy had, and he traveled directly to Shreveport to apply for the Hayride.

He was rejected.

None of the Pentecostals earnestly praying for the boys could ever have dreamed how firmly they would stay on these trajectories—nor how important either of them would become to American culture. A peek at the end of the 1980s would show that fundamentalist religions were stampeding the globe, and that none other than Jimmy Swaggart was leading the Pentecostal shock troops into the mushy ranks of Catholicism in Central and South America.

People would flock to his crusades in the tens of thousands. He'd walk the streets of the cities and be mobbed. Everyone wanted his autograph, and he'd sign his name and then put "John 10:10"—the passage where Jesus says, "I am come that they might have life, and have it more abundantly."

At the same time, fundamentalism's evil twin, rock and roll, was one of America's major cultural exports to the world. With many of his contemporaries in the grave, Jerry Lee Lewis had by the end of the 1980s become what they called early rock stars who had not yet managed to overdose fatally: a living legend. He sat in his trailer in the parking lot of the Palomino Club in North Hollywood, surrounded by admirers. The Palomino's neighbors on Lankershim Boulevard were video peep shows, live nude dancing, liquor stores, and the Foolish Pleasure Club, which advertised a woman holding a whip and a band named Buster Cherry.

He sang with the kind of hard, fuck-you sound you would expect from looking at early stills of him with his sour little mouth cocked open over the mike, what you would expect from someone married six times, rumored to have contributed to the death of one of his two deceased wives, someone who shot his bass player in the chest, who punched and slapped his sister onstage, who daily turned mean as poison from the poisons he ingested and the ones needled into his head from birth.

His face was bony and paste-white. His left cheek and nostril quivered involuntarily. It was 1973 that he got on the needle, according to his sister Linda. "Before that, he was just crazy."

His eyes looked fiercely out of their deep Lewis sockets as he told one dirty joke after another. The laughter was strained, and the grins were like the submissive fleering of chimpanzees in the presence of a marauding baboon, for Jerry could turn violent in an instant.

"My wife left me, THANK GOD!" he suddenly said. "I'm gonna have her head cut off." His small cold eyes swept over his audience. At times he despised his groupies, despised the drunken fans yelling "Killer!" But without them he was nothing, and he knew it.

"If you cut her head off, she still wouldn't die!" Nervous laughter.

"She's so fat she wouldn't fit in two coffins!"

He suddenly thought of Jimmy. "Jimmy Swaggart! Boy, that boy got caught big-time, didn't he?" He laughed weakly, then frowned, ashamed. "Naw, I shouldn't talk about him like that."

The look of genuine regret on his face gave a clue to why people stayed loyal to him and swore he'd give you the shirt off his back.

Then it was time to play. Inside, a great roar went up as he took the stage. "Killer! screamed the drunken crowd. "Killlllllller!" Jerry slammed into the first song. The piano made a sound like breaking glass.

♦   ♦   ♦

Some people later said they foresaw the cousins' success, but at 17, both of them felt completely trapped.

Other cousins seemed to be getting out of the trap. In August 1953, at 17, Mickey Gilley left Ferriday to follow a pretty teenager named Geraldine Garrette to Houston, where she moved with her family. Not only did he get out of Ferriday, he went to a huge, exciting city, where he was immediately given a good job by Geraldine's father, a contractor.

In January of 1954, David Beatty left for college in Springfield. Jimmy was only able to find part time pick-up jobs in the little nowherevilles around "Ferrity," as everyone called it, where the evening meal was still often a pan of cornbread, a pot of peas, and a big head of onion.

Jerry Lee spent 1953 with his parents at the Black River shack, divorcing, remarrying, being slapped and punched by women—including Mamie—and dodging the things they threw at him, doing it back to them, and squirting into Jane Mitcham the makings of a baby boy who would grow up tortured in his mind and who would never see 20. Jerry's sister Frankie never forgot the glimpses she got of her brother through the Blue Cat's door: hunched over the piano, he stabbed the keys in a trance of forgetfulness of what awaited him at Black River.

Jimmy and Frances were stable. They had saved enough money to buy a tiny trailer—28 by 8 feet—and they parked it at various locations between Wisner and Ferriday, finally settling in Aunt Irene Gilley's front yard. Irene constantly encouraged her nephew, and every other young person in search of God.

Frances had also become pregnant, but her son, born in 1954 a few months before Jerry Lee Lewis Jr., would be the polar opposite of Jerry's. A clue to the mark placed on these men by their families was the naming of their firstborns. Jerry named his doomed son after himself, giving Mamie back her Junior, while Jimmy resurrected his dead brother, too, naming his son Donnie.

By the Grace of God and Women

As Frances got closer to her due date with Donnie, Jimmy felt the pressure of work and responsibility keenly. He was immature and could not control his temper; in fact, Frances had warned him before they married that he was going to have to change his ways or she would leave him.

"I was fiery and explosive," Jimmy wrote years later. "I couldn't get victory over the small things."

"Jimmy was VERY high-tempered, he'd get mad, scream and holler," said a cousin. In later years, he told Frances' brother, Bob Anderson, that it had been a problem all his life. After Anderson went to work for the ministry, he saw it. "I've seen him throw a mike across the stadium because the sound wasn't right."

Once Jimmy had ordered thousands of Bibles printed, and wanted to see a sample before they went to press. He was brought a rough dummy rather than a finished product, because it was too expensive to print only one book. Before anyone could explain this to him, he stormed into Anderson's office, screaming about the ugly book, and hurled it against the wall. "He admitted his temper," said Anderson. "He told me he worked on it daily."

"I've seen Jimmy [at rehearsal] get mad at his road manager, yell at him," said a former employee. "Jimmy was such a perfectionist, the whole band would be playing, all the percussion, LOUD . . . it was already knocking you down, . . . and Jimmy could hear a gnat fly through." He would get angry and demand more of this or that instrument, and his manager would turn up the volume. "And then after a few minutes he'd turn it back down, and Jimmy would never notice."

He saw Jimmy get physical when he got mad; once he slapped a glass of water out of an assistant's hand. "He was just so UPTIGHT."

Their marriage began to sound like his parents' had, a big threat since Sun and Minnie Bell's worst fighting had always been attributed to the fact that they had been unsaved. Jimmy and Frances were saved, but it didn't stop the fighting.

"Demon oppression"—Jimmy's code for sexual appetites, lethal self-doubt, and depression—plagued him (it was almost certain the attacks had to do with sex, as Jimmy reportedly later admitted—and then denied—having a pornography problem that went back to childhood). He told himself, "God won't forgive you again . . . you've told Him you wouldn't sin again and yet you have."

Feeling there was no hope for him, he began suffering depression, sleeplessness, and weight loss. He got alarmed enough to visit a doctor, who was baffled at these symptoms in such a young man. Of course he couldn't tell the doctor he was suffering from demons. He confided in Ada that he doubted God, and of course she said such doubts were attacks of the enemy, Satan.

This continued for months, until the tension finally culminated in a predawn hallucination. The evening before had been one of the worst in his life. He could not clear his mind of unwanted thoughts, and the hissing condemnation in his head brought him to almost suicidal despair. Here he was, pretending to be a minister of the Gospel, when he could not even get free of his wicked impulses long enough to pray.

What was more scary, this powerful God of Ada's didn't seem able to help him. Could it be that Satan was more powerful in his own realm?

He tried reading his Bible, tried to connect with God, but he couldn't concentrate. Finally, after walking in the dark along the blacktop, he returned to the trailer and to bed. Almost immediately he fell into a lucid dream in which he found himself in the middle of a big, empty room with no windows. Its door was ajar. He felt evil all around. A creature weighing 600 pounds appeared in the doorway. It had the body of a bear and the face of an unspeakably evil male human. It advanced on him on its hind legs.

Jimmy sank to the floor. Then he whispered, "In the name of Jesus!" The beast, he wrote, "dropped like a tree that had been felled." As it writhed, Jimmy felt courage well up in him. He stood up, pointed at it, and said the words again. The beast crashed to the floor, holding its head.

Dream symbology says a bear represents something not to be trusted. The head represents the intellect. The open door represented opportunity, but it was blocked. All signs seemed to point to Jimmy not trusting himself.

But he awoke speaking in tongues, released from his depression. The beast's head was injured by mystical words. Magic words had slain the untrustworthy intellect, and the door was no longer blocked.

For now. But he had learned a lesson: God would get him out of severe pickles of guilt and sin. He would become accustomed, over the years, to sinning and then slaying the beast the sin finally grew to become in his mind. He probably even got used to it, maybe got hooked on it, sinning and letting the guilt and anguish and doubt build up and then slaughtering it in a surge of release.

◆   ◆   ◆

``Three of the most important influences in my life have been women," said Jimmy at the height of his fame. "They are my grandmother, my mother, and my wife."

Though Frances was the epitome of femininity, dignity, and grace on the outside, a weak father and a strong mother had made her tough. She didn't like bloodless, inept men. And she had faith in Jimmy's talents.

Frances was as close as any woman could come to a copy of Ada. As his grandmother's eyes blazed when Jimmy prayed timidly, and she would thunder, "You're not praying to a PUNY GOD!" so Frances' philosophy was, "Whenever you have problems, you learn to overcome them, to solve them, to knock the door down . . ."

The moment he married her, Jimmy surrendered himself to the fate thrust on him with Ada's conversion and the death of his baby brother 12 years before.

That Frances was a catalyst for this fate became clear shortly after the marriage, when she had a little chat with Jimmy's mother. Minnie Bell invited her into the kitchen one night and sat her down.

"The Lord called Jimmy into the ministry when he was eight years old," Minnie Bell told the 15-year-old girl. She told Frances he would "never be able to escape that call." He was going to preach the Gospel, she said.

"I was sitting shaking in that chair," Frances said. "I didn't know what was happening to me. It was like something was unveiled in front of my eyes."

She attributed it to the hand of God, but it was likely that she also had a realization of what Ada, Sun and Minnie Bell, Mickey and David and Jerry and the other cousins, sweet John Lewis and Aunt Reenie and Sister Wiggins, Brothers Janway and Roccaforte and all the preachers and family members and church faithful had invested in: the promise of Jimmy Swaggart, child prophet, tow-headed prodigy, anointed of the Holy Ghost, Chosen of God.

Years later, Frances added that she had heard a clear voice in her own head telling her that it was going to be difficult to honor Jimmy's Call, but she had been tapped; and if she didn't do right by the commission, "I'll remove you and replace you with someone else."

Frances didn't say whether it was a man's voice or a woman's. But if Minnie Bell had been blunt enough to say exactly what she wanted to, those would have been her words. In that moment, Frances understood that she had married into someone else's project, and that she'd better get out of the way or get on board.

She picked the latter. The next chance that presented itself, she went straight to the altar and got the Holy Ghost.

JIMMY RELIED heavily on Ada to encourage him. Every day after work, he would come home to the little trailer, get cleaned up, and he and Frances would take the baby over to Ada's. She would feed them, and they would study the Bible or read about the evangelistic movement in one of the publications Ada subscribed to.

Gordon Lindsay's *Voice of Healing* magazine contained news of the sensational healings still going on in the larger evangelical world. There were still many powerful and successful evangelists, if they were consistently dogged by the press. William Branham was packing in as many as 8,000 per night in Houston, where Mickey now lived. Branham then was invited to Europe; in Finland, 7,000 people attended the first night of his meetings.

Ada fed this news to Jimmy steadily, assuring him that one day he would preach to thousands, just like William Branham. He appreciated it. He didn't believe her at all, but sitting at her little kitchen table on Mississippi Avenue in 1954, "the call" was alluring. The alchemy that had attracted Sun five years before, the belief that true miracles of healing were happening out there somewhere, pulled at him.

The tales of top evangelists raising huge sums of money and attracting huge crowds fit right in with the conviction that God was blessing the evangelical movement and dovetailed with the "miracles" theme. As early as 1950, Oral Roberts was mailing out tens of thousands of books, anointed handkerchiefs, and other items. He was on 85 radio stations. His ministry magazine, *Healing Waters,* went out to 100,000 readers a year. He could not find city auditoriums large enough for his meetings.

A.A. Allen launched the "Allen Revival Hour" on radio the year Jimmy and Frances married, and regularly held huge meetings in Cuba and Mexico. By 1955 he was on 17 Latin American radio stations and 18 in America. Foreign crusades were expanding everywhere, and continued to be very successful even after the healing revival died down in the late 1950s. They were especially triumphant in Africa and Latin America, which held rich caches of "heathens" and disillusioned Catholics. People in undeveloped countries were good prospects because their lives and beliefs were simpler, they were closer to miraculous phenomena, and they were less educated, less skeptical, and easier to convert.

It was also encouraging that many ministries were raising large sums of money selling records. Jimmy had already learned the importance of music in attracting an audience. Now he was getting up the nerve to develop his voice.

The radio ministries that had matured during the war years were pushing into the new field of television. Bishop Fulton Sheen, who had pioneered the popular "Catholic Hour" on radio, was among the first to exploit the new medium of television, launching a series of highly-regarded religious talks.

The year before Donnie was born, Rex Humbard had gone on the air in Akron, Ohio; he was a visionary who had his church built especially for television production—long before it occurred to any sports league or municipality to design stadiums or coliseums around television. And even as Jimmy and Ada sat in the evenings, studying their publications, Oral Roberts began broadcasting over nine television stations with a revival-type show. In a year and a half, he had ten times that many, and by the time Jimmy decided to make his own full-time move into the ministry in 1958, Roberts had 136 stations. Clearly there was a bandwagon, and Jimmy wanted to get on.

He and Ada read T. L. Osborn's *Native Evangelism* and *Faith Digest,* which tallied the number of souls saved, lepers healed, and missionaries killed in various overseas efforts, and had photos with captions like "Over 300 hooks and pins are stuck into this poor, deluded heathen's body as he worships idols."

They read the serious, well-written *Pentecostal Evangel,* with article titles like "The Quiet Heart" and news from the spiritual battlefront: the Vatican's powerful new radio transmitters, the world expansion of Russia's League of Militant Atheists.

A.A. Allen's emotional tracts, with one cautionary tale after another and endless testimonies, all had the same theme and tone: "For years I've lived a drunkard's miserable existence; my past is dark and sinful. But tonight I'm saved, through the grace of Christ!" Even at 19, Jimmy could do better than that, much as he admired Allen's healing abilities.

Jimmy was an avid reader. He wasn't proud of dropping out of high school, but once out, he let his good intellect graze wherever it wished. He read at work during down times, and at home every evening.

He migrated toward the deeper, more intelligent treatments. He believed many of the miracles of the postwar years had been genuine, but he would belong to a different movement, and he already sensed it.

There was something deeply symbolic about the fact that a healing revival had followed a devastating depression and war. Once the poultice of general prosperity began to have its effect—a process that took about 12 years, from 1946 to 1958—postwar healing moved out of the hands of the evangelists. Rapid advances were made in medical technology, and healing as the main expression of God's grace in people's lives began to diminish as a result. Medical miracles would replace divine ones.

Money miracles would become the evangelical focus of the coming decades.

WITHIN A COUPLE of years of Donnie's birth, most Pentecostal denominations would be withdrawing their support of traveling evangelists. Disreputable and irresponsible evangelists had entered the field, and the Assemblies of God was trying to control its product. In 1953, the Texas District Council tried to discipline Jack Coe, who then attacked the denomination. It expelled him. Journalists who had made a living in the 1950s exposing the revival would find fewer stories to keep bread on the table, but the acrimonious synergy between the press and the evangelical movement would remain strong. On the one hand, preachers made good copy. On the other, even unkind stories were free ads for a revival. In the years of decline, the sting of public ridicule burned off all but the strongest ministers.

Jimmy watched the small-timers—Brother Kenneth and Brother Delbert and Brother Henry—strive for distinction, saying they were proud to eat bread and bologna after preaching an exhausting service that attracted only 23 people, including babies, and yielded only enough money to buy a meal or two. They said they'd *rather* eat this way, preferred it. Their defiance aroused pity and admiration.

He could see that even in these prosperous times, the preacher being poor was still a comfort to his flock. He saw that much of what passed for preaching was actually lullabies, to be crooned at the right time, magical chants that helped the trance. The brothers would move among the supplicants, eyes shut, saying the endless litanies: Hallelujah to God. In the name of the Father. And of the Son. And of the Holy Ghost. Hallelujah to the lamb. Praise God. Praise the name of Jesus. Glory be to God. Hallelujah. Thank you, Jesus. Thank you, Jesus, hallelujah. Praise the name of our Lord. Praise the holy name of our Lord. Glory to God.

He kept adding more preaching into his days, and grew more serious as he got glimpses of his own potential; he practiced constantly, preaching to trees in the woods, getting used to hearing his own voice, and starting to like it. Hearing himself master a surprising range of ideas, hearing his voice become more confident—it made the doubt and fear he'd lived with his whole life start to shrink a tiny bit. He was beginning to understand that he had a sexy voice. Frances knew that. She constantly pumped him up.

Shakin'

I n 1955, when Donnie was a year old, an obscure song by Roy Hall came out on the Decca label and flopped. Jerry happened to hear it. It was called "Whole Lotta Shakin' Goin' On." It was played in Memphis, but was banned in other places for suggestive lyrics and for sounding too "black."

Jerry had gone to Nashville a year before and had returned to Black River without a recording contract. By 1956, Elvis' "Heartbreak Hotel," "Don't Be Cruel," "Hound Dog," and "Love Me Tender" were all released to wild approval. Carl Perkins released "Blue Suede Shoes," Fats Domino cut "Blueberry Hill," and Chuck Berry came out with "Roll Over Beethoven." "American Bandstand" went on the air. That fall, Elmo sold 400 eggs to Nelson's supermarket on Louisiana Avenue and used the money to take his son to Memphis to audition for Sun Records, Elvis' and Perkins' label. Again Jerry was sent home without a contract.

In December 1956, J.W. Brown, the cousin who lived in Memphis, invited Jerry to come stay with him and try again. He offered to play bass for Jerry. Jerry took him up on it, and finally cut a song at Sun Records called "Crazy Arms."

Jimmy was sitting in a small Winnsboro cafe, taking a break from his job, when he heard his cousin's voice on the radio. Hearing it was unbelievable to Jimmy. All the times they'd talked about leaving Ferriday, about making it big . . . Jimmy had doubted either of them would really do it. It left him feeling he would never make it out of these backwoods.

Many felt the music was straight from hell. The country was psychologically volatile. The U.S. and Soviet Union both detonated thermonuclear bombs whose radioactive effects were far worse than the atomic bomb's. The legacy of Hiroshima was making itself felt in the psyches of the postwar superpowers.

Rock and roll was immediately linked to it. First, nationally televised Senate hearings were in full swing in which Senator Joseph McCarthy's inquiry into the Communist infiltration of the U.S. Army was casting its net wide, engulfing entertainment figures. Second, Rosa Parks' rebellion in Montgomery, Alabama in 1955—her refusal to move to the back of a bus in defiance of segregation laws—inaugurated two bloody decades of civil rights unrest and spawned white supremacist groups—White America, Inc., National Citizens Protective Association, National Association for the Advancement of White People, Pro-America, White Citizens' Council, Save Our Nation, Inc.—many of whom felt rock and roll was a specific tool of this evil called integration.

They said the new music had the goal of mixing the races by inflaming the passions of young people. It was being secretly subsidized by Communists, who hoped that a contaminated white race would be so degenerate and godless within a generation that they could easily take over America.

David Beatty remembered 1954 with a helpless laugh. "When I went to Springfield [to Bible college], I was just playing the piano at 19. And they run me out of the piano room. And I'd never BEEN in a honky tonk . . . all I knew was what we learned . . . growing up together as boys. But the music people in there run me out, wouldn't let me play. And I wasn't playing much of nothin'. But it had a beat. The music had a beat, and it came over."

Rock and roll, Jimmy later said, created "a new spiritual dimension to music [that] went beyond mere rhythm. It produced a driving, throbbing beat that stirred the sensual nature of man."

That driving and throbbing was coded into films like "Blackboard Jungle," a 1955 movie about drugs and rebellion in high school that aroused calls for censorship. Its theme song was "Rock Around the Clock."

IN JULY OF 1957, Jerry's star soared higher. He went to New York and performed on the "Steve Allen Show." He came back for an encore two weeks later—the first time that ever happened on Allen's show.

Jerry had performed "Whole Lotta Shakin' Goin' On," the Roy Hall song he'd heard two years before. In August, it hit like a tornado. Jerry was in demand all over the country. He traveled to Houston for a concert, and Mickey, still working for his father-in-law's construction firm, picked him up at the airport. When Mickey saw his cousin flash a wad of $20s and $50s, he made a commitment to get into music.

"Shakin' " went on to sell six million copies.

In November 1957, Jerry's "Great Balls of Fire" hit, becoming the best-selling single in the country.

That year, David Beatty was in Nashville at a revival. Jerry was in town. "The #2 page and the #3 page of the *Nashville Banner*, the whole layout—two pages, three pages of NOTHING BUT Jerry Lee and his concert. Packed it out, girls screaming . . . the whole thing," he said.

Mamie and Elmo were ecstatic. They moved to the new subdivision of Ridgecrest, into a decent, middle class home. Cadillacs began to fill their yard.

Jerry felt invincible. Smitten by his cousin J.W. Brown's blue-eyed seventh-grader, Myra Gale, who still played with dolls and believed in Santa Claus, he talked her into secretly marrying him.

Jimmy, at home in Ferriday reading the old-timey *Miracle Magazine* with Ada, was constantly tempted to quit after Jerry's blast to fame. He was driving a castoff car and preaching in the backwoods, thrilling repressed females with his music.

He knew all the moves, all the cues of his parents' generation—and oh, how the homefolks loved him for it. It was wonderful he could be trusted with the old forms, to keep them and pass them on to the next generation, in the middle of this chaotic time. Years later, his peers would come to like it, too: his style would remind them of what their parents had cherished, and what had brought continuity and security into the uneasy years of the Cold War.

No one could have predicted the siege that would tear apart the innocence of the fifties; no one foresaw the assassinations, the riots, the campus upheavals, the antiwar protests, but everyone could sense that the country was about done with unquestioned authority. Rock 'n' roll music was testimony to that.

The film "High School Confidential" opened with Jerry riding through town on the back of a pickup, playing piano and singing the title song, from Sun Records, in unintentional mockery of Jimmy's early preaching format from the back of Sun's pickup.

Awakening

The Great Awakening was a short-lived but potent Calvinist movement in New England that began about 1720 and gave birth to Methodism—the granddaddy of the Pentecostal movement. Its best-known proponent was Jonathan Edwards, a Yale graduate who later became president of what would be Princeton University. He made an intense argument for personal religious experience that galvanized the religiously moribund American colonies.

Edwards would indeed win many converts, but in the American way—by creating a market. From the fear generated by Edwards' haunting depiction of God's loathing for human wickedness was created a commodity to relieve the fear—salvation. Moreover, Edwards unwittingly introduced into the mix a sales feature that would stick with evangelism forever more, guaranteeing it both success and disparagement: entertainment.

In the colonies, preachers made a living off salvation, traveling and holding revivals where people could escape Edwards' vision of the flames of hell and the Lake of Fire if they came forward to be saved.

By 1750 the Great Awakening comet had burned itself out, leaving an ideological schism that spawned three new universities—Brown, Dartmouth, and Princeton—and gave the term "evangelist" a dramatic coloration that would never leave it.

But conditions were already ripening for another surge, one that would be the model for Jimmy's successful formula: Camp Meeting.

The American Revolution left the colonies profoundly demoralized. The religious establishment was in disarray, with many church leaders carrying the blemish of treason. At the turn of the 18th century, 95 per cent of Southerners were not affiliated with any church.

This spiritual apathy followed homesteaders west across the Appalachians, where they confronted a raw, primitive existence. Their life-and-death struggle against nature left them no time for refining morals or puzzling out how to govern their passions.

People on the frontier drank three times more grain alcohol per capita than they would when Jimmy was an adult, and drunkenness was rampant even among professed Christians. Drinking started early in the morning and went on all day. It was uncivil to refuse a "social glass," even for a minister. Customers at dry-goods stores were treated to a free shot after making a purchase, and liquor was a necessity at all social events, from childbirth and weddings and funerals to quilting bees and cabin raisings. Children and even babies were given alcohol, because water was considered to be without food value. Violence—domestic and public—and debauchery were commonplace, and men routinely neglected crops, work, and family. At one out of every three weddings, the bride was pregnant.

But by 1795, a new movement appeared, and this one would plow into the next century like a more vigorous strain of the same virus—the Second Great Awakening. Sometimes also called the Great Revival, this new movement preached the importance of free will in accepting or rejecting salvation, whereas the first had stressed the lack of free will and hence the need for grace.

Instead of settled colonists of the eastern seaboard, this movement's audience was the pioneers of the trans-Allegheny frontier. Thousands of people came from miles around to camp for days in woods or open fields, sleeping under the stars or in tents and listening to stormy, torchlit preaching deep into the night. As in the first Great Awakening, camp meetings included demonstrations of divine power, an element that was quickly inflated and misunderstood, and that drew skeptics and curiosity seekers.

At a peak in the preaching, several women might become hysterical and fall to the ground. This would give others permission, and soon the excited crowd would be leaping, clapping, shouting Glory! and Praise God! and Hallelujah! Then would follow the "spiritual exercises" or "bodily exercises."

In the "falling exercise," people filled with the Holy Spirit would swoon and fall to the ground and roll over and over. There were those who got the "jerks," as if they had been jabbed with a cattle prod. It started with the head involuntarily snapping backward and forward. Then it might jerk from side to side; soon the whole body would be whipping this way and that. People could be hurled into walls, flung over fences, and might have to be held down until the seizures passed. There were reports of lightning forking from head to head in the services. When the jerks "took" a crowd, bonnets, combs, and hats would fly, and unfurled braids would literally crack like whips. Some visitors came back with tales of heads rotating 360 degrees.

There were also the "barks," where people dashed out of the arbor in groups and roamed around camp, barking, growling, and snapping like dogs; the running exercise, in which a person would suddenly leap up and rush out into the dark, jumping over benches and crashing into trees, wagons, or fences; and the Holy Laugh, a loud, humorless bray.

In the eerie "singing exercise," vocal music would emanate, not from the singer's mouth or nose, but from the chest (these displays would usually bring the services to a standstill while people stared); often these sounds were of an unearthly beauty. In the "dancing exercise," people overcome by the spirit would skip and whirl like joyous children. But because secular dancing was morally tainted, this least peculiar of the spiritual manifestations was most suspect among believers.

These displays obscured camp meetings' anchor of rationality and inspired exaggerated rumors of sexual promiscuity. The release and abandon that came to be expected attracted predators who hoped rapture would be equally at home in the bushes. Drinking was forbidden at camp meetings, but it flowed surreptitiously around their perimeters, and men hung about hoping to exploit women overcome by their feelings.

Still, these features were a minor element of camp meetings; for the most part, the meetings were beginning to have a civilizing effect on the profane, alcoholic, degenerate atmosphere of the frontier. They were a practical way of getting the Gospel out to places that were untempered by any intellectual or professional life. They provided a way to keep in touch with people who kept moving west; family messages and news were often carried by preachers from meeting to meeting.

Families came from miles around and bivouacked outdoors together, listened to preaching, saw soul-saving, and came to believe enthusiastically in spiritual revival. Meetings became social occasions that were a constructive and positive foil to the hard life of the frontier. And within meetings, people who seldom saw their neighbors from even 10 or 20 miles away were able to commune in a setting whose purpose was high and positive. The nets of society were extended and repaired.

And despite the rumors of promiscuity, there were strict camp rules. Women were forbidden to enter the campgrounds during darkness—from an hour before sunset to an hour after sunrise. They stayed with neighboring families.

Camp Meeting's formula proved durable; services spread over the American frontier during the entirety of the 19th century. By the 1850s they were routine, held near rivers and creeks for bathing, drinking, and baptizing. Families would rise at 5 a.m. for prayer, cook breakfast, go to services, and then break up for individual prayer meetings and sessions where people could ask the preachers for advice. At night was the big service, where people got saved.

The highly organized Methodists dominated the frontier with their circuit riders—tenacious, devoted, self-sacrificing missionaries who rode through black, trackless forests and hostile Indian country, spending long hours in the saddle to reach the unschooled of the frontier. They were one of the few ways the "cabin population" got any relief from the life of unrelenting work. They preached at least once a day at cabin gatherings, taught weekly Bible classes on their circuits, and held two-day mini-revivals that cemented the lessons and faith in their supplicants until the next visit.

What the circuit riders did was remarkable. These men—Baptists, Congregationalists, Presbyterians and others as well as Methodists—were the glue that held the frontier together long enough for civilized practices to take root.

Camp Meetings weren't just rural or Southern; industrial workers in New Jersey and Massachusetts got spiritual renewal at permanent sites in fields with specially constructed pavilions. The movement gathered strength from the Industrial Revolution, as mechanized mining, weaving, and the factory system started to emerge. By 1859, when Charles Darwin's *The Origin of Species* was published, industrialization had become ugly in the cities and the mainstream churches were addressing themselves to social reform. Better labor conditions, abolition of child labor, non-exploitive wages and housing, and welfare reform were all attempts to apply Christianity in a competitive economic system.

THE FRONTIER CAMP meeting preachers were the forerunners of tele-vangelists. They were entertainers, they fed the spiritually hungry, and they traveled the country with the Gospel, selling tracts and begging donations to pay their way. Their electronic progeny travel the world via television and sell an array of items from refrigerator magnets to tours of the Holy Land.

By Jimmy Swaggart's time, sophisticated business principles would be applied to Jonathan Edwards' principles of fear and salvation in a highly effective formula; when the entertainment component was added, especially as practiced by one as talented as Jimmy, the sky was the limit. Jimmy would rise high.

But that mix also produced, from the very beginning of evangelism, an enduring enmity between press and pulpit. It surfaced in generation after generation; ever suspicious of what people were getting for their money, ever skeptical of the validity of religious transport, the journalists skewered one man of God after another over the generations. The "derision and ridicule" Jimmy suffered in his early preaching years were an organic, hereditary part of the movement he naively believed was only about God.

But the press often failed to take into account the lawless, undisciplined conditions that camp meeting attempted to bring order to. Reporters had little zest for stories of the homesteader's life of backbreaking work—hunting in the woods, gutting, skinning, cleaning, butchering, planting and harvesting, spinning, weaving, carrying water, beating grain into meal; listening in bed at night for sounds of Indians or ruffians who wanted to kill or steal, or animals who wanted to get into the smokehouse, seldom getting news of neighbors, never seeing a newspaper, never seeing a school—this life made the sight of a friendly man of God, cantering in the rain toward one's lonely, isolated cabin, enough all by itself to bring on tears. The circuit rider and camp meeting preacher represented a message of simple hope to thousands of people. Circuit rider Peter Cartwright was so well known by 1846 that he ran for Congress—losing to Abraham Lincoln.

The raucousness reported about camp meetings usually didn't take into account their context. First, the meetings were outdoors, which added to the sense of license but couldn't be helped; conversely, the open air and beauty of nature helped invoke a state of worship—even if there was a handful of drunks, whores, and scoffers laughing it up on the perimeter.

Second, meetings were often infiltrated by denominational rivals whose purpose was to heckle the preacher and disrupt the proceedings. Much of the recording of camp meetings came from non-Methodist church historians, and reflected their envy of the Methodists' remarkable success on the frontier. These judgmental and uncharitable accounts were in later decades some of the only historical sources of reporting about the meetings.

Third, camp meetings were easy targets. They weren't just attended by the faithful, or those who needed relief from drudgery, or people troubled in their souls by moral desolation, but by travelers, businessmen, politicians, fallen women, curiosity-seekers, drunkards, and anyone who might have a reason to create havoc. The services could easily be besmirched by hecklers who threw eggs, rocks, and rotten vegetables at the speakers.

The camp meetings' emotionality also had a practical function. Traveling preachers who were "spellbinders"—Jimmy Swaggart's direct spiritual forebears—were used to make converts; after they moved on, the circuit rider visited routinely to keep the new converts on the path. Too, services were emotional because many preachers were unschooled men who simply felt they were obeying a divine call. What they lacked in learning they made up for in passion and devotion.

Inevitably, the relationship between press and pulpit became synergistic: the exposés sold newspapers, and the publicity guaranteed crowds. Camp meetings continued to be ignored as a topic for serious historical study, even though they had, by the mid-19th century, helped swell church membership in all denominations by several orders of magnitude.

THE DEEP MEANING of Camp Meeting is in the ritual process that is universal to all cultures. Rituals help process transition and change, at both the societal and individual levels. One goes from death to heaven, from virgin to mother, from sinner to saved; music, dance, and action are used to heighten these moments and evoke their deep meaning.

Ritual, both societal and individual, has a narrative structure, a beginning, middle, and end. The beginning is segregation of a group or individual, focusing attention on it. In the case of Camp Meeting, a group of people in need of spiritual transcendence—homesteaders—selects itself out from the larger societal group and congregates under a tent. Then a sub-group—sinners—is segregated out and attention is focused on them.

These individuals then enter the middle state, liminality. They pass through a portal. This is where outbursts and bodily engagement take place, and also where every member of the group is fused into a community, where all differences are broken down. In this phase, the human mind is stretching, looking for connections to different parts of the cosmos. This is the moment those connections are being realized—literally given corpus—by being expressed through the body.

The liminal state, the state of ecstasy, that Jimmy seeks in his meetings is one that has been helped along in all cultures by music (and often drugs, including alcohol at early Camp Meetings). These states demonstrate how liquid speech can become, as it trails off into poetry, chanting, and song. Alone, words are just a formal, highly structured way of projecting meaning. But if you move from their formal to their symbolic character, where they evoke the most fundamental elements of existence—blood, birth, death, colors, sex, excrement—their structure breaks down. And music is perhaps the purest form of deconstructed language. It overwhelms formal meaning and moves people into symbolic meaning and ecstasy, where meaning is conveyed without words. Jerry, Jimmy, Mickey, and all musicians live and breathe this oxygen.

But even in trailing off, speech does not just dissolve into random sound. Whether it becomes chant or song, it retains a structure, a meter, and in following it from words into music or even dance, a person is submitting to a different kind of discipline, a different form than the linear one to which he or she submits all the rest of the days of the year, year in and year out. Words become a facilitative device to create community.

The purpose of the liminal state is to permit community to occur so transformation can occur, the kind of transformation that neither words alone nor music alone could bring about. No one, sitting on the log bench at a frontier camp meeting with a splitting headache from last night's skullbuster, knowing his crop was burning up because he was too drunk to get it in, knowing his children were without shoes, knowing he was the worst kind of sinner, could believe God's grace might turn him around just because a preacher said it. First he'd have to be segregated, singled out—he'd have to go down to the altar when the preacher called for sinners to come forward—and then he'd have to enter the community. He'd have to surrender to the music and start allowing his body—his carnal, fleshly self—to jerk, or fall to the ground, or allow sounds to come out of his mouth over which he had no control.

This liminal state is a time of meat—as in the root word of carnival—a state of the flesh. In the carnival tradition (in fact the phenomenon of carnival is a giant liminality state), role reversals are common, as the roles of church and state are relaxed or reversed; the king kneels to the commoner, the poor man is showered with gifts, church services are carried out by lay people, graves open and the dead live. In tribal societies, men are made to say things only women would say, or are made to speak like gods or animals. In the evangelical tradition, the liminal state is where a person who has sinned and lived only in the carnal world is transformed into a pure person again, where he is taken into the group after having been an outcast, where he surrenders his body—his flesh—to the community and the music. Like carnival, it has its own reversals, as when people walk in sick and leave whole.

Even if these are only symbolic reversals (especially in the healing realm, with its many failures), they serve their purpose: to turn things inside out so that differences are broken down and the third state—wholeness—can take place. Wholeness is restored, and people feel new, reborn, recharged, and more able.

One overlooked role of the church in general—whether through its ecstatic or its more disciplined forms—has been to provide some alternative to the grind of secular reality. On the frontier, and in the industrial-revolution cities, and in the sharecropper Depression days of Ada and W.H. Swaggart's marriage, right up to the frenzied scramble to live the good life today, many people either have drab, dreary lives or feel imprisoned by work, discipline, and necessity. They're hungry to release feelings of hopelessness, or of being ignored or imprisoned.

Camp Meeting still does this for people. In some parts of the South, meetings are still like huge family reunions, not nearly as religiously fervent as in the previous century, but still bearing the same social significance. People return year after year, and politicians regularly drop by to be seen by their constituents. Jimmy holds special five-day events several times a year, where the same enthusiasm and warmth and brotherhood is very much present. People stay in motels and eat at local cafeterias instead of picnicking in the field and sleeping in tents. But Jimmy still calls each of these special services a Camp Meeting, and people still yell out "Glory!" and "Amen!" in the middle of the sermon. They still come forward, kneel at the altar, shut their eyes and cry, and find cleansing and rest as others lay hands on them and murmur prayers into their ears.

Those early camp meeting forms are seen today in both gospel and rock forms, which align themselves with ecstatic states. They position themselves opposite the symphonic forms of classical music, which are mated with European imperial forms—highly controlled expressions, explicitly military, that were associated with formal institutions and evolved from the need for public spectacle.

The Protestant Reformation was about nothing if not the rejection of that formality. It sought specifically to take those forms—starting with the state church and the Bible—and turn them into the popular vernacular, which could be disseminated among everyone and owned by everyone.

The musical beat, which diminished in white worship after the Middle Ages and the rise of Christianity, seeped back in with the African slave trade to the Americas. Rock and roll made this a tidal wave. Before rock and roll, the beat was present in some form in both gospel and jazz, even though the South (unlike Brazil, which admits its roots) has repressed its close ties to Africa. But it broke through, especially in New Orleans.

Elvis allowed this primitiveness to break through, and so did Jerry. And, in the Pentecostal way, so did Jimmy.

Miraculous Healing

Nineteen fifty-eight arrived on a Wednesday morning, cold and forbidding. But Jimmy Swaggart awoke a different person.

A couple of weeks before this chilly New Years', he had preached in Wisner at Sun's church, and Jerry Lee had shown up at the house in his Cadillac before the service. Jerry's total record sales, including those for "Crazy Arms" and "Whole Lotta Shakin'," were at 21 million. Jerry wasn't a millionaire yet, but a million of anything was more than either of them could imagine. Jerry was on national TV, and his face was on magazine covers.

When he watched Jimmy preach in church that morning, Jerry wept. He had promised God a year before that if He gave him just one hit record, he'd take the money and set up a church and dedicate his life to God just like "Jimmalee." That was three hits ago. The church was packed—Jimmy made sure the word got around—and the crying was Jerry's testimonial to the correctness of his cousin's path and an affirmation to Frances, who had only one or two good dresses. Jerry was going to close a deal on a brand new house in Memphis in a few weeks. He was going to pay $12,000 in cash—more money than his father could probably make in half a decade—and plunk that angelic, blue-eyed, barely-13-year-old Myra down in it (they had married December 13, 1957, after he left second wife Jane Mitcham) and have so much money left over she could go out with a purse full of cash and buy leather chairs, linens, dishes, washer and dryer, dishwasher, clothes, anything she wanted.

He had brought Myra to hear Sun preach a few months before and seen her reduced to weeping by Sun's florid threats of hell for the unsaved.

"Jerry took me to church, and . . . I nearly came apart!" she said. "I was basically a little Baptist, I went to Sunday school, vacation Bible school. I colored the little pictures of Jesus, sang 'Jesus Loves Me.' . . . Thirteen years old, I was shaking in my boots! Uncle Sun was talking about dying and going to hell, and . . . 'you're not repenting, and you walk out of this building tonight and you may never see the sun come up again . . .' "

Jerry was now the big fish Jimmy and his father were competing to land. They wanted to bring their star relative to his knees on the altar. Minnie Bell went and put her arms around her weeping nephew, and it was a good display of the family bond for all to see. But when it was time for people to go down to the altar to repent of their sins and give their lives to Jesus, according to Jimmy years later, Jerry stayed put.

After the service, Jimmy started to remind his cousin that, although he had gained the world—Jerry had pointed to his Cadillac and mentioned a $10,000 performance fee—he could lose his soul. Humbly, Jimmy noted that he had given all his meager goods to the Lord. When he suggested that his cousin, 22 and only recently delivered of a lifetime of rank poverty, should do the same, Jerry didn't hang around much longer. Guilt was the only stick Jimmy had to hit him with, and all it did was make Jerry feel bad and resentful.

Now, on January 1, 1958, Jimmy had left his job as a swamper. He had talent, and he knew it; he had had several offers to play piano in gospel groups, and had declined. He was a preacher, full-time now, with Frances' wholehearted support. He wasn't going to be a minister in some little church somewhere. He didn't want to settle down. He'd lived in a small town all his life, and he wanted to roam.

Jimmy's first real gig was a revival in Sterlington, Louisiana, at the church of Jewell Barton, Jerry Lee's ex-father-in-law (the first of five such ex-in-laws). Jimmy had only preached two or three times as a full-time minister when Barton gave him a chance to appear. He started off well, but on the fourth night, he began to feel sick. He worsened rapidly, and Barton, worried, drove him from the parsonage where he and Frances were staying to a hospital at Monroe. He was burning up with fever.

Ironically, he was diagnosed with pneumonia, the illness that had killed his infant brother just as his own parents had set out on the road to Texas, "running," as the family all later concurred, "from God."

Now, after he had resurrected Donnie and set about to correct his family's path, to go back with a wife and a Donnie himself and do it right this time, Jimmy was ambushed by the old enemy. The new Donnie was about the same age Jimmy had been when his family made the ill-fated trip to Rio Hondo.

He was so weak he couldn't sit up in bed. Another old pair of enemies came to visit, too, even in the hospital: rivalry and depression. Never without a radio, Jimmy heard "Crazy Arms," "Whole Lotta Shakin'," and "Great Balls of Fire" constantly. Jerry's record sales were soaring, and he would soon be bound for Europe to perform.

And Jerry wasn't the only cousin making waves. Last fall, Mickey had cut "Tell Me Why" and "Ooh Wee Baby" on Minor Records and was circulating posters of himself sitting at a piano in a hip suit, looking suave. Mickey had then gone to Sun Records and cut "Come On, Baby" and a song he wrote, "Thinking of Me." Then he signed with a much bigger label, Dot, and produced two more songs; after appearing on Wink Martindale's television show in Memphis, he was headed for Philadelphia to try out for American Bandstand and then for New York to audition at William Morris. All this had happened in the past few months.

Another cousin, Carl McVoy, had joined the Bill Black Combo and had a song in the Top 40.

After being transferred to another hospital and running up more medical bills than he could afford, Jimmy checked himself out. One night, left alone for a few hours, he lay on his gloomy bed. The trailer was filled with depression and failure. He had had to cancel all the preaching dates he managed to set up before he got sick. The pneumonia squatted inside his chest like a wet sponge, waiting for him to surrender so it could sop up the rest of his miserable life. He was a high school dropout, a day laborer for five impoverished years. Elmo had bought him gasoline a few times, and groceries for his family—with Jerry's money. He had a three-year-old who would soon need schooling—and he'd made a decision to drag him out onto the road. He still took his formless, long-suppressed anger out on Frances. How long would his young wife look up to him?

Anxiety descended on him. Sinister thoughts, ones less formed into the familiar blame and scorn but more baleful, bloated with license, roamed freely inside his skull, looking for a catalyst to transmogrify them into a suggestion: suicide.

His only tool was prayer. A cry came from his mouth, and he grabbed his Bible. He let it fall open.

Joshua 1:9: "Have I not commanded thee? Be strong and of a good courage; be not afraid, neither be thou dismayed: for the Lord thy God is with thee whithersoever thou goest." He got up out of bed and walked around the little trailer. Ada's teachings of praying big prayers and her admonition of being God's chosen washed over him. The Pentecostal strategy set in: when you're depressed, it's from the devil. Just drown him out with praise. If there's anything wrong, just roll over it with your will.

He did. He got well.

His big step on January 1, 1958 had filled him with fear and doubt, and the pneumonia gave him time to rethink it. But once he made up his mind that God was his partner, he was cured.

◆   ◆   ◆

Jimmy started getting serious about the next phase of his ministry—the reality of traveling. Before he could build a revival schedule back up, he had to confront the highways in earnest. He and Frances traveled in a used Plymouth to little churches a few hours' drive from Wisner, often taking Donnie, preaching for pennies. He was bringing in $30 a week, barely enough to get enough credit to get into more debt, just for necessities.

One Sunday as he preached in Ferriday, Elmo arrived at the church in one of Jerry's Cadillacs, with stupendous news: Jerry had wangled him an audition in Memphis, at Sun Records, for a gospel line the studio was considering launching.

Visions of a home and new car flitted past, but, feeling faint, he said no. Later, he asked God why He'd wired his jaws shut, and God answered in the avuncular lingo of the Louisiana countryside: "Son, I'm gonna tell you two things about this . . ." and he told Jimmy to hang on, he wouldn't be disappointed. Jimmy later wrote that God had some contorted reason for keeping him from saying yes, but really it was likely that Jimmy simply had no confidence. He was extremely competitive with Jerry still, and he didn't want to humiliate himself.

Once after a road trip, Jimmy and Frances were invited to Elmo and Mamie's new house in Ridgecrest. Stay the night, Mamie invited. Jimmy appreciated it, but had an inkling what it would cost him, and he was right. The first thing his uncle Elmo did was point to the gaggle of expensive cars parked helter-skelter in the front yard. "Count 'em," he said gleefully. Jerry, Elmo told him proudly, rotated them, driving one of the Lincolns when he got tired of the Cadillacs, etc.

As for Mamie, she wasn't sure how to fulfill her social ambitions; she knew it meant having grace, hospitality, and charity, but she also had a notion that it meant being better than other people. For awhile, she put on airs before old church friends and family members; one day at Eva Gilley's Cozy Cafe, she peered at the outhouse a few yards out the back door as if she'd never seen it before.

"Eva," she said in front of the other patrons, "Do you think it'd be safe for me to go out there?"

"I imagine you've been to many a one outside, Mamie," Eva threw back tartly.

When certain people would drop in to visit, she'd snub them by hiding in her bedroom and having the maid tell them she was tired and had gone to bed.

Now Mamie ushered Jimmy into Jerry's room to change out of his one good suit while Frances helped with supper. The closet door had been left open, showing snazzy suits and box upon box of new shoes. She told him Jerry had another stash at his house in Memphis.

After giving Jimmy a little time to absorb the difference between what was in his closet and what was in Jerry's, Mamie tapped on the door and stuck her head in. Oh, by the way, she said, Jerry just signed another fat contract.

At first Jimmy took the bait. After Mamie left him alone once more, he started sinking into a black pit of depression. But after awhile, he pulled out of it by praising God, and was filled with warmth and supernatural affirmation. He began to shout that Hallelujah, God ruled the universe, that Glory, he belonged to that God, and so on.

He made enough ruckus to be heard in the kitchen, where Mamie and Frances were cooking, and sure enough, at the supper table he was rewarded with a query from the Lewises about his noisy tête-à-tête with God.

♦ ♦ ♦

In the first five months of 1958, Jerry made $75,000, an astronomical sum. After he made one appearance on "American Bandstand" in March of 1958, singing "Breathless," the record sold a million copies. Not long after the scene at Mamie's, Jerry released "High School Confidential," and concluded a smashing national tour with Chuck Berry and Buddy Holly that extended the entire month of April and 10 days into May. Jerry and Myra went home to Ferriday for a few days' rest before embarking on a six-week tour of England. Thirty-seven appearances were scheduled, worth $100,000.

Ferriday had proclaimed May 17th Jerry Lee Lewis Day, and held a parade at 2 p.m. That night, he played a benefit at the high school.

It was an unhappy reunion; the mayor and the Chamber of Commerce might have given him a key to the city and a plaque, but the citizens of Ferriday let him know they still considered him beneath them.

"Of course, being a hometown boy, we didn't overwhelm him with admiration, you know," said a Ferriday native years later. "We said, 'Let's don't show him that we really like him.' . . . we didn't jump up [in a frenzy], we just clapped, and he got mad and stomped off the stage."

"It's, 'who do you think you are, putting on airs like that! We knew you when,' " said another attendee at the concert. "Now Jerry Lee could care less if we all die down here. He feels like the people treated him like dirt all the time he was growing up, so he doesn't owe them a thing."

It was indeed generous of Jerry to appear in truculent Ferriday at the peak of his fame. And it was eerie that the sour visit took place only days before he would fall from that peak.

He and Myra, along with her mother and some other family members, arrived in London on May 22, 1958. While Jerry, dressed in sequins and velvet, was holding his first press conference, prying reporters ferreted out Myra and discovered her age ("15," she lied). The next morning, the papers were filled with stories about her, eclipsing news of DeGaulle's sweep of the French National Assembly.

Within a day, the press discovered that not only had she added two years to her age, she was Jerry's close cousin, and her marriage to him was bigamous, as his divorce from Jane Mitcham had not been final when he wed Myra. The Home Secretary's office, alarmed at the implications of pederasty and incest, sent police to the hotel to question Myra, Jerry, and other family members.

By the time Jerry went onstage on Sunday, May 25, the atmosphere was nasty. Rock and roll had suddenly turned into something more dangerous than a teenagers' fad, if this sordid product was what it turned out. Maybe there was something to this idea that Jerry was arousing the devil with a God-given musical gift, contributing to lust, immorality, and maybe Communism.

Headlines read, "Get Out, Lewis!" "Girl Victim," and "Clear This Gang Out!" Half the ticket holders didn't show up for the concert that night. The applause that did meet his songs was laced with catcalls.

The tour was cancelled, and Jerry's entourage flew home to Memphis the next day. Immediately Jerry was dropped from radio disc jockeys' play lists in the States. His bookings were cancelled, and he was similarly jeered by the American press. Undertones from his childhood in Ferriday, the opinion of him as white trash, had thrown out a massive echo. It looked like he was going to be dumped right back where he had started—playing in beer joints and stickerpatch ball parks.

Jimmy was preaching at a revival in Spring Hill, Louisiana when Jerry came home in disgrace. He called Jerry to invite him to the services, knowing curiosity would pack the house, and expecting to have the gloomy satisfaction of comforting his shattered cousin.

Instead of a broken and contrite man, however, he found Jerry as filled with bravado as ever. However, he was as willing a sacrificial lamb as Isaac, carrying the wood for his own funeral pyre: he promised to attend the next night and bring his notorious child bride.

Of course the place was packed. Of course Jerry was held up as an example of God's justification of sinners, and of course Jerry did not go down to the altar. But Jimmy got his mileage out of it.

While he had momentum with Jerry, Jimmy made a move that he had set up months before. David Beatty had confided to him that Jerry had promised to buy him a car when he came home from Bible college. But with the London disaster and the growing blacklisting, it was easy to see that Jerry's stash might quickly vanish, especially with the horde of relatives he was supporting and helping.

"Jimmy set in on Aunt Mamie to get a car," said David. "He'd go out there and butter up Aunt Mamie. And make Aunt Mamie think that I was a big shot 'cause I was goin' to college, and he was really havin' to struggle. And Jimmy had a better car'n I had!"

Jerry bought Jimmy a car instead of David.

In a folksy, airbrushed autobiography published by his ministry in 1976 (and re-issued in 1984), Jimmy wrote that he'd been praying for a new car for months, asking God to put the touch on Jerry for an Oldsmobile. After the revival meeting in Spring Hill, the family was eating steak on Jerry's nickel and Myra suggested Jerry buy Jimmy a car and take it off his taxes, Jimmy reported. Jerry complied; afraid he would only spring for a Ford, Jimmy wrote, he prayed hard.

Obediently, the Almighty screwed up negotiations at Ferriday's Ford dealership, and they headed for Natchez. On the way, Jerry commented that Jimmy's car wasn't really in such bad shape.

Again Jimmy went into action. "Lord, tear this thing up," he prayed.

Whereupon the ever-obliging Almighty made the engine cough and the brakes burn on the spot.

At the Olds dealership, when Jimmy trotted over to the car he had already pre-selected, God suddenly decided to rein in His greedy servant a tad. "You can have the car you want but not the color you want," He decided. "You can have the tan and white car."

How many of Jimmy's followers actually bought this treacle is impossible to say, but it demonstrated how comfortable he had become by 1976 with the assumption that his audience would believe anything he said about his relationship with God. However, it would be hard even for the neediest idolizer not to notice how Jimmy had abused prayer and trivialized the Creator of Heaven and Earth. And it showed the extent to which Jimmy had, by the time he'd spent 20 years in the ministry, managed to use the church's own dynamics to transform the harsh Pentecostal God of his childhood into an indulgent, supportive Daddy and executive producer. The transmogrification of Sun could hardly have been more clearly coded.

Jimmy really did need the car worse than David, however. He was in the field, and traveling with a wife and child. Often the accommodations they were offered by the churches where Jimmy preached after a grueling trip and a supper of okra stew were little better than sleeping in the car. A comfortable, reliable car was crucial for morale.

David forgave the perfidy, but he never forgot it. In 1982, the cousins were together for a funeral "at Aunt Reenie's house, four of us to the table. And we was just talkin' about old times, and cuttin' up and laughin', and Jimmy kinda got onto Jerry's case about not livin' for the Lord.

"And it kinda always irritated Jerry . . . He said, 'Jimmy Swaggart, I don't think you got a thing in the world to say about me, and the way I live. You're the very guy that conned David out of that car I was gonna give him.'

"And I'm tellin' you, Jimmy turned BLOOD RED! Well . . . the chickens come home to roost, see. And it'll catch up with him."

It actually caught up with him a year after he did it. Around the time he intercepted David's car, he recorded a song called "At the End of the Trail" at Ferriday's radio station, with the ever-patient David (probably still unaware that he was never going to get a car from Jerry) producing it. The record turned out terrible, but Jimmy kept emphasizing his music and advertising his relationship to Jerry. He wasn't aware of how damaging this was until he applied for ordination by the Assemblies of God in 1959.

The Assemblies had very lenient rules for ordination. "You were supposed to have read some stuff, but mainly you just had to have some ministry," said an old friend of Jimmy's who was ordained the year Jimmy applied. You had to have spoken in tongues, but there was no Bible school required. Sun had had no trouble getting ordained.

After working hard, traveling and preaching for well over a year, Jimmy and Frances drove to Lake Charles in the spring of 1959 for the meeting of his church's district council. The committee's questions were strangely vague. Ordination was denied.

Jimmy was stunned. He was the only applicant who was rejected, including some who had only been in service part time, while he had devoted full time to it, subsisting on $30 or $40 a week. Even his father hadn't done that. He should have been a shoo-in. He could not get a straight answer as to why he was rejected.

A clue could be found in the newspapers. A few weeks earlier, Jerry had performed in Baton Rouge. The crowd was only 1,000, nothing like his previous draws, but still large enough to make the local papers. Jimmy had heavily emphasized their relationship.

After the show, Myra, who had become pregnant shortly after she and Jerry were herded out of England, went into labor. Elmo and Mamie raced her all the way to Ferriday in one of Jerry's Cadillacs.

She gave birth to a son early the next morning, reviving interest in the international scandal of nine months before. Reporters from every newspaper and wire service in range converged on the little hospital, and photos of the 14-year-old mother were flashed around the world. The scandal was coughed back up for re-consumption and jokes flew about Jerry's inbred relationship to his new son. They named him Steve Allen Lewis, after the man who had given Jerry his first big break.

One of the new preachers who left Lake Charles with credentials was Gerald Wilson, who would later preach at Jimmy's church in Baton Rouge and become a beloved pastor near Monroe.

"Jimmy had every qualification, he was a full time evangelist," Wilson said. "They ordained some people that didn't have a scintilla of the ministry he had. . . . There was some concern about where is he going with this music because of the Jerry Lee tie."

"The Assemblies of God in those days was very conservative," said Jack Wright, an attorney and Nazarene minister based in the Lewises' ancestral home of Monroe, "and Jimmy's piano style was honky tonk blues. His left hand is where his trouble started."

Jimmy had also shown a taste for preaching on the edge, often just on the verge of doing something Jerry Lee-ish, of going too far. Later this envelope-pushing attracted millions and threw him into controversies he relished. But in 1959, his little boogie touch on the piano, combined with his fresh ideas and sex appeal, were just a little too juicy for the Assemblies.

But all he knew at the time was humiliation. The rejection was unusual and hurtful, said another Assemblies minister who met him a few years later. "It really hurts being told you just *don't quite measure up.*"

It had been very hard to get invited to enough revivals and churches to eke out a living for over a year. Now he'd have to do it all over.

Before the committee, Jimmy behaved with class, accepting his rejection with grace and humility, which went a long way toward mitigating the strikes against him. But it was a dismal drive back to Wisner, where he and Frances—who was uncharacteristically despondent over the rebuff—were met by a shocked Sun and Minnie Bell, who had expected a celebration. Jimmy had to pray for hours to get his equilibrium back.

That summer, Jimmy found a group of defenders who passed him from one venue to another, inviting him to preach revivals in Louisiana, Arkansas, and Alabama during the rest of 1959. Just after Christmas, he attended a preachers' seminar in Monroe. The speaker was A.N. Trotter, a famous missionary to Africa. Trotter told how he was rejected by his own brethren in the early years of his ministry, how they fought and discouraged him—all except for one kindly elder, who had laid hands on him and restored his faith. That man made all the difference. It was the kind of healing a young preacher could only get from an older man. No matter how strong the wife was, or how loyal one's peers or how supportive the family, there were times, especially for the sort of wounded men who often ended up as traveling preachers, when a loving father was the only thing that could restore the conviction of a loving God—it had to radiate from someone's flesh, somewhere. Trotter was such a father.

His sermon touched the crowd, and at the altar Jimmy wept with the other men, relieved he wasn't the only one who had suffered such rebuke. As he prayed, he felt someone touch his shoulders. Of the hundreds of men at the altar, Trotter had come to lay hands on *him* and pray for *him.* Jimmy felt warmth spreading through him. He felt God was telling him he was going to be anointed just like A.N. Trotter.

On the Road

Highway 65, Highway 15, Highway 80—they were big roads that went to big towns, while the little farm-to-market roads wound around rivers, pine barrens, streams, lakes, and bayous—Louisiana 128 through Jigger, Gilbert, and Saint Joseph; Louisiana 4 through Newlight and Newellton.

The little family, now more comfortable in the Olds provided by Jerry, rolled in the cold, silent, rainy countryside, heater blowing in the winter, through tiny villages with pioneer names—Duty, Enterprise, Fort Necessity—plain, sweet little communities built around a cotton gin or sawmill, with frame homes or trailers nestled into tall trees and big American cars parked in the yard. Trees—ash, maple, Tupelo gum, longleaf and loblolly pines, cypress, beech, red oak, chinaberry—rose unplanned among the houses and were left to themselves. Almost every porch had chairs, where people sat in the evenings in nice weather and shelled peas, or shucked dried corn as the sun went down.

Jimmy and Frances came around curves in harvest season and scared up flocks of tiny black birds hopping through the shorn stalks, pecking at fallen seeds. They crossed the muddy rivers on the new bridges made for automobiles, and saw the rusting railroad bridges off to the side, fast becoming relics good only for holding up fishermen with their buckets and stringers.

In spring, dewberry, stretchberry, and honeysuckle vines snarled on the fences along the water-filled ditches, where bracken fiddleheads and resurrection ferns shot up like coiled springs. The field-rows were soggy, filled with shiny water. Groups of carefree dogs seemed to lope along every roadway. Lives were informed by the moods of the land, the fields full of pumpkins or maize, the weather, and the rivers. But out of these places of silent beauty also came this wild, wild music that became rock and roll.

Jimmy wasn't really aware that the traveling revival of the great healing evangelists was over—the year he went on the road would later be deemed the official year of its death—but even if he'd known, he still would have gone out on the road. He was not cut out for some little pastorate and he already knew it. He loved traveling, and it was the only chance to really break out and make something of himself.

He didn't particularly plan to have a healing ministry anyway. "I wanted a genuine, deep moving of the Holy Spirit," he wrote, and though that included physical healing, what he knew best from his background was salvation. How to go in and touch people, how to push their guilt and grief and despair and failure buttons so they'd break down, and open themselves to the relief of being saved. That dynamic he understood, and he would spend the next years learning to play it like a violin.

He instinctively knew this arousal was a big responsibility; you weren't supposed to use it only to get money out of people. As his powers grew over the next few years, he consciously tried to be humble about them. His old friend Gerald Wilson explained why he was different from other preachers.

"He [had] stories and incidents people [could] identify with. And a feeling that he CARED. And he wasn't, in those days, self-righteous. A lot of the world can't understand—there's a ministry of the Holy Spirit: I'm not here to beat you down, I'm here to lift you up and help you. People sense that in him . . . Jimmy had a touch on his life.

"You had an old second-hand car, and a little suitcase, and you went wherever, whoever called you, staying wherever—with the pastor, in the back of the church . . . maybe after you had a few successes, they might get you a room in a motel." You got a hamburger and a coke when you could afford it, in places where the evaporative cooler spread a mixture of smells: swamp water, frying grease, and some unidentifiable bayou scent, like a wet dog.

"It's not as common now, you don't see the depth of commitment of people like Jim much any more. He was faithful, he gave everything he had, he did without."

Jimmy and Frances had no money, no guarantees of anything beyond a few days' subsistence. They took whatever accommodations were available— cold water, beds with springs sticking out. They lived in cheap cabins or courts that smelled of rat droppings and had roaches, stinky toilets, and scurrying sounds in the night, or in the basement of some church. Another friend from that period, Jerald Ogg, said church basements were "not fit to live in, most pastors wouldn't do it."

Jimmy and Frances did, though. "They'd come into that basement [at Ogg's Kansas City church] and clean it up and disinfect it enough to live in." It was damp and huge and cold, with roaches and cobwebs. "It was dark, you had to cross the whole basement to find a shower, there was nothing set up there for an apartment," said Ogg.

They discovered that evangelists were sometimes given the dreg accommodations with a clear conscience, because traveling preachers were supposed to suffer—first, because they were supposed to be doing the work of God, not seeking luxury; second, because Jesus had told his disciples to give up all they had to follow him, and someone willing to do that was a credible witness to God; and third, because the evangelist had to be assessed some price for not having the responsibility of running a church.

The traveling evangelists got to skirt the duties of the settled preachers, who were often so whipped down and tired of mind that it was hard to give a good sermon. As on the frontier, traveling evangelists enjoyed the luxury of being spellbinders. They could focus their energies on pleasing an audience, and they were a welcome respite, able to revive faith. Jimmy had a chance to make a reputation in a way he never could by sticking with some little clapboard church in Frogmore or Clayton or Wisner, like his father.

But even with the new car, life on the road was tough. "It was an exhausting, grinding, draining way of life," wrote Pentecostal historian David Harrell. "William Branham was a broken man after little more than a year; Jack Coe was physically exhausted at the time of his death; A.A. Allen, an incredibly tough campaigner, tottered constantly on the brink of psychological collapse; the resilience of Oral Roberts became a legend among his peers."

Jimmy liked to listen to the car radio while Frances and Donnie napped. He got ideas for sermons from the news and enjoyed discussions about current topics like the debate over the death penalty. Sermons dealing with such current events were always better than the "Jesus Loves You, Sinner" formula of so many preachers. And there were plenty of good issues. Birth control pills. The banning of *Lady Chatterly's Lover* from the U.S. mail. The shocking new magazine with page after glossy page of women baring their breasts—*Playboy*. Riots when black students demanded coffee at a North Carolina Woolworth's lunch counter.

Traveling with a small child in the back seat was difficult. "It got very discouraging," said Frances, "back in the early years, tremendously discouraging."

She had no nest to raise her baby. Donnie would get sick sometimes. When they traveled with him anyway, feeling that they shouldn't be taking him out with a cough and fever, they drove in silence.

"Jimmy and I wouldn't speak, we felt so guilty about raising him that way," said Frances. It was one way Southerners dealt with guilt: don't mention it. Just poach the family in silence. "We never had another child."

It was a mixture of love, discouragement, and excitement during those bittersweet travel years, when the sap was rising and God and demon oppression were tugging at him daily, and the thrill of new places and successful meetings brought return invitations and a sense he was really building a ministry.

But it would also echo that earlier time of cheap motels and death: Rio Hondo, Texas. Something precious and whole was lost when Donnie died. Jimmy had to go back out as an adult and finish what had been started.

Finding Donnie was one piece of unfinished business. Another was the flesh. The cheap motels he and Frances had to choose from while Donnie was a baby was where Jimmy saw the women hanging out. That's where he learned how to find them.

The Color Line

In the South, the old plantation-based social order, which had persisted in some ways more virulently after the Civil War than before, was about to enter a new and bloody incarnation.

Between 1950 and 1960 the South lost 10 per cent of its population, largely because of migration of blacks to the humming foundries and factories of the Northern cities. Now their left-behind kin, emboldened by *Brown v. Board of Education* and the new Catholic president who seemed bent on integration, arose like a sleepy dragon.

Before about 1957, there wasn't any trouble in Southern states, claimed Frank Rickard, the lawman who watched Jimmy and Jerry grow up in Ferriday. "Blacks just went up and voted if they wanted. It was when these Northerners came down here to fix things, and brought in a lot of trash, that it got messed up."

That may have been true of Ferriday and other small towns where many social strictures were more relaxed. But the idea that it was true everywhere was shot full of holes when, on January 31, 1960, a black college freshman sat down at a bus terminal lunch counter in Greensboro, North Carolina and was refused service. Day after day groups of students sat at the counter for two hours, then went outside and prayed the Lord's Prayer loudly on the sidewalk. The experiment spread to other towns, and soon it became obvious that a black person's inability to get a cup of coffee at a lunch counter had nothing to do with "Commies and outside agitators."

By 1965, Frank Rickard was a police officer in Natchez and up to his ears in racial violence on both sides of the river. A black store on Highway 84 in Ferriday, Frank's Shoe Store, was firebombed. The culprits, said Rickard, were "a splinter branch of the Klan called the White Dollar Club. They were violent, nothing but trash. So was a splinter called the Minute Men. The Klan wasn't violent until this bad element got in. Neither was the N.A.A.C.P., but they had violent elements, and those were S.N.C.C. [Student Non-Violent

Coordinating Committee] and C.O.F.O [Congress of Federated Organizations].

"The White Dollars set Frank [Frank Morris, the store owner] on fire with kerosene, and he ran down the street. He burned to death . . . He was a good fella, had as many white customers as black ones, and they thought the world of him . . . [So then] C.O.F.O. burned a house in Natchez, a furniture store, and a sporting goods store after Frank's was bombed."

The White Dollars, Rickard said, also "got a cripple-legged little colored boy, he was about 14 years old, in Bunkie, Louisiana, and tied him to a tree, and beat him and left him tied there. It was in the winter, and he almost died."

Sammy Davis, Jr., the black principal of Ferriday Upper Elementary School who would later be mayor of Ferriday, formed the Deacons for Defense. The Deacons armed themselves with pistols, shotguns, and machine guns.

Two opposing groups marched in Natchez under a court order that said they were supposed to walk two abreast on either side of Rankin Street. Instead, said Rickard, "they got out there and started swaggering down the street any old way."

About eight of the troublemakers on each side were arrested, and Rickard put them all together in the same cell in the jail and turned the fire hose on them. "I told them, there! If you wanna fight, fight!"

In 1960, as Jimmy fought his second battle for ordination, the era of sit-ins, marches, and rallies erupted in Louisiana. Governor Jimmie Davis, who owed his election to the wealth and influence of white supremacists, was swearing he'd go to jail before allowing Louisiana's schools to be integrated.

Driving from town to town, Jimmy and Frances often found the news on the car radio utterly discordant with what they were seeing out the windows. It was hard to believe, driving past the orderly farms, the pastures dotted with Guernsey milk cows, the houses with picket fences and neat brick chimneys, that only 30 miles down the highway, New Orleans was on the verge of riot.

Having come from the wrong side of Ferriday, Jimmy had rapport with blacks, as did all his clan. He and Jerry owed their music to Old Sam and some of the regulars at Haney's. Before he became mayor, Sammy Davis, Jr. told young Jerry Lee, "Get as rich and famous as you want, but don't get white on me."

The Swaggarts, Lewises, and Gilleys "were a friendly buffer zone between us and what I call the *real* white folks," said Davis. "They were the closest thing to being black without being black." He was sure they were called nigger lovers.

Jerry's sister, Frankie, remembered Mrs. Thompson, the black lady who practiced voodoo on the bank of Black River, a mile or so from the sharecropper cabin where the Lewises lived.

Mrs. Thompson loved and befriended the child, who could not relate to anyone in her troubled family. She gave Frankie voice lessons, and gave her a spell to help hit high notes. Frankie also had her eyebrows arched by Mrs. Thompson. She sat the girl down on a stump, put her hand into a pot, and wiped some stuff that was hot and tingly on her eyebrows. Are you sure this is the way you want it? she asked. Frankie's eyebrows came out in a thin, arched line, she said, and never grew back the way they had been.

But the families were racist, as well, in ways that seemed normal to everyone in those days.

"I remember growing older and finding out a few things," said Mickey, "and I said, 'Mother, how could you teach me that all men are created equal, and on the other hand, that I shouldn't associate with blacks?' Her comeback was that all creatures on the earth should seek after their own kind. You know—the sparrow doesn't mate with the blackbird. That was just their type of mentality back then." One of Mickey's father's bars in Ferriday welcomed both blacks and whites—but the place had a color bar, a rail that ran down the middle separating the two groups.

It was not uncommon for white men to have second "homes" in the black part of Ferriday. One night during a racially tense period, the men of Bucktown decided they'd had their fill.

"They went from house to house," said a relative of Jimmy's, "saying they were going to string up any white men they found. Twenty-five white men ran out of Bucktown with only the clothes on their backs. If Pa Swaggart [W.H.] wasn't one of them, it's only because he had made up with Ada for the time being."

But Pentecostalism kept its equilibrium. A.A. Allen, one of Jimmy's favorite evangelists, held an integrated revival in Little Rock in 1958, and another in Atlanta in 1960. A year later, he added a beautiful black female singer to his revival team. He told blacks they should want to be black, to be glad of it, because, he said, you'll never be at peace if you want to be something other than what God made you.

Oral Roberts insisted that blacks be allowed into his meetings as early as 1948. His revivals were supported mostly by poor whites, and in their context, racial boundaries were simply ignored. This toying with taboos had long been a feature of Pentecostalism, whose preachers had conducted integrated services since the days of Azusa Street.

Christian journalist Larry Thomas was a Missouri native who worked for Jimmy in the 1980s. "The [ministry] leadership didn't have the racist attitude by and large, but they still had some good old boys with gun racks. You [could] still tell that many folks weren't happy that blacks came to the Family Worship Center. [Blacks] get more excited in their worship; you could look around and see [disapproval] on some people's faces . . ." But Jimmy, he said, got excited in worship too. "There were some of the biggest surprises from him." Jimmy had a black organist for awhile, and under his influence, "Jimmy liked vamping on the organ, putting soul into his playing."

On June 23, 1960, Jimmy was accepted for ordination by the Assemblies of God.

39

Being Seen

A white Methodist minister walked his little daughter into a segregated Louisiana school. He was attacked by screaming, spitting women, as was a mother bringing her child in. Her neighbors told her she was disgracing the neighborhood and making a spectacle of herself.

The thing that made this Louisiana scene—and the terrible convulsions to come—a display of massive proportions was the new medium of television. One thing Jimmy saw more and more, even on the roofs of isolated little farmhouses, were television antennae. He was not in a position to watch daily, but all across the land he was crisscrossing, Southerners were seeing themselves for the first time as others saw them. They saw their governors and legislators, grown men and leaders, declaring war on wide-eyed six-year-olds. They saw a mob screaming "nigger-lover" at a priest as he escorted his five-year-old into school.

In 1961, news cameras sent the dissonant images out to the world: Freedom Riders beaten, kicked, and stomped at a Birmingham bus station, in a beautiful city full of magnolias and antebellum homes, now crawling with jeeps and federal troops in combat dress, forcing screaming civilians away from the bus station with rifles and bayonets.

The fear and guilt of the entire nation were being laid bare by television over the next several years as fire hoses and police dogs were unleashed on students and civil rights demonstrators. Medgar Evers' 1963 funeral turned into a riot of dogs and nightsticks—with the police cutting the power cords to the news cameras and microphones.

It was played out in the South, and the out-of-control Southerners bore the shame and scandal, but the integration of blacks and whites held a primordial *dis-ease* for whites all over the country, as if they were watching the mating of Satan and God. As if whites were realizing, to their horror, that they had shadow selves, that their Calvinist cop self who kept things under control was balanced by a dark, sensuous, creative, drumbeat self.

"Civil rights was the biggest issue [for preachers], especially in the South, with the changes in the social structure, jobs, schools," said Gerald Wilson. "Some people said the churches were being 'invaded' by people who just wanted to see if they'd have trouble getting in. [Jimmy and I] took the stand that the church was not to exclude ANYBODY, not the vilest sinner, and certainly not on the basis of color."

By the mid-1960s, Southerners were sick of being on national television. Television had savaged some of their most cherished images of themselves. They were gracious. They lived in lovely settings, they made their peace with blacks and didn't have racial problems like in the Northern cities, and their hospitality in spite of their Civil War defeat was legendary. They were jealous of the daily interviews with Martin Luther King, disgusted with the way the media fawned on him and scribbled his every utterance, while their own accusations of Communism and manipulation went unheard by what they felt was the uncaring, punitive, vicious Yankee press.

Well-meaning whites, no more racist than their Northern counterparts, were genuinely baffled that blacks felt they had been treated unjustly. White Southerners had given up their slaves and lived side by side with the black freedmen. They'd made a reasonable accommodation, and felt blacks were satisfied with it and ought to be. It was upsetting that Northerners were coming down and telling their "decent Nigras" how to claim their rights. It really stung. They asked their decent Nigras over and over, why do you need someone from Massachusetts to come down here and tell you what to do. You don't need that now, do you?

King touched on the core of their distress when he talked of dignity. "[The Negro] has come to feel that he is SOMEBODY," he said. "And with that new sense of 'somebodiness' and self-respect, a new Negro has emerged with a new determination to achieve freedom and human dignity whatever the cost may be."

That observation evoked something about the South that seemed deep: many people didn't seem to feel they'd ever really been seen. It echoed what David Beatty said about a teenager feeling at last that he was SOMEBODY when he got the Holy Ghost. Something had taken away many Southerners' sense of self. What King and Southern blacks had in common with David Beatty and Jimmy Swaggart and Jerry Lee Lewis and their Ferriday clan were, first, that nobody-ness; and, second, the Pentecostal church—which gave them back their somebody-ness through emotion, ecstasy, and community.

The irony was that the church (in addition to the obvious culprit, the Civil War) was a prime suspect in the robbery of selfhood in the first place. Jimmy's brand of Pentecostalism was the church of the South's sharecroppers and lintheads and wage slaves, and its Holy Roller format kept them an underclass.

It was one of the many strange reversals of Pentecostalism that it provided such an intense experience of being both seen and unseen. The problem was not how to get attention—the pressure to get saved put the spotlight ruth-lessly on children and adults alike—the problem was how to be seen and accepted just as you were. The church purported to do this, claiming to love sinners, but the reality was that this love was conditional. If you wanted a place, a sense of community and belonging, you'd better get saved and start speaking in tongues pretty soon. No one ran you out if you didn't, but it was clear there was something wrong with you.

40

A String of Tragedies

So far, Minnie Bell had escaped the fate of her mother—the mental illness of rages and despair that the family called "it." Mercifully, in 1955, Theresa Herron had died—claimed, said a grandchild, by a voodoo curse invoked in desperation.

Sun and Minnie Bell moved to Baton Rouge, where Sun pastored a depressing little church in a gritty, blue-collar area in the northern part of the city. Minnie Bell's father, William Herron, had died of stomach cancer, and when Minnie Bell developed a growth in her throat, she was in a quandary.

She believed strongly in prayer and miraculous healing, but eventually she traveled to a hospital in nearby Centreville, Mississippi to have the tumor removed.

Jimmy was 25, and the horizon had cleared with his acceptance for ordination. Once again, the faith of women—Minnie Bell, Frances, and Ada—had pulled him through a dark time. In late June of 1960, he and Frances left for a revival in Alabama, planning to return for his ordination ceremony in July. Minnie Bell's minor throat surgery had healed well, and she looked forward to the celebration.

Not long after Jimmy and Frances left, Minnie Bell began having what the family later referred to as female problems. A hysterectomy was recommended, and she and Sun prayed about it. She kept putting it off, hoping the situation would correct itself.

Finally she decided she would rather go through the expensive process than risk putting anyone through what her mother had gone through, possibly as a result of the "change." She went to the hospital, back to the doctor in Centreville. Stella and Mamie accompanied her.

"They gave her a big old white tablet," said Sun's uncle, John Lewis. "She swallowed it. Then in a few minutes, she started to get sick. She told her sisters to pray—'somethin's happenin' to me,' she said—and they started praying hard. She got sicker and sicker. Stella and Mamie ran and got Sun and they [kept] praying. Then the doctors came to get her. 'She'll be all right as soon as we get her on the operating table,' they said. They gave her some more shots."

Minnie Bell's girlhood friend and sister-in-law Arilla had just finished dressing, and was leaving for the hospital, when her brother-in-law Jack Wells arrived from the sawmill where he worked.

"I guess he didn't know how to give the news," Arilla remembered. "He just came up and said, 'Guess what? Minnie Bell just died!' "

Arilla rushed to the hospital to find Stella, Mamie, and her brother Sun in shock.

"She never woke up," said John Lewis. "They never put a knife to her."

Jimmy and Frances got the news over a roadside gas station phone. Stella had called them in Alabama; unable to break the news, she had told them that the surgery had gone badly and Minnie Bell was unconscious. They immediately started home. Unable to drive even for an hour, Jimmy pulled over and called. Crying, Stella told him the truth.

Minnie Bell had died on July 9, 1960, under anesthesia. At the time, such accidents were not uncommon. But the doctors told the family it was a heart attack. Her sisters didn't believe it; they'd seen her get sick after taking the big white pill, and they'd seen the doctors give her another shot in spite of that and wheel her in for surgery.

"But the doctors had got Sun's consent to go ahead with the surgery, so they were off the hook," said John Lewis. "Jimmy Lee took it real hard."

"It was so senseless," said a niece. "Aunt Minnie Bell was sweetest, the nicest, of all of them. She was precious. She was just as good as gold. I know it just nearly killed Jimmy to lose his mother."

Her funeral was large. People came from all over. Jerry cancelled bookings, Mickey and David traveled from out of town. Jimmy looked for some meaning to it, but there was none. He had to settle for meaning's shadows; later, remembering the last time he'd seen her, he mulled over their goodbyes as if they had the weight of prescience.

Sun was broken, his dependence on her laid bare for all to see. All those years ago, when they had both gotten saved and the fighting had ebbed, it had been because Minnie Bell made up her mind to put a stop to it, whatever the cost. She had let Sun take the credit for everything, for leading them into church and getting them saved. She had stuck with him through everything. Now anyone could see that it had been her that propped him up.

"It like to run Sun crazy," said John Lewis. "He ain't been the same since."

Ada saw it, too. The only thing that had held Sun together was this woman. Until the funeral, Ada was proud of the role she'd played in pressuring them to get saved and get the blessing of the Holy Ghost; it had probably saved their marriage. She had kept up her own spiritual work, preaching fiery sermons at the church in Ferriday and traveling to nearby towns with her sister Irene to hold tiny, fierce revival meetings, as if she hoped to become an avenging version of Mother Sumrall. But at the funeral, she suddenly under-stood something about her pushy, determined style, and it humbled her.

"When she saw so many people crying and going on," said Arilla, "she realized that she'd preached against so many things—makeup and stuff—they'd take a whole sermon out on how somebody wore a pair of [bobby] socks or something—she said she realized, 'I shoulda been preachin' love,' " as Minnie Bell had.

When she was buried, Sun fell on the grave.

After the funeral, Sun asked Jimmy and Frances to come back to Baton Rouge with him. Sun needed help pastoring his church; without Minnie Bell, he was unable to manage. Jimmy and Frances considered it. Life on the road had been hard. It would be nice to put six-year-old Donnie in school and let him make some friends and have a more normal life. Jimmy's sister Jeanette lived next door with her husband and two children. Jimmy could concentrate on his sermons instead of worrying about bookings. They moved in, and Jimmy preached nearly every service.

But they left Baton Rouge after only six weeks. Jimmy later said he was just restless, he didn't feel he was "called" to preach this way; he was an evangelist. But there were other reasons.

There was talk in the family that cheapskate Sun took his wife to a cut-rate welfare doctor instead of the good one in Natchez, that he pressured her to have the surgery so she wouldn't turn out like her mother. Those cruel rumors are unlikely to have much truth to them. Minnie Bell's sisters were sure they'd seen the doctors make a mistake. And Jimmy and Jeanette blamed the doctors, not Sun.

But the murmuring in the family wouldn't die: why, the Herron sisters asked, had Sun taken her to Centreville? Why that little place, in the middle of nowhere, why not at least the big hospital in Baton Rouge? They couldn't help rehashing it, wondering what would have happened if he'd said no, let's make sure she recovers from that pill first. It was like he hadn't been looking out for her—or like, because her sisters were there, he had to overrule them or something.

These currents were exacerbated when, very shortly after Minnie Bell's funeral, Sun started seeing another woman. Before the year was out, he had remarried. The new wife, Jeanette Wimberly, was a missionary, a woman more educated than Sun. David Beatty met them for dinner at the Piccadilly Cafeteria in Baton Rouge one evening shortly after the wedding and left feel-ing it was not going to work. Indeed, it was soon annulled.

Sun stayed single several years. Then one day David Beatty casually men-tioned a widow he knew, Dorothy Sharp from Covington, Louisiana. David noted that her situation was similar to Sun's, that she had married rapidly on the rebound, to a Baton Rouge preacher, and it hadn't worked out, either. Shortly after that, David got a call from Dorothy; Sun had simply shown up at her door in Covington. She liked him.

She and Sun were married about five years, but Sun's stinginess reportedly killed it.

"She was a wonderful lady. If Uncle Sun had been just halfway normal, but he was so TIGHT. She made a cake for someone—she was a wonderful cook—and it cost about ten or fifteen dollars," said David Beatty. "That was the catalyst." Sun's tantrum over the cake was the last straw; he and Dorothy were divorced.

"Jimmy got mad, because he thought she was wonderful, too, he tried to get Sun to stay with her. Right away, within a year, he married again."

The next wife was a shy, more submissive woman, also named Dorothy. Sun hung onto this marriage.

Though Sun kept trying to put back together what he'd lost when Minnie Bell died, the truth was that the family disintegrated after her death. From that time on, Jimmy and Frances' days of going home to rest up from the road, to eat chicken dinners with the family and hear the Herron sisters and Ada laughing in the kitchen, to leave Donnie playing at Minnie Bell's, comfortably supervised, while he and Frances attended a conference or nearby revival, were over.

The next year and a half would rain more trials and ugliness down on the clan.

SEVEN MONTHS AFTER his mother's death, Jimmy experienced an eerie *déjà vu*. Again he was preaching in Alabama. Again he received a telephone call from Louisiana.

His aunt Jane Brown, Ada's sister and the grandmother of Jerry's wife Myra, worked in the charity hospital in Monroe. That morning, February 19, 1961, Ada had entered the hospital, complaining of a severe headache. This was most unusual for his grandmother, who had spurned doctors and medicine since her conversion. Her twin siblings Jane and John watched as she was given a shot. Arilla sat by her mother's bed. Sister Irene Gilley arrived, but Ada had fallen asleep. Shortly, Arilla noticed her mother's fingers and feet had turned blue.

"She made that awful sound," said Arilla. "They went and got a machine and put it on her to keep her alive."

After a long time, Arilla told them to take her mother off the machine. She left to get a cup of coffee so she wouldn't have to watch. A stroke, the doctors said, had killed Ada at 65.

Another funeral took place in Ferriday, this one rather rowdy compared to Minnie Bell's. Jimmy chose to see it as akin to a camp meeting, with people singing and praising God, but there was quite a bit of drinking to grease the praise along. The Lewis clan tended to celebrate life's passages by taking liquor. John Lewis called it "getting on the devil's string."

Jimmy grieved. But there was a liberation. These two strong, loving women had also been his captors.

Frances glided into the empty slots. She was more than capable of filling both of them.

SUMMER PASSED, and Minnie Bell and Ada were missed. As chilly fall northers blew in, the family drifted farther apart. Mamie, feeling ill and depressed because Elmo was talking divorce, took a piece of paper and pen and recorded a sense of foreboding on October 27, 1961.

She wrote that it had been a "long dreary day," and reflected that there was nothing to live for now but her children and grandchildren. Sadly, she ruminated about Elmo—that they would never live together again, that she couldn't take back the cruel things she'd said and done, nor could he—and about how life pretty much ended at 49. She ended by apologizing to God for not doing much with her time on earth. He had been so good to her, she wrote, and she had given back so little.

Three months later, Elmo's mother died at 87, which was expected. But nobody expected what happened three months after that, on Easter Sunday, 1962.

Jerry was away in Minneapolis. Seventeen-year-old Myra was cooking dinner for Elmo and a visiting Herron cousin after taking three-year-old Stevie to church. Myra assumed Elmo was watching his grandson, but Elmo was reportedly drinking with his in-law. After awhile, she called Stevie. There was no answer. After a frantic search, she saw the hose running out in the back yard, into the swimming pool. She looked in the water and saw her baby five feet under in his new Easter suit, a purple bruise on his forehead.

Mamie blamed Elmo for Stevie's death. Jimmy wrote to the elder Lewises from Sun's address on Truman Street in Baton Rouge, finding the right words both to comfort and to tap into the black ooze that engulfed the family. The letter said that his and Frances' hearts bled at the family's sorrow, and suggested that maybe God had meant it to bring the errant Elmo back into the fold.

He then wrote sweet, comforting things, referring to when they would all meet each other and Stevie in heaven; he referred to his mother, knowing how Mamie missed her sister. Then some salt for Jerry: God had been good to Jerry, he wrote, and he hinted that perhaps Jerry was being punished for his Godless ways.

Myra and Jerry, broken, were advised to leave town and plunge into work. A second tour of England had been arranged. This time Jerry took Myra, introduced her to the audiences, and played to wonderful, soothing acclaim. He had completely reversed his disaster of 1958.

They stayed in Europe for a month, but in June, six weeks after Stevie's death, Myra was still unhinged. She traveled to Baton Rouge to Sun's church to speak to him about the possibility that Stevie might be resurrected. With either the cruelest cynicism or the most astounding show of faith, Sun affirmed it was possible. He drew audiences, preaching two harsh sermons about the lesson of Stevie's death, what God was trying to say to Jerry Lee Lewis about his evil doings and abominations, with Myra weeping in the audience for all to see. She allowed Sun to baptize her, and then returned home to pray for three more weeks, day and night, for Stevie's return.

Jimmy and Sun had made all their moral points to the Lewises, and though their work was harsh and smacked of the family rivalry, some good came of it: Stevie did return, in a way. Myra was finally released, by her intensive prayer, into a dream where she saw that Stevie was actually being spared a life of suffering.

IN AUGUST 1962, Jeanette Swaggart Ensminger's baby, one-year-old Tamela Dawn, was playing at Sun's house. He sent her home to her mother, next door. Jeanette dressed her, and saw her toddler go outside. She thought Sun was waiting for her.

It had rained, and water washed through the culverts running alongside the uncurbed street. The baby was nowhere in sight.

They searched for hours before someone noticed that Tamela's little dog had been sitting next to the culvert in the same spot, staring down at the water, for the entire time. They started looking downstream, and found her body blocks away.

As one life exited the family, another entered: the same month Tamela drowned, Jerry's sister Frankie gave birth to a son, Michael Lee New. Two months later, Michael accidentally smothered to death in his crib.

Mickey Gilley had left the girl he'd chased to Houston and married nine years before, Geraldine. Before he remarried in December 1962, Geraldine shot herself, permanently damaging her shoulder.

Also in December, Mamie and Elmo were divorced, ending years of bitter fighting. Elmo moved to Memphis, and Mamie, lonely, started drinking, smoking, and dating, keeping it a careful secret from Jerry. She quietly married a man named R.V. Harper from Ferriday—another secret well-kept from Jerry, who had met Harper once when Mamie brought him to Memphis; Jerry had kicked him out of his house and he'd hitchhiked back to Ferriday.

Jimmy immortalized his mother and grandmother in his sermons, repeatedly citing them as inspirations. Their status as Good Women was assured. Jerry would not be able to do that for Mamie; all he could do was defend, threatening violence to anyone who hinted that she might not have been as perfect as her sister. His attempt to mold young Myra into a more virtuous

Mamie showed in Myra's divorce petition, where she described, among many other acts of violence during their 13 years of marriage, his jerking a cigarette out of her mouth and threatening to stick it in her eye, and then putting it out on her arm.

Jerry hated women to smoke, because he remembered his mother picking him up from school one day when he was a child in Ferriday. She was waiting for him in the car, a cigarette hanging out of her mouth, stuck to her lip. The smoke curled up and got into her eyes as she was backing the car up, and she ran into another car. Jerry was horribly embarrassed. It was hypocritical of her to smoke and then harangue him about not living for God like Jimmy, but he couldn't admit that.

Keeping the Faith

With little now to keep them bound to Ferriday or family, Jimmy and Frances trotted from city to city on the evangelical trail. Frances packed and unpacked, loaded and unloaded. She cleaned and disinfected the areas where they quartered. She cooked their meals, took care of laundry, grocery shopping, arranging accommodations, and Donnie's education. Every day she tutored him, using the Calvert Correspondence School of Baltimore, a Bible-based home teaching program aimed at migrant workers.

Jimmy and Frances often stayed with Jerry and Myra while they were traveling, and the temptation to compare was powerful. They had watched as Jerry's career soared, sank, and inched back up. He wasn't playing $10,000 gigs like when he first burst onto the scene, but he was still rich compared to them. He still owned half a dozen gaudy vehicles, and he still had a swimming pool styled like a piano, and the world still knew who he was.

"I remember Jimmy coming to . . . Memphis," said Myra, "passing through and spending the night at our house, when he didn't have anything except what was in the trunk of that car. Him and Donnie and Frances. They didn't have money for a hotel."

Once while they were staying with the Lewises in Memphis, Jimmy was suffering from a case of nerves, the recurring problem to which he had come to ascribe his depression and his Sun-like rages. Seeing Jerry's newest purchases around reminded him to ask Frances where his wallet was. It was out on the car seat, she told him. He slapped her across the face and ordered her downstairs to get it, then felt terrible.

He knew he had to get a grip on his temper. He preached and wrote about it, saying God would only use an undisciplined preacher for so long. If he doesn't "buffet this sinful body and subdue it," as Paul told the Romans, God will cast him away, Jimmy preached.

He got into another argument in downtown Ferriday at about this time, yanking his coat off and chasing a man named McKnight down the street, yelling, "I'm gonna whip your ass!" Another time, at a camp meeting, a hypochondriac tagged along behind him, whining about her nerves until his own were raw; he turned and snapped at her to shut up. Contrite, he tried to explain his feelings about self-pity and positive confession.

Around the time of the slapping incident—a rare occurrence but a revealing one as it centered on his wallet—he was in a Bible seminar with a preacher he admired. The man said that the biggest compliment a preacher can be paid is for people to say he's a good man. It impressed Jimmy. He made up his mind to try harder—this was what he wanted people to say about him, and he knew it meant governing his temper.

Frances forgave his lapses, preferring to see him as the good man he wanted to be. She never complained about the moving, the charity. She never said she wished Jimmy would pick another career, and she was always firmly reassuring when he was depressed and discouraged. "Frances was very ambitious for Jimmy," said her brother, Bob Anderson. "[She] wanted to make him the biggest preacher in the world."

Her only doubts—and they were less doubts than guilt and regret—were about the effect on Donnie of having no home, no roots in his life. "It was a hard life for the little fellow," Jimmy said later. "[Much of Donnie's] time was spent either on a church pew or in a car on the way to a meeting." At first, when he was very small, it had bothered her mostly when he was sick or upset. As he got older, she saw him suffer because he wasn't able to make friends. She and Jimmy weren't enough; he sorely needed peers.

Donnie was about the same age as Myra's little brother, Rusty Brown. In Memphis, they would drop him off to play with Rusty, but there were few other playmates.

Of course Donnie wasn't the only child being raised on the road. Other traveling evangelists—including Jimmy's friend Gerald Wilson, for awhile—had children too, and even ministers with a settled pastorate might move every few years: "Kids just became part of the partnership," said Wilson. "And I'm sure Jim and Frances put a positive spin on it . . . plus Donnie was an only child—he had a lot of advantages other kids didn't have."

Too, the schools were becoming unfriendly; in 1962, when Donnie was eight, the Supreme Court struck down prayer in schools. Frances, having abandoned her own education, worked hard on Donnie's. He claimed later that he put in at least eight hours with her in school every day until fourth grade.

"Frances is an outstanding person," said Jerald Ogg, an old friend who would later join Jimmy's ministry in Baton Rouge. "She did all the teaching of Donnie, he attended very little school the first 10 or 11 years."

"[She's] a very strong lady," agreed Wilson. "But that's true of all preachers, the woman is a steadying hand, she's the one who says it'll be all right. It wouldn't be possible without her. And when the kids come along, they just say 'this is what we do'—and the family gets support from them, too. Donnie was a real little trooper. It's a team, they're all in there together."

Donnie didn't rebel. If the kids were rebellious, Wilson said, if they hated the evangelical life, it wouldn't work. "It would be more than a guy could carry."

Frances always found an upside. Donnie got to see the country, meet people, and learn to be flexible, she told a reporter years later. Wilson concurred. "A lot of other kids, struggling in some little old church somewhere, they were the only C.A.s [Christ Ambassadors]. And I'm sure Jim and Frances put a positive spin on it. We always told our kids they were pretty fortunate. And they were."

Donnie was a trooper, but Frances decided to allow him to go to public school, even if only for short periods. He had to learn to interact with other kids sometime. She started in Baton Rouge, in familiar surroundings to ease the transition. They were staying with Sun, resting for a few days after being on the road. Frances enrolled Donnie in fourth grade at Brownsfield Elementary.

He was pleasantly surprised. Public school was so much easier than being taught by the iron-willed Frances.

He managed to make the grades, despite moving schools every few weeks, except for once in Alabama. He failed several subjects, and Frances immediately felt there was something fishy. Donnie suffered the same derision and ridicule Jimmy had suffered growing up, and it often made public school very hard on him. She drove to the school, suspicious.

The teacher was defensive, and refused Frances' demand to see her gradebook. They argued, and she revealed her disapproval that a young niece had been going to Jimmy's revival. Frances insisted she was taking it out on Donnie, and the teacher—probably feeling it didn't matter anyway as long as these Holy Rollers moved on in a few weeks—changed the grades.

But Jimmy was moving up. He had cultivated the professional demeanor and smile of the showman. He was slender and handsome, with a strong, square jaw, straight teeth, and a faint dimple. He became aware of how important it was to look not only clean and decent, but fashionable.

Concerned that there be nothing about their appearance that would mark Donnie and make it even harder for him in school, Frances cultivated the kind of respectability that would not only impress Jimmy's audiences, but hers and Donnie's, for they were the ones that had to deal with the real world. Jimmy was always in his own milieu, praying or crafting a sermon or dealing with other ministers.

There would be no giving in to the temptation toward show-business clothes like some of the other evangelists wore, though. By the 1970s, some Pentecostals and religious conservatives had a face which was an unambiguous reversal of everything that Pentecostalism's traditional severity in dress stood for. That doomed tradition held, said Christian journalist Larry Thomas, that women had to pin up their hair, forego makeup or jewelry, and "men had to *pin* their collars closed when they came to church so that if their top shirt button accidentally popped off, a sex orgy wouldn't break out."

But televangelists would go far the other direction, their sets frequently resembling bordellos, and stars like Tammy Bakker and Jan Crouch wearing bizarre makeup and gaudy getups—accouterments severely condemned in the churches of their youths.

Television was the perfect medium for evangelists because it did what they did: simplified and magnified the message for easier digestion. Both painted in broad, colorful strokes. The Protestant format, because it concentrates authority in the preacher (as opposed to Catholicism, which diffuses authority into vestments, incense, chants, statuary, ritual, and so on) also played a role in the marriage of television and evangelism. Setting up one person as the authority makes personality all-important, and can lead to cults. Evangelicalism in particular stresses individualism and personality.

Theological simplicity made it easy for ministers to toggle back and forth between religion and free enterprise, which is why the Bakkers could be unapologetic about opulent shooting sets and Rolls Royces. While Bakker's followers thought the tiny, doll-like Tammy Faye was adorable, secular and mainline religious viewers were mesmerized by her flashy clothes, gaudy jewelry, and weeping confessions of her drug and marital problems. Tammy's makeup, with false eyelashes caked into mascara spears so long they reached her eyebrows, became the subject of a T-shirt featuring huge smudges and the caption, "I ran into Tammy Faye at the mall."

Jimmy established a reputation for sobriety, and Frances only mildly flirted with sensational clothing after they got on television. The strictures, obsolete or not, were the moral center of the Pentecostal faith, and it was to that center that Jimmy stayed fastened. In his own way, so did Jerry Lee. The rigid inflexibility of his church was the only strong morality he knew, the only institution that ever gave him any standards to live up to. That was probably one reason he never returned to the church: he didn't want to see it all corrupted, the women with their red salon fingernails and fluffed, fragrant hair, cherry-lipped and stiletto-heeled like the whores of his youth.

JIMMY'S REVIVALS started taking him out of the South; he appeared often in Ohio, Indiana, Illinois, and Michigan—places where his association with Jerry wasn't so devastating. As soon as his ordination came through, he went right back to using Jerry's name prominently in his posters. In fact, Jerry's name was printed so much larger than Jimmy's that some of the posters looked like advertisements for a Jerry Lee Lewis concert. They would have some statement such as, "Bro. Swaggart is a first cousin and former music associate of Sun Record Star Jerry Lee Lewis."

More and more frequently, the closing date was scratched out on Jimmy's posters and an extension penciled in.

Gradually, he got some perspective on his religious tradition. He began to see things about these familiar people who streamed into the tents and sanctuaries for services, filling the air with the smell of Lilac Vegetal, the men with their booze-crumpled faces and leathery skin from working in the sun, hair combed back, plaid shirts with pearl snap buttons stretched always too tight, either over bellies swollen with the comforts of fried chicken and cream gravy or over skinny work-hardened thoraxes; the women so focused on virtue as to totally miss the point of salvation at times: there might be a buzzing for days when a sister would fall, slain in the spirit, and be lowered to the floor, and it be seen that she was wearing a black lace slip. To church! There was always a church contingent that was nosy, wanted to know did Sister Swaggart make that cake from scratch or one of them mixes.

He also saw wonderfully wise men and women guiding the little churches, anchoring a warm, loving community in which the preacher was pivotal, immersed in weddings, funerals, baptisms, all the rites of passage. This was the quiet heart of his faith—the sweet grass-smelling springtime of community, the little table with the family praying over dinner, the team that the father and mother put together, the way the preacher and his wife created a little space where the world could not come in and corrupt.

He saw how the homebound preachers' humility often came from clinging to their poverty, and how that could lead to poverty of ideas; the window would open right in front of them many times, and they didn't want to go through it. Maybe he wouldn't have either, if it hadn't been for Frances. I'd rather dig ditches, they'd say, and do just what I'm doin', preach what I'm preachin', than try to fool a bunch of people like that Father Sheen.

There were dilemmas of faith; people who stayed away from doctors and kept prayer cloths in the medicine chest instead of aspirin, but then fretted about whether to go bothering God just to heal a little headache. God was busy, maybe they should go ahead and take an aspirin. But then maybe it was good to ask God to heal the little things; then it would be easier to trust Him for the big things, wouldn't it? Their confusion about how to apply huge principles to small matters was moving and exasperating.

Jimmy was intellectually curious, and he gave thought to the deeper problems of the human condition. He took on big questions—where was the line between faith and superstition, why does prayer fail—and found that people were hungry for it. Though he knew all the forms—the crooning phrases, the Holyghost jig, the tongues in the middle of a sentence, the dragonbreath vilifications and jeremiads—he genuinely wanted to understand what the Bible was telling people. He was an interpreter, anointed far and above the preachers who would never ask why faith healing or miracles worked for some but not others, who were content that God worked in mysterious ways.

And anyone could see that his father, though his preaching was impassioned, was no different from these others. Sun gave three-foot candy canes to members who brought five or more visitors, and his typed newssheet was full of tired platitudes: We want a Holy Ghost church and we believe the Lord will give it to us, if we pay the price. The eyes of the Lord still run to and fro throughout the whole earth to show himself strong on behalf of those who put their trust in him. $58 was taken in at the fundraiser for the new Sunday school annex.

Jimmy felt willing to go anywhere the Lord said he was needed, but the thought that it might be in a place like this, bribing people to visit and praising God for $50, was deeply depressing. Donnie or no Donnie, he needed to stay on the road.

Just Do It!

Recordings were becoming more and more common at revivals. Every preacher who had ever sung in church seemed to be scrounging up the resources to cut a little 45 to sell. They all hoped to hit the big time, of course, but the technology allowed anyone to record who had a few dollars to pay for the wax.

In 1960, Jerry again offered to help Jimmy cut a gospel album at Sun Records. But, as in 1958 when Jerry offered through Elmo, Jimmy refused.

Jimmy never gave a good explanation of why he twice refused such a generous offer, citing only those avuncular chats with God where the Almighty gave a contorted explanation that added up to Jimmy having met some test of faith.

But most likely he was simply intimidated. He had already been denied ordination because of music. And he wasn't about to walk into a famous, highly professional place like Sun Records, where his cousin had mounted a massive triumph of world fame, and embarrass himself. He needed practice first. That was the objective of the primitive recording in late 1958 with David Beatty.

Jimmy decided to enlist Mickey's help. Mickey had been playing regularly at a club called Nesadel on Spencer Highway in the Houston suburbs, near where his Gilley's Club would later be located. He could help Jimmy without the threat of comparison that Jerry presented. Mickey found a studio and Jimmy borrowed from the bank in Wisner to pay for it and some session musicians. He was going to have to sell some albums to pay it back.

He recorded "Some Golden Daybreak," "What a Day That Will Be," "He Bought My Soul," and "Stranger" on a little 45 rpm. This was far better than the record he'd made in Ferriday, but he still didn't like it. He touched it up, recutting some tunes at a different studio. Frances, mindful of the money they'd borrowed, urged him to send it to gospel stations, but he refused. They argued about the record's quality; he was unwilling to humiliate himself by sending it to stations that played major gospel singers like the Blackwood Brothers and the Statesmen.

"But she kept on, she kept pounding and pounding," he said later, until he sent copies to several stations. If Frances was going to be paying back a loan, she was going to make sure every penny was maximized. She wasn't going to just give up without a fight because of some male pride.

He was satisfied enough to present it for sale at his meetings alongside the albums of other preachers. People bought it—because it had become traditional to purchase a souvenir at revivals, because he was Jerry's cousin, and because his live music had become one of his big draws.

By 1962, he had sold enough copies of the record to bolster his confidence—and Jerry made the offer a third time. Jerry's offer was incredibly generous. The musicians, studio time, and engineers were free.

Jimmy declined. This time it was his singing voice; he had suffered a four-year battle with allergies that cropped his breathing so he could hardly speak, much less pour himself into a sermon.

Frances, always the one to keep pushing onward, said the allergies were just another of Satan's tricks and they'd beat it, and make the recording. Sure enough, in the Pacific breeze of California a few weeks later, the allergies cleared up. But he was still insecure about sounding stopped up. He was running out of excuses, and Frances would not be turned aside this time. "Just DO it, make a record!" she said.

She wouldn't let him back down. They traveled to Memphis to Sun Records.

Jerry had his old friend Cecil Harrelson arrange the session. Cecil was married to Linda Gail, Jerry's youngest sister, and Linda was to sing a duet with Jimmy on one of the songs. The afternoon before the taping, Jimmy went to the studio to look over the setup and warm up on the piano.

As Jimmy tells it, he took in the legendary studio smelling of stale cigarette smoke, the place that, he later wrote, "seemed filled with power." A man walked up and asked him for his union card. No one had remembered this detail. The union supervisor refused to let him use the studio.

The deal was off. Jimmy and Frances went back to Jerry's house and sat around, discussing farfetched ways of getting the recording done. That evening, among the hangers-on who never left the comforts of Jerry's orbit was a guest, a gangster type who Jimmy later reported owned a casino in Las Vegas.

However seedy the man was, something about him inspired Jimmy to start walking up and down the hall, praying out loud. Finally the man asked what the situation was, and Jimmy explained what the Lord wanted. Gimme that phone, the man said, and get out of the room.

They recorded the next day with no interference from the union. At the end of a six-hour session, Jimmy had an album he called "God Took Away my Yesterdays."

After the album was released, Frances and Jimmy once again fought over whether to send it out. He was still loath to be compared to other gospel singers, but this time he capitulated with little resistance.

The record got played on a Michigan gospel show, and calls started coming into the station. Jimmy and Frances were amazed and delighted. They ordered copies and carried them in the trunk, unloading them into their rooms to keep them from the hot sun. They filled orders from wherever they were camped on the road, and announced them at revivals. Stores that stocked religious music agreed to carry them.

Once the record broke through the membrane of resistance into industry channels, it had enough credibility that a distributor finally picked it up.

With this new success, Jimmy's revivals started to go from one or two weeks to four and six weeks. Music added another dimension for audiences— the performance they seemed to crave and that seemed to drive home his points in a way that words couldn't. His confidence rose, and he realized something about his Pentecostal upbringing.

"It seemed as if I never quite measured up to what God wanted from me," he wrote. "I had been taught what not to believe in—smoking, dipping, chewing, cussing, drinking—all the don'ts and none of the do's. There wasn't a positive element to it, and practically no faith. In the process, I had been filled with such negativism that I lost my confidence."

This was an insight to be grateful for, but he never went further. He didn't draw back like Mickey and contemplate whether maybe they overdid it, or whether it was what Sun, not God, wanted that he could never measure up to. He would never call that hellfire terrorizing "child abuse" like Mickey did, but was always impressed with the power of that seedy Vegas club owner to get the work of God done.

"He made a phone call," Jimmy still marveled years later, "and after that it was, Mr. Swaggart, is there anything we can do for you? Co-cola? Coffee?"

Demon Oppression

espite his growing reputation as a show-stopper, Jimmy continued to suffer debilitating seizures he characterized as "demon oppression." Later, he would strongly hint that these were sexual cravings that usually started out as a case of "nerves."

As with his camp-meeting predecessors, he was pushing himself physically with a brutal appearance schedule. He and Frances needed secretarial help with the mail orders, bookings, Donnie's ever-shifting school arrangements, living accommodations, and cultivation of future contacts. The relentless work and travel schedule left Frances tired as well, and since she took on all the logistical matters, she was constantly busy.

Their living arrangements still often meant there was no separate room for Donnie (or that members of the host family were sleeping through the wall, if they were in someone's home), so privacy was out of the question. Even with privacy, though, it was becoming clear that sexual tension played a large role in Jimmy's product.

Anyone could see how women responded to him, especially when he sang. They stood, swayed, closed their eyes, and held their arms high and wide. When he preached, they were transfixed. When he cracked jokes, they giggled, tossed their heads, crossed their legs. A rival minister, jealous, assumed this appeal was the reason Frances stayed with Jimmy too: "If she didn't have her *piano man* there, I mean—why else would she stick around?"

Jimmy could spot such tension in others. Once, he wrote, a man and his wife came up to congratulate Jimmy on the service. Jimmy had an overpowering feeling that the woman was having an affair. As Frances chatted with the husband, Jimmy took the wife aside and said, "You are being unfaithful to your husband and it is going to destroy your life and your home . . ." He told her to let the Lord deliver her.

Her jaw dropped, but several days later she wrote him that it was true— she was actually seeing several men.

It didn't help that they stayed with Jerry as often as possible. It saved money, but it always aroused gloomy feelings. Doubts would plague Jimmy as he wandered around at night or in the early morning while others slept, stroking the leather chairs and listening to Satan hiss that he would never have anything like this. Myra had had another child, Phoebe, and it seemed that Jerry was providing much better for his family with Satan's music than Jimmy was with God's word.

During his stopovers at Jerry's, Jimmy always felt a strong desire to bring Jerry back to God, and his failure to do so seemed related to his states of religious arousal. Once, he wrote, he and Frances were on their way to a revival in Ohio. As usual, Jerry's house was full of people, and Jimmy played some gospel songs for them.

Afterward, in private, a platinum-blond woman told Jimmy of her Pentecostal background, and confessed she felt guilty about the way she was living. Jimmy tried to get her saved again right there, but she fled from the room. In a few minutes, he heard her laughing and talking with the others. He had had no impact on this crowd. Apparently they had just asked him to play to be polite.

He went outside to contemplate that, and talked to God about how sad it was that those rich, sexy people seemed to have everything, "but once you get beneath the surface there's nothing but loneliness, disappointment and heartache." As soon as he said those words, he found physical release. "Joy flooded my soul and I began crying."

Jimmy has told many, many times about a state of great arousal that begins with what he calls "feeling the presence of the Lord," feeling the Holy Spirit moving through him. It always culminates with him breaking into tongues, praises, shouts, or tears. Something happens to him physically, something he always unwittingly describes as a kind of climax.

It happened one day, when he felt the close, foreboding presence of God after a night at Jerry's. It was still there when he and Frances and Donnie got out on the road, where, he wrote, he felt God was warning him that the devil was going to try to kill him.

Not long after, he topped a rise at 65 to see a stalled car at the bottom of the hill. He braked, plowed into the hill, and flipped his U-Haul. Frances and Donnie were shaken, but they and the trailer contents were unharmed.

As he stood by the road among the crowd that had gathered to help, he felt tension building that he characterized as "the Lord's presence." "I could hardly stand there." In that tremendous state of arousal, he righted the trailer, thanked them for helping, and drove off. "Almost instantly I began speaking in tongues."

This is one of many instances in which Jimmy associates depression (the rejection by Jerry's followers) with arousal. And though he said the devil had tried to kill him, he was also asking whether the world cared if he killed himself.

ALL PREACHERS' WIVES have to deal with the idolatry of needy women. The Assemblies had inadequate training at the time about how to deal with women getting a crush or developing a dependency on the minister. Jimmy was under Frances' constant watchful eye and his meetings only lasted a few weeks, hardly enough time to get into trouble. But there were gaps in Frances' surveillance, and emotional factors were at work whose power no one in Jimmy's growing circle of evangelists really fathomed.

There was a sexual revolution going on that was connected with the civil rights movement and rock and roll. The conservative Assemblies ignored it and clung to a format that attempted to control libido by giving it a highly structured place to be expressed, and then controlling the forms of that expression.

The unseen part of that format was what it cost the preacher, especially a showman like Jimmy. Of course Jimmy has never written about his love life; all that exists is the public record of immorality in his later years, juxtaposed against decades of observations by those close to him and Frances. Almost without exception those observers report strong love and partnership between them. What the nature of their bargain was or is no one can know, but it is clear that some of Jimmy's power in the pulpit came from sexual tension. And to the extent it did, cravings in the bedroom would threaten it—for where did that power come from in a Pentecostal, if not from governance over the flesh? The lack of privacy in their nomadic life may actually have been a factor in keeping Jimmy's power intact—even if it also led to "demon oppression."

Jimmy was sensitive enough to recognize that Frances' great admiration for his mastery of his audiences' emotional states was the linchpin of all the huge sacrifices she made for him. It would be dangerous to tamper with that sort of bargain. A normal, active sex life was probably impossible in their circumstances, but the compensation would be an incomparable passion in the pulpit.

And for her, too, it was probably better not to go into certain things. If she stumbled across evidence that he was using pornography, what would be the point of making a big issue of it? Jimmy was bringing people to Jesus, in growing numbers. God worked in mysterious ways; if He was blessing the ministry, and He was in charge, how did some man-made rules about smut stack up against that? Sex was a commodity, like meals and rooms: it had to be dealt with. It would be Jimmy's problem, as it is mostly men's problem.

But the pressures were becoming too great for tongues, tears, praise, prayer, and the occasional temper tantrum to give him release. To the extent he backslid, his confidence suffered. He often slipped into a state of unrelenting anxiety.

"I was sick almost constantly," he wrote, "a series of nagging problems which seriously hindered my victory . . . I focused on my faults and the failures . . . I would walk the floor half the night . . . I did, deep down, doubt the capacity of the Lord to love someone as imperfect and flawed as I."

God intervened, in the form of a little book given to him at a service one night. It was about thinking positively instead of negatively. The effect of the book was to liberate him from an idea of God he'd had since childhood that doubtless reflected his relationship with Sun.

"Suddenly I saw God," he said, "not as a cruel taskmaster but as a living, divine Heavenly Father, who loved me. Suddenly the picture of a judgmental God evaporated." That was a turning point. He let go of some of his self-judgment, and more success started to follow.

But Satan was more devious than even Jimmy thought, for this positive and healing concept also played into one of the diseases of Pentecostalism, the suppression of unwanted emotions and desires.

One night, hard in prayer over demon oppression, he applied the marvelous new positive confession dynamic. The Lord spoke. "When you feel this thing coming on you again . . . start praising the Lord . . . It will be hard at first . . . but don't admit to that thing. Don't say it with your mouth."

Just deny the problem, God seems to have said. Jimmy would use this coping strategy over and over through the years, but it would never solve his problem.

44

A Good Man

Sun was leaving the Calvary Assembly of God in Baton Rouge for good. He offered the job of pastoring it to Jimmy, but Jimmy declined. He was making a strong reputation now as a star at camp meetings, and that required travel. It was another chance to settle down for Donnie's sake, but he hadn't come this far to lose momentum now.

His sister Jeanette and her husband, Bobie Ensminger, took over the church. Bobie preached, and Jimmy and Frances attended often when they were in town.

Jimmy had a large room on the back of Sun's house in Baton Rouge, where he could have quarters for his family when they needed it, and to service his growing ministry—posters advertising his meetings, albums, mailing materials, order forms, and a one-page newssheet that would one day grow to over 50 pages to be sent out to more than half a million readers—the *Evangelist* magazine. In the big room, he and Frances would wrap albums and send them out. Frances read and answered the mail—prayer requests, record orders, complaints—and handled the logistics of bookings.

Jimmy and Frances met Jerald and Janett Ogg in May of 1963. Jerald, a Nashville native, was associate pastor at the Sheffield Assembly of God in Kansas City. Sheffield was one of the denomination's largest churches, with 650–700 members. On big days, 1,000 or more would attend.

The first time he met Jimmy, he was impressed, and recommended extending his booking. "Jimmy came for a 10-day revival and stayed six weeks," said Ogg. "He got stunning results. Over 100 people were saved."

The Oggs were a model family, loving and positive. Janett Ogg was well-read and versatile; their three sons and daughter were good students and good kids. Jerald's sister Jenelle was involved in the ministry and made a gospel album with her brother of which he was quite proud. He was a warm person and an utter straight arrow—the epitome of the "good man" Jimmy strove to be.

Jimmy's father had stayed stuck in the small-church rut and couldn't seem to find his bearings without Minnie Bell. He was retreating back to Ferriday, where he would dabble in rental houses and open a furniture store, car wash, and other small enterprises, still preaching here and there and trying to make a go of marriage. His floundering with women had hurt and embarrassed Jimmy. "Dad just isn't like that," he told Ogg. It was doubly embarrassing because the Assemblies took a very strong position against divorce, forbidding its ministers to perform marriage ceremonies for divorcees.

Touched by Jerald's closeness to his sister, Jimmy tried to include his own sister in the ministry, but it didn't work. Jeanette was fun-loving, attractive, and vivacious, with the booming Herron laugh. She was a very gifted pianist who had played for Jimmy in the early days when he was going from one tiny church to another around Ferriday.

"She could play the hell out of a piano," said her cousin Linda Gail Lewis, Jerry's sister. "I remember being really impressed with her and wondering, God, can a WOMAN really play like that? She'd beat the hell out of it, just like Jerry and Jimmy did . . . She had a more aggressive style than most women. She really got down on it."

That was the problem—Jeanette was not submissive. Because of that, she didn't get along with strong-willed Frances, and neither did her husband Bobie. The deaths of her mother and baby daughter, and a few years later, a son who had a wasting disease of the brain stem, also worked on her. The first two deaths, so close together, had both involved Sun, and though no blame was put on him, a strain developed that was never normalized.

"Jimmy's family is not a real close family," said an in-law. "Those people aren't very compassionate [with each other] . . . even his daddy is jealous of him. Jimmy and Donnie aren't very close to anybody [except] maybe each other." Mainly, he said, "Frances wouldn't have the Ensmingers."

Though Jeanette remained well-liked by cousins and kin, they hinted at other darkness in her life: sexual confusion, a loner husband, maybe a touch of the madness the family called "it" from her grandmother Herron. When Jimmy declined to take over Sun's scruffy Calvary Assembly of God, she obliged, preaching there for a tiny congregation with the help of her husband and only remaining child, a son named Daryle. Eventually she became something of a recluse, refusing to answer her door or telephone, according to a cousin. A tabloid reported that she had screaming battles with Frances, and a relative close to the ministry confirmed that Frances blocked Jeanette's calls to Jimmy during a ministry crisis that involved a family member.

But the Oggs weren't comparing Jimmy's family to theirs. They valued him as a gifted preacher who could pull in the crowds and help people get saved. He was unique.

"There weren't a lot of preachers who played piano when they preached," said Ogg, who felt Jimmy's music was a critical part of his ministry. He also admired Jimmy and Frances for their dedication, for sticking with the grueling road trips and roach motels and bad weather and unfriendly journalists. He made sure Jimmy was invited back frequently to the church in Kansas City. "He'd pack that thing out at night. He was turning people away. It was the results—people were saved, they were healed, they experienced the baptism of the Holy Spirit . . . [I'd] see Jimmy come into the church there in Sheffield in the morning and pray all day. Literally."

Ogg continued to press his colleagues to pass the word about Jimmy. These were influential men in the denomination; they could open doors for Jimmy and provide him venues, and Jerald Ogg opened this great resource fully to him.

"Jimmy would get recommendations from them, and he would begin to hit the best churches in the movement." Brightmoor Tabernacle near Detroit, the Assembly of God Tabernacle in Atlanta, and the Oak Cliff Assembly in Dallas were all prestigious, well-funded churches with big congregations and guaranteed large crowds during revivals. These gatherings produced record sales and, more important, mailing lists where Jimmy could advertise his services, send his newssheet, and offer items for sale. He and Frances and Donnie now traveled with a U-Haul at all times.

Jimmy preached at these churches every year from the time he met Ogg until he started experimenting with bigger venues—City coliseums and auditoriums—around 1973. Ogg helped Jimmy get on a Tennessee radio station in the early 1960s, and even booked Sun for a revival or two, and he made sure Sun was treated with respect—good parking, prime seats, meals out—when Jimmy preached in Kansas City.

Ogg's church rented an apartment for Jimmy and Frances when Jimmy preached in Kansas City—a far cry from the castoff rooms they were used to. As associate pastor, Ogg usually entertained visiting evangelists, and the Swaggarts came over every night after the service. Donnie was eight and Jerald, Jr. seven.

One day they would work together in one of the biggest ministries in the world, the Jimmy Swaggart Ministries. Jerald, Jr. would become a journalist and attorney, and work for Frances—carrying out orders that would be pivotal in the downfall of televangelist Jim Bakker. Donnie would be the trooper he'd always been, taking this job or that according to Frances' directive.

The adults played board games —Sorry!, Monopoly—or sat around and talked after the services.

"They usually stayed at our house 'til nearly midnight," said Jerald. "Jimmy preached every night 'til 9 or 9:30, then they'd come't the house for fellowship and food. One night they locked themselves out of their apartment. They didn't want to wake up the landlord that late at night for the key, so they came back to spend the night with us."

Ogg was a few years older than Jimmy, just enough to take pride in using his position to help a younger man build his ministry. Later, after the Oggs began to work for the Swaggarts, he remained proud of his role in Jimmy's success. He resented the battering Jimmy took from the media. "My wife and I have nothing but praise for Jimmy," he said. "He treated us great."

◆   ◆   ◆

Downtown Baton Rouge had an air of benign neglect, and yet there was a cosmopolitan feel to it, like New Orleans. The bridge across the Mississippi River sat on enormous concrete pillars rising up out of the gray-green water. It arched massively into the sky, and driving across it, you could see for miles. At night riverboats would splash golden light over the water as the river held their travelers in its jaws—gentle for now, but with rain, capable of breathtaking tantrums fit to split the cosmos. Those pillars that held up the great bridge over the Mississippi would appear and reappear in Jimmy's dreams, rising out of the great unconscious of the water.

Jimmy continued making albums, one a year, and by 1967 his five records were selling well. Donnie was 13 and in dire need of stability. Despite his constant exposure to the religious life, he still hadn't gotten the Holy Ghost. Jimmy and Frances had saved up several thousand dollars and wanted to buy a house in Baton Rouge. It was a damp, subtropical place, often dripping with rain, but it teemed with life and beauty, and they had church connections there.

Jimmy and Frances explored a growing area a few miles east of downtown. Passing mixed retail—little flat-roofed printing places and muffler shops alongside antique stores and insurance storefronts—they selected a decent, middle-class subdivision called Tara, near the old highway to Hammond, Louisiana.

They settled on a lot at the corner of Tara Boulevard and Trinity Avenue—a nice evocation of fictional Old South and Old Time Religion and a symbolic site for their first home.

Preachers were notoriously bad credit risks. Jimmy couldn't get a home loan. But he was bringing in a pretty good income from camp meetings, and his record albums were selling well because they were being heard on the radio. In the fall he started building, hoping the money would come in to pay the contractors.

It did; Jimmy was invited to preach a revival in Detroit, and his meetings went on for a phenomenal eight weeks. He was a guest on a local radio show several times during the revival, and he did very well. Suddenly his records started getting more air play, more people came to the Detroit revival, and the money came in to pay his contractors. The tab came to $32,000.

Jimmy and Frances' first real residence, finished in the summer of 1968, was brick, with a slate-colored roof and brick columns. Their neighborhood was a well-groomed one of one-story ranch homes. Most had brick facades and token slab porches. On them hung porch swings bought in memory of a rural ideal whose death no one seemed willing to accept.

Sure enough, as soon as the money came in to pay the house off, Donnie got the Holy Ghost.

"What Hath God Wrought?"

— Samuel Morse, reacting to the first telegraphic transmission.

Radio station KDKA in Pittsburgh, the first to be issued a broadcast license by the Department of Commerce, broadcast the first church service in 1921 from an Episcopalian church, disguising the Jewish and Catholic engineers in choir robes. Radio was still an amateur fad until Westinghouse, which owned KDKA, pioneered the manufacture of ready-made radios; by 1924, more than three million were in use.

Though some religious leaders warned that radio was a tool of Satan, preachers were among the first to experiment with it; in 1922 Paul Rader of the Chicago Gospel Tabernacle attracted huge audiences who heard his broadcasts from atop city hall. Other electronic preachers followed rapidly, not always understanding the new technology. R.R. Brown, a Nebraskan with a popular following who earned the nickname "the Billy Sunday of the air," used to shout into the microphone as if he didn't trust it to carry his voice all that way without help.

It was relatively easy to get a license, and by 1923, at least ten churches had their own stations; five years later there were 60. Stations were allowed to operate at virtually whatever power and frequency they wanted, and by 1927, the airwaves were chaotic. Congress formed the Federal Radio Commission and started assigning frequencies, channels, power modulation levels, and broadcast schedules.

That decimated religious broadcasters, who couldn't afford equipment for the changeover. At first the FRC wouldn't grant licenses to religious broadcasters anyway, claiming they were nothing but "propaganda stations."

That slightly unconstitutional stricture was short-lived. But the religious community responded to the blows of FRC regulation by using the airwaves to raise money for their stations.

Early efforts were modest, mostly focused on buying equipment to comply with regulations. Venerable stations like KPCC in Pasadena, California and KFUO in St. Louis—among a handful that have stayed on the air since the 1920s—were started by staid Presbyterians and Lutherans who were often highly educated. Walter Maier of "The Lutheran Hour," for example, held a Ph.D. from Harvard in Semitic studies and taught Hebrew. Against the Elmer Gantry stereotype were people like Charles Fuller, the independent evangelist who started a radio ministry in Southern California during the Depression and founded the well-respected Fuller Theological Seminary in Pasadena. By 1937 his "Old Fashioned Revival Hour" had become a coast-to-coast syndicated broadcast over the Mutual Broadcasting System, with millions of regular listeners; eventually Fuller was heard all over the world.

The advent of commercial radio networks in the late 1920s brought big money into the medium, creating power and influence (two commodities to which preachers were usually strangers). The commercial networks had to operate in the "public interest, convenience and necessity" to stay licensed. They met that obligation by offering free time during the 1930s and 1940s to mainline churches. They spurned the ones that had marked themselves as "evangelical"—even though churchmen like Walter Maier were just as evangelistic in their way as leaping, shouting Billy Sunday, the premillinarian traveling evangelist whose talent for invective drew huge crowds. (To evangelize simply means "to announce good news." To be an evangelist was part of the five-fold ministry outlined in the New Testament.)

In the late 1940s during Jimmy's adolescence, however, the frontier was television, the exciting new technology that was expected to create a world language, bring world peace, and correct eye defects.

About the time the war ended, a struggle was going on between liberals and evangelicals for the control of religious broadcasting. The battle was forming between mainstream churches—Catholic, Jewish, and established Protestant denominations—and evangelical groups whose programming was technically crude, and whose bawdy methods of raising money for air time did not inspire confidence in their ability to pay the bills (Fuller, of course, was among the exceptions). The Communications Act of 1934 replaced the old FRC with the Federal Communications Commission, which had the power to license individual stations (first radio, and later television). No station had to interpret "public interest" as religious programming, but the FCC always recommended religion as one of the programming categories, and most broadcasters didn't want to ignore a suggestion from the entity that renewed their licenses.

So the television networks, ABC, NBC, and CBS, loaned studios, crews, production time, and air time to the three mainstream religious groups to produce shows every week—ignoring, as radio networks had, the evangelicals. The networks preferred to give the free studio time as well as air time so they could control the product (CBS was last, only getting involved in program production after its broadcasts of activist priest Charles Coughlin got the network into legal trouble).

Even with the mainstream churches, though, there was constant tension over content. The networks wanted the message bland and non-threatening.

The churches wanted the freedom to rattle viewers with content like prophecy and criticism, so they could fulfill their mission to disturb, warn, and make converts.

It was a fight for the ground between revolution and irrelevance, and frequently the churches, complaining that the faith was too alive to be shoehorned into the networks' narrow commercial spectrum, thought of leaving the suffocating embrace of public service and simply buying air time. But it was too expensive.

In 1941 an academic group that called itself the Institute of Education by Radio made recommendations to the FCC that would have killed religious programs, even making it illegal to sell air time for them. Evangelicals responded by forming the National Association of Evangelicals (NAE), and demanding that the Institute accept a delegate from their organization. The FCC agreed, and the NAE succeeded in partially defanging the recommendations. In 1944, the NAE formed the National Religious Broadcasters, supposedly a regulatory arm, but actually a business association aimed at making sure evangelicals were not shut out of radio and television.

New FCC rules and competitive pressure from new independent UHF stations caused the networks to consider making all religious programmers pay for air time. This came as a shock to the mainstream churches, and they resisted. But the evangelical denominations, used to having to raise money, paid up, and by the 1960s and 1970s, they were dominating the airwaves.

This takeover was invisible at first, but was pretty complete by 1976, when criticism by mainline churches of the evangelicals' gaudy, shallow programs and incessant begging became strident.

But the stations said paid-time programs attracted more viewers (presumably because they *were* gaudier) and so were meeting the needs of the viewing public better—a complete reversal of their position about evangelicals in early radio and television.

Evangelicals had always embraced technology enthusiastically, being the first to innovatively use printing to produce their tracts, developing sophisticated distribution networks, and being among the first on the air when radio became commercial. Jimmy's ministry would become one of the most advanced users of computer technology.

By 1960, there were over 200 million radios and televisions in the US. FM frequencies came to be used more by religious broadcasters as car radios and home stereo systems started being manufactured with FM receivers. The gospel music recording business, centered in Nashville, started to grow in the early 1970s. Evangelical publishing was well established, and records were distributed through Christian retail bookstores. There was already an audience, too, of fans who had been buying their favorite religious singers' tapes and recordings from revivals and church services. Nineteen-sixty was when some independent evangelical groups began to raise money to buy their own television stations and start their own networks. This was fueled by the expansion of licenses granted for UHF stations.

The most far-reaching posture of the FCC in the early 1960s was the distance it kept from religious fundraising. The regulations governing money-raising by non-commercial stations were strict, but the FCC, zealous about church-state separation and having no clue that piety would someday have the capacity to raise billions of dollars over the airwaves, didn't enforce them for paid religious programs. The FCC's ruling, based on the fact that religious programs weren't commercial-length shows, made it much more profitable for stations to sell time to religious programmers, because they didn't have to worry about whether those programs conformed to restrictions.

The unpopular hours were sold to religious programmers, who were free to solicit over the air and sell religious merchandise. It turned out that the ones who were least shy about doing that were evangelical or fundamentalist preachers. The mainstream churches simply refused to stoop to competing, and long-standing, respected shows like CBS' "Lamp Unto My Feet" and "Look Up And Live" began to disappear.

Then the FCC ruled that the Fairness Doctrine (which says that all viewpoints on controversial social issues must be aired) didn't apply to religious programs, because they just weren't controversial enough. So there was no regulation to assure that mainstream churches would still be heard in proportion to what they viewed as the evangelical clamor.

But the evangelicals had their own troubles. Government at federal, state, and local levels began to interfere more and more in church affairs—they wanted to eliminate tax exemptions for evangelical associations, they wanted to deny permits to erect revival tents, they wanted to reclassify revivals as business meetings instead of church services so they could get license money and sales taxes, they wanted to stop evangelists from using the mails to send healing items.

There were three main ways to get money over the air: ask for contributions, offer incentives like gifts, or offer the incentive of special prayer or counseling. Solicitations could be very manipulative, involving begging, weeping, and testimonials.

The incentive example included belonging to a select group of some sort: Oral Roberts had "prayer partners," Pat Robertson had the "700 Club," Rex Humbard had a "prayer key family." And of course there was the "PTL Club," which offered a partners' card, a lapel pin, and a magazine to donors.

Many media-watchers called the direct-mail appeals manipulative. Oral Roberts, for example, wrote: "Dear Brother [name], I must tell you an overwhelming feeling has come over me about you, something tells me you're hurting in some way, either spiritually, physically, or financially . . ." and then a request for money.

From Rex Humbard: "I've got some very bad news. My heart is broken, and I have not been able to eat or sleep." Why? He was going to have to take his program off the air in your area.

Computer technology allowed religious broadcasters to handle huge volumes of mail. While the mainline churches were debating the ethical implications of computers, the evangelicals were learning and using them.

IN 1960, after failing the New York bar exam, Pat Robertson moved to Virginia Beach, Virginia, and bought a defunct television station. By 1961, Robertson was ready to go on the air. In 20 years, he would be head of the Christian Broadcasting Network, CBN.

Oral Roberts added television to his radio ministry in the mid-1950s. He had 350 employees and a budget of $3 million a year, and was an inspiration not only to Jimmy, but to all aspiring evangelists who looked hungrily at television and radio. But Roberts' supernatural-healing format was so controversial he was refused air time on networks.

Oral Roberts shut down his television show in 1967 and started to reconsider how he'd been using the medium. His faith healing was way too raw for the intimacy of television, and he sensed he was slipping away from the mainstream approval he wanted. He would reappear two years later with an overhauled image. Gone were the long lines of trembling supplicants and the sweaty sessions where Roberts would press his hands urgently on people's heads and bellow, "Heal! Heal!" in his Oklahoma accent.

Marvin Gorman became the pastor of the First Assembly of God in New Orleans in 1965, the same year Jim and Tammy Bakker joined Pat Robertson as guest hosts on the "700 Club" at CBN, and started a children's puppet show there. In November, Jim and Tammy took over the "700 Club"—three years before Jimmy went on radio.

In 1972, Pat Robertson's WYAH (for Yahweh), Channel 27, started syndicating Tammy Bakker's children's puppet show to stations in Charlotte, North Carolina, Canada, and the West. His CBN was growing and quietly acquiring other television and radio stations.

Camp Meeting Hour

J immy was now booked a year in advance for revivals. Frances was furnishing their new home and concentrating on stabilizing Donnie's life, and couldn't travel much. But it was risky sending him off on the road alone, to build his reputation without her. They had been on the road together nearly ten years, and she knew where his weak places were. But she really wanted to settle down, and he was considering cutting his revivals back to please her.

Jimmy was mulling over his radio success in Detroit. Many people had come up to him and urged him to get on radio after hearing how well he handled himself on the air. He had seen how Jerry's career depended utterly on radio air play, all through the blacklisting after his marriage to Myra, through the ups and downs of his career in the years since.

And in 1968 Jerry was once again proving how vital radio was. After a dreary, drunken 1967, a year of bombed songs and gritty road tours through blue-collar America, Jerry was finding his career again—this time in country music. In January, he went into the Mercury studio in Nashville and cut "Another Place, Another Time." It stayed on the country charts for four months and crossed over to the pop charts. It was his biggest hit in 10 years.

Four more hits followed during the year. Apollo 12 astronaut Charles Conrad, Jr. announced he was taking a 90-minute Jerry Lee Lewis tape with him to the moon.

Jimmy had a hurdle: radio Pentecostals had a bad reputation as hicks and hucksters. So he decided God wanted him on radio to nullify the hucksters. Again, God spoke to him in the chattiest manner: "I want you to stop this other kind of programming where the Holy Spirit is being hawked like a piece of cheap goods," said God.

Jimmy thought big, too: God told him He was going to "send a wave of the Holy Spirit like the world has never seen before."

Frances didn't want to be associated with hucksters, either. She had worked hard to climb up to the middle class. Her son was going to finish high school, like she and Jimmy never had. She had a brick home in a new subdivision. She liked the role of preacher's wife.

But she was ambitious, and she probably realized the power of the media before Jimmy did. Years later, after she had become the CEO of the Jimmy Swaggart Ministries and had earned the nickname Dragon Lady, she sought to defuse that image by hinting that Jimmy's whole media career was a fluke. She had never wanted him to go on radio in the first place, she said.

But when "I sensed in my spirit that the radio ministry was God's will," there was no stopping her.

Not many people questioned Frances when she spoke of will. By her Dragon Lady period, she was well used to mingling God's will with her own.

It wasn't likely that Frances, who "kept pounding and pounding" on Jimmy to make a record, was ever indifferent about radio. She didn't plan to just drag boxes of records around in a car trunk for the rest of her life. In a fundraising appeal a few years after her statement that she'd never wanted him on radio, Jimmy, forgetting she'd said it, wrote, "In 1969, I knew the Holy Spirit had told me to go on radio. However, Frances was the driving force, constantly asking, 'Have you ordered the radio equipment yet?' . . . I was fearful, but Frances wouldn't let me back out." It wasn't going to be easy for Frances to hide her ambition.

In the fall of 1968, Jimmy bought some equipment and hired an engineer to set up a makeshift studio. At one of his meetings, he made connections with radio hosts, shortly signing agreements with stations in Atlanta, Houston, and Minneapolis to send them tapes of his 15-minute show (a song, some preaching, and an ending prayer).

He and Frances named it the "Camp Meeting Hour," and it went on the air January 1, 1969, exactly 11 years after Jimmy first started out on the road.

There was hardly any response to it. His chronic discouragement returned. When someone suggested he make a harder pitch for money, he declined, concerned about the huckster reputation he was trying to avoid.

Against Frances' will, Jimmy considered canceling the show. Frances dug in her heels and said she'd sell the furniture to stay on the air. Maybe they should make a harder pitch for money. Even though the broadcast included some old-fashioned elements—tongues, miracles, and healing—it was a class act compared to a lot of other radio ministries.

That summer, the Swaggarts, traveling, were caught in a flash flood that destroyed their belongings and equipment. At the end of summer, unable to pay his bills, Jimmy made a decision. While preaching in Louisville without Frances, he wrote the stations, canceling the shows.

The station managers promptly called Frances. She vetoed Jimmy, making arrangements to keep the shows on the air, and got the Atlanta station to do her a special favor: it told the story of the flood, beseeching listeners to help and promising to play the tapes it had on hand until they wore out.

The harder pitch for money had been made. Within three days, $3,000 had come in to pay the bills. Years later, discussing how she addressed problems, Frances said, "knock the door down."

This was the beginning of Jimmy's public life, and when he had to deal with the major media in later years, he and Frances had trouble reconciling themselves to the assaults on their privacy. They never seemed to get over the fact that the medium they had chosen was a two-edged sword. Like the Bakkers, they felt it was okay to share personal stories like the flood to get donations, but that the press, the FCC, the IRS, and their nosy followers, who wanted to know personal details about Frances' clothes and jewelry and cooking and furniture and leisure, were shockingly intrusive. They were so used to just taking things up with God; they never fully reconciled themselves to the loss of that autonomy.

In July 1969, while Jimmy was in the midst of an attack of nerves over the status of his broadcast and whether to add more stations, he was asked to preach at his denomination's national General Assembly, which included the top brass among the 10,000 attendees. The 34-year-old was the youngest preacher ever to appear before them, and the invitation was a tremendous tribute. He had to follow speakers he admired—Bible college presidents, world-known missionaries, and leaders of large congregations.

He brought down the house. Never had he had such a triumph.

Though he was ecstatic, Jimmy vowed never to "share God's glory." Even though hundreds of people were swooning, singing, dancing, and praising God in response to his preaching, he was scared he might give himself too much credit. Pride was how Satan got in.

It was wise, this humility, but of course pride wasn't the only way for Satan to get in. Anti-pride offered a door, too. If Jimmy couldn't claim his success and become confident, he was left open to more battles with nerves and demon oppression.

He was driving back to Baton Rouge alone, with no Frances to monitor him, no one to recognize him, past cheap motels and stores where *Playboy* sat on the shelves. Who would know, if he stopped and took care of some business? Only God. God would hate the deed, no question. But He was a forgiving, loving God. All have sinned and come short of His glory.

♦　♦　♦

In the fall of 1969, Jimmy again suffered from nerves as he prepared to add ten stations to his list of broadcast outlets. It cost $500 a day—a preposterous figure. Again he sat on the edge of the bed night after night, unable to sleep, worried about going broke and becoming a laughingstock. One night God pointed out to him he was already broke, and he was released from his worry in a lighthearted moment.

There were few of those moments regarding money, however; money was his crucible. Like Sun, he could be pathologically thrifty. But he made a virtue of it—his insistence on fiscal responsibility would earn his ministry a sterling reputation over the next years.

Yet he was influenced by the health-and-wealth gospel, the belief that God wants His children to be materially well off, and only failures of faith keep it from happening. In 1976, he wrote that the Bible showed a "simple three-point plan" . . . [for] "asking God for whatever I needed, and receiving it."

The plan: 1. Check with God or the Bible to see if what you want is God's will; 2. You don't have to tell God twice, just start thanking Him right after you ask; 3. Don't let the devil block the answer from God.

Jimmy wrote that he put his formula to work back in 1969, asking for an office building, because his house was overflowing with radio equipment and supplies, and Frances was getting tired of it. In a few weeks, he was shown two vacant lots on Goya Avenue.

Goya was a little one-block street like its brothers: Renoir, Cezanne, Rembrandt, Titian, Van Gogh, and—right in the middle of this pantheon—Harry. The area was a jumble of minor retail and mixed residential, unfettered by zoning laws. On Goya and the surrounding streets were vacant lots overgrown with waist-high weeds full of stickers. Hidden in them were water-logged tires and broken appliances shoved off the backs of pickups in the middle of the night.

But he liked the location. It was only a few miles from the house. It was near a major thoroughfare, and the approach to it along tree-lined Donmoor Avenue, with its decent, well-kept homes, white picket fences, and big, shaded lots, was pleasant.

At a service in Houston a couple of weeks later, he finally got up the nerve to ask for the money, something he hated because it was what the hucksters did.

The congregation provided it.

Once he had the land, it came time to get bids on the building. He and Frances prayed hard, and then he gave the job—again with no money to pay for it—to a contractor who bid $50,000. Asked about financing, he said he had it. This lie he rationalized years later by going back over the dynamics of the three-point plan, and telling himself, "I don't know where the money is coming from. That is God's problem."

But if God was really his business partner, why couldn't Jimmy just tell the builder that God was going to finance the building—like Leona Sumrall had done? That was faith. He was distorting faith to engage in deception.

He wrote that his conscience bothered him about that fib, and then the three-point plan dropped out of his writing. If he really actually used any elements of it as far back as 1969, it soon failed him and would continue to fail him. Though in his belief system, doubt and even caution were seen as lack of faith, he never ceased to suffer depression over this conflict when he was about to make a big move.

He was fearful that when he had to abandon the project for lack of money, everyone would know he'd lied. His reputation would be ruined. Again, his greatest fear was derision and ridicule.

By 1981, he was telling readers, "Fiscal carelessness will ruin a preacher . . . [he] should have the money before he spends it, or else know it is coming. He shouldn't run up a charge account and say, 'I will trust the Lord about this' . . . if you cannot pay cash, don't buy it!"

Voices

By 1971, Jimmy was on 50 radio stations. That year he had the best-selling gospel album in the country, "This is Just What Heaven Means to Me." All he and Frances had to do was sit down and crunch a few numbers to see that if some was good, more was better. The record royalties funded more stations.

He and Frances had a few luxuries for a change. The ministry could afford its own attorney, and hired photographers, secretaries, and radio and recording professionals.

Over the next months, the Goya offices would be refined, and redecorated. Jimmy's office would eventually be outfitted with paneling, naugahyde chairs and sofas, floor-to-ceiling bookcases, orange drapes, and orange carpet, one of the trendy interior decorator colors of the 1970s. Jimmy finally sat in a green leather chair like one he had envied at Jerry's house a decade earlier. An American flag hung behind his desk, and on the wall was a large painting of Jesus descending from the sky. The brick building was neatly groomed outside, with white plantation shutters and white columns.

Frances loved shopping, and bought herself and Jimmy stylish clothes, and had her hair colored and done in one of the cast-iron "bubbles" that were the rage. She defined the family to the world, and the image she projected was of winners—well-groomed, hard-working, loyal, and self-sacrificing. Jimmy wore three-piece suits, tinted aviator glasses, and a diamond ring, and carried a briefcase.

It was becoming clear that they could be as rich as Jerry Lee. And how much more good would be done in the process.

Nineteen seventy-one was starting out badly for Jerry. On April 21, Mamie died of cancer. Jerry was not at her bedside, as he had been unable to stand the sight of her ill. He was also in a state of despair too black to drink, needle, fight, or screw away. After 13 years—half her life—of abuse and tragedy, sprinkled with unforgettable times of tenderness, Myra, the love of his life, was divorcing him. He was cut to ribbons by what was now so clear about the woman dying and the one leaving: one of these women had loved him only for himself, and he had treated her like dirt and driven her away.

Mamie's funeral was held at the Church of God on Mississippi Avenue instead of her old church, where she no longer felt she belonged.

With Mamie barely buried, in May of 1971 Jimmy's grandfather suffered a fatal stroke at the Baton Rouge nursing home where he had been living for several years. Jimmy went to the hospital where W.H. had been taken, and found him under an oxygen tent, unconscious. A black woman he had taken up with while Ada was still alive had arrived at the hospital too. Sun, embarrassed, tried to obtain a restraining order barring her, said a relative, but it was denied; the court deemed her W.H.'s common-law wife.

Jimmy arrived in time to bid his grandfather goodbye and pray that he receive Jesus Christ at last on his deathbed.

ONE SUMMER DAY not long after the Goya building was complete and humming with activity, God told Jimmy, in the conversational lingo to which Jimmy had become accustomed, to expand his radio ministry in a hurry.

Frances was always happy when Jimmy would finally hear God say something she had been trying to tell him over and over. Jimmy leaped into action, hiring a Boston firm to start booking him on every station that would play gospel music. As usual, he didn't have the money to pay for air time. That was God's problem.

That was when God started nudging him about the royalties. "Now about these record albums," he reported the Lord said to him one day. God wanted the royalties signed over to the ministry. "Father, would you take ninety percent and let me have ten percent?" Jimmy dickered. God said no.

Jimmy was becoming ever more comfortable marbling his own and Frances' thoughts into his prayer life, and squelching deep inner voices if they didn't fit the game plan.

"I think what happens with this kind of person," said William Martin, a Rice University sociology professor and televangelism expert, "is that he begins to think, 'I couldn't have come this far if not for God.' Then he begins to say, 'Well, if I have this idea to build a Bible college or a mission, it must have come from God.' Next he starts to say, 'God told me this. God told me that.' And the next step [is] . . . 'I think what God meant to say was . . .' "

But Jimmy's audiences were willing to believe in his casual and chummy powwows with God which cast God and Jimmy as coach and quarterback, or God as Boss grooming his prize employee, taking him more and more into confidence and expecting Jimmy to "get it" when He made some sign or nudge. And, of course, God the Father, with Jimmy as God's oldest boy who has more responsibility than the other kids but also more access to the power structure. Every Pentecostal wanted to keep believing in miracles—it was such beloved doctrine that, if it had been practical, the church would probably at one time have made performing a miracle one of the prerequisites for ordination, like speaking in tongues was. It was unlikely Jimmy was going to get much objective input except from his own instincts, but they were usually demonized as satanic doubt whenever they popped up.

Jimmy turned all the royalties over to the ministry. Now he had the money to pay for his radio expansion. It was a gamble on record sales, because there wasn't nearly enough money to pay the stations' bills without extra sales, but he had enough confidence in their track record so far to believe it would happen. And it did; sales tripled.

But once he expanded his listener base, he found that not everyone liked the voodoo feel of his tongues speech coming into their homes and cars. Many urban listeners associated Holy Ghost possession with the hucksters. A station in a major market—one that brought in many record sales—cancelled him even after he attempted to make his broadcast more dignified. Others threatened to follow suit. He modified his message and only lost one other station.

By 1972, Jimmy's meetings were so popular he couldn't find churches big enough. He tried to stay with Assemblies of God facilities, he wrote later, but they weren't very big. Jimmy had been watching Billy Graham's success, and he saw that thousands of people who would never set foot in a Pentecostal church would come to auditoriums and stadiums. If he could attract them, it would blow his ministry wide open.

He did, and it did—they came. Jimmy's show lost the rigidity of its denominationalism and slipped some of the bonds of the Holy Roller image. He patterned his weekend crusades on Billy Graham's, with local steering committees for matters such as advertising and transportation. He still had his eye on that "good man" model, and Graham, who never let himself be alone with a woman, even in an elevator, epitomized it.

He started overhauling his music, too, building a crusade orchestra. He was concerned that visitors who had bought his albums, which were made with studio musicians and full orchestration, would be disappointed if they didn't find the music as good when they attended crusades. He put together a talented choir and bought a huge truck and trailer to haul musical equipment, albums, books and tapes for sale, while the singers and crew followed behind in a touring bus. Finally, in the late 1970s, he purchased the ultimate: a DC-3 to haul the entire crusade team.

David Beatty had started pastoring a small church in Baton Rouge and had been occasionally invited to travel with Jimmy and sing at the services. However, David would soon be phased out as Jimmy sought to polish his sound. He hired a young guitarist named Dwain Johnson to play bass and sing harmony with him—a decision he would come to regret.

"People Always Kill God"

Though the Jimmy Swaggart Evangelistic Association on Goya Avenue was not yet sophisticated—in 1973 Jimmy only had one crusade assistant, longtime associate Harry Bouton—it had grown into a business that grossed $3 million a year. His staff fielded 5,000 letters a day. In 1975 Pentecostal historian David Harrell called the JSEA "the most spectacular new revival ministry of the 1970s."

Guided by Frances' unerring sense of what the public wanted to see in its preachers, Jimmy had adopted a conservative-mod look, with well-cut suits with faintly belled pants and wide ties; he even grew modest sideburns for a brief period. He acquired a professional smile, and album and publicity photos showed a handsome, confident man with bright eyes and softly coiffed hair, straight teeth, full lips, and a strong chin. Frances wore expensive double-knit and wool outfits that were matron-chic and kept her dark hair coiffed in the bouffant flip that was *de rigueur* for wives of rising executives. Though it was invisible to their followers, she was involved in every facet of the ministry's operation.

The ministry was called "determinedly honest and clean" by reporters—albeit mostly ones friendly to the movement. Except for the *Charlotte Observer*, which was doggedly tracking the doings of Jim Bakker's PTL network, the mainstream press hadn't discovered televangelism yet and wouldn't for two or three more years. Those reporters he did know Jimmy cultivated with care. His operation was considered above reproach; its appeals for money were classy and calm, a deliberate contrast to the more hysterical elements of his tradition.

"Preachers, painters, and prostitutes," Jimmy's banker told him, had the worst reputation for repaying money. Preachers were notorious for piling up debts which their churches then had to pay. There was an attitude that God would provide. Underpinning that was the tax-free sinecure the church had from the U.S. government. And there was probably an even deeper-hidden feeling that they were already paying, by having to be clean-living role models for everyone else.

Jimmy himself noted that preachers don't report to a boss, don't put in a set number of hours a week, don't work regular hours except for services. But he was an exception, and his banker knew it. He kept his skirts out of the mud, even paying bills he thought were questionable so his operation would keep its clean reputation.

In 1972, Jimmy announced his intention to start a television series, and, taking a cue from Oral Roberts, started toning down his services. He didn't try to work people up or let the services become unruly, even though he still preached with the flavor of the oldtime camp meeting spellbinder.

He was good at walking the line: he still believed strongly in healing, and his audiences loved his many tales of miraculous healings. But he admitted he didn't know why some people didn't get well. He also abolished the prayer line, where people queued up to receive on-the-spot prayers for specific illnesses, substituting instead a simple mass prayer for the sick at the end of the service. He taught the gifts of the spirit, but curbed their expression: "The old-fashioned whoop and holler has its place," said Jimmy, "but people want something deeper."

Jimmy "brought mass revivalism back to life in the major Pentecostal denominations," wrote historian David Harrell; his appeal was in all directions and he seemed destined to "rescue charismatic campaigning from its reputation of radicalism and irresponsibility."

He was also drawn into the positive-thinking fad that was sweeping the country—"The only thing you cannot do is what you say you cannot do," he preached in a more trendy version of his three-point plan—but he took care to lace it with plenty of Pentecostal doctrine so as not to be associated with one of the emerging class of mystics that would soon be known as New Agers.

He discouraged love offerings, the practice of people coming forward after the sermon and stuffing money into his pockets. Besides being a rather crass expression of love, they were a sour reminder of the days when he hardly got enough money from preaching to buy a pound of lunch meat. It also allowed people to make tiny contributions, as opposed to what they gave when he asked specifically for a twenty-dollar bill or a check for $50 to keep the radio broadcast on the air.

His decision to donate record royalties to the ministry had met with approval from secular writers on the lookout for religious scams. In return for the royalties, the ministry paid for repairs, insurance, utilities, and maintenance of the house at Tara and Trinity, and gave him a "parsonage allowance," which he deducted from his taxes—at that time, in complete compliance with the IRS.

SUCCESS BROUGHT trials that flowed from the age-old problem of exhaustion and pressure: the evangelist on the platform carried everything; the emotional pressures on him were tremendous. Evangelists were lonely people, targets of adoring fans who demanded that they be Jesus or the father that wouldn't fail them. They had few outlets, were not allowed weaknesses. Few people could understand how hard it was to live with their public image. "Burdened by work, adored by their disciples, tempted by floods of money, the successful revivalists became trapped men," wrote David Harrell.

Sometime in 1973, the Assemblies of God admitted there was a problem and instituted a formal rehabilitation program for wayward or disturbed preachers. About this time, Jimmy became very interested in the subject. He sought out the story of his old hero, A.A. Allen, who had been arrested for drunk driving and then lied about it, saying he was kidnapped and knocked out, and had awakened to find men pouring liquor down his throat. He ended by leaving his affiliation and launching an independent ministry. Jimmy found Allen's old pastor, who still led the church where Allen had preached before his drunk-driving arrest in 1955.

Jimmy asked him about Allen's demeanor before the arrest. The pastor had known there was something wrong, but didn't want to believe the rumors of Allen's drinking were true. So he ignored it. Jimmy sought out other elders, asking a trusted older minister how Allen could have had such a successful ministry while being a hypocrite. How could he keep preaching? For his own reasons, Jimmy needed an explanation of how someone who was such a sinner could still have the anointing of God.

The older man didn't really have an answer. He assured Jimmy that Allen had probably "wept many tears over this terrible evil within his life. I am sure he promised God many times to stop." Jimmy was sure of that, too, because he'd done it himself so many times. But it didn't explain why God tolerated hypocrisy; it seemed God was either ignoring or blessing it. All Jimmy could conclude was that God was being merciful to Allen, giving him lots of rope as long as he saved lots of souls.

Jimmy consulted Gordon Lindsay, the Dallas-based evangelist who had become a linchpin of the postwar healing revival. Lindsay had tried to persuade Allen to come clean back then, but he wouldn't. He clung to his lie, and lost his ministry. Jimmy asked Lindsay what the turning point had been for Allen, as well as for another evangelist of that period who had been brought down by moral problems.

When Lindsay answered thoughtfully that many preachers can't stand prosperity, Jimmy understood immediately; most of them came from poor backgrounds and couldn't believe their good fortune. They eventually acted that belief out.

Jimmy then decided the devil targeted preachers more than other men, that more temptations were cast in their way, because in destroying a powerful

evangelist, he has destroyed God's entry into millions of lives. Preachers have
to keep their distance, he said, and they start to feel that "nobody ever gives
back to him in return." He admitted that he felt at times a great loneliness.

No matter how good his wife is, a preacher is alone, especially inside his
head. Other women feel the glamour of this; they admire the scholar and the
man of God. They unburden themselves to such men because they trust them
not to take advantage—at the same time giving off signals that they wish they
would.

Lindsay had also reminded Jimmy of the ego problem of fame: "They start
to think they are God."

Jimmy never noticed how this approached his own ever-chummier conversations with God, in which he and God became partners in a joint venture.
"There's a great danger in becoming God," said Jimmy's friend Gerald Wilson, "because people always kill God."

Things moved too fast for Jimmy to get derailed by these warnings, however. He had continued to sin, had continued to hear voices of doubt and
believe them, but the fact was, God went right on blessing his ministry.

God seemed willing to give gifted preachers immunity for some time, but
how long would it last? How would Jimmy know when God was about to
crack down?

◆   ◆   ◆

In April of 1973, Jerry Lee had brought his surviving son, troubled, drug-
addicted, and sometimes violent Junior, to one of Jimmy's meetings in Ft.
Worth. After the service, the-18-year-old came up to Jimmy. "I wish I could
go with you," he said. Jimmy told him fine, pack your bags and come on. Of
course Junior hadn't really meant it, even though Jerry hoped for nothing so
much as that Jimmy might be able to straighten the boy out. But it was just
Junior's idea of good manners. He wasn't even really considering it.

After they left, Jimmy prayed. "Father, that boy can't live for you in the
atmosphere he's in. I don't know what will have to be done. But if you have
to take him home to heaven to insure his salvation—please do it."

Eight months later, Junior was at Jerry Lee's office on Brooks Road in
Nashville.

"Junior, where are you?" called Marion Terrell, his uncle.

Junior came out of Jerry's office, but didn't say anything.

"What are you doing with that knife?"

Marion looked his nephew right in the eye. Junior was usually fried from
LSD and PCP, and Jerry Lee was afraid of him. Marion, a powerful, gentle
soul with years of karate, wasn't.

This night, Junior had drawn a knife and run Jerry and his entourage out
of the office. Marion had been called.

"I'm gonna kill ever one of them up here, and then I'm gonna kill you."

"Put the knife down, you don't want to make Uncle Marion hurt you."

"He reared back," said Marion, "and here he come with that big knife. I grabbed him and took the knife and throwed him about ten feet over in the corner. He got up and said, 'Uncle Marion, that was slick, wasn't it?' Then he got up, went out to his car, and drove out to [Jerry's house at] Coro Lake."

Marion followed. When he got there, it was as if nothing had happened. Junior was calm.

A short time after this incident, Junior was killed when his Jeep overturned on the highway near his father's home. It was November 13, 1973—a few days past his 19th birthday.

Ironically, Jimmy got the news in Waxahachie, Texas, preaching at Southwestern Bible College, from which Jerry had been expelled in 1952 for playing boogie music in chapel. A couple of days later he read an interview with Jerry about the influence of rock and roll and the drug scene. Did he have any idea that his pioneering music would affect so many lives for generations?

Jerry replied that if he'd known what would happen in only a little over a decade—that there would be "millions on dope today who were influenced by the music . . . countless others who've gone off on every possible emotional trip"—he'd never have played his first note on a piano.

Leroy Milton Lewis, Jimmy's great-grandfather and the grandfather of Jerry Lee Lewis and Mickey Gilley, in the early part of this century. Marginal farmer, wastrel, poet, teacher, alcoholic, and lover of music, he married his 14-year-old cousin in 1888. Their stormy marriage yielded 11 children. Photo: courtesy Myra Lewis Williams.

Foreground: Jimmy's maternal grandparents, William Herron and his mentally ill wife, Theresa, in about 1953, with some of their children (*from left:* daughters Viola and Mamie; son-in-law Elmo Lewis; one of the Herron sons and his wife; and daughter Stella). Theresa's violent episodes drove her husband from the house. Her insanity was never fully diagnosed, even though she was committed to East Louisiana State Hospital in Pineville for several months. Photo: courtesy Lewis House Museum.

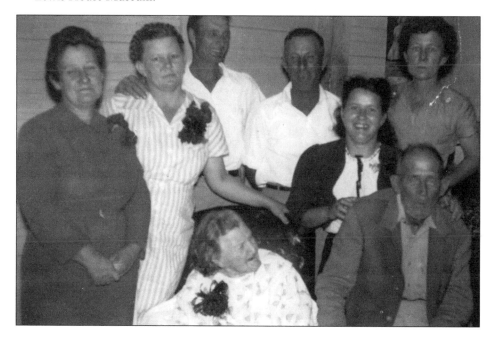

Three of the Herron sisters—Minnie Bell, Viola, and Mamie— with their husbands, their sons, and a group of cousins, in about 1949 or 1950. Jimmy (in striped T-shirt) and Jerry are at the extreme left and right, in almost identical postures, each standing next to his parents. Jerry's mother, Mamie, is holding a child; her husband, Elmo, is behind her. In front of Elmo is Viola, partially hidden behind her son David Beatty; husband William Beatty is behind her and to her right. Photo: courtesy Lewis House Museum.

Jimmy, about age 13, in a school photo from Ferriday. It was at about this time that his parents began to leave him alone for weeks at a time while they traveled the Louisiana backwoods as evangelists. Photo: Christopher Bell/Liaison Agency.

At left is Jimmy's paternal grandmother, Ada Lewis Swaggart, circa 1954, in Ferriday. Born-again Ada was a powerful influence in Jimmy's life, steering him toward the ministry. With her are her brother, John Lewis, and her sister, Irene Lewis Gilley, Mickey Gilley's mother and also a pillar of the church in Ferriday. Photo: courtesy Lewis House Museum.

Jimmy's parents, Willie Leon ("Sun") Swaggart and Minnie Bell Herron Swaggart, a few years before her tragic death in 1960, when Jimmy was 25. Minnie Bell was the sister of Jerry Lee Lewis's mother, Mamie Herron Lewis. Sun was the nephew of Elmo Lewis, Jerry Lee's father. He was also the nephew of Irene Lewis Gilley, Mickey Gilley's mother. Photo: courtesy Lewis House Museum.

The seedy Blue Cat Club at Under-the-Hill in Natchez, circa 1955. Jerry began playing there as a teenager, bringing needed money to his sharecropper family. His sister Frankie remembers waiting at night in the car with her parents for him to get off work, a loaded gun on the dashboard in case of trouble.
Photo: courtesy Lewis House Museum.

Jimmy circa 1958, when he began preaching full time, traveling throughout the South with wife Frances and baby Donnie, raising the child in the car and living in church basements and cheap motels, while his famous cousin made thousands of dollars per performance. Jerry Lee bought him a new Oldsmobile the year he went on the road.
Photo: courtesy Lewis House Museum.

Jerry Lee Lewis and his famous "child bride," cousin Myra Gale Brown, in 1958. Myra's paternal grandmother and Jerry's father were siblings. Myra was barely 13 when she and Jerry married in December of 1957. Five months later, his skyrocketing career was ruined when the press learned her age, her relation to him, and that he was still married to Jane Mitchum when he married Myra.
Photo: courtesy Lewis House Museum.

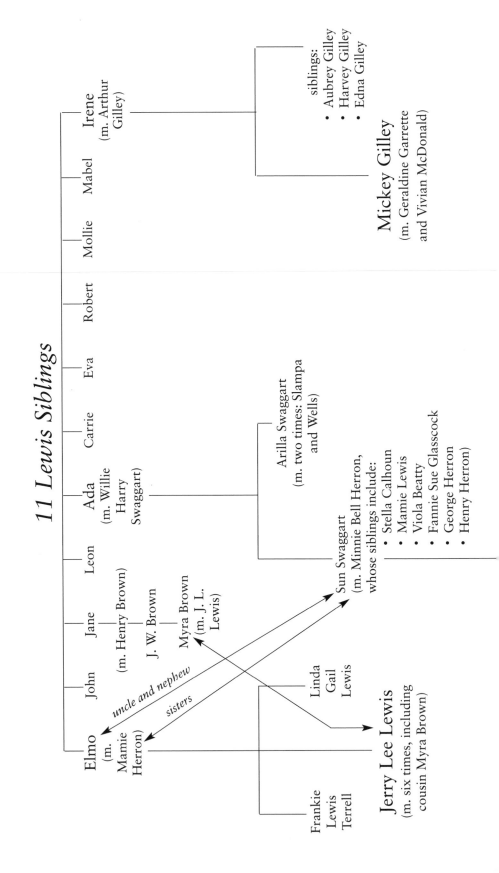

11 Lewis Siblings

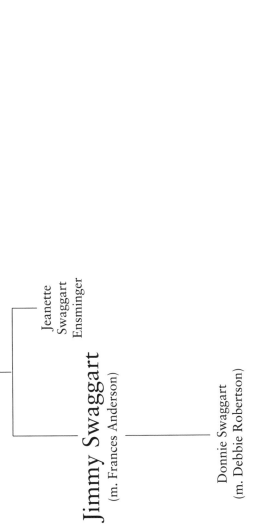

Jeanette
Swaggart
Ensminger

Jimmy Swaggart
(m. Frances Anderson)

Donnie Swaggart
(m. Debbie Robertson)

Partial Lewis / Swaggart / Gilley Genealogy

Jimmy in vintage form in 1987, a year before his first "moral failure." His decision in the early 1970s to move from preaching exclusively in churches to secular settings, such as stadiums and city auditoriums, greatly increased his following. Photo: Anthony Suau/Liaison Agency.

Jimmy plays piano for Frances in their stylish living room on Highland Road in Baton Rouge, near the ministry compound, in 1987. When the Swaggarts moved from the humble "rectory" at Tara and Trinity into this 9,300-square-foot home across the road from the Country Club of Louisiana at the end of 1984, Jimmy got rid of his modest Volkswagen and both he and Frances began driving Lincolns. Photo: Anthony Suau/Liaison Agency.

Jimmy jogs near his home for a *Life* magazine photographer in 1987, at the height of his international visibility, wearing the same "uniform" that prostitutes said he wore when soliciting them down the highway in New Orleans. This and other behavior led to speculation that, unconsciously, he wanted to be caught. Photo: Anthony Suau/Liaison Agency.

Evangelists Jim and Tammy Bakker, of whose entertainment focus the Swaggarts disapproved, in 1986. The Bakkers' followers were enthralled with Tammy's heavy makeup, flashy clothes, and tearful personal confessions. In 1987, under pressure from the Swaggarts and the *Charlotte Observer,* Jim Bakker resigned from PTL, his North Carolina ministry, under allegations that he had paid hush money to church secretary Jessica Hahn, with whom he had had a sexual encounter in 1981. Bakker went to prison in 1989 for fraud and conspiracy. Photo: AP/Wide World Photos.

"I have sinned against you"—
Jimmy's February 21, 1988,
confession was called
"fabulous television" by
Professor Quentin Schultze,
"more dramatic than any
evening soap opera." A decade
later, it would be repeatedly
suggested that President
Clinton should "do a Swaggart"
to defuse the uproar over his
affair with White House intern
Monica Lewinsky.
Photo: courtesy ABC News.

Jimmy and Frances are photographed haggard but stoical at Civil District Court
in New Orleans in July 1991. Fellow evangelist Marvin Gorman's $90-million
lawsuit against Jimmy, Frances, their ministry, and other individuals culminated
in a 10-week trial whose testimony drifted from conspiracy and unbridled adultery to illegitimate children, New Orleans mob connections, and exorcism.
Photo: AP/Wide World Photos.

A Radio Station

In 1973, Jimmy made a radio coup of which he was very proud. He had tried for years to get one of the Baton Rouge stations to launch a gospel music program, but without success. Baton Rouge was, after all, more than one-third Catholic. Now a local station, WLUX, was in bankruptcy court. The FCC had ordered it auctioned for debt.

"They wouldn't let you bid over what was owed on the station," remembered David Beatty, "and it was $80,000, that's what the station owed. For you to be able to get it, you had to be able to pay off all the debts.

"[Jimmy] went by the Savings and Loan and he got 80,000 dollars. And slipped it in his coat pocket. When he got out there, he told them he wanted [the station]."

There was another buyer, too, one Jimmy remembered as wanting to make WLUX "the number one rock music station in Baton Rouge." Both men told the court-appointed referee that they could pay off the station's debt, said David, and the referee said, "Well, you both qualify. I'll have to go and determine which one of you we're gonna let have the station."

That was where Jimmy rose out of his chair, said David, and kicked the props out from under his opponent. "You oughtta let the person have it that came prepared to buy it, y'know," he said Jimmy suggested. The referee asked what he meant.

"Well, I am here, prepared to buy this station." The other man protested, saying he too could offer a check, "and Jimmy said, 'yeah, but a check is negotiable paper; I mean I came to *buy the station*.' And he just laid his $80,000 on the table," said David. "And he said, 'Now, I think, if this man can match my $80,000, THEN you oughtta go back and consider it. But if he's just gonna give you a check, and he don't have the money in the bank, and he's gonna have to go get it, then I oughtta be the one to get the station.'"

Jimmy wrote later that he handed his bank bag to the referee, who counted the money and then asked the other buyer if he could match it.

"No," the man answered, and picked up his briefcase to leave. "Obviously I'm in the wrong business. I ought to be a preacher."

Jimmy got the station, but the FCC turned down his license application. He appealed, the referee agreeing to an operating permit and appointing him the station manager until the appeal was decided. Jimmy gave the job to David Beatty, and David ran the station part time, understanding that he would quit his own ministry and run the station full time if they won the appeal and the license was granted.

On Jimmy's orders, David immediately dumped the station's country-rock format and started playing gospel. Jimmy felt a thrill the first time he switched on the station after the change.

For six months, David ran the station at a profit. Jimmy pulled together whatever local support he could to vouch that he would be a responsible steward of the people's airwaves. He flew to Washington to talk to FCC appointees and found them lukewarm about a religious station. He engaged the help of Senator Russell Long (son of slain populist hero Huey Long). But the situation looked bleak.

He prayed hard, but finally one day God hinted he wasn't praying for the right thing. "There are some FCC members who are totally in opposition to My ways and My Word," God murmured. The nickel dropped. Jimmy understood. Instead of praying that he'd win the appeal, he started praying that the offending commissioners would be removed.

One of Richard Nixon's first acts after taking the presidential oath of office in January 1973 was to remove liberal FCC commissioners and replace them with conservative ones.

After six months of sweating it out, word came down that the Court of Appeals had overturned the ruling against Jimmy. He had his station.

But it cost him his closeness with David Beatty. One day, shortly before Jimmy got his license, "it just ended, abruptly. Without any—just BAM. I wasn't the radio director any more," said David.

He had no idea why he was fired. He'd kept the station on the air during the crucial appeal. The station's income had increased during his tenure. He was counting on making it a full time thing, maybe even being on the telecast.

"[Jimmy] never did explain it to me. There was no warning, nothing. Two weeks before, he'd told me what a tremendous job I had done, part time. But he didn't want me to leave my church until he'd gotten the license to the station. And somewhere in those two weeks, I fell from grace."

After that, their relationship deteriorated. "Frances used to cut my hair, and I'd go over there and eat all the time, and we had great fellowship, they came to my church." That all died.

Beatty always suspected it was Frances that was displeased with him, either because he wasn't as sophisticated as she'd like—he had been accompanying Jimmy on crusades, where he was often invited to participate in local church services—or because she was jealous. Or because he'd served his purpose: Donnie had graduated from high school and had started attending Louisiana State University, leaving Frances free to travel with Jimmy again, and apparently she didn't want David along any more.

There was no love lost on his side; he didn't like Frances and vigorously resisted whisperings that she was the brains behind the ministry. Drop Jimmy off anywhere with ten dollars and a pickup truck, said David, and he'd soon be a millionaire. He got that straight from Uncle Sun. Frances, he said, would be making four dollars an hour in a drugstore somewhere without Jimmy.

"Frances is a manipulator, and she knew a good thing when she saw it. She just got on Jimmy's bandwagon." He said Frances always encouraged Jimmy, she pushed him, she always told him it could be done.

Interestingly, in Jimmy's writing it is he and God who sound like an old married couple, tussling over how to proceed. Jimmy reports the usual doubts, despair, double-minded prayers, failures of faith, followed by round scoldings from God. Hardheaded Jimmy wouldn't put the lid on the toothpaste, wouldn't put the toilet seat down. He'd say he was sorry, behave for two weeks, and then do it again.

A Huge Burst out of a Shotgun

Gail McDaniel was the babysitter for her minister's three children. Now, in 1973, the troubled 18-year-old's life had become intertwined with his.

Gail and a 16-year-old girlfriend were in a deep crisis with their Pentecostal families. Her friend's brother-in-law was suspicious of Gail. He accused her of being a lesbian, and threatened her with criminal charges for contributing to the delinquency of a minor. Gail denied it, but she was terrified, especially of the effect of such a scandal on her critically ill father.

She consulted her minister and boss, Marvin Gorman, 40. Gorman had done much pastoral counseling in his eight years leading the First Assembly of God church in New Orleans, and a lot of it had been for sexual problems. When Gail went to see him in his office at church, he told her that he had influence with her friend's family, and could help.

He also told her the only way she could straighten out her life and nip her lesbianism in the bud was to have sex with a man. He persuaded her to do it with him, right there on the floor of his office, implying it might influence whether he cooperated in defanging her girlfriend's family.

She did what he asked, several times over the next few months. Sure enough, charges were not pressed against her. Then her father died, and she stopped seeing Gorman.

At least, that was the story she told in court 18 years later.

MARVIN GORMAN had been saved at the age of 16. Two years older than Jimmy, he grew up in Hampton, Arkansas, and by age 19 had hit the road preaching, like Jimmy. He was a personable man, friendly and ambitious.

Gorman soon married, and found that neither he nor his wife were cut out for a road life. After about two years, he took an assistant pastorship at Crowley, Louisiana. He soon became pastor, and stayed three years, looking for opportunities to move up in the Assemblies of God organization. About the time Jimmy and Frances went on the road full time in 1958, Gorman began working for the Assemblies as state youth director, with oversight of Sunday schools. Based in Alexandria, he traveled the state, crossing Jimmy's path many times and even staying with Sun a time or two.

Jimmy knew Gorman, but not intimately. He was a pastor; Jimmy was an evangelist. But Jimmy became very aware of him in 1972, because that was the year Gorman went on television in New Orleans, on WDSU Channel 6.

Jimmy was not confident about preaching on television. Live audiences he knew he could enchant, but when he compared himself to the other television preachers—Oral Roberts, Rex Humbard—he wasn't sure he could compete. The usual posse of demons gathered to hiss doubts and fear of being a laughingstock into his head.

Nevertheless, everyone else was doing it. Jim Bakker and Paul Crouch out in California started their new show, "Praise the Lord," in May of 1973 under Bakker's Trinity Broadcasting Systems nonprofit corporation; Pat Robertson had bought WYAH in the 1960s. Richard De Haan, Jerry Falwell, James Robison, Robert Schuller of Orange County, California's Crystal Cathedral—were all in various stages of television ministry.

But even if he was scared, Jimmy was lured by the promise of television—reaching huge numbers of people, making a good living, acquiring fame equal to Jerry's by countering Jerry's messages from hell. In 1973 he started making videotapes, staying in his comfort zone by doing lots of music. He taped first at an inferior studio in Baton Rouge and then at another in New Orleans. He couldn't get a polished product, and became discouraged.

He later told how he had said to Frances over and over, "I can't do it"—a phrase that would send her into a tailspin. Then he was riding in the car with her one evening and heard a stern voice in his head: "Next time you say you can't do something . . . it will be like cursing me." It's impossible not to imagine that that was Frances, not God, thundering in his head.

He started taping his crusades, where he really shone, and augmenting them with music tapings done at a rented studio. He tried sending the raw footage to a production house on the west coast, but the result was crude and unsatisfactory. The Californians didn't understand Jimmy's kind of ministry. Finally he visited the "Hee Haw" studio in Nashville, and made a deal to tape there. He decided to upgrade his sound, and hired professional engineers and back-up singers who knew their way around the Nashville sound.

To get the best rate, he had to tape 24 half-hour shows in a week—an unbelievable schedule. But he did it—and delivered every time. Like the "Camp Meeting Hour," it was essentially a gospel music show—15 or so minutes of music, eight to 12 of preaching, and the rest selling albums and advertising upcoming crusades.

He bought air time on one station. He would add stations and the response would become more solid over the next several years; after he built his own production studio and started making his own tapes in 1981, it would go through the roof.

As he acknowledged a few years later, "Radio is like a rifle . . . television is like a huge burst out of a shotgun."

♦   ♦   ♦

Mickey Gilley had recorded "Roomful of Roses" in 1974 with Jerry's old producer, Eddie Kilroy. It became the No. 1 country hit; by the fall, Mickey had two more number one songs. Three number-one records in a year: even Jerry had never done that. Jimmy's gospel albums outsold Jerry's records that year, too. By the end of the year, Mickey had been named Most Promising Male Artist by the Academy of Country Music, No. 1 Most Promising Male Artist by *Record World,* and No. 1 Top New Country Singles Artist by *Billboard.*

It was a dismal year for Jerry; two of his musicians quit and sued for back wages; his Jerry Lee Lewis Enterprises collapsed; he was evicted from the building where his late son had threatened his life, and sued by the building's owner; he was ordered by a court to pay for a no-show in Virginia the previous year; and he was sued for $100,000 owed on a jet he'd bought before Jimmy bought his. Early in 1975, he would be greeted at the Denver airport by federal agents, who arrested him for drug possession. Later he would assault a fan at a Memphis club; see his fourth wife file for divorce; and be sued by a man he had hit with a mike stand during a performance several years before.

Mickey's club, Gilley's, was becoming famous. He had teamed up with a club owner and welder for Shell Chemical named Sherwood Cryer in 1971. Cryer had taken him out to see a club he owned on Spencer Highway in the Houston suburb of Pasadena, called Shelley's. It was a wreck, lit by kerosene lamps, and the sky visible through the tin roof. "Just a bunch of tin, and an old bandstand, with a bar sitting over to one side," he described it later. He told Cryer he ought to just take a bulldozer and push it over.

Instead, Cryer and Mickey formed a corporation, Gilley Enterprises, and set about fixing the place up. The building started out at 48,000 square feet and, 10 years later, was estimated to have grown to 70,000. They installed 40 pool tables, and furniture to seat over 2,000 people.

Betraying his Pentecostal roots, Mickey wanted to call it the Sin Den, but Cryer vetoed that. Everyone always referred to Mickey as "Gilley," so the club became Gilley's.

Gilley's became the biggest honky-tonk in Texas, and famous the world over. Its congenial atmosphere was legendary. The rural highway setting made people feel free. Mickey beamed at his audience, talking to them from the stage ("Hey now! Watch your hands!"), and, during breaks, wandered through the club and chatted with people at their tables. "None of that star stuff," was his policy.

The patrons ranged in age from young teens to couples old enough to be their grandparents—several generations all doing the whip, the twostep, the cotton-eyed Joe together across the huge dance floor. Clothing ranged from cowboy to hippie to urban attorney. Gilley's would eventually have its own shooting gallery, punching bags, video games, and five mechanical bulls to test people's rodeo skills. It even installed showers for truckers. A sign at the entry said, "Check guns, knives, chains, knucks, all weapons at the front door" and meant it.

Gilley's, open 24 hours a day, would pull in 5,000 people on big Saturday nights.

A FEW HUNDRED miles down Interstate 10 from Gilley's, the Jimmy Swaggart Evangelistic Association employed 150 people. Jimmy's "Camp Meeting Hour" was the largest daily gospel radio program in the world in 1975, broadcast on 550 stations.

But it was television that would make his name. By 1975, his Jimmy Swaggart telecast was on 200 television stations with 2,000 cable outlets. Record and tape sales were topping a million each year. The $500-a-day budget that had caused him such anguish in 1969 had ballooned to $35,000. The ministry was receiving more mail than any other entity in Louisiana. That had real meaning: a ministry's mailing list was its lifeblood, the source of orders for records and tapes and donations. Once a postal employee stole bags of ministry letters, took the money out, put the gutted letters back in the bags, and tossed them into bar ditches all over Baton Rouge. It took the ministry six months to track all the lost orders and make good on them.

He had expanded his broadcasts overseas, buying radio time in Africa, India, Ireland, East Asia (Hong Kong, Taiwan, and the Philippines), and Central America.

Jimmy owned five gospel radio stations now, in Dallas-Fort Worth, Oklahoma City, Pensacola, Baton Rouge, and Bowling Green. He was holding 35 crusades a year, and accepting scores of other invitations.

Jimmy's friend of 15 years, Richard Dortch, now superintendent for the Assemblies of God's Illinois District, had been inviting him to preach at the posh summer family camp Dortch had developed at Lake Williamson Christian Center, the district's 350-acre retreat. Dortch invited big-name evangelists, and Jimmy was one of them. In fact, Jimmy (like Jerry) always closed the show, performing on the last three nights of camp, because he drew the biggest crowds.

Dortch also saw to it that Jimmy was invited to preach at many other Assembly conventions, and he visited Baton Rouge to sit in Jimmy's Amen

Corner numerous times after Jimmy opened a church and founded a regular local congregation.

Several thousand miles away from Baton Rouge, two events took place that would involve Richard Dortch and ripen over the next decade to loom large in Jimmy's life. He was aware of the first: Jim Bakker had started broadcasting his "PTL Club" from Charlotte, North Carolina, with wife Tammy in 1973. The second was that a Southern traveling faith healer named John Wesley Fletcher was ordained in the Assemblies of God. Fletcher started appearing on Bakker's show in 1978, and by 1980 the two men were inseparable. Soon, these events would cost Jimmy his longtime friendship with Richard Dortch.

Jimmy's operation on Goya went largely unnoticed by the local press. Of course, he had no local congregation with the traditional bulletin board announcements to publish, but mainly, the coverage of religion was ghettoized by the media.

But in 1976, Jimmy Carter, the Democratic nominee for President, announced he was a born-again Christian. When he was elected, the media suddenly realized it had better check out the evangelical movement.

Newsweek called born-again Christianity the most overlooked religious phenomenon of the decade, and the term "born-again" promptly migrated for good into the secular world, being applied to everything from Macintosh fans to broccoli enthusiasts.

That it could have failed to notice a faction that might be key to a national election stung the mainstream media, and journalists hurried to dissect this "new" phenomenon. Though they found what they expected—corny and boring local programming—they also found large followings for Jim Bakker's PTL network in Charlotte and Pat Robertson's Christian Broadcasting Network in Virginia Beach, Virginia. By early 1976, PTL had 46 affiliates carrying it. Other players were Oral Roberts, Rex Humbard, Jerry Falwell, and Paul and Jan Crouch.

Jimmy was now building his own television studio at Goya, planning to add more stations and worried about funding as usual.

The media also immediately found something else it expected—hypocrisy. In 1976, two students at the American Christian College of Tulsa televangelist Billy James Hargis, whose patriotic, Communist-baiting broadcast was carried on 140 stations, confessed to each other on their wedding night to having had sex with another person. It turned out the be the same person—their leader, Hargis. He was accused of sexual impropriety by a total of five students, four of them men. He vehemently denied the charges but, as always, such stories made it easy for some in the media to dismiss the movement.

◆   ◆   ◆

It was Christmastime in New Orleans, 1978. Marvin Gorman was at his new Airline Highway location, the bankrupt Baptist church he had bought and occupied in about 1973. In the office where he had seduced Gail McDaniel five years ago, according to her, he continued to do pastoral counseling, including consulting with church members about sexual problems.

One of his clients, Lynda Savage, was not a member of his church. She was married to another Assemblies of God preacher, David Savage, and was having marital crises. She would end up having affairs with her brother-in-law and another minister.

One day she called Gorman, distraught. She was in a New Orleans motel. She was going to kill herself, she said. Marvin rushed over.

He found her sitting on the edge of the bed, and he sat down beside her. There were pills on the night stand.

"All at once she turned around, her blouse was unbuttoned," he said. "She grabbed me and started kissing me and grabbed me in my crotch."

Here their stories diverged. "I was overcome by guilt," Gorman would tell a jury more than ten years later. He lost his erection after penetrating her. "I stood up, zipped my pants, told her I was very, very sorry and walked out of the room and left."

But Savage would claim she had a three-year affair with Gorman, during which they had sex eight to 12 times.

Three other women would come forward and say he had kissed and fondled them during counseling sessions in his church office. A fifth would say she had sex with him over a three-month period. All but Savage were members of his church. All were testifying in the late 1980s on behalf of Jimmy Swaggart.

``Don't Ever Let Me Get Like That''

Jimmy's cousins were making headlines again, and it was bringing attention to him. Mickey had been named 1975's Top New Male Vocalist in the Album Category by *Record World,* and in 1976 was named Most Promising Male Artist by *Music City News,* and both Best Male Vocalist and Entertainer of the Year by the Academy of Country Music.

Those triumphs made another bad year for Jerry look even more like the hand of God punishing him, and Jimmy used some of Jerry's headlines in his sermons.

In February 1976, Jerry had his nose fixed from a beating he'd taken several years before when he called a fan's wife a whore. He got bad reviews when he appeared at Gilley's, loaded, in June; in April, he had been sued for unpaid rent on two houses leased the summer before. By summer his sister Linda, who sang with him, had a nervous breakdown. At the Palomino Club in North Hollywood in August, he vilified his two cousins from the stage and announced he was divorcing his fourth wife; six weeks later he shot his bass player in the chest with a .357 magnum. In a period of a few days, he was arrested at his estranged wife's house for yelling drunken obscenities at her neighbors; he overturned his Rolls driving his daughter to school while intoxicated, and was jailed; and he was arrested again when, on release from jail, he drove to Elvis Presley's Graceland mansion and waved a pistol at the gates, demanding to see Elvis. The next day, he entered the hospital for ulcers. Before the year ended, his wounded bass player filed a $400,000 lawsuit.

Jimmy was asked for his reaction to all this. In December of 1976, he dedicated a song to Jerry and made a grave plea over television for prayers for him. A few days later, he gave an interview to the *Nashville Banner,* saying, "I almost hate to answer the phone sometimes, because I know somebody is going to tell me Jerry is dead." A month later Jerry entered the hospital again, this time to have his gall bladder removed; he had to cancel an important European tour. A few months later, the hospital that had treated him for ulcers sued for unpaid bills. Shortly after that, he was arrested for driving intoxicated.

A real rift between the cousins occurred in July of 1979. Elmo Lewis died after a month-long illness. "Jerry Lee came to the funeral wearing a long fur coat to the floor," said his cousin Arilla Wells, and reportedly loaded on alcohol and drugs. Jimmy was traveling, and could not make the funeral in Ferriday. He sent Frances, who also showed up in mink, hugged Jerry's sisters, Frankie and Linda, and went over to speak to Jerry.

Frances was speaking to him in an undertone, explaining Jimmy's absence, when suddenly Jerry's voice rose above the gathering. "You tell Jimmy Lee Swaggart to kiss my ass! This is my father's funeral and he's not here!" After Frances left, things deteriorated, and the day reportedly ended with sibling threats of violence toward Jerry, who fled.

By the end of 1977, it was almost becoming a joke to use Jerry in sermons any more. His old friend and manager Cecil Harrelson sadly remembered being in Nashville with Jerry in the early days, and seeing a billboard touting a new Johnny Cash album. Cash was rumored to be using heroin, and he looked terrible. He had the back of his hand on his forehead like he had a headache, and his wrist was so skinny. "Promise me, Cece," Jerry said, "if I ever get to looking like that, will you just chain me to a table leg. Don't ever let me get like that!"

Now he was like that. Though those who knew him privately often saw endearing and generous things, his drug use had gutted all but the most stubborn or exploitive relationships, and his public stunts had surpassed everybody's saturation point.

One day Sun visited the Goya Avenue complex. He had never totally recovered his equilibrium after Minnie Bell's death. He strolled through Jimmy's complex, examining some new additions. The place was sprawling over both sides of the street now. He went to Jimmy's office. It had just penetrated, he said, how big this thing was. He had been in such a fog it hadn't really hit him. Now he seemed to realize his son was a winner—a huge winner.

The Principality of the
Powers of the Air

> *"Wherein in time past ye walked according to the course of this world, according to the prince of the power of the air, the spirit that now worketh in the children of disobedience: Among whom also we all had our conversation in times past in the lusts of our flesh, fulfilling the desires of the flesh and of the mind . . ."*
>
> —Ephesians 2:2–3

This prince is known as Satan.

Once he made a commitment, Jimmy was passionate about it. Now he saw in the Bible his personal mandate to get on the air over the entire earth in order to bring about the Second Coming of Christ. But he didn't seem to remember that the same Bible warned that "the air" is the principality of Satan.

Maybe he misunderstood the battle. Certainly he fought ideology battles over the airwaves, dueling with Catholicism and pornography and sin; but the fleshly battles he fought in his head, in his demon-oppressed thought life and in the competitiveness he felt with other broadcasters, were also battles with the prince of the power of the air. Centuries of Christian grappling with the meteorology of heaven, from Tertullian and St. Jerome to St. Augustine through Cotton Mather and beyond, perhaps conditioned him to write off the prince as merely the entity who brought hail to punish the Egyptians and who threatens to unleash the winds of the apocalypse on humans of the future. Or maybe he wanted success so badly that he ignored the warning in Ephesians.

Jimmy never seemed to consider that the airwaves he coveted might turn out to be a magnifier of his battles with the flesh, a bigger arena to play them out, with bigger consequences.

In fact, it turned out exactly that way.

NINETEEN SEVENTY-SEVEN began a 15-year media spurt for the Assemblies of God. By the next year, one in four Assemblies churches was sponsoring its own local radio program. There were 30 religious television stations that year, with 30 more applications pending before the FCC. Most of the air time was for evangelical or fundamentalist programs. A 1979 Gallup poll commissioned by the magazine *Christianity Today* showed an astonishing 19 per cent of American adults considered themselves Pentecostal or charismatic.

Reagan's landslide victory in 1980 encouraged the fundamentalist Christian right to molt into its political persona. Sixty-two percent of white evangelicals voted for Reagan. (In 1984, it would be 80 per cent of all evangelicals; in 1988, the Christian right would help put George Bush in office, with one poll indicating that up to 93 per cent of them supported him.) Reagan had long courted them; in 1971, he had spoken of the book of Ezekiel at a fundraiser, saying that the fire and brimstone promised in Ezekiel must be nuclear weapons, and that the nation of Gog was probably the godless Soviet Union. "It can't be too long now," he told his audience, apparently referring to the end times. The next year, Oral Roberts addressed the Democratic National Committee.

In August 1980, Reagan had addressed 15,000 evangelical leaders at the National Affairs Briefing in Dallas, and openly endorsed their aims. He also met with Christian leaders at the Republican National Convention in Detroit that year. Their certainty that he supported them kept them focused on their political agenda for the next 12 years.

In 1979 the term Moral Majority had been coined for the new Christian right by Jerry Falwell, whose Thomas Road Baptist Church in Lynchburg, Virginia had over 15,000 members. His "Old Time Gospel Hour" television broadcast was culled from the church services. With Reagan in office for his first term, Falwell declared war on abortion, pornography, homosexuality, socialism.

There appeared to be a worldwide fundamentalist movement afoot, with the murder-suicides of over 900 American followers of Jim Jones' People's Temple in Guyana in 1978 and the taking of American hostages in Iran in 1979. The press coverage of those events, along with the explosive growth of satellite and cable television, gave the televangelists sudden visibility. Some of them would prove ill-prepared for this, but others would take to it readily. Pat Robertson was one of the latter. In April 1977 his CBN television network had dedicated its satellite earth station, the first owned and operated by a Christian ministry. Within a few years, he was being seriously considered as a presidential candidate.

Jimmy had no political aspirations, either in secular life or in the Assemblies of God. His old friend Richard Dortch, however, had risen high in the Assemblies. A respected district Superintendent for five years, Dortch was nominated for a top position at the denomination's headquarters in Springfield, Missouri in 1975. Though he withdrew from that competition, he was expected to eventually move into the top slot, General Superintendent.

In the fall of 1977, Dortch and his wife Mildred flew to Baton Rouge to visit the Swaggarts. For several days, they helped Donnie plan a big celebration of Jimmy and Frances' 25th wedding anniversary. The evening, hosted by Dortch, was a tribute to the Swaggarts' faith and tenacity.

Not long after that, Dortch made a decision that would bring him wealth and power and put him in the limelight, but would cost him his credibility with the national organization, require him to lie to Jimmy, require Jimmy to publicly rebuke him, and lead him to prison. In January of 1979, he accepted a position on the board of PTL, Jim Bakker's booming North Carolina television network and ministry.

Jimmy made *Time* magazine that year; it named him one of the country's six most popular electronic evangelists. He now had 600 radio stations airing his program in 25 countries (a total of 15,000 airings a month), and was broadcast on 250 television stations and several thousand cable outlets. His telecast was also being distributed overseas; in August it went from a half-hour to an hour. Seven hundred fifty thousand of his 34 gospel albums sold per year, for a total of over eight million.

Reporters materializing at Goya Avenue found most of the street taken up with ministry buildings and the television studio. Brisk, dedicated workers trotted everywhere, filling orders, filing, opening and sorting tens of thousands of letters, and packing albums, preaching and teaching tapes (three quarters of a million a year), lesson guides, books, and Swaggart-annotated Bibles.

People now attended his crusades every year in the hundreds of thousands. He conducted more than 30 exhausting crusades in 1979, some of them abroad. Less than four years before, his daily budget had been $35,000; now it was $75,000 and pushing toward $100,000 in the next few months as he planned to add 50 more stations.

Mickey continued to give Jimmy momentum. He was nominated for 1978's Best Male Vocalist by the Academy of Country Music. A major article appeared in *Esquire* about Gilley's, with its mechanical bucking bull and subculture of oil field workers who had found a sense of belonging at the cavernous club. In September, the "Today" show's Tom Brokaw visited Gilley's and did an interview with Mickey. It was like a shot of jet fuel to his, Jerry's, and Jimmy's careers. Mickey appeared on "Hee Haw," "Grand Ole Opry," "Pop Goes the Country," and other television shows that year. Jerry performed with him at several, stung that he was only an adjunct star but grateful for the lift, especially because he had faced another barrage of self-inflicted misfortune: emergency room visits, arrests for driving intoxicated, IRS liens, and lawsuits. In April, onstage at the Old South Jamboree in Walker, Louisiana, he had cursed the audience, kicked his stool into their midst, refused to sing, and then fainted onstage.

The national attention was flattering, and Jimmy wanted the exposure, but he didn't relish giving interviews. He was scared of the old bugaboos, derision and ridicule. He willingly gave interviews to the gentle Christian press, and of course he would never turn away publications like *Time*, but when the Baton Rouge newspapers or magazines showed up or a reporter called from New Orleans, he was often too busy, dashing off to Nashville, where he still taped his television broadcasts (though post-production now took place at the Goya Avenue studio), or off on a month's tour of Africa.

Frances didn't like the media, either. She was highly suspicious of secular reporters from the first, and instructed her office staff to fend them off with official ministry figures and a handful of *Evangelist* magazines and other publications, and then to find out where else they might be publishing the information they got. The important thing was to keep them away from Jimmy. He didn't understand how venal they were, how they could twist his words, or blow some little thing out of proportion.

"My mother saw through that game much quicker than he did," said Donnie later. "She can spot a phony twenty miles away. It doesn't matter how much sugar and spice is flowing."

Frances knew from years of publishing the *Evangelist* —gone from a folded sheet of typing paper to 24 pages that had a full staff, printed several signatures in color, and went out to half a million readers every month—how you can present information and arguments to maximize the effect you want but still stay on the right side of the truth. If she hadn't had the *Evangelist* to instruct her, though, the Pentecostal fiat of attributing every impulse to God would have conditioned her to the ways in which the truth can become soft and pliable in the hands of an able communicator.

Frances very much wanted to control the way she and Jimmy were seen by others. Knowing what the press had done to other evangelists, and knowing the potholes in their private life, she didn't want anyone to get any clues about anything. She handled the press.

"[Frances] is very businesslike," said Ed Pratt, a local reporter and long-time observer of the ministry. "She would only answer the questions I asked and no more. She was very cold. But she was a brunette then. Maybe she's warmer now that she's a blonde."

Indeed, by 1979 Frances had given herself a sleeker, more sophisticated look. Her round face became leaner; she lightened her hair, slimmed down, dumped her matronly double-knit dresses for more flashy, feminine garb, and started trying to get Jimmy into a diet and exercise program. A photo from that period showed Jimmy looking virile and handsome, and Frances the perfect preacher's wife, with ruffles and a casual blond coif. Jimmy projected openness, humor, and honesty in all the photos of him from that period. He came across as the straight arrow he wanted to be.

It made Frances angry that the news media seemed so cavalier with its power. Jimmy took the job of stewardship of the yearly $30 million or so in donations extremely seriously. It was one of the things about him that Frances most respected and admired, and it made her furious that so many in the media didn't see more of a difference between him and someone like Jim Bakker.

In March of 1978, Bakker had announced plans for his PTL organization to build Heritage University, which he projected would open in only five months with 300 graduate students and be an accredited, four-year university in five years. But instead of building a school that year, he came up with Heritage USA, a Christian theme park in Fort Mill, South Carolina that featured a huge water slide and shops full of kitschy merchandise.

And while he was hatching plans to expand the park with Christian time-share vacation condos, a 19th-century shopping village, a huge Christmas display including a giant whale, a 1,000-square-foot Wendy's shaped like a sand castle, and other frivolities, Jimmy was busy beefing up the services of his foreign missions and staffing what he proudly referred to as "the West Point of Bible colleges"—the new Jimmy Swaggart Bible College—on his ministry grounds in Baton Rouge.

In January of 1979, about the time Richard Dortch joined PTL, the *Charlotte Observer* broke a story about how Bakker had used hundreds of thousands of dollars, which had been donated to PTL for overseas missions, for other projects in the U.S. that he was more interested in. The law forbids anyone to raise money over radio or television for one purpose and spend it on something else, and the FCC started an investigation into the misspent money.

Bakker ranted to PTL's faithful that the government and the *Observer* were out to get his ministry, and that if anyone needed evidence that Satan was trying to stop the spreading of the Gospel, they need look no further than those two bodies. He threatened to march on Washington with 100,000 Christians to protest the FCC investigation.

Most Pentecostals were ready to believe it was Satan attacking, using reporters, revenuers, and commissioners—watchdogs that could easily be transmogrified into hellhounds. The Bible was literal, Bakker and Jimmy and other preachers were interpreting it for people, and if they said the devil was working through the news media, it was probably true. And it was self-feeding: camaraderie was cemented by the feeling of being an outsider, under attack. We expect to take some arrows for God, they said to each other. The apostles did it. It's the least we can do.

Bakker's viewers swamped their congressmen and the FCC with letters and calls about the FCC's witch hunt. Over the next three months, they gave $5 million more than PTL needed to cover expenses.

For years Billy Graham, worried that the feds would soon be prying into all areas of ministry and distressed at the lack of any display of accountability by most media evangelists to their constituencies, had pressed for a self-regulatory group. The Evangelical Council for Financial Accountability (ECFA) was founded in 1979, forbidding family-dominated ministry boards or bait-and-switch tactics to raise money, and requiring audited financial statements. Its parent arm, the National Religious Broadcasters, urged Bakker to cooperate with the FCC.

Jimmy, alone among the major televangelists, immediately published his financial statement. It had the effect of setting him apart from Jim Bakker, a distinction he welcomed. He disliked Bakker and his talk-show format with gaudy guests, often washed-up entertainers, gushing testimonials. Still, the loyalty of Bakker's viewers in the face of his misuse of funds must have been secretly encouraging. It indicated that if anything bad came out about Jimmy, he'd probably survive.

Jimmy didn't engage in bait-and-switch. He set limits on purchases and monitored budgets. He didn't buy expensive homes and cars and vote himself outrageous bonuses like Bakker. He took a $15,600-a-year salary, plus $400 expense money per month, which he used on the road to buy meals and incidentals. The ministry provided a car (in 1982, he still drove a Volkswagen) and a house allowance. He ate at drive-through hamburger stands. It made Frances angry that the secular press underplayed these factors.

Jimmy was proud to offer his financial statement. He was proud of the way he'd spent the money. As with the historical thrust of Pentecostalism, missions were his most important work, and his organization was spending hundreds of thousands of dollars to build churches and Bible schools abroad. Jimmy made the outlandish prediction that someday his ministry would funnel as much as $10 million into world missions. But in seven short years, he would make that pronouncement come true.

His overseas programs were models of good management, as was his operation at Goya Avenue. The staff—200 by 1980—met with Frances and Jimmy at 11:30 for daily prayer and meditation, an updating on activities, and prayers for whoever requested them. Everyone was kept informed, and communication was open.

Though he was unable to resist telling a reporter a schmaltzy—and probably apocryphal—tale of a torn-down old scrubwoman who handed him a whole week's salary, $32, for God's work, Jimmy ran a squeaky-clean operation aimed at one thing: spreading the Gospel.

Whether Frances liked it or not, though, evangelists were natural targets for skepticism. There was the old love-hate relationship with the press, time-honored from the days of the frontier. It was irritating to Frances how the local reporters kept writing about how nobody knew Jimmy in his own stomping grounds. ". . . most of Louisiana is unaware of [him]" said one, and another extended it to his public: ". . . to thousands in the evangelical church community, Jimmy Swaggart is an unknown." They mischaracterized him as distant and preoccupied to his staff, when he was actually well-liked among them.

Reporters who were given access to the merchandising operations and to Jimmy's, Frances' and Donnie's offices seemed to always end up looking for something bad to publish—his leather chair was a little opulent, and was it seemly for a preacher to have a *mahogany* desk? His magazine staff "packaged" his message instead of simply editing it. Or the *Evangelist,* filled with sermons, interviews, and essays, would be dismissed as a catalogue of gifts and trip offers.

The thousands of letters that arrived every day, ripped open and tossed right and left by sorters, might be portrayed as meat for the grinding maw of holy commerce, when the truth was that Jimmy had every letter read and categorized and responded to whether there was money in it or not. A staff of special counselors dealt with letters requiring personal answers.

If he had state-of-the-art musical equipment, there might be a snide comment about how "the Lord" wanted only the very best. The Swaggarts were never allowed to forget they were high school dropouts. They were portrayed as secretive if they declined interviews or refused to reveal expansion plans. Their name was misspelled.

The journalists covering the evangelical movement were surprised at the technological sophistication of the religious broadcasters. Billy James Hargis, before his downfall in 1976, had pioneered direct-mail methods of soliciting money, and was one of the first, in the 1950s, to get one of the machines that made it appear he had personally signed each letter to donors.

Reporters tracking Jimmy found an advanced computer system for direct mail and a well-run television post-production studio with the best video and musical equipment money could buy. His crusade video crew could handle audio, video, and lighting in the most challenging settings.

Given that televangelists had weekly shooting schedules (and often daily promotional chores), said religious media historian Quentin Schultze, the quality of their productions was extraordinary—easily as good as the production values of the networks. That, said Schultze, made critics uneasy. Technical competence and financial success did not comport with the hayseed image that separated evangelists from the mainstream. If the evangelists weren't easy to spot any more, they could insinuate their values into the mainstream.

The problem with their critics in the media, retorted the evangelists, was that they were used to having that seductive power all to themselves, and they didn't like it when some linthead from Alabama or Mississippi had as good a shot at defining American values as they did.

Ironically, Jimmy agreed with the media critics on one point: He couldn't stand the entertainment-driven formats of people like Bakker and Paul Crouch. They were supposed to be preachers of the Gospel, not talk-show clowns. In a few years he would rail about "pompadoured pretty-boys with their *hair* done and their *nails* done who call themselves preachers." The wives of those men—chiefly Tammy Faye Bakker and Jan Crouch, grotesquely mascaraed and wigged, and bedecked with gaudy outfits built around feathers, rhinestones, organdy, and sequins—were so far distant from the solid decency of women like Minnie Bell that they were beneath mention.

The Mission of the Air

Premillenialists like the Pentecostals focused not only on preparing the world for Christ's return, but on hastening it: they took to heart the words in Matthew 24:14, which said the end of the world would follow the preaching of the Gospel to all nations. Evangelizing the world was one of the main missions of the first General Council that formed the Assemblies of God in 1914 in Hot Springs, Arkansas.

In 1976, Jimmy expanded his radio and television shows to Africa, India, Ireland, Hong Kong, the Philippines, Taiwan, the West Indies, and Central America. He didn't go overseas himself much until about 1977. When the Oggs joined the ministry in 1980, Jimmy hadn't done a crusade overseas except in Africa and Australia. He had a strong mission in India, and was providing one meal a day for 7,000 kids in Calcutta, and helping missionary Mark Buntain build a 2,000-seat church there.

By 1979, Jimmy was saying that missions were his most important work. Third world populations, he said, were becoming more and more literate, and he had to get God's Gospel into their hands before, he said, Communism inserted its "gospel."

He had already built two churches in Mombasa, Kenya, and laid out $87,000 toward a Bible school in Nairobi. In late October 1980, he met with East African U.N. ambassadors to discuss the distribution of funds to address hunger, which he planned to start sending at the beginning of 1981.

He was also buying property for a Bible school in Brazil and had plans to distribute literature in the Philippines and China, and to help construct a church in Madrid.

The missionary work wasn't just to feed the hungry—it was to spread the telecast. Jerald Ogg, who had become Jimmy's crusade director, would contact an Assembly of God missionary in the targeted place. The idea was to first get on television and let people learn who Jimmy was and get familiar with his message. After a few months of airing tapes of the telecast, Ogg would organize a crusade there. After a presence had been established, the ministry would spend some money—set up a mission of some kind, help build a church or school or provide children with food and clothing. The mission might come before the crusade sometimes, but the advance guard was always television.

When Jimmy arrived, he would be approached with requests. His reputation for delivering on his promises was pristine.

"A missionary might tell him, we need $350,000 for something, and Jimmy would say, 'You got it,' " said Ogg. "And he meant it. He came through."

"When Jimmy made a promise like that," said a pastor of a large denomination, "it was like money in the bank."

The Assemblies of God had the largest missionary program in the world by the early 1980s, and Jimmy became no small part of it.

By 1981, Jimmy's telecast was on nearly 700 television stations. He worked from before sunup until the wee hours. The "Campmeeting Hour" morphed into a 30-minute teaching program, "A Study in the Word" which ran as a simulcast on WLUX.

He was creating controversy. There was a very negative reaction to a series of *Evangelist* messages in late 1981 and early 1982. Jimmy had written that dishonesty was showing up in the "positive confession" doctrine he'd benefited from himself for several years. He now felt that the message was exploitive and deceptive, and dishonest.

"Great announcements of mighty miracles and healings were being made to the public when, in fact, few healings or miracles were taking place," he said. He later disgustedly reported watching "a husband and wife team" who called out people with illnesses and reported that they were seeing these people healed. "The man closed the scenario," said Jimmy "by stating that somebody out there had a certain number of stocks (stocks and bonds), and they were supposed to give them to the work of the Lord, etc. I do not believe God was telling these people anything of this nature." Jimmy was almost certainly taking aim either at the Bakkers or Paul and Jan Crouch.

He feared speaking out would hurt his own ministry, and sure enough, other preachers who listened to him over his 600 stations let him know they weren't pleased—they were benefiting greatly from preaching the prosperity gospel and didn't like him putting it down.

He had a kind of vision during this period. It took place after a typical morning when he had arisen after midnight and again before dawn to pray and ponder his problems. He saw a great light with God-consciousness at its center, moving toward him.

"The closer the light came to me, the uglier I became. There were flaws that I had not seen before."

♦ ♦ ♦

Gilley's Club was so successful and its mechanical-bull-riding competitions so notorious that Mickey bought the business of the inventor, Joe Turner. His club sold Mickey Gilley belt buckles, windbreakers, designer jeans, and beer.

In 1980, *Urban Cowboy,* the story of the oil refinery workers who found a home at Gilley's, was released, starring John Travolta and Debra Winger; Kenny Rogers, Linda Ronstadt, and Johnny Lee all performed in the film. Mickey also had two hits in the top five country charts, to cap a triumphant year.

A script chronicling Jerry's life was rejected by Hollywood that year as "too dark," but the idea knocked around for years, with Mickey Rourke or Sean Penn playing Jerry. Jerry continued to invoke darkness; in January of 1980, he was booked for 10 nights at a club called dB's in Dearborn, Michigan. There he met 23-year-old Shawn Stephens, who would become his fifth wife—for three months, before she died under suspicious circumstances whose investigation by the Mississippi police seemed less than thorough, according to a *Detroit Free Press* investigative story in October 1983. Jerry wasn't charged.

It was 1980 before Jimmy held a major service in his adopted home town. His first Camp Meeting in Baton Rouge was at the Riverside Centroplex in July. Followers came from as far away as Canada, Hawaii, and Australia. Six thousand people showed up, a respectable number considering they were staying six days—though Jimmy had hoped to fill the auditorium's 13,000 seats.

The local ABC affiliate, WBRZ, did a special on him one week, wondering if it was okay for a churchman to be such a successful businessman, and asking whether he was more a preacher or an entertainer.

"I wanna put out the hook, the bait," he replied. "I don't care [why] they come. It's not my ministry, my music, my preaching, my praying . . . but I can be a channel to spark an interest. . . . If people are just hooked on Jimmy Swaggart, they will be sooner or later very disappointed."

Local papers compared him to Graham, Robertson, and Falwell, and marveled that he was right here, the best-kept secret in Baton Rouge. Of course, they found problems with his "healthy ego" and hinted that it might be unfair for him to have his little tract house on Tara and ask for donations. They called him "a wealthy man." They reported his controversies: he called most preachers "dead" and said they reduced the Bible to "nothing but dusty old book reports."

Donnie introduced him onstage as "my daddy." Jimmy introduced certain members of his entourage as being "saved from dope addiction," or "saved out of rock and roll."

Living, he said was simple: no smoking, drinking, lusting or other aspects of the "vile, profligate, debased, filthy, rotten, dead-relating" secular world. No movies, not even G-rated ones, because they feature Coming Attractions.

At that first camp meeting in Baton Rouge, he collected $120,000 in fifteen minutes one day, asking for 1,000 believers to write him a check for $100. Then he passed plastic buckets around, asking those who could give anything at all to just put it in.

Outside the auditorium, albums sold for $6, tapes $5. Also for sale were books, pen sets, bowls, paper weights, belt buckles. In a fundraising brochure, beautifully written and designed, Jimmy asked for $500 chunks for a new ministry headquarters to be built on Bluebonnet Road. The brochure said it would be a sacrifice, he knew it and God knew it. But God would reward you for it. The brochure ended with the utter pragmatism he mixed in with his lofty goals: "We must have the funds in soon, because I refuse to waste the Lord's money on high interest rates."

The press clucked at the cheekiness of it, but they didn't understand: people *wanted* to give to the Lord's work, and *wanted* to pay for the places Jimmy had taken them with music and words and passion over the past few days.

"I been watching him a lot on TV," said a woman. "Me and my boys all took our vacation at the same time so we could come down here. Say, I don't guess anybody'd know if I could go up and talk to Jimmy, you know, touch him."

♦   ♦   ♦

It was 1981, said Donnie later, that the ministry hit warp speed. " . . . all of a sudden somebody pulled open the blinds, the light hit us, and we just exploded across the nation."

Jerald Ogg remembered what it was like at Goya Avenue when he and his family arrived in 1980. He had called Donnie around Christmas of 1979, and the Swaggarts had immediately hired him as crusade director. It was a hive when he got there with his wife and children. Each week a special U.S. Postal Service 18-wheeler was sent down from Memphis to the ministry's shipping dock to deliver the 70,000–100,000 pieces of mail the ministry took in. Then every month, the *Evangelist* was shipped to its more than 600,000 readers worldwide. Janett Ogg was the magazine's first managing editor. She took it from 12 or 16 pages to more than 60 over the next eight years. Jenelle Ogg, Jerald's sister, eventually became Dean of Women at the Jimmy Swaggart Bible College.

There were two huge buildings and a storage warehouse, no room for an office for Jerald. Then Jimmy rented an office complex across the street, and put the crusade office there. Jerald had never seen a more sophisticated computer operation. Jimmy and Frances had the best of everything. "I left town for a week," he said, "and when I got back, I'd lost my office to computers." Averaging 35 crusades a year wasn't unusual, said Ogg. "One year we did 20 or so one-nighters." They cut back when television responsibilities got too heavy.

Pat Robertson was now an inspiration; in 1981, as head of CBN, he commanded a $50 million headquarters, four television stations, six radio stations, a missionary radio station, a recording company, a programming service that provided shows to over 3,000 cable systems, a news network, a university, and a satellite earth station. He built it all from one television station. One of the first cable networks, CBN would soon become The Family Channel.

ON MONDAY, March 30, 1981, the ministry received a piece of mail that said, "Ronald Reagan will be shot to death and this country turned to the left." It was mailed from Grand Junction, Colorado, in a pre-addressed "Jimmy, please pray that —" envelope torn out of the *Evangelist*. That was the day John Hinkley shot the President, his Press Secretary Jim Brady, and two others outside the Washington Hilton Hotel. Hinkley's parents lived in Evergreen, less than 200 miles from Grand Junction. Jimmy turned the notes over to local FBI authorities, but first fed the zip code into the ministry computer and came up with a name. The FBI asked him not to reveal it.

Even though there was no direct link between Hinkley and the Swaggart ministry, it seemed to be another indicator of some connection between political majorities and religious movements. Pope John Paul II was also wounded by a gunman in an assassination attempt two months after Reagan—who was the first president to establish diplomatic ties with the Vatican.

The previous year both presidential candidates, incumbent Jimmy Carter and Ronald Reagan, had sought the "born-again vote" by courting leaders like Bakker, Falwell, Robertson, and Jimmy. In April 1980, for example, the Bakkers had been invited to a White House reception held by First Lady Rosalynn Carter, and Bakker had spoken at a Washington For Jesus rally, excoriating the government's actions on school prayer, abortion, and the FCC's investigation of PTL. The day before the election that fall, Bakker was invited to fly aboard Air Force One from Memphis to Jackson, Mississippi and pray with President Carter.

TEXAN-TURNED-CALIFORNIAN Zoe Vance, 13 years older than Jimmy, had inherited royalty interests in an oil field from her father. Her only child, a son named David Malcolm, had died of kidney disease at age 16 after a painful illness. Then she was widowed, and she entered a life of thoroughbreds, parties, vodka, and younger men who took gifts and money from her, including a house and an Italian sports car for one of them. One beat her up.

In 1976, she made out a will leaving most of her estate to a medical research facility established in David Malcolm's name.

A couple of years later, lonely, ill, and suicidal, she started watching Jimmy. He reminded her of her late husband, Dude, who had been a musician. Her donations to his ministry quickly caught Jimmy and Frances' attention. First she donated her house, then all her jewelry, and then some $2 million in cash.

She was thanked at a crusade, brought up to the front to be hugged by Jimmy and Frances in front of the congregation—a small, frail woman with gray hair and a shy smile. She looked so ordinary and—as her only relative, a wealthy sister, would later claim in a lawsuit against Jimmy—vulnerable. Because of cataracts, she could no longer drive, and she walked hesitatingly. She looked at least 70, even though she was only in her late 50s. She had lost a lung to radical cancer surgery, and it was hard to imagine that she had lived a wild life and could, as her executor would later say, drink and cuss like a sailor.

She became attached to the Swaggarts, growing more distant from her old social companions, some of whom had perhaps hoped to inherit part of her considerable remaining fortune.

In August of 1980, the Swaggarts were invited to visit Vance at her $1 million California beach house. They gave her solace, showing her how to surrender to the Holy Spirit, to die to the world and to understand that Jesus was the bringer of a great gift: her eternal life. They taught her that none of us can do anything to earn this gift. Jimmy sang and played the organ in her home, the first time a man had sat down and made music at it in the 11 years since Dude's death. Jimmy baptized her in the Pacific Ocean, a bold and rather erotic impulse, as the waves affirming life and creation washed over them.

A year later, she died of lung cancer. She had changed her 1976 will a month after Jimmy baptized her, leaving her entire estate—worth $7.6 million—to the Jimmy Swaggart Evangelistic Association instead of to the medical research institute. It was the largest donation the ministry had ever received.

Zoe's wealthy sister, Mary Leone, challenged the will in Texas and California courts. An Episcopalian who detested evangelicals, she claimed a "systematic, sophisticated, and manipulative effort" by Jimmy to get her sister's fortune.

Bill Treeby, the ministry's longtime lawyer, rebutted that her interest in Jimmy was a last-ditch effort to find something meaningful in her last years, and that she'd quit drinking and become healthier after becoming a regular follower of his crusades. But the bottom line, Treeby said, was that she was of sound mind when she made out her will.

The suit dragged on for over two years, finally settling 70 per cent of the money on the ministry and 30 per cent on the research foundation. The Swaggarts got none of Zoe's gold, diamonds, or pearls, some of which were family heirlooms. But the Vance case had a classic exploitation profile, and Jimmy would have to watch it presented several times in the media in a way that made him look as bad as possible.

Guarding the Temple

B y this time, a needed shell was being built around Jimmy. Frances made sure there were plenty of layers of personnel and rules between him and reporters, followers, and employees. Jimmy's crusade schedule was already killing. He didn't need to be dealing with people's problems, ambitions, or crushes.

In 1979 he had outlined exhaustive plans for expansion: First, he wanted to increase his overseas spending from a few million to at least $10 million per year. "We plan to become involved all over the world," he said. But don't think he was going to slow down his radio, television, or crusade efforts, he said. On the contrary, he was expanding them.

He was doubling the telecast to an hour and expanding the number of stations and cables on which he was buying time—a huge financial commitment that would bring his daily expenditures to $150,000. He was continuing a commitment to release a new gospel album every year, and he would hold one of his elaborate crusades three weekends out of four. He was planning the Bible college and seminary. He was doubling the ministry's office space, already the size of two football fields. He was going to build a 1,000-seat on-site chapel for employees and their families and friends. The *Evangelist* was also doubling in size.

Those were just the projects he allowed to be revealed to the press. He had not even told them the extent of his plans for a huge new ministry complex on Bluebonnet Road.

He had learned a big principle: get on the air, everywhere you can, as fast as you can, and the money will come.

Frances was fiercely protective of him. He was even more someone to look up to than ever. He used his talents honorably. He had many flaws, but she saw him cultivating the good things about himself, choosing good role models and working on his weaknesses.

In his 1976 autobiography, Jimmy portrayed her as always going along with him, being continually supportive and encouraging. She prayed and fasted alongside him, took huge burdens off him, and raised his child under extremely difficult circumstances. Over and over she provided critical strength, patience, and judgment. He admired her at least as much as she did him. "A woman can either make or break a man's ministry," she reflected. "You can help your husband excel or you can hold him back."

He had to be protected from women. By now, Jimmy had learned the hard way not to take any telephone calls at revivals. All of them went to Frances, Donnie, or other crusade team officials. This created grudging feelings among followers who felt Jimmy thought he'd gotten too important to deal with them. They didn't understand how tiring the crusades were. It was impossible to be accessible to anyone who called.

But mainly, it was because he had found that "too many times the telephone would ring and when I picked it up, it was a young lady who had a 'problem.' " His old mentor, A.N. Trotter, had pointed out that corruption can leach into even the most healing and well-meaning mission, he remembered. " . . . preachers, sitting for hours listening to one sad tale of woe after the other—garbage, filth, all the problems befalling the human race—are bound to be affected. It gets into their subconscious and many have fallen because of it. Temptation becomes great. The husband does not understand, but the *pastor* will understand. So the lady makes her appeal and the damage is done."

In late 1980 and in 1981, trouble of this sort reared its head in his denomination. Two events happened that would become very important in Jimmy's life.

One he didn't know about at the time. It took place on December 6, 1980. In Room 538 of a Sheraton Hotel in Clearwater, Florida, near Tampa, Jim Bakker, 40, engaged in sex with 21-year-old church secretary Jessica Hahn, starting the chain of events that would lead to a huge collision with Jimmy in six years. This liaison was arranged by John Wesley Fletcher, the Assemblies of God preacher who had become a Bakker protégé and around whom rumors of homosexuality and drunkenness were already swirling.

The second was that Lynette Goux, yet another member of Marvin Gorman's New Orleans congregation who had consulted him about her marital problems, went to Gorman's motel room during a 1981 telethon, laid on the bed, took off her blouse, touched his crotch, and pulled him down and started kissing him. Though they extricated themselves without committing adultery, Goux felt guilty and scared because she had, in fact, been seeing Gorman for several months in an improper way, meeting him for counseling and driving with him to remote places to talk in the car. It had started with friendly and affirmative hugging, then moved to kissing and fondling.

Goux's husband, Ronald, was Executive Vice President of the Jimmy Swaggart Evangelistic Association, the only top official who wasn't a family member. Lynette called Frances and poured out her troubles.

Frances advised her to speak to Jimmy, who questioned her and found that Gorman had bought her gifts, and that her husband Ronald had tapped the phone, recording long, intimate conversations between her and Gorman.

She confessed to her husband. Jimmy felt satisfied that no adultery had taken place, but he resolved to speak to Gorman.

A short time later, he ran into Gorman at the airport and asked him to drop by the Goya Avenue office next time he was in Baton Rouge. In a few weeks, Gorman showed up, and they went into Jimmy's office and closed the door.

Jimmy told him what he'd heard, and asked him it if were true. Gorman, he said, wept, and admitted to kissing and petting in the car. He denied he'd tried to seduce Goux in the motel room, though. Jimmy felt he was lying, and tried to worm it out of him, telling him he just didn't believe a man would be in a situation like that and not even try to "get her in bed." Gorman was silent, so Jimmy let it go, moving on to the next question: was this the only woman? Was this it? Gorman said yes, absolutely.

He asked Jimmy if the District Superintendent of the Assemblies needed to know about this. Jimmy said no, if he would promise it was over and Marvin would go straight now. Gorman assured him it was just an insignificant departure. "I don't want this to come back and haunt me," he fretted. Jimmy agreed to keep it to himself.

Marvin left, having failed to mention that an almost identical motel-room-blouse-off-grab-crotch incident had taken place in 1978 with Lynda Savage. Nor did he mention that that incident had bloomed into a three-year affair that was going on at that very moment.

DONNIE'S HIGH SCHOOL graduation had been a triumph for Jimmy and Frances, healing some of their dropout stigma. It was a tribute to Donnie's Frances-like toughness, for he had found secular school rough sledding.

As an adult, he was constantly compared to his father, and blamed for returning the press's hostility. "He has zero—none of the charm—of his father," said a reporter. "You know, his father is a commanding person, he has this deep voice—when he talks, you listen." Donnie didn't inherit the voice, but that wasn't his fault.

Donnie had not lasted long in college, transferring from Louisiana State University to Southwestern Bible College in Waxahachie, Texas in 1974 and then dropping out to join the ministry as crusade director, planning 30 or more crusades a year. It was a big job for a 20-year-old, and twice Jimmy got mad and fired him. Donnie took a job selling shoes. But under Frances' tutelage, he hung onto the position until 1980, when Jerald Ogg, Sr. took over.

While he was in Waxahachie, he met a Mississippi girl, a preacher's daughter, and fell in love. Debbie Robertson was fragilely elegant, very feminine, with high cheekbones, black hair, and brown eyes. They were married at a small Assemblies of God church outside Louisville, Mississippi in 1974. Debbie began working in the office and playing piano with the crusade team.

The year before the wedding, Jimmy had started a serious overhaul of his sound. One of the musicians he hired was Dwain Johnson, who played bass guitar and sang harmony with Jimmy. It was a union that would last nine years, perhaps bittersweet ones for Donnie, who had to sit back and watch another young man become his father's musical protégé.

In 1974, the ministry bought a house on Cyndal Street, in the East Baton Rouge subdivision of Sherwood Oaks. Dwain Johnson and his wife Janet moved into it.

Everything was fine for at least four years. In February of 1978, the Johnsons purchased the house for $55,000—a very reasonable price—with the caveat that the ministry could take it back within the next six years if things didn't work out for some reason. Janet gave birth to a son, Kristopher, in 1980.

Around that time, Debbie Swaggart and Dwain Johnson began having an affair.

It eventually surfaced, and in June of 1982, there was a big confrontation at Donnie and Debbie's house. The two couples involved were there, along with a friend of Janet's and two of Debbie Swaggart's relatives.

Jimmy arrived, furious, fired Johnson on the spot, and demanded that he vacate the house on Cyndal Street. Johnson left, and Jimmy turned to Janet.

"Tell that no good husband of yours if he is in town tomorrow I'll kill him!"

Janet Johnson believed him. She rushed home and told her husband of the threat. Then she took her son and went to stay with a friend.

Dwain Johnson also took the threat seriously. He was packing to leave town when he heard a car drive up and saw Jimmy get out. He fled out the back, hid in the neighbor's bushes, and watched through the windows as Jimmy went inside and stomped through every room, looking for him.

The next day Jimmy called Dwain. "I want to tell you something. I want you out of that house. I'm going to give you until Monday morning. If you're not out first thing Monday I'll have you taken out on a stretcher. I won't do it personally but I'll have it done."

Jimmy had taken in Dwain Johnson and worked with him like a son for nine years. Their relationship survived a drinking period Dwain fell into before his son was born. He also admitted smoking marijuana sometimes. Neither Jimmy nor Frances would have tolerated those for long, but moving in on Debbie Swaggart was downright treachery.

Jimmy's outrage might also have been on behalf of Frances; he always went to bat for her, and her guilt about the way Donnie had been raised made her fierce. Dwain had usurped Donnie's rightful place in a way; maybe if

Donnie had had a more normal childhood, he could have had music lessons and developed whatever talent he had.

Whose idea had it been to keep Donnie imprisoned in that car for over 10 years, subjecting him to constant ridicule and rejection at school and wiping out his childhood? It was Frances who mentioned guilt about Donnie in an interview, saying it was why she and Jimmy never had another child. But why feel guilty if you know you're doing what the Lord wants? No wonder Frances insisted her work was all for the Lord. It would be unbearable to think she had sacrificed her son for her own ambition. It was Jimmy who said the reason he stopped traveling and bought a house was because he couldn't bear seeing Donnie suffer any more.

A source close to the ministry said that when Frances first found out something was going on with Dwain and Debbie, she isolated the two, instructing the staff and employees not to speak to them.

That October, the Johnsons sued Jimmy and the ministry for $2.5 million, alleging wrongful termination, humiliation, mental anguish, trespass, and deprivation of their home. Johnson complained that the ministry had never paid him royalties on any of the music he recorded, nor given him any vacation pay; nor did the ministry give him severance pay nor any information about what might be owed him under the ministry's retirement plan.

Debbie Swaggart was replaced by another pianist.

"Their affair upset Jimmy because it would cause distrust, and negatively affect the ministry," David Beatty surmised about Jimmy's rage. "People would quit sending in money."

ON FEBRUARY 4, 1982, four months before the showdown at Donnie's house, Jimmy flew to Ferriday. Arthur Gilley, Mickey's father, had passed away at the age of 84. Jimmy preached at the service, along with his cousin Gerald Lewis and two other ministers. His cousins had been in Baton Rouge only days before—Mickey had performed at the Centroplex on January 22 and Jerry at the Texas Dance Hall on the 29th.

The one p.m. services were held at Evangel Temple Assembly of God in nearby Crestview, the Gilleys' adopted church. The church was packed with relatives because of the draw created by Jimmy, Jerry, and Mickey.

The services were a little chaotic; the highway patrol stopped the entourage on the way to the cemetery and informed Mickey that he'd driven off without his mother. Jerry had arrived so wired that he didn't recognize some of his relatives. At the end of his sermon, Jimmy gave the altar call, aiming a special arrow at Jerry as always: "Whosoever among you believes you wouldn't go to heaven with Uncle Arthur if you died today, come forward." There was nothing Jerry could do but come forward. When Jimmy asked him point blank in front of the crowd if he would accept Jesus as his saviour, Jerry turned and left.

Shortly after that, Jerry was onstage at a club in Columbus, Ohio while Jimmy was there on a crusade. He was playing a raunchy song, "Meat Man," with a Bible on his music rack, so bombed that Jaren, his fourth wife, called Jimmy at his hotel, hysterical. Jimmy drove over to the club, walked onto the stage, and took the mike away from Jerry's face in the middle of a garbled song. Jerry was flabbergasted. "Why Jimmy Swaggart! Son, what are you doing here?" Jimmy told the audience who he was, and said he was taking his cousin home. He paid the promoter in cash and took Jerry back to Baton Rouge with him. After seven sober days, Jerry left.

At the time of the struggle with Dwain Johnson in the summer of 1982, the Baton Rouge news media started getting serious about covering the ministry. Again, it was partly because of notoriety brought on by Jerry—on June 8, two days before Jimmy's confrontation at Donnie's, Jaren Lewis, Jerry's fourth wife, was found drowned in a friend's swimming pool, just before final divorce papers were to be served. She had been on food stamps for two years because Jerry refused to support her; she left a 10-year-old daughter, Lori Lee, whom she had always said was Jerry's but whom he refused to claim.

During 1982, Jimmy's preaching reflected the strain of dealing with the Johnson and Gorman sexual affairs. He said Pentecostal churches were winking at dancing and movies. He lamented that they'd become self-conscious about members getting the Holy Ghost because it wasn't good for the denomination's new, more upscale image as its leaders became a force in politics. An appalling number of Pentecostal preachers had drinking problems now, he claimed.

"In the last few months," he wrote, "I believe I have witnessed the fall of more Christians to sin and adultery than in the last five years put together." The sexual revolution was doing its job.

◆　◆　◆

The Bluebonnet Road project was what woke the reporters up.

The plans for a huge new complex near Interstate 10 southeast of downtown had not been publicized. If you weren't a subscriber to the *Evangelist*, or hadn't picked up a brochure at a camp meeting asking for money for a new facility on Bluebonnet Road, you wouldn't know. "See, this wasn't taken seriously early on," said Ed Pratt of the *Baton Rouge Morning Advocate*. "Swaggart started grabbing attention when these great huge enormous holes started appearing in the ground."

By May of 1983, two white concrete administration buildings were finished and ready for occupancy on 100 acres on Bluebonnet. They contained

100,000 square feet and cost $5 million. The floor space was only one-fifth of what was planned for Phase One of the Jimmy Swaggart World Ministry Center. The broad concrete walkway up to the front doors had brass-lettered Bible Scriptures set into the sections. The flags of 40 nations—everywhere the telecast went—flanked the walkway.

Inside, the ministry's tape production, dubbing, shipping, packaging, and mailing were already underway. WLUX had been moved to the grounds. Jimmy's spacious second-floor office, lined with best-selling albums and decorated with photos, plants, and discreet lighting, was flanked by a dozen other private offices, carpeted and equipped with nice furniture and computers. A large secretarial pool stood in the center of the second floor. Downstairs in the designer-decorated lobby, a fountain splashed and a big red book memorialized donors of $500 or more who had helped build the center. Security guards guided visitors to a desk to register and obtain a badge, because, as Jimmy said, "There is nothing like a religious kook."

A million-dollar warehouse for Jimmy's five 18-wheeler mobile television trucks sat next to the site of a second warehouse, to cost $2 million. Also planned for Phase One were the Zoe Vance Teleproduction Center, another $5 million, and the octagonal Family Worship Center, $8.9 million. The new center was dedicated on Sunday, May 8, 1983.

Near the end of 1982, *Newsweek* had prepared a feature on Jimmy, noting that he was reaching 1,880,000 households, had sold more than 12 million record albums, and had taken in more than $60 million in 1982. It touted the new World Ministry Center complex, citing a $30 million price tag for the completed project. The *Evangelist* now had a circulation of 800,000—close to that of a major urban newspaper. In fact, *Newsweek* noted, Jimmy's appeal was no longer so much to the "biscuit and syrup kind of folk" who had formed his message as to the largest urban markets—Los Angeles and New York. It noted that in September, he had to turn away 5,000 followers at Madison Square Garden.

The writer, Kenneth Woodward, admired his "left-hand 'walks' up the keyboard, surprising arpeggios and tremolo flourishes" and his ability to "speak for hours without notes—shouting, crying, whispering into the microphone as if it were the ear of Lazarus."

ON THE FRIDAY morning before he was to preach in Columbus, Ohio, where he pulled Jerry offstage, Jimmy awakened at 2 a.m. He'd had a nightmare, he wrote, a graphic vision of the message he was planning to preach. It was about the Biblical rebellion of Korah, the Levite who conspired to challenge Aaron's priesthood and Moses' authority, and the destruction that ensued—Korah's followers were swallowed up by the earth and other rebels visited by a plague that killed over 14,000. He wrote that he had a vision of people "screaming and crying out, clutching their throats and gasping for air—as the plague of sin strangled and ultimately destroyed them."

He had the powerful conviction, he wrote, that the same thing was happening all over America at that moment, and he identified with Aaron, who ran among the people with his censer of atonement. Jimmy got up and stood next to his hotel bed and doubled over sobbing. Sin was killing people all over the world. "You've got to warn them," God said. "You've got to run as fast as you can." But Korah's rebellion had to do with power, not sin. It seemed Jimmy was hunting for any sign that Minnie Bell and Ada and Frances were right, that it was up to him to evangelize the whole world.

Petra

The central place on earth for a preacher of the Gospel was Israel.
"Seeing the place where Jesus walked, the garden, the tomb—it really [did] something to [Jimmy]," said Jerald Ogg. "The Via Dolorosa, Gethsemane, Calvary . . . it comes alive, Golgotha, the garden, the empty tomb, the Upper Room." Jim Rentz, co-pastor of Jimmy's local congregation in Baton Rouge, had done a small tour before 1980, and set up a 1980 service in the Upper Room. Israel needed dollars, said Ogg, and its tourism department had opened things up. "You bring 500 people in, they eat a lot of food, pour a lot of money into the local economy, so it's pretty easy to get cooperation for something like a service in the Upper Room."

But the Middle East was not an easy sell. Though Israeli Premier Menachem Begin and Egyptian President Anwar Sadat had shared the Nobel Peace Prize in 1978, the Shah of Iran was forced into exile in 1979 by the Islamic fundamentalist coup led by the Ayatolla Khomeini in which Americans were held hostage for over a year. The U.S. Embassy in Tripoli was attacked by an angry mob, and the U.S. ambassador to Afghanistan was kidnapped by Muslim terrorists and killed in a gun battle.

The next year, the Palestinian mayors of Israeli-occupied towns were injured in bomb attacks; the Turkish government was upset by a military coup; Iraq invaded Iran. A few months later, Israel bombed an Iraqi nuclear plant near Baghdad and was unanimously condemned by the U.N. Security Council. Then U.S. jet fighters shot down two Libyan planes over the Gulf of Sidra; shortly after that, Egyptian President Sadat was assassinated.

Still, the ministry sponsored a major tour in 1980, with 500 pilgrims. The ministry planned several tours a year, canceling only one after Libya shot down an American plane. Jimmy produced videos there for fundraising purposes and to promote future tours.

Jimmy was inspired by every spot he visited. He stood on top of Masada and looked out over the Dead Sea at Jericho, one of the oldest cities on earth. Contemplating the lush plains around the buried sites of Sodom and Gomorrah, he reflected on the wickedness of those prosperous towns—so much that God had removed every speck of them from the planet. He imagined Moses and his sister Miriam, singing and dancing unto the Lord as they celebrated the parting of the Red Sea. His denomination was the only Christian one left that had any form of sacred dance at all.

He especially identified with David, the sweet psalmist, slayer of Goliath, carver of empires unmatched in ancient Israel, adulterer who paid dearly. The places and characters of the Holy Land were vivid to Jimmy from childhood—Nazareth, where Jesus spent his boyhood; Capernaum, the village on the Sea of Galilee where Jesus found Andrew, James, Peter and John; Hebron, in the hills of Judah where Abraham built an altar, and where he, Sarah, Isaac, Rebekah, Jacob, and Leah were said to be buried in the cave of Machpelah.

Jimmy was returning from Israel in 1982 as Zoe Vance's sister and Dwain Johnson prepared their lawsuits against the ministry. On this trip, he had visited the ancient Jordanian city of Petra, the capital of the Arabic kingdom of Nabatea from the 4th century B.C. to the second century A.D., that Jimmy felt was filled with evil. It was on a major caravan route, and Jimmy called it "similar to Las Vegas, Atlantic City, the movies, or pay TV of today. In it were concentrated the gambling dens, the floor shows, and all fleshly sins common to that era."

Esau had lived here. Rethinking the story of Esau and his estranged brother Jacob, Jimmy wanted to visit the place where the wicked, worldly brother had spent his time. Esau would have been a talk show host or MTV star today, wrote Jimmy, and Jacob would have been "one of those 'odd' Jesus people—those people who aren't really 'with it.' " But the man of God is always reviled, he wrote, while "The rock star staggers across the stage with eyelids drooping, overcome by the effects of drugs, almost unconscious in his performance of songs that deify adultery, fornication, and rebellion."

He was struck by the beauty of the abandoned city, now a major archaeological site. You have to walk a narrow path through a deep cleft in rock walls that tower hundreds of feet on either side to get to the city. He noted predictions that Israel would take up residence in Petra during the Great Tribulation of the Antichrist because it is a naturally defensible spot. But, climbing the narrow path to the city, it didn't occur to him that Petra could also have symbolized reconciliation—of mind and body, desire and detachment—as easily as symbolizing sin, lust, and fornication. As the Book of Matthew says, "strait is the gate, and narrow is the way, which leadeth unto life, and few there be that find it." That statement is a metaphor for the process of physical conception as well as for spiritual rebirth.

He stood in the place, conjuring instead the sin that had happened there. "One could sense the dancing girls," he wrote, "the torches as they illuminated the great broadways, the huge buildings carved out of solid rock, the soldiers laden with the spoils of war, the gambling, sinning, and wallowing in the filth of the flesh."

Anyone looking back could see a shift in Jimmy about this time. Evidence would surface in a few years that he was deeply into pornography by now. Perhaps he had made some rationalization that it would be good to really know this matter of the flesh fully. He had already noticed that his own difficult childhood had helped his sermons immensely. He understood meanness, parsimony, lust, drunkenness, cheating, envy, pressure, even madness— because he saw it all growing up. His compassion for people who were in sin, broken and humiliated, pierced his listeners to the heart. He truly did know the blessing of forgiveness, of sweet relief in confession and prayer and submission to God. He was no phony—he knew exactly what he was talking about, and it gave him credibility.

But there was something about the story of Jacob and Esau in particular that invited a marvelous rationalization. Just before he reconciled with his brother, whom he had tricked out of his birthright, Jacob had a waking dream in which he wrestled desperately with an angel, pinned him, and made the angel bless him before he would let him go. The angel did, and Jacob was transformed into Israel, Prince of God.

But first the angel wounded Jacob in the thigh. As with the Fisher King in the myth of the Holy Grail, wrote Robert Johnson in his 1974 book *He,* this was "a wound to his maleness, his generative capacity, his ability to create." This wound meant a haunting incompleteness, the inability to touch happiness. The only relief the king felt was when he went fishing—the fish being one of many symbols of the Christ nature and also of the subconscious. Like Jacob and like the Fisher King, Jimmy was happiest when seeking his Christ nature. But that also meant fishing around in his subconscious for his carnal one.

Jimmy could identify strongly with Jacob. He had had many battles with the flesh in his life. Perhaps he could bring this flesh business to a conclusion once and for all by going into the crucible of his own Petra and confronting it, and then wrestling it to the ground like Jacob. He would demand its blessing, and be transformed. If he could be cured of that sexual wound, and be freed of the attraction pornography held, he could preach mightily about this sin without being touched by it any more, as he had done with so many other subjects. He would actually have credibility from God.

In its own way, it was a positively soaring ambition.

He was aware of the dangers. In "Victory Over the Flesh," a booklet he wrote at that time, he said that once you dabble in sin, you're hooked, there's no middle ground. The flesh "attacks the Christian with terrible, lustful desires that seem to choke off the victory of the child of God; a war he wages constantly. . . . This is war to the death."

He knew all the traps: even the great men of God, he said, think they're immune from sin; if you don't believe it, look at David, Moses, Solomon.

And he knew the inevitable outcome: "Oh you may get away with it for a time. It may seem you can 'play both sides against the middle.' But it will eventually take its deadly toll . . . We cannot defeat [Satan] at his own game, for he is the master of it."

Despite this, he did what he'd always done: took risks, went out onto the edge. It was a year or so after his visit to Petra that he was first rumored to have been seen in one of America's juiciest Petras right down the road—New Orleans.

Brimstone

Jimmy's writings in the *Evangelist* dabbled in a wide range of issues. He lamented the lack of leadership. Where are the Pattons, the MacArthurs, today? he asked in 1982. "Oh, there are plenty of *males* around," he wrote, "but not many men! Today, the world's picture of an 'American man' is the long-haired, dope-saturated, draft-dodging, nicotine-filled, effeminate, lazy degenerate . . ."

He railed against lawlessness: for every criminal executed in California in the past 20 years, he wrote, 40,000 citizens had been executed by criminals. "I've got an answer to uncurbed lawlessness," he declared: "The side-by-side answers of a double-barrelled shotgun!"

He preached vehemently against the Methodist Church's ordaining homosexuals, and he spoke out against the issues facing fundamentalists: abortion, feminism, Communism, secular humanism. He displayed contempt for the Catholic mass, but took on most mainline Protestant services too, as well as onstage healings.

Jimmy published a tract in the January 1983 Evangelist entitled "A Letter to My Catholic Friends," which he had issued the year before as a booklet. In it, he stated Catholic errors in thinking: that the pope was infallible; that sins could only be forgiven through a priest; that Mary, not Jesus, was the main intercessor with God. He said Catholic doctrines came from mythology and tradition, not the Bible, and that Catholicism led to a belief that it was the pope, not God, who saved people's souls. Catholicism, he wrote, was a false religion, and not a Christian one. Catholic tradition is in "complete contradiction to the Word of God," he wrote.

Catholics squirmed when he described them as "pitiful" for "[thinking] they have enriched themselves spiritually by kissing the Pope's ring." Catholic writers accused him of being arrogant and ill-informed, and much was made of the fact that he was a high school dropout. At one point a couple of Atlanta television stations even dropped his 30-minute weekly broadcast under pressure from the archdiocese. But most of his comments about Catholics were consistent with Pentecostal doctrine. When he said things like "Catholics . . . believe that they will get into heaven through their works. You won't get into heaven through works. You have to accept Jesus Christ as your savior and be born again," he was relaying the belief of his church. But he also had a gift for rubbing it in: "Most Catholics are Catholics two times a year: once at Mardi Gras and once at . . . I can't think of the other."

He further attacked priests, saying they pestered survivors to pay for prayers for the dead; that bordered on heathen ancestor worship. He said that in countries where Catholicism had dominated, "the people have been led into ignorance, superstition and sin." In those countries, he said, one saw "the vilest immorality and intellectual apathy."

His bold attack in a city that was more than a third Catholic was too much. It immediately produced a front-page response in the Baton Rouge Diocese's *Catholic Reporter,* from where it spread to other Catholic publications. It was reported in the local secular media, and then picked up by the national media.

These were only skirmishes in what was to be an ongoing war. He found his viewers liked his jeremiads against the "cult" of Catholicism, along with his attacks on secular humanism, the press, rock and roll music, and other targets.

He realized that the Catholic church's concern about his doctrinal accuracy and propriety were in direct proportion to its nervousness about the inroads Protestantism was making into traditionally Catholic countries. And Jimmy was huge in Latin America. He had funneled $8 million into El Salvador and Costa Rica alone. As one cleric said, "sects [like the Jimmy Swaggart Ministry] have taken advantage of the weaknesses of the Catholic church, and the church doesn't know what to do." Several years later, Pope John Paul visited Chile a few weeks after Jimmy had preached to an overflow crowd there of 80,000; it was in question whether the Pope drew a crowd much bigger.

WHILE PHASE ONE of the new World Ministry Center was being finished in early 1983, Jimmy was cooperating with WBRZ-TV on a documentary. Frances wasn't happy about it, but Jimmy felt strongly that they should cooperate with WBRZ if they wanted any control over how they were seen.

In late 1982, WBRZ had hired John Camp, a respected investigative reporter who had built a career in Boston and Miami, though he had lived and worked in Baton Rouge in the late 1960s. Shortly after he arrived back in Baton Rouge in 1982, two disillusioned ministry employees contacted him, concerned about what they perceived as a hard-edged business trajectory in an organization that was supposed to be concentrating on the Lord's work.

The ministry did have a huge marketing component. It would mushroom even more over the next few years, selling books, audio and video cassettes, record albums, the *Evangelist,* pamphlets, refrigerator magnets, mugs, book marks, jewelry, Bibles, songbooks, study guides, sweatshirts, cookbooks, and other items. It sold spaces for singles conferences, senior citizen convocations, ministry specialization conferences, children's camps, Holy Land tours, Hawaiian retreats, youth camps, domestic outreach programs, and prayer breakfasts.

It solicited money for natural disasters, planned giving, World Outreach partnerships, the upcoming Bible College and planned Seminary, and of course support for overseas missions, children's programs, and the television ministry. It had will and tax planning departments and offered to set up trust funds. At services, visitors filled out cards whose information was entered into the computer and then passed along to regional "missionaries" living in the visitor's area who would make follow-up calls and visits. These missionaries received computer printouts containing names, addresses, telephone numbers, and amounts of past donations, which they tried to persuade the brothers and sisters to increase.

Camp contacted other former employees, and found that most had left because they were disillusioned. Many had come from other ministries, envisioning the Swaggart organization as a huge, dynamic new force for bringing hundreds of thousands of souls to Jesus. But instead they had found a business, focused on dollars and cents, and a not-always-rational attitude toward employees.

Camp became intrigued. He realized, he said, that "there had been little real critical study of televangelism in print or broadcasting" up to that time. He decided to do a story.

He met George Journigan, the ministry's recently fired accountant and ex-Director of Finance. Journigan charged that, in the move from Goya Avenue to Bluebonnet Road, the ministry changed from "a very efficient, Spartan type operation" to mindless spending, repeatedly upgrading inexpensive functional buildings and building a "grandioso" television studio.

"I went from a $350 desk to a $1,700 desk" said Journigan, who estimated that the offices of Frances, Jimmy and Donnie cost $100,000 to furnish, while Jimmy "was on television crying for money for the starving children." Journigan said he was fired for questioning expenditures. He had asked Jimmy if he realized that only a third of the $3 million that had come in had been sent to the network of missionaries handling the monies in the field. The staff felt that if they were out there collecting money, they had a right to know how it was being spent. Jimmy disagreed. Journigan was told that, since he didn't seem to have anything better to do than worry about things that weren't his business, the ministry didn't need him.

Harry Bouton, Jimmy's longtime road manager and associate, was fired around the same time. Jimmy had also gotten angry about something one day and fired the whole development department.

"Harry Bouton was the most devoted, true blue—he'd stay up 'til four in the morning counting the money or something, and then be ready to go again the next morning," said David Beatty. "He and his wife Margie [a ministry pianist], they never would say a disparaging word about Jimmy." The Boutons and their children had worked for Jimmy more than ten years.

As Camp developed his investigation, it seemed to him that "Frances, principally, felt herself and the ministry to be above accountability." When employees showed concern about how rapidly the organization was expanding, Frances came down hard. She didn't think that was anyone's business. She seemed to have a fundamental disagreement with the media about how many questions evangelists who wanted to use the public airwaves should have to answer.

The more Camp learned about the Jimmy Swaggart Ministries, as the old Jimmy Swaggart Evangelical Association was now called, the more it reminded him of a cult: a group feeling of marginality and political disenfranchisement, a frustration with society and a desire to replace a lost sense of community and idealism, a deliberate separation from the mainstream, an unwillingness to share information about the leadership's finances and membership.

Camp acquired an audio tape of a ministry staff meeting in which Jimmy put him in mind of Reverend Jim Jones. Jimmy was bearing down on rumors of discontent at the way the ministry was run. He didn't take kindly to questioning of his decisions and actions. "Lemme tell you about the chain of command here: I'm *every link* in the chain!"

But when Camp had laid enough foundation to call Jimmy in early 1983, he found him surprisingly receptive. "Been waitin' for your call," he said to Camp. "Been hearin' you been talkin' to people all over the place. We live in a glass house here, we want to help you any way we can." Once Camp asked a few questions, Jimmy realized his adversary had a huge amount of inside information, so he decided to be open.

"There was no hint," though, said Camp, "of Jimmy having any involvement in sexual peccadilloes. There were rumors [outside the ministry] of Jimmy hanging out in cruddy motels with hookers, but everyone discarded them . . . I was dealing with insiders . . . They said such a thing was not possible with Swaggart."

The WBRZ special, "Give Me that Big Time Religion," aired May 19, 1983, shortly after Jimmy's World Ministry Center was dedicated. It won major broadcast awards—Peabody, DuPont Columbia, Scripps-Howard— but it inaugurated an era of bad feeling from Jimmy and Frances whose cloud only lifted a few times in the next decade.

The documentary's largest question, triggered partly by the ongoing FCC and IRS investigations of Jim Bakker's PTL, and partly by the disgruntled calls to John Camp from ministry insiders, was how money raised from donors was spent. George Journigan, who had come to Baton Rouge from Pat Robertson's CBN, said more than half the ministries' money was raised from children's appeals, but was diverted to luxuries; Frances' desk, for example, reportedly cost $11,000.

Siding with Journigan, and also fired, were the ministries' Director of Counseling, Noble Scroggins, and another employee who accompanied him to talk to Jimmy.

The documentary noted that Jimmy's gold record albums, which purportedly brought in much of the ministry's money, represented sales figures that weren't monitored by anyone except the ministry itself. It reported the purchase of land and plans to build a large residential compound on a toney stretch of Highland Road.

It said that seven members of the Swaggart family reportedly received $400,000 in salaries in 1982. It mentioned the Dwain Johnson case—which Jimmy would soon settle out of court—and described the settlement of the Zoe Vance case, which Jimmy felt the film tried to make look as bad as possible.

Frances was furious about the documentary, both when it was being made and when it aired. She was mad at Jimmy for cooperating with Camp. Several years later, she said, "I always say to the Lord, before he takes me to heaven, let me have it with the reporters."

In one segment, Camp was asking something delicate about the finances. Frances, wrathful under her pretty coif, said in an angry twang, "Jimmy, I don't like this, now this is just ridiculous!" Jimmy froze, his mouth open. He bit his cheek; alarm bells were clanging in his head. He shut his eyes, held his palm up, shook his head no.

"Frances was [called] the Dragon Lady of the whole operation," said Camp later. "She didn't have a lot of intimate friends. She was just a country girl cast into the role of running this huge company . . . Her attitude was, 'the money's comin' in, let's spend it.' This was a period when the ministry was expanding, expanding, expanding, and they had no fallback position, no reserves."

"Jimmy wanted everything the best, the fastest, the quickest," said Bob Anderson, who worked at the ministry for 14 years, mostly as purchasing agent. "If something was a day late, Jimmy and Donnie were on the phone [yelling]." There was huge pressure as the ministry expanded. "Some people couldn't take it, because they were scared to talk back to Jimmy or especially Frances. When Donnie and Frances gave conflicting directions sometimes, . . . they'd just try to comply, and get yelled at." Once an elderly employee who worked in shipping was told by Jimmy to destroy some tapes. Later Dennis

Westbrook, Jimmy's brother-in-law who was in charge of shipping, told the man not to do it. "Jimmy went into a rage," said Anderson. "He beat his chest, and yelled several times that HE was the boss, not Dennis, not Donnie. But he didn't mention Frances."

Another time, Anderson remembered, the ministry's printer discovered that the post office had botched a third-class bulk mailing. "He sent a driver six or seven hundred miles through a big snowstorm, driving like crazy," to the mail station where it should have been flown, so it would go out on time. But when the printer produced a clumsily-trimmed direct mail product one time, "Donnie knocked $12,000 off the bill." The printer bent over backwards to give the ministry breaks, according to Anderson. "They'd pay [the printer] $18 for Bibles and sell them for $100. Why did they have to act like that? It was Frances and Donnie, primarily."

Within two years, said Anderson, "I almost cracked up from the pressure from Jimmy and Frances."

WBRZ's documentary aired on a Thursday. In the pulpit the next Sunday, Jimmy lashed out at the station. He promised to buy time on the other two commercial stations in town to rebut the program. He put the reporters in his audience on notice that news coverage would be monitored. Tape recorders were confiscated at the entrance. He brought delighted laughter from his audience, calling WBRZ "that bunch down there [at Channel 2]," and vowing to "break that dog from sucking eggs." He noted that Camp had left town on vacation after the show aired, implying Camp was a coward who wanted to escape the reaction to it. Then he declared that the ministry loved Camp anyway.

He turned the media's secular methods back on them, citing a Gallup poll showing that 80 per cent of the 300 or 400 news officials who controlled what everyone read, heard, and saw didn't attend church or synagogue. Ninety percent of them were liberal, he said; 45 percent favored Socialism.

He didn't fall into the trap other besieged evangelists did, acting wounded and wrapping himself in Scripture. He didn't retreat into praying for his enemies. He didn't act bewildered and petulantly call the reporters "mean" like Jim Bakker did. He met his enemies on their turf. Christians were treated like a bunch of nuts, he said. He managed to see to it that whatever nuttiness the charismatic churches did actually possess was nullified by the unfairness of the media.

Newsweek was kinder to Jimmy than WBRZ. It quoted him saying, "This ministry is totally honest. There are no stocks, bonds, investments or secret slush funds. I do what God calls me to do. . . . Even though it takes business sense and many of the tactics used by the Fortune 500, it's the Holy Spirit that is guiding us."

On June 9, 1983, Jimmy bought an hour on WAFB-TV in Baton Rouge for his rebuttal, called "Give Me that Old Time Religion." He opened with a clip of his angelic lead singer, John Starnes, singing "God Bless America." He explained that John Camp had misinterpreted the information he was given. He aired clips of his work in underdeveloped countries and said the news media were constantly attacking religion and especially his ministry. His body language was the shrug-and-twitch of the boxer he had once hoped to be.

Repeatedly saying, "to be frank and honest with you," he admitted Frances had been given clothes and gifts, but said a Phoenix businessman had paid for her desk—which did not cost $11,000 as Camp claimed.

Jimmy finished his rebuttal of "Big Time Religion" by asking for money for a school in El Salvador. With characteristic chutzpah, he invited WBRZ to make a sizeable contribution and then keep tabs on how the money was spent and how the school was doing.

A few days later, Jimmy took out a full page ad in the *Baton Rouge Morning Advocate* and refuted WBRZ's accusations about the Children's Fund, the Swaggart family salaries, and Frances' desk. Less than three percent of 1982's fundraising, he said, dealt with Children's Fund specials.

Jimmy concluded by citing the 1981 *Washington Post* scandal in which a reporter, Janet Cooke, won a Pulitzer prize for a faked story about a drug-addicted child that got past her editors and the Pulitzer committee. He said the victims of WBRZ's attack would be the very children WBRZ was supposedly so concerned about.

The ad was clearly written, but filled with italicized words like the letter of a nut.

THE WBRZ FLAP pushed Jimmy around a corner, into an even tighter alliance with Frances. Never again would he feel he could trust the press. He had felt a certain prickly camaraderie with John Camp, Camp said later, because of the reporter's well-publicized bout with alcoholism, which had caused him grave family problems that he'd faced publicly. Jimmy had created a ministry program for alcoholism, "running full page ads in the paper for it, advertising a Christian cure, as opposed to A.A.," said Camp, who was chair of the Baton Rouge Council on Drug Abuse at the time. Jimmy's rival program attacked secular cures and Camp had to recuse himself when the Council responded to Jimmy's attacks.

"Jimmy carried a certain resentment that I had overcome my alcoholism," said Camp. Frances, coming from an alcoholic father, was grimly dead-set against drinking and perhaps similarly resentful at Camp's success. "I hate alcohol," she said in an interview. "Any preacher that wants to say it's all right to drink, I'd love to wring his neck."

Later, when the news of Jimmy's sexual addiction surfaced, Camp would understand that Jimmy's resentment of him was partly that of a man who had watched someone defeat an addiction using secular methods when he was unable to no matter how hard he prayed.

But Jimmy didn't get the reciprocity he'd hoped for from WBRZ, and Camp did have some misgivings about his documentary. "Jimmy was providing a high level of spiritual sustenance. Am I going to undermine him?" But he couldn't forget something Noble Scroggins, the ministry's Director of Counseling, told him.

"At one point, [Scroggins] had received a letter . . . from a woman in Texas who said she and her sister had been sending monthly contributions to the Children's Fund. But now inflation was eating up their checks. . . . What they wanted to know was, if we committed suicide, and had our [insurance policy] willed to the Jimmy Swaggart Ministries, would that be a sin? Scroggins immediately took the letter to Jimmy and said, 'You've got to do something.'" Jimmy, Scroggins said, replied "Yeah, you're right" and dropped the letter in his in-basket. "[He] put it somewhere along with all the other stuff he had to do. Noble said it should have been dealt with immediately." That was Scroggins' epiphany, and Camp relied on it every time he wondered whether he should pursue his slant on the documentary.

During the shooting of "Big Time Religion" there was a meeting with Camp, news director John Spain, and Jimmy—for once, Frances was excluded—after which Jimmy draped his arm around Camp and said he expected him to become a Prayer Partner.

Camp joked that he already was one, since Jimmy had used his name attacking WBRZ to raise at least $3 million.

"No, John," Jimmy shot back, "it was probably closer to $10 million."

If Jimmy felt a bond with Camp based on their "sinning" past, Camp also represented a dangerous combination of an addict's insights and a reporter's instincts. He well understood how an addict can rationalize the harmlessness of one little beer. If he had pursued any of the rumors about Jimmy being seen at motels in New Orleans, he would surely sniff out more.

However, he didn't. And Jimmy knew that even if he had, who would believe some drug-addicted streetwalker? "I always thought that was why Jimmy didn't get a high-class hooker," said a family member, "even though he could have easily afforded it."

JIMMY REALIZED that no matter what he said or did, he'd never be able to seduce the media. A few weeks after the WBRZ tape aired, *Newsweek* called him "king of the TV evangelists," saying he had surpassed Robert Schuller, Oral Roberts, and all the others. But it also dwelled on the Vance case, the WBRZ show, Jimmy's new Lincoln Continental and his Rolex, his will-planning department, and his tax-sheltered trusts, part of whose interest went directly to the ministry.

As communications professor Quentin Schultze, author of numerous books on televangelism, put it, "The pervasive net of the news media seems to secularize and politicize virtually everything in sight."

Jimmy tried for years to meet his secular critics on their own terms, but one of his most revealing accusations was that reporters "try to pick apart and take apart the ministries. They try to analyze them." He implied that analysis was the enemy, that the mysticism in religion should not be scrutinized, nor anything in his religion quantified. That had some truth in it, as spirituality does elude reductionism, but from there it was only a step to the notion that all enemies were Satan, that doubt itself was demonic, and that no outsider should try to understand the cult because unless you're in it, you can't. He wasn't alone; Christian magazines were full of admonitions to preachers not to give secular interviews.

Now, instead of making his points inside his traditional Pentecostal refuge, where his audience understood what he meant and how he wanted to come across, Jimmy found himself very much in The World. He had to defend his remarks to a bigger audience—one that had been, as Schultze said, secularized and politicized. He tried to live up to that challenge.

But Jimmy was learning something else about the media that earlier evangelists had learned: even adverse publicity was good for business. Accordingly, he continued to attack the Supreme Court over its decisions on school prayer, and he told the justices they'd burn in hell for their stand on pornography. His skirmishes with Catholicism continued; his remark to a crowd in early 1983 that "None of the things Mother Teresa does will add one thing toward her salvation," was widely criticized—and, he claimed, misunderstood.

In October of 1983, Jimmy decided to show gruesome pictures of Auschwitz and other Nazi death camps to underscore a sermon on salvation, an exercise in poor taste that anyone could have seen would be "misunderstood." Though he explained that when a person "does not accept Jesus Christ, he takes himself away from God's protection . . . [and] places himself under Satan's domain," it was a theologically mushy and unsatisfactory justification for what was an unfortunate dramatic gambit.

The Roman Catholic archdiocese for Atlanta had already complained to the stations that carried Jimmy about his anti-Catholic statements. In November, two Atlanta stations, WAGA, a CBS affiliate, and WANX, owned by CBN, dropped his weekly 30-minute program over the Auschwitz pictures.

Jimmy didn't know how to handle the onslaught, because he was an avid supporter of Israel. At first he was silent. For a month he refused to comment, hoping it would blow over. Finally, his information director, Jerald Ogg, Jr., said the cancellations were a result of misinterpretation. "It was a distortion. It was inaccurate. It has hurt him personally. It has hurt his ministry. And he wants to go back and try to . . . work this thing out any way he can." But despite a clumsy attempt to explain in a letter to Rabbi Howard Singer of the Anti-Defamation League, the chorus of repudiation continued.

"Christians never agree on these things anyway; but Jimmy was a BIG supporter of Israel, very pro-Israel," said Larry Thomas, Jimmy's writer and researcher.

By the end of 1983, his remarks about Mother Teresa had metastasized in the press to "Mother Teresa is going to hell unless she has a born-again experience." Other articles accused him of saying that "Catholics, Jews, and some Protestants won't get to heaven." His remarks about the Holocaust seemed, in the words of a journalist, "to suggest that the extermination of 6 million Jews was the result of their failure to believe in Jesus Christ."

He tried to clarify. On his November 6, 1983 broadcast, he said, "I admire what Mother Teresa does . . . but none of those things that [she] does will add to her salvation." He also added that nothing he did would add to his own salvation, either, but that was little reported. Regarding Jews, he had actually said, "Because of their rejection of Jesus Christ . . . they have known sorrow and heartache like have no other people on the face of the Earth."

He tried to refine his position, explaining that "the Jewish people started trusting so completely in their system of law to save them that they forgot what the system represented." The law, he said, was only a prototype for the real law, the real thing, the One that was to come. He was trying to say, he explained, that blind trust in the law, whether done by Jews or Catholics or anyone else, no matter how sincere, was putting your trust in the wrong place: "Millions who are trusting in man-made laws will be eternally lost."

It helped some. And it was actually a pretty sophisticated quest, seeking to find the law beneath the law, the deep meaning of morality and good works. But it wasn't enough. Stations kept getting protests about him.

Finally he sent out a mailgram in November 1983 asking supporters to help. Thousands of letters protesting the ban flooded into WANX and WAGA in Atlanta from Jimmy's donors.

The National Religious Broadcasters declined to comment, apparently feeling the line had not been crossed into religious intolerance as the storm gathered momentum.

After Christmas, WLVI in Boston announced Jimmy's broadcast would be taken off the air on February 1, 1984 because of the holocaust episode. His other Boston outlet, WXNE, cancelled everything except his Sunday broadcast. Channel 4 in Miami threatened to cancel his telecast because of the holocaust matter. The stations were inundated with angry letters and calls charging censorship and demanding that he be put back on. One of the Atlanta station managers said some callers cursed them and told them they were going to hell.

All the while, money was pouring in. In the March 1984 *Evangelist*, he published a collage of all the headlines vilifying him, and maintained that the

telecast was bearing fruit because the "uncompromised" Gospel was going
forth. "The tree that bears the most fruit gets the most rocks thrown at it,"
he said, and one day he was going to have to stand before God and give an
accounting. And he didn't want to be faced with thousands of souls saying
"you had the media power and you knew the truth, and you didn't have the
guts to tell the world about real salvation because you didn't want to offend
anyone."

His television ratings were not really hurt by the controversy, and just after
Christmas, he bought time on Ted Turner's Atlanta superstation.

"The Mother Teresa thing—he wasn't trying to shock anyone," said Larry
Thomas. "The media was just looking for ways to embarrass him and make
him into a buffoon the way Hollywood likes to portray ministers like him.
He was not against Catholics. He was against Catholic doctrine. It wasn't
personal. The press personalized it, not Jimmy."

During 1984 and into 1985, Jimmy wouldn't back off of his positions on
Catholicism, but, distressed by the holocaust flap, he did back off of anything
that might become inflammatory regarding Judaism.

A Son of the Reformation

In August of 1983, James Watt, Reagan's Secretary of the Interior and a member of the Assemblies, spoke before the General Council of the Assemblies of God in Anaheim, California, confirming the growing political influence of the Christian right; excerpts from his speech were reprinted in the *Evangelist*.

A year after that meeting, Democratic presidential candidate Walter Mondale excoriated President Reagan for allowing the likes of Jimmy Swaggart to be a "policy adviser" at the White House. Speaking before the Jewish fraternal organization B'nai B'rith in September 1984, Mondale cited the Jewish and Catholic flaps of the past two years, accusing Jimmy of saying Jews were damned to hell and accusing the President of blurring the boundaries between church and state.

"Jimmy got a laugh out of that," said Jerald Ogg, Sr. "He just came to the White House to meet with Falwell and a couple of others. Jimmy wasn't an advisor to the White House." Jimmy's 1984 visit, though, prompted numerous editorials; WNBC-TV in New York compared him to Louis Farrakhan, who called Judaism a gutter religion, and the *Baltimore Sun* called on Reagan to "show as much courage as Jesse Jackson finally did in [renouncing his association with Farrakhan]" by jettisoning Jimmy Swaggart.

Jimmy wrote Mondale and demanded an apology, saying he had been quoted out of context and that it was low to use theology to score political points. Mondale refused. "An apology is definitely not in order," he said.

But political courtship of the Christian right was still strong. Television preachers offered access to a big voting bloc, and by 1983 all the candidates had caught on. Reagan addressed the National Religious Broadcasters in 1983. In 1985, Vice President George Bush met with Jim Bakker and did television spots featuring conversations with an evangelical—who later became a special assistant to President Bush—about the subject of being born again.

"Jimmy actually influenced *them,*" said Thomas. "Once Reagan quoted Jimmy in a speech; he said it was out of the *Evangelist* . . . Reagan was reading the *Evangelist* to see what Jimmy thought." Jimmy's 1982 book *Rape of a Nation* had in it everything he felt the American people were concerned about, and the candidates read it and other prominent evangelists' literature to keep a finger on the pulse of that constituency.

"Jimmy couldn't publicly give an endorsement," said Thomas, "or he'd violate his IRS 501(c)(3) [tax-exempt] status. He could say in a private church service who he would vote for, but he couldn't endorse anyone. All the candidates . . . wanted to know what he thought. If they could win him over, they figured, he'd preach on 'their' topics and people would make the connection."

If there was a courtship of the Christian right, there was equal courtship *by* the Christian right of the celebrity factor in politics. It brought tremendous credibility to someone like Jimmy to be associated in any way with the White House. About the Mondale matter, Jimmy said he had "been to various meetings with Mr. Reagan" on "issues pertaining to morality and traditional values.

"If I have anything to offer in respect to moral choices and traditional values, I would be available to any and all in government on a non-partisan basis." Jimmy was allowing the media to exaggerate his meetings with Reagan, leveraging a few ceremonial events into "advice." But the inflation was coming from the media; Jimmy was just riding in its slipstream, getting out of it what there was to be got.

Around the end of 1984, Jimmy went to Communist Mozambique. He found the place paralyzed because of "Communist insurgency," and used Reagan's term "evil empire" to describe Communism's grip on the world. In the *Evangelist* later, he gave seven steps to overthrow Communism: don't enter any more agreements with the Soviet Union; get out of the U.N.; boycott Communist-country products; export no technology to Communist countries; use "Voice of America" and "Radio Free Europe" and any other media to let the world know Communism is bankrupt; keep America militarily strong. The only non-secular step was number seven: come back to God. Those were hardly non-partisan comments on "moral choices and traditional values."

In that same issue, Jimmy printed a chapter out of the book *Window of Opportunity,* by Newt Gingrich, U.S. Representative from Georgia. The article, about the balance of tensions between conservatives who fear nuclear destruction from other countries and liberals who fear that a nuclear-muscle-bound U.S. is a threat to itself and all other nations, was erudite and well-written, the sort of thing to give a strong underpinning to Jimmy's claims of political connections. The *Evangelist* also gained credibility by publishing bibliographies and footnotes with many of its articles.

In 1985, Jimmy was using his new political muscle to urge his readers to picket Seven-Eleven and other convenience stores that sold smut; *Playboy* and *Penthouse* were chief targets. Be firm, he said, and just insist that the manager stop selling them. He published the names, addresses, and telephone numbers of company officials.

In an essay in *Commonweal*, an author intrigued by Jimmy but wary of compromising his liberal credentials called Jimmy "pig-ignorant, as stupid about the limitations of . . . religion as a man could be and still be able to get dressed in the morning." The author, John Garvey, attacked Jimmy's Southern accent, and said his emotionalism was an embarrassment. Then, slowly, he pondered whether "we liberals" might do well to understand why so many people were drawn to the Jimmys of the world. Some of Jimmy's observations, in fact, echoed those of a thinker who did have unimpeachable credibility with the author: Flannery O'Connor.

He finally concluded that maybe even the wrongheaded, embarrassing, sweaty, weird vision of people like Jimmy Swaggart was no worse than the "relativism of a lot of modern secular folks."

"Jesus really does present us with hard choices," he marveled, and they might make us "look funny to some of our friends." To the extent Jimmy was saying that, he allowed, Jimmy was, "damn it all to hell, telling the truth."

♦   ♦   ♦

During the Catholic fray, Jimmy had fought back by publishing letters he'd received from former monks, priests, and even a bishop. Many had left the church after decades of study. They wrote of misgivings about papal power, of the useless intermediaries between an individual and the Saviour, of the Bible being reduced to a trivial devotional. They wrote movingly of feeling like hirelings, not shepherds. Their spiritual hunger was not satisfied by the trappings of the Roman church. They saw corruption and hypocrisy in the confessional that simply "rendered the commission of sin easy."

It would be hard to imagine Jimmy having time to spearhead a search for such testimonials. It smacked more of someone used to war, able and ready for it, someone of crack judgment on how to attack adversity: Frances. If there were any doubt she had the skill, savvy, and killer instinct to do it, it would be erased by seeing the way she handled PBS when, in 1984, "Frontline" sought to do a documentary about the ministry.

She agreed to let Jimmy and other ministry officials give interviews on two conditions: that they be given a specific time period in which to answer and that their responses not be edited. PBS refused. Frances refused the interviews.

When PBS ran its story anyway, using footage borrowed from WBRZ's "Big Time Religion" to probe the ministry in a way Frances saw as critical of

Jimmy, she requested an audited financial statement from PBS, and wrote in the *Evangelist* that she got a massive runaround and had to solicit an attorney. She scrutinized the statement and found IRS violations; she published them in her *Evangelist* column. She reported that the ministry had three times the number of employees PBS had in its national headquarters, but PBS' payroll was larger.

She also skillfully defended Jimmy about the Catholic uproar. "They tried to portray my husband and me as money-hungry individuals living off the donations sent in by supporters of the Ministry. In Baton Rouge, it is not my husband who rides in a chauffeur-driven limousine—it is the bishop of the Catholic church."

Catholics were up against a formidable foe. When a Florida magazine laid out what it considered seven of Jimmy's most egregious statements, Jimmy and Frances reprinted them in the *Evangelist* and defended each one by referring to Catholic literature, from Vatican II to the Dogmatic Canons and Decrees. Jimmy defended his statement that Catholics had been discouraged from reading the Bible by citing a decree of the Council of Trent that said that anyone who might "presume to read or possess [the Sacred Books] without [the bishop's written] permission may not receive absolution from their sins till they have handed them over to the ordinary." That was hard to refute, and many of his detractors had to retreat to calling him a high school dropout.

Finally, he was articulately defended by a Catholic writer, Barbara Nauer, who asked her readers to consider what the word "protestant" meant. She called Jimmy a committed Son of the Reformation, and said Catholics traditionally call this "holy zeal," and revere it. Jesus' mission, she said, was to save souls, and she didn't see the Catholic church doing much of that. She hadn't seen a Catholic cleric preach from a Bible in 20 years. Instead, priests gave "the bright thoughts of their old seminary professors" or literary criticism or quotes from self-help books by Ivy League professors.

It helped, and at a three-day crusade in Milwaukee, Jimmy told 10,000 visitors that God had told him, "preach what I tell you to preach" and ignore the consequences. "If you don't like what I say, talk to my boss!" The crowd leapt to its feet, cheering.

Sociologists noted the success of his iconoclasm: "Swaggart, more than any other of the real pros," said University of Virginia sociologist Jeffrey Hadden, "has this populist Huey Long-type appeal. He goes after pinhead intellectuals and politicians. He's the only one that does."

Jimmy called his religious adversaries "Mr. Mohammed, Mr. Moon, Mr. Buddha," and his secular ones—journalists—dolts and simpletons for not seeing the truth in the Bible, and his public loved it.

While clergy and press reacted to Jimmy's theological positions, the organism that was Baton Rouge was reacting to the upside of Jimmy Swaggart.

Jimmy was doing so well for the Baton Rouge economy, said one magazine in 1985, that "economists might suggest Louisiana forget hi-tech and get another evangelist." Jimmy was the largest local employer of unionized construction workers since 1981. He refused to let his contractors talk to the press, still miffed over an uncomplimentary article about the ministry four years before.

However, a local magazine revealed that the contractor, Tudor Construction Company, and ministry employees had agreed to talk off the record—which must have infuriated Frances, who was soon to experiment with lie detector tests in a bid to stop leaks.

"I Don't Want This Thing
to Come Back and Haunt Me"

The early 1980s were full of juicy rumors in the Assemblies of God. Pastors everywhere seemed to be sinning. Nineteen eighty-three was the year when stories about Jim Bakker that had been wriggling for years in the muck began surfacing. That was the year John Wesley Fletcher, who was now defrocked but who had been Bakker's constant companion on the air and off for several years, called the *Charlotte Observer* anonymously three times.

The first call was in February 1983. He told a reporter that two brothers who worked at PTL were getting housing from Bakker because one of them was Jim Bakker's lover. He said to remember the name Jessica Hahn. After two more calls, when the reporter tried to set up a meeting, Fletcher stopped calling.

Though Fletcher was a handsome, dynamic preacher, he had been kicked off Bakker's show in October 1981 after a security guard complained he'd made homosexual advances. However, Bakker had promised to "take care" of Fletcher in return for his silence—about the brothers, about setting up Bakker's tryst with Jessica Hahn in 1980, and about the numerous times Fletcher himself had had sex with Bakker.

Homosexuality was about the worst offense in the Pentecostal world. Shortly before Dwain Johnson's suit was filed against Jimmy in 1982, Richard Dortch, who was serving on PTL's board, arranged to meet Fletcher at the St. Louis airport. Dortch had decided to do something to distance Fletcher from Jim Bakker. There were numerous other rumors of Fletcher's drinking and bisexuality, though he was married and had children. At the airport, Dortch told Fletcher he was dismissed from PTL and would face charges by the Assemblies, mandating a two-year rehabilitation period during which he could not preach.

On probation, Fletcher expected to use Bakker's influence to get preaching gigs. For a while, he did. Fletcher traveled as he had before joining PTL, and audiences liked him.

One of the doors Bakker opened for him was in New Orleans, at Marvin Gorman's First Assembly of God church. Gorman and Jim Bakker had been close pals for years. Now Gorman was a rising star in the national Assemblies of God. By the mid 1980s, he would hold a position as one of the denomination's 13 Executive Presbyters—a select group out of some 232 General Presbyters.

Gorman was a regular on the Bakkers' popular show on PTL. His own daily talk show, "Marvin Gorman Live," was broadcast over PTL and on 37 independent stations.

Jimmy accepted occasional invitations to preach at Gorman's church. He had preached there more in the 1970s, before Lynette Goux had her fling with Gorman and then told Frances about it. "He packed the place out," said a member of Gorman's church.

Fletcher and Jimmy knew each other well, too. Jimmy saw in Fletcher oratorical and charismatic talents equal to his own, and he had urged Fletcher to be more combative and forceful about sin. Jimmy felt Fletcher's years at PTL, pandering to the prosperity gospel and Hollywood celebrities, had made him soft. He had no idea.

Fletcher was invited to stay with one of Gorman's flock—as luck would have it, the troubled Goux family, now grappling with marital problems. He knew that the host couple were friends of Jimmy and Frances Swaggart, 60 miles up the highway in Baton Rouge. But he didn't know that the phones in the house were tapped. Ronald Goux was sure his wife was carrying on with their minister—Marvin Gorman—and he recorded many hours of their conversations.

One day while the husband was playing back his tapes, he found he'd netted a very different fish. He'd taped Fletcher murmuring sexual things over the wire to none other than Jim Bakker.

It wasn't long before that news made its way to Baton Rouge.

Inevitably, it reached Bakker, who apparently decided Fletcher was now a huge liability. Not only was he Bakker's apparent lover and procurer, he was a quintessential insider, and there was a lot to say about PTL—outrageous spending unapproved by the ministry's financial officer, sweetheart deals to contractors and favorites, misleading reports to viewers about PTL's missions efforts, drinking, marital discord, affairs by both Bakkers, condoms and liquor given as gifts, extravagant dinners, parties, and trips, vacation homes, huge bonuses for the Bakkers.

Bakker started isolating his old cohort. The invitations to preach dried up.

In February of 1983, when Fletcher anonymously called the *Charlotte Observer,* he was on the verge of a nervous breakdown. He was depressed, and feeling increasingly guilty about the legions of fans who thought Jim Bakker was just the nicest thing, and what a heart for God! And that Tammy—what an imp.

In August of 1983, Jimmy was at the Assemblies' biennial general council meeting in Anaheim. His old friend Richard Dortch was also at the meeting. Dortch had been on PTL's board four years now, and the assumption was that his presence was helping stabilize the troubled ministry. However, the telephone-tap story destroyed that illusion. When Dortch and Bakker, trolling for PTL staff in Anaheim, attempted to recruit a respected missionary named Sam Johnson, Jimmy warned Johnson against it. He said Bakker's ministry was rotten, and to stay clear of it.

At the end of 1983, Dortch disappointed Jimmy. He left his position as superintendent for the district of Illinois, where he oversaw 700 ordained and licensed Assemblies ministers, to work full time for Jim Bakker. Bakker, in need of the respectability Dortch could bring, had offered him more money than he'd ever made in his life. He would be Co-Pastor, Senior Executive Vice President, and Corporate Executive Director.

In spring 1984, shortly after Dortch joined PTL, Bakker's new water park, fake volcano, and Victorian shopping mall at his Heritage USA theme park were set to open, much to Jimmy's and Frances' disgust. At the same time, Marvin Gorman's Christian Family Television began running on Cox Cable, seen in New Orleans and Jefferson Parish. Gorman also bought time on PTL's Inspirational Network—as did Jimmy. Jimmy bought time on Paul Crouch's TBN in California as well, despite the fact that the Crouches had a format similar to the Bakkers' and dressed even more like country music stars. More and more, Jimmy felt walled in by the feel-gooders.

Jimmy was about the only prominent Assemblies preacher still willing to talk about sin and wrongdoing. Yes, you were supposed to unflinchingly hate the sin but love the sinner; but Jim Bakker was preaching about loving the sinner—the homosexual, the alcoholic—in a way that sounded like he didn't really hate the sin very much. The rumors continued to fly about PTL, including tales of Tammy having a nervous breakdown and being addicted to tranquilizers. This seemed to be all just fine with Marvin Gorman; and, after a year working for Bakker, Dortch didn't seem dismayed, either.

Richard Dortch got a phone call just after Thanksgiving in 1984. He had only been working at PTL for a year, and he was about to be dealt a blow. Jessica Hahn was on the phone, saying she'd been drugged, raped, and assaulted by Jim Bakker.

Dortch immediately flew to New York, where Hahn lived, recruiting an Assemblies pastor from the area to assist him. After meeting with Hahn, the two men decided it was a shakedown, though, Dortch wrote later, he wondered. Dortch gave the other minister $2,000 to give to Hahn for "medical expenses" she said she had incurred since the 1980 incident—presumably, fees paid to a counselor she had consulted for trauma.

Dortch flew back to Charlotte, satisfied the fire had been quenched.

In a few days, on December 3, Hahn called Charles Shepard, the *Charlotte Observer* reporter who had done many PTL stories, and told him her story.

When she sent a draft lawsuit to Dortch, he realized the problem was not going to go away.

Dortch was still an Executive Presbyter of the Assemblies of God at that time. He knew his duty was to set in motion church discipline of Bakker. But instead, he consulted an attorney. By the end of February, 1985, he had hammered out a trust fund for Hahn with a Los Angeles attorney and had $265,000 of PTL's money wired into the account.

He hoped that would do the job, because Heritage USA had finally opened after a false start, resulting from unpaid contractors, and its growth was shooting out in every direction. With the popular Christian theme park's unpaid bills, he didn't need distractions. But by the fall of 1985, other insiders were calling Charles Shepard, not only about Hahn's affair with Bakker, but about the trust fund. They were calling it hush money.

◆　◆　◆

In 1984, Marvin Gorman started hearing rumors about himself. Among them was that he'd been sexually involved with a number of women, and that he'd fathered an illegitimate child by one of them.

The only person who had confronted him about sexual impropriety had been Jimmy Swaggart, two and a half years before, over his fleeting liaison with Lynette Goux. And Jimmy had promised to keep it quiet. Gorman remembered saying, "Jimmy, I don't want this thing to come back and haunt me." After tracing a rumor to Jimmy, he called. Jimmy denied violating his confidence.

He wouldn't be able to deny it for long. In mid-July, 1985, he got a call from Bob Schmidgall, soon to be an Assemblies Executive Presbyter like Gorman and Dortch. Schmidgall told Jimmy that Gorman was being considered for a very high position in the national organization—General Superintendent or Assistant General Superintendent. As they both knew, the election for this position was three weeks away, at the biennial convention in San Antonio, Texas. But Schmidgall had heard that Gorman had once had a moral failing, and that Jimmy knew something about it. True?

Jimmy said later that he struggled with himself. "I realized I either had to say nothing—in effect lie—or else tell him what I knew." But the real question was why Schmidgall was calling Jimmy. "Dozens of others knew Marvin Gorman's reputation," said Larry Thomas. "Several people were actively spreading the word about him because he was being considered for that top AG position. Jimmy got [asked] because he had credibility, contacts in every state and district, and was very concerned about the Assemblies of God."

There was also talk that Jimmy wanted to hold high office himself in the Assemblies of God—or Frances wanted him to. If that were true, this was an opportunity to remove a competitor. On the other hand, Jimmy was aware that Bakker and Gorman were political insiders with many friends in Spring-field. It was possible that Schmidgall was trying to find out if he was the source of the rumors about Gorman. He had to decide whether to trust Schmidgall—or, if he was a Gorman plant, whether to use him to send a message to Gorman and the whole Executive Presbytery.

Whatever his reasons, he decided to break his silence about Lynette Goux.

On August 8, 1985, the Assemblies held its biennial convention in San Antonio. Richard Dortch had been a favorite for General Superintendent be-fore he took the job at PTL, but his association with the Bakkers had taken a toll. He not only didn't get the top spot, he wasn't re-elected to the Executive Presbytery. He was badly shaken, but Jimmy had predicted two years ago to Sam Johnson that any association with Jim Bakker was trouble.

Marvin Gorman quietly withdrew his name from consideration for General Superintendent.

The Highland Road

Though Jimmy had let it be known to reporters covering the Zoe Vance case that he still lived in the tract house on Tara and drove a Volkswagen in late 1982, that was the last mileage he would get out of the humble car and he knew it. Soon he would drive a Lincoln, and move out of the Tara house into an estate.

In the previous year, he had spent nearly $400,000 to purchase 18.25 acres on Highland Road, an ancient thoroughfare running alongside Bayou Fountaine, cleared when Louisiana was under Spanish rule. During the Civil War, its nine miles meandered through cotton and sugar plantations.

Now that same dirt was expensive real estate and ran through the campus of Louisiana State University. The road started near the state capitol, the old part of the city that housed the mansion district. Driving out from this heart toward Jimmy's new purchase, you left behind the cosmopolitan feeling of downtown, and with it the sense of decay around Louisiana politics and the weird, seductive energy given off by things decadent. Bogs and waterways darted among the ugly, paralyzed-looking buildings of urban renewal, and then the songs of nightbirds, frogs, and insects abounded at night among the shreds of beautiful forest along Highland Road—giant sycamores, live oaks bearded with Spanish moss, pine trees, hackberries, cottonwoods and fragrant magnolias. It wound through comfortable homes set back from the street on big grassy, shaded lots. There were no curbs, giving a breath of the countryside. Houses had porches with columns, white picket fences, awnings, and deep green shutters.

Almost all the way out to the end of Highland Road was the Swaggarts' new spread. Their land was across from Jack Nicklaus' heavily wooded planned community, with its artificial lakes and uniformed guards, called Country Club of Louisiana. Their neighbors were politicians and corporation heads.

Nineteen eighty-three was spent building three houses on the acreage: a 9,300-square-foot one for Jimmy and Frances, 8,000 square feet for Donnie and Debbie and their three children, Jennifer, Matthew, and Gabriel, and a 4,372-square-foot residence for Frances' brother, Bob Anderson, who was the ministry's treasurer.

"I don't want any walls except what has to be there to hold it up," said Frances to a friendly interviewer. She wanted a lot of glass, and no fancy entrance. "One little door is all I want." But Jimmy's model for someone who had arrived was plantation-style columns, and he prevailed.

As always, Frances had a good reason for wanting a simple front. She was concerned about drawing the kind of attention Jim and Tammy Bakker were getting for lavish spending, along with Falwell, Robertson, Roberts, and other television ministers who lived behind guarded walls and gates. The Bakkers took expensive vacations and had just bought a luxury condo in Florida, spending $22,000 just for mirrors.

Frances and her decorator, Ken McKay, were at the site every day. Construction began about the time WBRZ aired its documentary in the spring of 1983, and Frances was still mad about it. She would get upset, seeing WBRZ's cameras set up on her property line and its helicopter flying overhead. She forbade workers and contractors to speak to any members of the press, and identification was removed from Tudor Construction Company's trucks so reporters would not speculate in print that the house was a gift in return for Tudor getting the contracts on most of the ministry's work.

Rumors flew about sunken rooms, marble floors and hallways, secret passages, Frances having things torn out and rebuilt, Roman-style columns inside, and solid gold swan-shaped Jacuzzi faucets. There were ordinary tensions and misunderstandings in building a home, but the plan changes and tug-of-wars between McKay and the builders (who liked Jimmy but detested McKay) were the sort of gossip Frances knew the press was salivating for.

A quick decision was made to construct a privacy fence. It would turn out to be the kind of tongue-clucking expenditure the media expected; it reportedly ended up costing $250,000, enough to build three average three-bedroom homes. The tall wooden fence was hung on brick posts two feet thick and spaced a few yards apart; heavy steel gates shut off the sweeping driveways leading to the houses. The Swaggarts installed a guard house, security cameras, an alarm system.

Frances had learned the emblems of wealth and taste; in her home there would be no hint of the 28-foot trailer parked next to the blacktop in Wisner, Louisiana. Eventually the news of polished wood floors, oriental rugs, and an antique piano with heavy, ornate legs surfaced in the press.

There were heavy drapes, gilded mirror and picture frames, ormolu clocks, wavy-legged Louis XV furniture upholstered in peach, blue and white, and delicately flowered lamps with tasteful shades. Gilded wall sconces held electric candles, and from the ceiling hung ornate candelabra. Geegaws of gold, porcelain, and ebony sat on shelves and walnut stands; there were statues of marble, and the formal fireplace had a freeform walnut-and-marble frame around it like a soft open mouth.

As they expected, Jimmy and Frances were questioned about the opulence and price of the house and furnishings. The attention focused on PTL and other television ministries for the past several years made him vulnerable, since his ministry board was, contrary to the rules of the Evangelical Council for Financial Accountability, completely dominated by rubber-stamp family members. That rule, in fact, was one reason Jimmy had never joined the ECFA. But when the press questioned his followers, they came through for the Swaggarts: there's no law, they said, that says Christians should have to live in poverty.

In fact, the house exemplified one of the double-binds of Pentecostalism: as an ex-Jimmy-watcher put it, "[They] say it's all dust and ashes, your reward is in heaven, and then they turn around and say, 'look at Preacher's new Lincoln, the Lord has blessed his ministry.' "

Estimates for the entire compound, including land, houses, and presumably furnishings, ran between $3 million and $5 million. Jimmy didn't want the house to become an issue and tried different tacks to downplay it. "It only has two bedrooms," he said, though one of them was reported to be nearly 2,000 square feet. "It is nice, [but] I don't want to appear to be something I'm not." He had borrowed the money from the ministry, giving it the interest instead of a bank. It was all he and Frances had, he said. "We have no investments. I have no savings accounts."

Finally he claimed the old house on Tara was plagued with security problems. "Crazies," he said, had tried to break in. People had hidden in the bushes to spy. ". . . we're like public property. People don't just drive by— they'll come into your house!" He had started getting violent threats when construction on the new house started, he said.

But most of the security problems he referred to actually pertained to the Highland Road house, and he and Frances got their wires crossed on the story; in 1985 she would write in the *Evangelist* that they had never received a threat or been bothered by curiosity seekers while living in the Tara house.

The house construction and WBRZ drew attention to his ministry and helped it grow. The dizzy notoriety, however, would last only four years before scandal would erupt.

60

Gorman and Bakker

By early 1986, Heritage USA was the third largest theme-park attraction in the country, behind Disney World and Disneyland, with nearly five million visitors a year. PTL reached 13 million households, and Bakker brought in more than $100 million a year—about two-thirds as much as Jimmy.

During the summer, Richard Simmons, the evangelist of exercise, appeared on Tammy Bakker's show, offending Jimmy. Simmons was effeminate and a secular celebrity, two things Jimmy despised about PTL's trajectory. But more, he was a reminder of a serious problem: the more ministries like Bakker's got away from preaching the Gospel and got into matters of the flesh, the more they tended to not guard their flanks from the IRS, now wanting to look at sales of religious merchandise, and the liberals, who wanted to tax the churches (backed, Jimmy felt, by money from drugs and pornography).

Jimmy had reason to rant: Bakker's troubles with the FCC had aroused the IRS; in October of 1985, after an audit, the IRS had decided to revoke three years of PTL's tax-exempt status and had begun examining records from 1983 on. If the IRS extended this kind of examination to other ministries, everyone could get burned.

But as if to flout the audit, in 1986 Bakker planned a religious home shopping network that practically invited the IRS into church. Instead of ceramic Jesus lamps or embroidered Bible covers, he wanted to sell items like "a TV and VCR for playing a videotape of [Heritage USA's] Christmas City"—presumably exempt from sales tax. Kodak and K-mart were reportedly interested in rights to the PTL "market."

The leaders in the national Assemblies of God were doing nothing to rein Jim Bakker in, and other ministers were turning to Jimmy for the leadership to do what their superiors would not.

On Sunday, July 13, 1986, Jimmy preached to his congregation—now about 5,000 regulars—at the Family Worship Center and then he and Frances boarded a plane to San Jose, Costa Rica to dedicate a church. His attorney and board member, Bill Treeby, went along, with his wife Nancy.

Treeby was not a member of Jimmy's church. He lived in New Orleans and attended the Lakeview Christian Center, whose pastor was Michael Indest. On the plane, Treeby told Jimmy and Frances that a woman in his congregation had approached Indest, in need of counseling. She was married and had had several affairs with other men. One of those men was Marvin Gorman.

This wasn't the 1981 Lynette Goux affair; this was a different woman.

Pastor Indest could have taken the matter up with the head of the Assemblies' Louisiana District Council, Cecil Janway, and let Janway send it up the line to the national level for discipline. But he wanted Jimmy to handle it. "I didn't know who else to bring it to," he said later. He had a lot of respect for Jimmy, he said. Maybe it could be handled Scripturally, without need for interference from church authorities.

Jimmy learned from Indest that the woman was Lynda Savage, whose husband David was a music minister in Gorman's church. She had gone to Gorman for counseling in 1978. She was the one who had threatened suicide in a hotel room and then unbuttoned her blouse and grabbed him between the legs.

On July 15, back in Baton Rouge, Jimmy had Indest on the phone, telling him that Lynette Goux had also sought counseling with Gorman, visited him in a hotel room, taken off her blouse, and grabbed his crotch.

The two preachers hung up. At about 5:30, Jimmy's phone rang. It was Indest again. Marvin Gorman was standing there in his office, he said. He had confessed his misdeed to David Savage. Could they come over?

At 8 p.m., cars drove through the gate and pulled into the sweeping drive at Jimmy and Frances' house on Highland Road. Jimmy's co-pastor Jim Rentz, Treeby, Indest, Gorman, and David Savage, the wronged husband, went inside. After Jimmy greeted them, they all made their way into his study, which looked out over the large, free-form swimming pool. Frances left.

Marvin Gorman's peers and brethren, whom he had known for years, prayed for him. They asked God's guidance.

Jimmy turned to Marvin and asked if he had had an affair with Lynda Savage. Yes. Jimmy asked if there had been any others. No. You sure? Jimmy asked. Gorman vehemently said he was sure. Yeah? What about Lynette Goux, back in 1981? Gorman had vowed back then that there were no other women, too, said Jimmy—"and at that very time you were involved with [Savage]."

Gorman was extremely unhappy with the direction this was taking. He hadn't wanted to drive up to Baton Rouge in the first place; he'd resisted when Pastor Indest suggested it. He had confessed to David Savage, but Savage had insisted on bringing Indest into it. He went along with that because he'd wronged Savage and he owed him. That's where it should have rested—it was between him and the Savages.

But Indest had insisted on bringing Jimmy Swaggart in on it, threatening to call Gorman's wife, Virginia, if he didn't go to Baton Rouge—Swaggart, the source of rumor after rumor he'd been hearing about himself in the past couple of years. The rumors had seemed to intensify with his rise in the national Assemblies hierarchy and the growth of his television ministry. His local congregation was actually larger than Jimmy's now; of course he had spent two decades staying at home building it, while Jimmy had traveled. But tomorrow, he was supposed to close a loan for $16 million for a new church and two television stations and satellite uplink.

This scene was extraordinarily bad timing, and now Jimmy was dragging up the Lynette Goux business—which had happened seven years before and hadn't even led to a sex act—in front of these men. And Jimmy had promised back then to keep it quiet.

He was beginning to feel a trap close on him. He was well aware of the rules: the Assemblies offered two choices for a minister caught in adultery—a two-year rehabilitation, with no preaching, or dismissal.

But the denomination's bylaws also said that the district had the sole authority to discipline its ministers, and its decisions weren't subject to review by the Executive Presbytery or anyone else (though a proposal to change that would soon be put before the leadership in Springfield). The Louisiana District Superintendent, Cecil Janway, might cut him some slack, but Jimmy Swaggart wouldn't.

There was not much he could do but say okay, he had lied back in 1981, he had been seeing both women, but he was telling the truth now. When he said that, he later claimed, Jimmy called him a liar and said he "had not repented and that he needed to come clean with his confession, leave the ministry, and seek rehabilitation."

Jimmy then accused Gorman of affairs with seven women, some of them members of Gorman's congregation and some ministers' wives, Gorman claimed later. It was an important accusation, because the denomination's penalty depended to some extent on the severity of the moral failing. If a minister dabbled in pornography, for example, but didn't commit adultery, it could mean the difference between two years out of the pulpit and only a few months. Gorman denied it.

Then Jimmy opened the Bible to I Timothy 5:20. He made Gorman read aloud what to do when an elder has sinned—"Them that sin rebuke before all, that others may also fear." What should you do? said Jimmy. Silence. Finally, Jimmy said, "You're going to have to call Brother Carlson [General Superintendent G. Raymond Carlson, the denomination's leader in Springfield] and Brother Janway."

Marvin begged for a break, for time to close the $16 million deal tomorrow. Jimmy said no, that would amount to defrauding the lender if Gorman's ratings dropped because of a scandal. The others agreed with that.

The solution, suggested Jimmy, was to just tell the lending agency of this impending change. "If they still want to loan the money, that's their business, but they must know about this."

Humiliated, Gorman asked them to at least keep quiet until he had had a chance to tell his family. And *he* would call Carlson and Janway. He didn't want any of these people in the room to do it; it was his place.

They all prayed together in Jimmy's study. The other men were concerned about Marvin's mental condition, Jimmy said later. He had taken a devastating blow, and Jimmy didn't want him driving back to New Orleans by himself. He asked Rentz to drive Gorman's car down and deliver it to David Savage's church in New Orleans; he would drive Gorman there himself to pick it up. Along with Marvin and Jimmy rode David Savage, the cuckold who had forgiven, but demanded a huge price for it.

In the car, Gorman asked Jimmy about one of the rumors. Had a third woman, who had worked for both Jimmy and Gorman, claimed to have had an affair with him, too? No, said Jimmy.

When they got to David's church, it was after midnight. They prayed together again. David went home. Jimmy and Rentz headed back to Baton Rouge, and Marvin got in his car and drove home to face his wife.

Back in Baton Rouge, Gorman later accused, though it was very late, Frances was on the phone, calling members of Gorman's church.

THE NEXT DAY, Wednesday, July 16, 1986, Marvin Gorman stepped down from the pastorate of the New Orleans First Assembly of God, the church he had guided for 21 years. The next Sunday a statement was read to his stunned congregation that he had had "numerous adulterous and illicit affairs."

Pastor Michael Indest announced to his congregation at Lakeview Christian Center that Marvin Gorman had been involved in several illicit affairs and had voluntarily resigned from his church, though why it was their business was never explained.

Fireworks erupted in several pulpits that day. Bakker spoke furiously at his Heritage Village Church, enraged at Jimmy for, as he saw it, running Gorman out of his ministry. He didn't mention Jimmy by name, but, it was just as clear that he was the target as it was that Bakker was Jimmy's, when Jimmy shot back that "millions are deceived [and] duped" by "pompadoured pretty-boys with their hair done and their nails done who call themselves preachers."

"I don't know how much longer I can go on," Bakker wailed.

But his diatribe had some truth in it.

"We drive our preachers until they break and then we kick 'em out," he said. "[And] I want to tell you who destroyed him. You say, himself? No. The church. The church. The church."

Bakker was saying these things unwittingly, not understanding their deep truth—that the Assemblies of God was not sophisticated about how to handle sex. It was a forbidden topic, a huge strike against the possibility of helping preachers. Christian counselor Raymond T. Brock wrote that fallen ministers "report feelings of shame, guilt, fear, anger, and depression"; the fact that they sinned threatens everything they believe and say to their flocks about deliverance and forgiveness and God's love. Their only refuge, Brock said, was to believe it was demon possession or oppression.

Some ministries had programs for sexual addiction, and members found liberation in the fellowship. But preachers like Gorman, Bakker, and Jimmy felt there was no such fellowship in the Assemblies for ones who had risen as high as they had. It was almost impossible to humble yourself when hundreds of people were counting on you for their jobs. Confessing, which removes the element of secrecy and thus the element of shame, was something these preachers simply couldn't do.

Bakker continued to staunchly defend Gorman on his television show, and Jimmy continued to fire volleys back. A few weeks after Gorman's resignation, PTL arranged a $75,000 loan for Gorman against a Certificate of Deposit. Gorman ended up defaulting and PTL had to forfeit the CD.

BAKKER WAS ALSO greatly upset about Jimmy's enthusiasm over a book called *The Seduction of Christianity,* an attack on the prosperity theology Bakker preached. Larry Thomas had given it to Jimmy.

"That was one of my jobs, to screen materials like this. I was so engrossed I read all night . . . at first I had doubts about my own reaction: was it really on the mark, or did it just sound like what I wanted to believe? I took it to a prof at the Bible college." He read it and told Thomas Jimmy should see it right away.

"Jimmy . . . was flying to Denver that day and he read the whole book on the plane on the way. . . . within two weeks he had ordered all the college staff to read it. We felt it showed how modern church ideas could be traced to occultic roots. Jimmy really took off on it, and used parts of it as points of departure for sermons. Dave Hunt [the author] came, and taped several shows for 'A Study in the Word.'"

Bakker saw the book as a slap at him. "The book mentioned people who appeared on PTL," said Thomas. "It raised questions about the practices of [some] Pentecostal preachers . . . In fact, Paul Crouch ran a crawl message across the bottom of the screen on Jimmy's show that said, 'TBN doesn't endorse or agree with the ideas in this broadcast.' "

One day Bakker muttered something overheard by an employee that gave a hint of what the real warfare was. "If he gets Gorman, he'll get me," Bakker said. Gorman's slip was seven years ago—when Bakker himself had had sex with Jessica Hahn. That probably meant he was still fair game to Jimmy.

But Gorman was far from defeated; he was going to fight the charges against him and go full steam ahead with his television ministry, which was not under the Assemblies' jurisdiction.

About two weeks after the confrontation in his study, Jimmy flew to Springfield for a conference with the Executive Presbytery, presumably to use his leverage as a generous supporter of Assemblies overseas programs (he would give more than $10 million in 1986) to go after Jim Bakker. He had acquired a lot of dirt on Bakker by this time.

In 1991, he denied that he'd discussed Bakker much during that meeting, claiming that the four hours he, Frances, and Donnie had spent there were spent talking about a draft policy paper. His account isn't convincing—such a discussion could be held by phone, wouldn't take four hours, and wouldn't require that three people fly to Springfield. By 1991, Jimmy was trying to soften the posture he'd been taking about his own infallibility during the PTL crisis. The September 1986 issue of the *Evangelist*, for example, contained a letter from a distressed minister who wrote scolding him politely but firmly for endorsing *The Seduction of Christianity*. Jimmy scored the writer for questioning him at all. "You know, it's a strange thing," was Jimmy's response, "Even though God has given me the responsibility of touching this world for Christ, you show absolutely no respect whatsoever." He blasted the writer for being sarcastic and slanderous, when the letter was neither.

Actually, Jimmy's response had far more the flavor of Frances' wall-eyed lunges at people who questioned her husband. Jimmy was too busy to author everything in his column. Given her active involvement in every facet of the ministry, especially the magazine, her authorship is far more likely.

A few days after his return from Springfield, Jimmy sat down and wrote a five-page letter to Cecil Janway, the Louisiana District Council Superintendent, detailing his confrontation with Gorman in 1981 and three weeks ago on July 15, 1986. The letter read like a deposition, as if he were expecting legal trouble.

A few days later, Jimmy was livid. He heard that Gorman was minimizing his dalliances, confining his confession to only the Lynette Goux affair so as to escape the stringent penalty for adultery and suffer a lesser one. And he heard that the national presbyters were probably going to buy it. Apparently his trip to Springfield warning them about Bakker—and by extrapolation, his buddy Gorman, whom Bakker was so vociferously defending—had meant little. Marvin was popular in Springfield, he had lots of friends. They were probably going to keep him out of the pulpit a few months, slap his wrist for kissing and petting Lynette Goux, and then let it blow over, ignoring the three-year affair with Lynda Savage. Jimmy felt he had other ammunition against Gorman. No one was even talking about the 1973 affair with young Gail McDaniel yet.

Jimmy didn't know it yet, but Gorman was dismissed as an Executive Presbyter on August 14. He was fighting for his life, and had every rationale for minimizing his trifling. It was extremely suspicious that his affair with Lynda Savage suddenly cropped up again just when Gorman was about to hit warp speed with his satellite uplink and new stations. How convenient for Jimmy that Marvin would be kicked out of competition the week he was supposed to sign his big deal.

The way Jimmy pitched it, Gorman was not showing the slightest repentance, much less rehabilitation. "I want it clearly understood," he wrote Janway on August 20, "that I will take whatever steps I feel are necessary to see that this situation is not covered up and that Marvin is not treated differently than any other minister would be treated." Gorman only confessed because the women came forward and gave him no choice. Jimmy wanted the full two years of rehabilitation—the Assemblies' harshest admonishment for straying preachers.

Jimmy's old friend and board member Janway obliged him. On Tuesday, September 2, 1986, Janway read another statement to Gorman's congregation, stating that Gorman had engaged in "unscriptural lascivious conduct" and offering him the two-year rehabilitation.

Gorman refused.

Things deteriorated rapidly after that. Jim Bakker flew to Springfield a few weeks after Swaggart, to present his side. His visit contrasted sharply: instead of taking a strong stand for anything, he offered platitudes about unity and harmony and prayed they could all work together in the body of Christ, etc. Then he went back to PTL and fumed, debating whether to pull Jimmy's daily half-hour show, "A Study in the Word," off PTL. It came on at nine a.m. and its attacks on people Bakker admired always left him fuming. But it brought around $50,000 a month into PTL, which badly needed the cash.

And the money came on time. Television ministries were rated in the industry by their reputation for payment; Robert Schuller, Oral Roberts, and Jimmy were all known for paying well and had excellent ratings, though Jimmy was sometimes a little slow. The undisputed worst were Jerry Falwell and PTL.

It took Bakker six days to decide. To hell with Jimmy's $50,000—he couldn't take it any more. In mid-September, Dortch pulled "A Study in the Word," off the network, but left Jimmy's weekly broadcast from the Family Worship Center in place. Jimmy was given an excuse about slot availability, but no one in Baton Rouge was fooled.

"PTL dropped Jimmy because of his embracing of *The Seduction of Christianity*," said Larry Thomas unequivocally. And of course because of Jimmy's trip to Springfield. Dortch later said it was because "Foolishly, Jim Bakker and I were watching Jimmy Swaggart attack us each morning at 9:00 a.m.," but PTL also dropped another show whose host, Tennessee minister John Ankerberg, had discussed the *Seduction* book.

At about this time, Jimmy's phone rang; John Wesley Fletcher was on the line. It had been two and a half years—February of 1983—since Fletcher, depressed about being jettisoned by Bakker, had called the *Charlotte Observer* and told the reporter who answered to remember the name Jessica Hahn. Between 1983 and the autumn of 1986, Fletcher had been preaching wherever he could get gigs. Though he could have ruined Jim Bakker at any time during those more than two years, he chose not to. Whether it was as he told *Penthouse* in 1989—that he really believed PTL was helping people despite Bakker's depravity—or whether it was that he felt he had no credibility because of his own participation with Bakker in things the Pentecostal world abhorred, he had been silent.

Now, with Bakker under siege by the IRS, the FCC, Jimmy, and the *Observer,* which knew about the Jessica Hahn payoff but hadn't been able to document it yet, Fletcher wanted to tell what he knew. Like Michael Indest, he picked the most powerful member of the Assemblies he knew: Jimmy Swaggart.

Jimmy's and Fletcher's later accounts of their conversations differ. Jimmy said he was hesitant to accept Fletcher's calls, because Fletcher might merely have an axe to grind because of his falling out with Bakker. He also said Fletcher's relationship with Bakker and PTL "was an unsavory situation and I did not want to become involved"—a disingenuous-sounding piety considering how willing he and Frances were to root around in the ashes of Marvin Gorman's years-old dabblings.

Fletcher's version was that he called because he'd heard the Swaggarts were actively seeking dirt on Bakker; he later said Jimmy promised him a "safe haven" in return for inside information about PTL.

Fletcher had many lurid stories about Bakker, not only the incident about Jessica Hahn and the fact that there was a threatened lawsuit and payoff, but story after story of Bakker's lusting after young men (indeed, many photos of Bakker during the days Fletcher was at PTL showed a marked effeminacy), drinking, and spending donor money on outrageous luxuries for himself and Tammy.

Around the time of Fletcher's calls, two men, Charles Cookman and Cecil Janway, decided to try to put out the rapidly escalating conflagration between Jimmy Swaggart and Jim Bakker. The two men were equal in status; Cookman was on Bakker's board and was the Assemblies' district superintendent for North Carolina. Janway was on Jimmy's board and was the superintendent for Louisiana. Cookman suggested they bring their warring charges together for a truce.

Jimmy agreed; PTL needed his money and he needed the network slot. But he wanted Richard Dortch there, too, he said. From what Fletcher had told him a few days earlier, Jimmy's old friend Dortch certainly appeared to be covering up for Bakker.

The last thing Bakker wanted, however, was to be in the same room with combative Jimmy Swaggart, who would ask him point-blank about Jessica Hahn, Fletcher, Tammy's drug use, his celebrity guests, and his homosexual encounters. He refused to attend the meeting, but agreed to send Dortch. It was specifically understood, Dortch said later, that the meeting would consist only of the two teams: him and Cookman, and Jimmy and Janway.

Cookman and Dortch arrived at the Baton Rouge Hilton on September 22, 1986. Janway was there, and the three men secured a hotel suite and waited for Jimmy to arrive. He did, shortly—bringing with him Frances, Donnie, and Jim Rentz, contrary to their agreement.

Dortch was furious. It was five against two. He kept his mouth shut, but he did not feel he particularly owed Jimmy any candor now.

After tense amenities, Jimmy turned aggressive. He demanded to know what Dortch was going to do about Bakker embracing a sinner like Marvin Gorman on his show. And why, asked Jimmy, was PTL still running Gorman's broadcast as if nothing had happened? Dortch told him it was none of his business. Gorman was a Louisiana preacher, not a North Carolina one. "Your superintendent [Janway] is sitting beside you. Ask him," he told Jimmy curtly.

Jimmy then attacked Cookman, Dortch later said, asking the older man the same question. Cookman rose and stood in front of Jimmy, jabbing his finger at him, according to Dortch. "Jimmy Swaggart, you are discourteous; you are rude; you are mean-spirited . . . You are going to be brought down if you don't get control of your spirit." Jimmy barked back that he intended to be rude, bringing tears to Cookman's eyes.

Jimmy turned back to Dortch, pressing him about the rumors of Bakker's homosexuality. Angry, Dortch demurred. He also feigned ignorance when Jimmy asked about rumors that a woman had been paid $250,000 in hush money. After Jimmy had complained about Richard Simmons being on Bakker's show, Donnie started to attack. Jimmy suddenly silenced him. "You be quiet, I've already made a fool of myself," he said to his son. Then he apologized to Cookman for "rebuking an elder."

When Jimmy asked about Jessica Hahn and the hush money and lawsuit, Dortch lied, saying he'd heard there was a lawsuit against a different man, a Jim Baker, with one *k*. And that no payment of hush money had ever "crossed his desk" or some other term that allowed him to claim later that technically, he'd told the truth.

That was Dortch's account of the meeting. Jimmy's was much milder, saying basically that things had started courteously and had briefly gotten a tiny bit tense at one point, and that he had told them about Fletcher's phone call about Bakker. He said he left convinced that there was no truth to Fletcher's gossip and that he put PTL out of his mind.

But his bland rendition wouldn't get past anyone close to the situation. "There wasn't enough truth in [Jimmy's account of the PTL affairs] to fill a thimble," said Larry Thomas.

The meeting broke up. The PTL men left, shaken at Swaggart's extreme hostility.

Jimmy went back to his office and cancelled his remaining show on PTL.

◆ ◆ ◆

Perhaps Jimmy violated the terms of the meeting, bringing his entourage, because Bakker had bailed anyway and because he had just been notified that some of his programs would be pulled off PTL; that may have seemed a betrayal that invited a corresponding betrayal. But once there with Frances, some of his aggression certainly seemed to be for her benefit and, to some extent, Donnie's. Jimmy's reputation for unquestioningly deferring to Frances, and vociferously defending her positions, was getting worse.

"Jimmy was good to work around, really personable," said an ex-television producer for the ministry. "His wife got hardened; she was tough to deal with. Jimmy changed around her, he was subdued when she was around. I remember some of those rehearsals, Jimmy and the musicians were rockin' away!—not like something Jerry Lee would do, [but] Jimmy would be banging away! on that piano. And then Frances would come in and give him one look, and it was over. Jimmy was just a big kid."

Once, he said, Frances and Jimmy were at Ralph and Kacoo's, a restaurant on Airline Highway near the ministry that was a hangout for staff. It was after an Easter Sunday camp meeting, and Frances spotted one of their longtime producers shaking hands with a former pastor of Jimmy's who had started a rival church.

The next day, the producer was fired.

Shortly after that, Frances fired another good employee—a television engineer—for questioning the first firing. Several employees stormed into her office.

"Jimmy . . . heard the ruckus and came through the [connecting] door," said an ex-television cameraman for the ministry. He pointed to one of the employees and asked if the ministry had ever done anything to hurt her. Yes, she said.

"You're fired!" said Jimmy. Then he turned to another and asked him the same question. The answer was yes. "You're fired!" said Jimmy. Frances' honor had to be protected.

"She was still his wife," said the ex-cameraman, "love or hate. He had to take up for her."

Back at his office on September 22 after the meeting with Dortch and Cookman, Jimmy had to choose who to believe: Dortch, who was an old friend, after all, or the debauched Fletcher. He believed Fletcher. Clearly preachers like Gorman and Bakker had been getting away with stuff like Lynda Savage and Jessica Hahn and homosexual massages and drinking and drugs for years, and now that it was coming out in the open, they whined and tried to weasel out of it. There were probably tons of other preachers getting away with these things, and they would probably go right back to doing it as soon as the heat was off.

He continued denouncing Bakker from the pulpit and in print. One *Evangelist* article would contain firm words: "if a preacher of the Gospel is caught . . . in an immoral situation . . . this pastor or evangelist must be placed on probation for a period of a year. . . . During this time, he cannot preach anywhere. . . . [to allow him to] would be the most gross stupidity."

Do Not Fail

Any evangelist worthy of the title salivated at the prospect television offered for saving souls, and at the prospect of hastening the Second Coming of Christ by harvesting enough of those souls. Around 1985, workers at CBN began secretly planning to televise the Second Coming, so convinced were they that television was the medium that would spread the Gospel throughout the world as prophesied before the millennium.

For some time, Jimmy had been becoming obsessed with a notion: that he, and perhaps he alone, was God's choice to evangelize the whole world. Over and over from 1985 on, he would tell of his ever-increasing sense of urgency.

"God has . . . given me a commission to reach the world by television. . . . He said TV will reach the millions and hundreds of millions and reach them quickly. That's what He's ordained me to do and I'm trying to carry it out. I need your help. And He told me you would help me. You've got to help me."

Numerous times over the next few years he would tell of walking near a cotton field on July 1, 1982, at 9:15 a.m. The field, he said, was ready for harvest. God spoke to him, saying He was ready to destroy America but would delay it while Jimmy spread the Gospel to all corners of the earth like the Scriptures said would happen in the last days.

It would be a kindness to call this an apocryphal story. Over the years Jimmy changed it. Stephen Winzenburg, an Iowa communications professor who monitored Jimmy's broadcasts for various purposes, remembered a slightly different version: Jimmy told of a dream he had had of threshing wheat. There was only one other minister out there doing it (Winzenburg was sure it was supposed to be Billy Graham) "and Jimmy said that only he and one other electronic minister were ordained of God."

In 1988 he said it was Monday, July 1, 1985—not 1982—at 9:30 a.m. that "God spoke to my heart that we should put the telecast on every station throughout the world. Do this immediately! Do not fail!"

Wherever Jimmy was on July 1 of any year, there was probably no cotton field anywhere near him ready for harvest, but in 1986, he and Donnie launched a mission styled "D-day or Delay," a plan to package his broadcast for consumption by every free nation on the planet, and eventually every nation, free or bound. Though it was outrageous that "D-day or Delay" referred to the Second Coming of Christ—which evoked an image of Jesus Christ hanging around heaven tapping his foot and waiting for Brother Swaggart to get wired into every hut in the world—Jimmy had convinced himself it was his job to convert everyone he could reach by television.

During the D-day campaign Jimmy's show was the highest-rated weekly broadcast and a top fundraiser at $500,000 a week. His sermons were translated into a hundred languages and dialects, "every man in our own tongue" as at Pentecost. The fitness of that thought must have been one of the things that cemented in his mind that he was the one chosen to hurry Christ's coming.

♦   ♦   ♦

As the pressure to evangelize the whole world became heavier, events were slowly coalescing around a dark-haired young woman in Nashville. She was a few years younger than Donnie and, in fact, superficially resembled his wife. Like his wife, her name was Debbie. On January 28, 1985, the 24-year-old pled guilty to prostitution in Nashville and was fined $50. Less than three months later came another guilty plea and another $50 fine. She packed up and headed south, to Tampa.

Tampa, near where Jessica Hahn and Jim Bakker had come together in Room 538 of the Sheraton Sand Key Resort in 1980, was not friendly to the young woman. She was arrested in July and charged with "a prostitution-related offense." She would be arrested and charged six more times for the same thing by February 1986, spending a total of 14 days in jail in Tampa.

Debra Murphree was very feminine, with black hair, black eyes, high cheekbones, and a sexy little gap between her front teeth. She was from southern Indiana, but had a Cajun-girl look, with a slightly concave mouth and strong chin, and a Southern accent. Her engaging little sneer was reminiscent of Jerry Lee Lewis', and her smile was a knowing one.

In the fall of 1986, she gave up on Tampa. Maybe the Big Easy would be more forgiving. She moved into a hotel across from the New Orleans Baptist Theological Seminary with her boyfriend, a coke dealer. She worked the streets at first. It took her two months to build enough of a clientele that she could stay inside—at the Starlight Motel, then the Travel Inn, across town in Metairie. While she was building this clientele, she met her most famous client.

The street she picked to work was Airline Highway, Business Route 61, that ran from New Orleans all the way upriver to Natchez, Mississippi. Airline Highway was nonstop commercial all the way through Baton Rouge, the sort of strip-commerce that had once fed the cities—before freeways—and that now kept a death-grip on the tired remains. Of those, there was a certain kind of motel that sat among the used-tire emporiums, liquor stores, and dance clubs.

Such a motel was the Travel Inn. Debra was able to set up shop there after a couple of months commuting by bus from her boyfriend's hotel room across town.

It was during those first months that Jimmy first spotted her. A week or so after his angry meeting with Dortch and Cookman, she stood on a corner on Airline Highway, wearing slacks and a sweater. A tan Lincoln Town Car crawled past and slowed. She was new to the area, but had seen the Lincoln a few times before. She had assumed it was an undercover cop and moved on. Maybe not. The car stopped, and she walked over. "Do you want a date?"

It was comical: he assumed the same thing she had; he asked if she was a cop. "No," she said, "I can prove it." She got into the car and raised up her blouse.

He was wearing a tee shirt, headband, and baggy jogging pants slit—ripped, she said later—at the crotch, with a white handkerchief over the opening.

"All I want to do is jack off awhile . . . look at your tits," he said, according to a 1988 *Penthouse* article. He offered her $10, but she said no way, she did nothing for under $20.

"That's all I've got."

She told him to pull over and let her out. "Let me see what I've got." He found another ten.

She hung out at the London Lodge Cafe. She told the regulars there that she was dating Jimmy Swaggart, but nobody cared.

THOUGH DEBRA HAD A lot of rough edges, including a crude cross tattooed on one arm and "Debbie" on the other, there was something about her that stood out to Jimmy. He didn't just choose her randomly and then stick with her because it was convenient. He pursued her, trying three times to pick her up before she decided he wasn't a cop.

There was something that made him want this woman, and this spot on Airline Highway, out of all the other choices he had.

It was understandable that he would be tempted. Between Marvin Gorman's illicit sex life and Jim Bakker's peccadilloes and his own gnawing obsession that had led to demon oppression his whole life, Jimmy was hearing nonstop stories of women taking off their blouses, people touching each other's genitals, people getting massages, people having sex. Besides being titillating, these stories were confirming something he'd known for years: in the atmosphere of the sexual revolution, preachers were getting away with murder.

He had evidence that Marvin Gorman had not been truthful about all his dalliances, and the rumors about Jim Bakker made Bakker sound like the emperor Tiberius. Doubtless the revelations at hand were only the tip of the iceberg. And if these guys had been getting away with it, how many other preachers still were? It was already a common failure among men of God, one of the most notorious pitfalls of power and charisma even before the sexual revolution.

There was something in the air, something about New Orleans, about motels, about Debra—her name and the color of her hair and her age—that aroused an unfinished, dishonored part of himself.

The biggest clue was in the Travel Inn itself. Its sidewalk split with dead brown grass growing in the cracks, its tiny, dreary office with a slab of tin jutting over the roofline and fluorescent lights squatting on the soffit, its downspouts for soggy, mildewy days, and its courtyard filled with old faded cars, had a ring of familiarity.

These women at the Travel Inn were one tired sigh away from the kitchens and bedrooms and rutted mud lanes and sticker-patch yards of places like Rio Hondo, Texas, and of the little town 150 miles up the Mississippi River where he had always found refuge from the demons of hell and this world by closing his eyes tight and whimpering help me Jesus, oh, praise Jesus, praise God.

ON JANUARY 1, 1985, at 9:30 a.m., wrote Jimmy, God again told him to "put the telecast on every station throughout the world. Do this immediately, and do not fail!" Jimmy fell on his face and told God it was too hard. God replied, "I will give you a face as flint! I will give you a head like steel! I will give you a tongue, . . . a mouth, . . . you will say what I tell you to say!"

The biggest obstacle to God's command was Communism. The Soviet Union was a challenge equal to getting Jerry Lee Lewis saved. In need of dollars, the Soviets had opened the country to tourism for some years, and Jimmy traveled there and to other eastern bloc countries in the late summer of 1985 to investigate broadcast possibilities. On his return, he called the U.S.S.R. a "charnal [sic] house of the damned."

The number of Christians behind the Iron Curtain was so small that the government had not expended much energy trying to suppress their worship. As long as it didn't cross over into menacing social or political activity, it was tolerated. The church was a competitor, no more nor less. The word "minister" had no religious connotation, but it carried an aura of respect, and preachers were allowed in under tight strictures and heavy supervision. There often had to be a secular intermediary, such as a cultural or business exchange program. And enough dollars had to change hands.

The job of Jimmy's international ministries director, Jim Woolsey, was to try to secure television time. As elsewhere, the general format was to make a donation to obtain help in setting up a meeting with the official in charge.

In 1986, they let Jimmy preach in Siberia. He flew to Novosibirsk. The officials who gathered to meet Jimmy were not sure who he was; until they saw him, all they knew was that he was an American who had been brought in by a missionary. But one of them recognized him and let him know that he knew Jimmy had harsh things to say about Communism. Jimmy disarmed him with his knowledge of a famous World War II tank battle in which the man had been wounded, and tension subsided.

Jimmy was allowed to be interviewed on Soviet television. He said Christians made the best citizens because they didn't smoke or drink, they worked harder, and they didn't lie, cheat, or steal. But he was still not allowed to preach on Soviet television.

Finally Woolsey was permitted to meet the Soviet head of church activities in Moscow. After he agreed to buy video playback equipment for several churches, they allowed him to leave dubs of a demo tape translated into Russian. Jimmy still wasn't on the air, but at least the tape would be played in a few churches, and possibly dubbed for distribution to a few more.

A year later, a group of Russian officials visited the ministry in Baton Rouge during a U.S. tour. They asked for more tapes, and Woolsey complied. Jimmy then announced he was "on the air" in the Evil Empire.

Francesville

> *"Uncle Sun said they should call that ministry Francesville down there."*
>
> —Frankie Terrell

As 1986 opened, Jimmy's ministry had 751 employees in Baton Rouge. The Bible College, launched only a year before, had an opening class of 426 students, a healthy start. A shopping center on the corner of Bluebonnet built a footbridge across a muddy sump to Minnie Bell Swaggart Hall, the dorm.

The city's Chamber of Commerce estimated that Jimmy had created 1,502 new jobs in the city, three new retail stores, $33.1 million in personal spending, $15.75 million in retail sales, $17.2 million in bank deposits, and $3.3 million in state taxes. The city and parish aimed to get more, claiming the ministry still owed sales taxes for the books, Bibles, records, tapes, cross-shaped pins, and other items—"the perfect marketing mix," according to sociologist Jeffrey Hadden—it sold through the *Evangelist* and in its stores. Jimmy argued that these were gifts given in return for donations.

Jimmy was now bringing in $128 million a year, and had assets worth $142 million.

The stakes weren't fried chicken dinner-on-the-ground and chocolate cake and $2 in the offering plate any more. The stakes were really big now. Politics, Marvin Gorman and other rivals, world power, were all lined up outside Jimmy's door. Frances was as equal to it as Tammy Bakker to a Saturday at the mall. But Frances wasn't going for press-on nails and breast implants. She was the tailored, coiffed, tastefully jeweled Chief Executive Officer of the Jimmy Swaggart Ministries.

"I have heard Jimmy . . . a hundred times say that if it was not for Frances he wouldn't have had the drive and the desire to get into radio and television," said Bob Anderson, Frances' brother. "If it wasn't for her he would have quit years ago."

Donnie felt his mother was the most disciplined person he'd ever met, and the toughest.

"Frances is a tough broad," agreed Skip Haley, an assistant news director at WBRZ who had done so many stories on Swaggart that his office bore a sign saying "Thank You For Not Speaking in Tongues." "She's the business brains behind it."

"I'm not a weakling," admitted Frances. "I don't keel over and pass out at opposition."

In an interview with *Baton Rouge Magazine*, she came across as ladylike and unpretentious. The photos she permitted to be used showed a pretty woman standing on the winding staircase in her large home, playing in the yard with the three grandkids and their puppy, laughing with Jimmy at the breakfast table, working in the ministry office. She was dressed freshly, nails polished, ruffled spring frocks at home, suit and pearls at the office, hair fluffed and curled in a very feminine style.

"The women [employees] tried to emulate her, but no one had as many dresses as Frances," said a ministry employee. "She was the Classy Southern Belle, even the Yankees tried to copy her, but they couldn't hide their Boston accents. On the platform, Frances could project that, but talking in front of groups or [staff] meetings, etcetera, she was tough, firm, every inch the executive."

Frances liked the image of belle and behind-the-scenes minister's wife; she shunned the term CEO. But as the ministry grew, she inched from belle to steel magnolia to the closed, shrewd "Dragon Lady" of the organization, finally supervising 1,500 employees, spearheading the ministry's marketing efforts, and alternately rebuffing and attempting to manipulate the despised press.

Frances reviewed all the ministry activities, scanned the mail for criticism, and planned counterattacks. She participated in all the crusade services, appearing onstage for announcements, sitting through the sermon, and laying on hands at altar call. She critiqued Jimmy afterward, giving him feedback on the effectiveness of both message and music. She trouble-shot all day and trained Donnie in his new duties as "Chief of Staff." She supervised all personnel, negotiated television contracts with networks and stations, juggled the bills. She dictated articles for the *Evangelist* and planned future expansions.

The Northerners who worked at the ministry all noticed Frances' preoccupation with appearances. She jogged six miles a day and advised her employees to do the same. In early 1985 she instituted a weight policy, explaining that it had to do with insurance rates. Everyone had to go down to the basement and stand in line to be weighed once a month. There were departmental competitions, and individual "losers" were recognized in chapel; big losers got to travel with Jimmy and Frances to the next crusade.

The explanation about insurance rates appeared to be a fiction when the Bible college students were also pressured to lose weight. And of course there was favoritism, said Larry Thomas—"If a four-dollar-an-hour employee got fat, there was pressure to lose the weight. If a family member or a very, very valuable employee got fat, there was no pressure."

The weight program was eventually dropped, mostly because the administrative hassles weren't worth the payoff of not having fat people at the ministry. But it cinched Frances' reputation for giving free rein to her appetite for control, and she furthered it by making staff members take lie detector tests when she suspected they had been talking to the press.

Reporters who questioned Jimmy's ethics or theology in print often got a call from an agitated Frances demanding a retraction. Stephen Winzenburg, who had painstakingly compiled statistics on how televangelists used air time, received three calls from Frances after his research appeared in *USA Today*. "She wanted to either fly me to Baton Rouge or she and Jimmy fly to Florida to 'set me straight,' " said Winzenburg. He declined.

She was a workaholic and expected others to be, too.

"The administration tended to expect you to make sacrifices, to act like missionaries and deprive yourself," said Larry Thomas. "You were supposed to be willing to go off on a three-week crusade away from your family, come back Monday morning at three a.m., and be at work at nine. You were expected to push into 60–80 hour weeks without comp time or overtime. If you worked 80 hours one week, you didn't not work the next, you worked a regular 40 or 50 hour week. On the other hand, the staff expected a Christian work place to maybe be 'forgiving,' meaning lenient about when you came and went."

"They paid poor salaries," agreed Bob Anderson, "but most religious organizations do. They feel like people should be dedicated to doing the Lord's work."

The ministry had informal compensatory time; if someone left early for a dental appointment or kid's soccer game it was "overlooked"; but comp time was not coded into personnel policy, and you couldn't be too obvious about taking it. All in all, the "Christian" theme worked far more on the side of the administration than on the regular employees' side.

Then a young man was hired as a kind of aide-de-camp to Frances. The new lad would come in late, take long lunches, and leave early. "Rather than confront him," said Thomas, "they just made a new policy that everyone had to start punching a time clock. That was insulting. I'm an adult, I know when to come and go."

Frances' aide wasn't the only case; this was their way of dealing with problems. "If one department was doing something they didn't approve of, like, 'you're not supposed to eat at your desk,' they wouldn't deal with that specific department, they'd issue a blanket policy. It was like the whole class gets punished because Johnny did something wrong."

If Frances thought someone was sinning or if someone made a mistake, said a source close to the ministry's inner circle, "it was automatic—you're outta here."

Frances tried a few cosmetic magazine interviews, but they didn't work the way she wanted. Reporters from the mainstream news media continued to monitor the ministry's problems, and the negativity increased.

"Frances is driven by anger," said Ed Pratt, a local newspaper reporter who did dozens of stories on the ministry. "She is just enraged all the time." She had passed this on to Donnie, said Pratt. "One day there were some reporters and cameras out in front of the ministry watching [Donnie and other family members] load stuff into their cars—you know they have this fleet of big Lincoln town cars. Donnie came over and spit into the cameras and said, 'get off my property!' You know his father has always said anyone is welcome on the grounds, it's God's house and all that, and here's his kid's attitude: 'get off my property!' "

People, Frances said, thought working for the Jimmy Swaggart Ministry was "just praising the Lord all day. Unfortunately, it's not that way. We're here to work just like in any other business." She told her brother, Bob Anderson, not to be so nice or friendly with his staff. "If they don't fear you," she said, "you're not a good supervisor." He vehemently disagreed. "If you want someone to respect you, you can't buy it and you can't [get] it out of fear. You got to earn it," he told her. When he said he wanted his people to respect him instead of being afraid of him, Frances retorted, "They're not YOUR people."

A Bible college professor who left in 1988 felt Donnie and Frances were "rather arrogant, especially Frances—strong-willed, domineering, makes snap decisions."

"If you put a notion in her head, *it never leaves*," agreed Bob Anderson. He was speaking of the positive as well as the negative aspects of that, but the professor said that a complaint to her from someone she wanted to believe might very well result in a summary firing, without anyone asking for the context or the whole picture.

"I've heard first-hand accounts of people being chewed out by Frances, and of her literally cussing, you know, using 'damn' and 'hell' and so on," he said. "I asked, you mean she was very angry, and they said no, I mean she *cursed* me." But Bob Anderson said he never heard of her using profanity in the 14 years he was with the ministry. Fury, yes, but not profanity.

However, "Frances is one of the big problems with how people were treated by the ministry," Anderson said. A 15-year trucking crew employee asked Jimmy for a raise and Jimmy complied. "Frances found out and took it back," said Anderson. "I've seen her do things so cruel and cold-hearted. [She's] as cold as ice water, I don't care about your Christian this and your Christian that . . . The only time I had a problem working with Jimmy was when I had to go through Frances or Donnie . . . and Donnie doesn't know enough to come in out of the rain . . . [he's] just a mannequin they wind up and he hopes he doesn't run down before the sun goes down. There's not a real bone in his body."

He said his sister hired an employee for Bob whose real job was to spy on him. The man reported to Frances. Bob knew it and made sure the spy had complete access to the file Frances suspected him of mishandling.

"Frances runs the whole show, Jimmy is merely the onstage performer," said Winzenburg, who became negative about the ministry after Frances called him when his study appeared in *USA Today*. Her first question, he said, was "do you have any dirt on Billy Graham." We have plenty, she said; we monitor him. She told Winzenburg that if he didn't use what he had, she was going to use hers.

"Jimmy's heart seems to be in the right place," said WBRZ's Skip Haley, "but he's got some people around him that should be fired."

Jimmy's cousin Frankie Terrell, a businesswoman herself who owns a convenience store in Ferriday, called Frances a dictator and said nobody dared question her, but she agreed with many of Frances' business decisions. "She's usually right . . . you've got to be very careful about things like [the WBRZ documentary]. As far as opening the books [to WBRZ]—I sure wouldn't do that."

Larry Thomas agreed. "My experience with her was that she didn't play favorites, didn't play games . . . She would listen, but she was rarely convinced that what she'd already decided was wrong . . . She was just a very, very strong individual. Jimmy always said, she could run General Motors."

An observer close to the ministry said, "Jimmy gives her the credit!? He BETTER! I feel for Jimmy, not Frances. She saw to it that Jimmy was motivated in the way *she* desired. She is very controlling. I don't have any respect for Frances, don't have much use for her. And who was in charge of counting the MONEY up there? Her Mama! I mean, I've got no problem with a family ministry, but . . . well, I guess she took care of her own, didn't she?"

The WBRZ documentary back in May of 1983 had revealed that many family members worked in the ministry, but none of them seemed to be from Jimmy's side. The highest number noted by 1988 was about 27—but Jimmy's relatives implied they had been elbowed out. There were no sinecures based on blood, at least not Swaggart blood. Family might be given preference, but, once in, either you performed or you were out. And it seemed the Anderson clan was more able to perform than the Swaggarts.

Frances' brother Bob Anderson was treasurer; her mother worked at the ministry; her sister Linda Westbrook was Jimmy's secretary; Donnie held various positions, from crusade director to chief of staff to titular editor of the magazine; his wife Debbie was on the board. Other Andersons and their in-laws were provided for as well, but neither Jeanette Ensminger, Jimmy's sister, nor her husband Bobie played a role, and Sun was not invited to preach. Finally Bob Anderson, the subject of several exposés regarding financial irregularities (Anderson firmly denied the charges, and none ever held up), left the ministry in 1994 in disgust after his sister took sides against him in a dispute.

The Ensmingers, said the elder Jerald Ogg, were "loners. They didn't come to the church—her husband pastored an independent church . . . [Sun's old Assemblies church in Baton Rouge]." But in the early days of the television effort, said Ogg, Jeanette would come in the studio and help out. "She played, helped out in the telecast, she was a good piano player." Like others, he liked her.

"Jeanette's been outside the family," said David Beatty. "[She] played on television, sang a time or two, but Jimmy didn't want any competition. Jeanette was a good musician, a good singer, she was electrifying. But Jimmy didn't share the glory with anyone."

Plus, he said, "Jeanette and Frances would easily clash—you got two strong-headed women, two abundantly strong-headed women there. Jimmy was concerned about [Jeanette's] behavior back then, [but] it was more Jimmy, the jealousy factor" that derailed the relationship.

There was some vague, unspecified "problem" with Jeanette's and Jimmy's relationship that had to do with her children. No one could put it into words; one ex-employee said it had something to do with whether Jimmy and Frances showed enough compassion when her infant daughter, Tamela, drowned; another said it concerned some problem with her surviving son, Daryle, who reportedly has been quietly hired and fired numerous times over the years by the ministry.

Sun was reluctant to speak of his own isolation from the ministry, saying only, "Men has wives, you know. And wives has husbands. I'm gonna put it like that."

David Beatty put it more bluntly. "Frances didn't trust anybody on Jimmy's side of the family. All of the Andersons and none of the Swaggarts worked at the ministry. She wanted ultimate loyalty. Somebody on Jimmy's side would have been more loyal to him than to her."

But Larry Thomas disagreed. "Frances' family is well taken care of—the ministry is family oriented, and it's pretty well understood that anyone whose spouse needs a job, something will be found . . . There were a few questions with unqualified family members, but most employees were fully able to do their duties . . . Frances had firm control, but she wouldn't have denied any of his family members jobs."

"When you have 1,500 employees to manage, someone's going to call you a Dragon Lady," said Jerald Ogg, Sr.

Frances' fierceness had its endearing side, too. Not many men had the kind of defender Frances was for Jimmy. After the PBS "Frontline" show about the ministry ran, she took an unusual four full pages in the *Evangelist* for a two-fisted rebuttal that essentially called anyone who had criticized or even questioned her husband a liar, hypocrite, or tool of Satan.

She made sure her message was smooth and literate, so she wouldn't come across as a nut, but the strength of the arguments was their intelligence. She was very right about much of what she said, and so passionate it was impossible not to admire her. The only impeaching factor was her absolute refusal to give any credence to her enemies. But for believers who didn't particularly care to hear the other side, that was because there was a war, and Frances was a warrior. "There's superwoman!" a follower murmured once when Frances walked onstage at a camp meeting; the fan leapt up, clapping madly.

Frances respected Jimmy for spending hours and hours in his study, working on his messages and praying. She never made him feel like he was neglecting her. He liked her style, she was sure of that—"He'd notice if I didn't look nice." She and Jimmy were a team, utterly single-minded, with no hobbies, movies, athletic events outside Frances' attendance at the grandkids' baseball or basketball games, no parties or social events. Other ministers who spoke at the Family Worship Center said they saw strong love between them.

"I wouldn't change my life for anything in the world," she said. "Everything I do has a purpose. It's not trivial. It's helping people." She never prayed for herself; her prayers were for the ministry and to give thanks to God for blessing it so.

Frances talked only to friendly reporters and gave out the official ministry homespun. She jogged before daylight; Jimmy wouldn't jog or diet. They liked to read in bed (when their schedules allowed them to retire in the same bed), talk about the day, discuss problems, plan the future. They liked "20/20" and "60 Minutes." Frances used to cook every night before 1984. Now, no time. She still baked chocolate pie, bread pudding, pound cake, Jimmy's favorites. They spent almost no time in their beautiful new home. She hadn't been back to Northern Louisiana for years. Shopping was her only recreation.

Jimmy's comments about Frances focused on how heavy her responsibilities were, how he would have quit without her, and how hard it was to talk about her. The impression was that he had an incredible best-friend powerhouse in her. She even seemed flexible, despite her rigidity with the press. Suddenly you couldn't blame her for the Dragon Lady image—she seemed to be protecting all the right things.

"[The Swaggarts] were very kind to us," said Jerald Ogg, Sr. "They had a wonderful warm side and they shared it with their employees." They furnished the Oggs with a car, and once Jimmy called in the 12 or 15 male department heads and told them to go to a nice store in Baton Rouge and pick out three suits, three dress shirts, three ties, and three handkerchiefs and charge it to the ministry, and don't look at the price.

"There was that sweet old missionary, big and long and tall, he had to have a big car," recalled Anderson, speaking of Morris Plotts, who worked in Africa under great hardship for many years. "Jimmy bought him a brand new Mercury Marquis . . . we took him out back and showed him that brand new red [car] and he broke down and cried. That's the kind of person Jimmy was."

Most of his staff and employees liked Jimmy very much. He had a reputation for hiring an unusual number of women in executive positions—about half his top staff—and was easy to work with. In the opinion of many, he and Frances made a good, balanced team as employers; the imbalance that crept in during the early 1980s seemed to come with expansion and their inability to accept the public scrutiny it brought.

His flock loved Jimmy's sense of humor; most of the humorous, affectionate things he did to make people feel a sense of belonging never got on television. Once he baptized a tiny baby dressed in a long white lace gown. The parents stood quietly; it was a solemn moment, with the thousands of visitors in respectful silence as Jimmy spoke the requisite words. Then he took the baby in both hands, begging it not to cry, and turned and held it high above his head to the audience and waved it back and forth like a banner, its white gown trailing. It was inexplicably comical, and the laughter and applause welled as he kissed the baby and handed it back to its parents. As they walked back to their seats, laughing, he asked his people: "I wonder if any of you were ever that pretty? Certainly you were!"

Another time he announced a tape that featured Dwight Jones, his blood-and-guts-blues harmonica player who had been "saved out of rock and roll." "And if you don't buy this tape," said Jimmy, shaking his head and fumbling a moment at the thought of what might befall anyone so dense, "God's gonna cause all your babies to be born nekkid!"

He went too far in telling the congregation about one of Frances' three face lifts, however. "She like to killed him," said Anderson.

Even though it didn't show up in print, Jimmy typically charmed his adversaries, the reporters, on the rare occasions when he gave an interview. When he, Jerry, and Mickey gathered for a 1986 magazine spread, Jerry sighed, flashing his piano-shaped diamond ring. "I guess this will go straight to the IRS," he said.

"I *told* you to go into the ministry!" Jimmy shot back.

It touched people the way Frances always referred to Jimmy as "my husband" instead of "Jimmy"—in her *Evangelist* columns and letters, in interviews, in conversation. She referred to him that way so much it was striking.

Yes, Jimmy was *her husband,* and that husband-ness of his was what actually defined her and gave her strength a trajectory. "My husband" was a constant touchstone for her.

Who else Jimmy was, she was not telling. Nor was he. But very soon, they would both have to admit that there was another Jimmy, one they had both tried hard for many years to keep out of sight.

IN THE JULY 1985 *Evangelist,* Frances foreshadowed the beginning of trouble. She wrote that Jimmy just couldn't go on, he was staggering under the burden of trying to keep so many enterprises going just on his own mettle. He had been doing it for years and years without cease. She had seen him, she said, so tired he literally couldn't stand up.

One would think this would be a prelude to an announcement that Jimmy was taking a well-deserved rest and the flock would be watching tapes for three months. Instead, she asked for more money.

As if that would create more hours in the day for Jimmy to somehow catch up on a lifetime of disturbed sleep; as if that would lessen his real burden—living and breathing and embodying Jesus' teachings for all to see; as if that would cure the terrible demon oppression that woke him from his sleep.

Over and over during the years Frances had been spearheading the ministry's growth, she and Jimmy had proven that they would just take any such extra giving, or extra time, or extra media coverage, and immediately leverage it into more debt. Time debt, energy debt, family-time debt—Frances was worse about running up her tab, in a way, than Tammy Bakker. At least Tammy acknowledged she had "shopping demons." Jimmy and Frances said it was because God was in such a rush.

As Frances took over more administrative responsibilities, the ministry seemed to go from a solid operation that had a clear message and a firm grip on its spending and debt to an unrelenting monster that ate up people's time, peace of mind, health, and futures.

Compromises started in little ways, as the desperate need for money started leading them toward the manipulative and deceptive fundraising turf that had lured other ministries, but not theirs. "You choose words carefully in raising money," said Larry Thomas. "Jimmy never compromised his message just to get money, but it's incredible what they would do to get money in."

When people fell off their pledges—the typical attrition rate was 30–50 per cent—the ministry started to send letters that were like late payment notices. The implication, said Thomas, was that "you might lose your salvation, because you've broken a vow with God."

At first Jimmy felt it was unethical to allow people to use their credit cards for pledges; it just contributed to their debt, and he wouldn't do it. But he finally changed his mind in about 1986. "It was just too much of an advantage," said Thomas, "to be able to have the money in the bank, drawing interest that day, instead of waiting weeks or months to get it in."

Jimmy didn't belong to the Evangelical Council for Fiscal Accountability pioneered by Billy Graham, nor did most of the other big ministries. It was because of "a silly rule that you can't have a family member on the board of directors," said Thomas. "That's stupid, because most of these ministries did have a family member on the board, and those probably needed watching more than any other."

But the IRS "came and stayed a whole year," said Bob Anderson, "and they hardly found anything to disallow. They disallowed some expenditures, like Jimmy's fence."

Between July 1984 and the beginning of 1985, about 60 employees had quit or been fired, because, sometime after the WBRZ story aired in May of 1983, the ministry quit providing workers with information about how money was spent, according to some who left. After that, beginning in 1984, was when the lie detector tests were instituted. "The overall temperature of that ministry is boiling," said an ex-employee. "The feeling when you walk in the door is, will you have a job at 5 p.m. You don't say anything. You just come in and do your job and that's it."

"Two years from now, that ministry will be running on one leg," said a former executive in 1985.

He was wrong. The ministry was making money hand over fist two years later, with more than twice the employees it had in 1985. But he was only about a year off.

The "Hostile Takeover"

Jimmy spent the fall of 1986 traveling, preaching, and doing battle with a wide array of secular enemies. He took on numerous speaking engagements, hosted visiting missionaries at formal dinners, supervised his international missions program, wrote columns and articles for the *Evangelist*, and supervised and planned for expansion of the Bible college, which had a healthy 1,451 students enrolled for fall.

He also conducted his traditional Thanksgiving Camp Meeting in Baton Rouge, which drew thousands of visitors from all over the U.S. for several days' stay. He kept up his Sunday and Wednesday sermons at the Family Worship Center and prepared for 12 major crusades scheduled for 1987, most of them abroad. Getting his 82 tons of equipment and scores of crusade team members past customs was a chore that could usually be left to his assistants, but only he could attend to rehearsals, preparation of sermons, meetings with government functionaries and Assemblies of God missionaries, and visits to projects needing funding.

He attacked pornography, supporting an injunction to keep publisher Larry Flynt from sending free copies of *Hustler* magazine to all the members of Congress—a practice Flynt had started that year. (The injunction was blocked by a court order ruling Flynt's First Amendment rights were at stake.)

In the past year, the National Education Association had lambasted Jimmy and people like him as "fanatics, extremists, and ideologues who will say anything and stop at nothing in order to achieve their goals." These people, the NEA spokesman said, were bigots with big bucks and powerful friends in Congress and the White House, and were a threat to democracy. He also included Jerry Falwell, Phyllis Schlafly, Jesse Helms, the Bakkers, Pat Robertson, and others, including *Readers Digest*.

But the month of April had been declared Jimmy Swaggart Month by the Kentucky Legislature; Jimmy was cited for feeding children over the globe, for his attacks on abortion, and for filling "a vacuum of leadership" in keeping up the pressure against Communism.

On October 6, the House Ways and Means Oversight Subcommittee heard testimony from Ole Anthony, founder of Dallas' Trinity Foundation, about abuses of televangelists.

Anthony, a Norwegian-American ex-undercover intelligence operative, ex-Republican fundraiser, ex-evangelist, and avowed Muslim, Jew, and Christian with a background in geophysics and electronics, lived under a vow of poverty. Backed by an eclectic group of supporters, he conducted sophisticated demographics research and investigations into the excesses of religious broadcasters. He had founded the Trinity Foundation in 1973 to monitor televangelists, and in 1976 had started a talk show on Jimmy's Dallas radio station. The station had a low market share—0.1—but within two months, Anthony's intelligent, high-level broadcast had an 8.6 share. Unaware of who owned the station, he once made fun of Jimmy's style. His show was abruptly cancelled.

Anthony told the subcommittee that Jimmy, Roberts, Falwell and others were breaking IRS laws by issuing certain tax receipts, skirting local laws requiring solicitation permits and financial disclosure for solicitation over television, and engaging in false advertising by telling donors their contributions would be returned "a hundredfold." He said taxpayers were subsidizing this nonsense and that the promises of self-policing were a sham because most evangelists' boards were made up of relatives and lackeys. He said religious broadcasters could not meet the community standards section of the FCC code.

This was the sort of trouble Jimmy had feared Bakker would unleash, and indeed, Anthony cited PTL's troubles to underscore several points.

Before leaving for one of the overseas crusade tours, Jimmy had a dream that seemed to presage the terrible scene that was soon to be played out at the Travel Inn.

He was in a large house, he wrote in his 1991 book *The Cup Which My Father Hath Given Me*, fighting a huge serpent with a sword. It was standing upright, taller than him. Its head darted back and forth as it tried to bite him. He fought mightily, sweating, panting, as it came horribly close to sinking its fangs into him with lightning speed. A man dressed in white watched the battle serenely from the side of the room, hands behind his back. Jimmy wondered why he didn't help. At that moment, Jimmy saw an opportunity and slashed the snake's head off. The man did not congratulate him; he just nodded to Jimmy to follow him through a door. Elated at his victory, Jimmy followed.

They left the house and went outside into a yard. The ground shook as if an earthquake had struck. The man was peering into the distance. Jimmy looked too, and saw something that looked "like a huge stanchion—the type that holds up great bridges." It was 100 feet tall. When he was finally able to see the top of it, he realized it was another snake, its huge head darting back and forth.

Jimmy turned to the man. "I have to fight this, don't I?" he asked, and the man nodded. Jimmy turned toward the snake, sword in hand, repeating, "I have to fight this thing." He woke up.

JIMMY ALSO SPENT the fall shoring up his case against Gorman, who was proving a slippery catch. Michael Indest, the preacher who had come to Jimmy for advice when Lynda Savage confessed her affair, started making a chronology of Gorman's alleged affairs. Later two church members would say he claimed to have an inch-thick file on Gorman, though he denied it. But rumors flew, and Jimmy and Frances would be accused of fueling them.

Reverend Andy Harris, a onetime marketing director for Jimmy Swaggart Ministries, said later that even after Marvin Gorman had left his church, he heard the Swaggarts tell ministers numerous times that Gorman had had repeated extramarital affairs.

It got out that Gorman might have a spare kid running around; Lynda Savage told Indest that she had had sex with both Gorman and her husband the same day, and wasn't sure which one was the father of her third child.

In September 1986, Tom Miller, pastor of the Canal St. Assembly of God in New Orleans, told a meeting of about 20 Assemblies of God ministers that he had performed an exorcism on a deaf-mute woman who began speaking in a male voice that he recognized as Marvin Gorman's. The entity emitted a foul odor and threatened to cause a spiritual war in the church if Gorman, Satan's messenger, was not left alone. Even that outrageous tale circulated enough that it ended up in court testimony.

By the end of 1986 Gorman's two admitted 1978–1981 indiscretions—Goux and Savage—had mushroomed into rumored affairs with over 100 women, including the wife of reputed New Orleans Mafia boss Carlos Marcello. As Gorman was blackened through Assemblies of God channels across the country, the Carlos Marcello rumor even reached an overseas missionary. By January, when the annual convention of the National Religious Broadcasters was to take place in Washington, D.C., Gorman was certain the source was Jimmy and Frances.

"The whole Gorman thing stemmed from stupid jealousy," said David Beatty. "I mean, Gorman was just a little television preacher down in New Orleans."

Gorman had returned from a session at national headquarters, where he had gone to answer the charges against him about Savage, "chewed up so bad; he wasn't even allowed to present his explanation or defense. [He] was a beaten down little puppy when he came back," said a family member. Gorman left the Assemblies of God.

Stripped of his denominational base and plagued by the escalating rumors of his affairs, he was unable to maintain his television ministry, which he claimed later had revenues of $4 million a year, but had been in financial trouble when the confrontation in Baton Rouge in July of 1986 took place. The $16 million loan Jimmy torpedoed was supposed to fix that, but the loan went away. Now, in January of 1987, Gorman filed personal bankruptcy, with debts that would balloon to more than $3.5 million.

By the time the National Religious Broadcasters' convention rolled around at the end of January, 1987, Jim Bakker was convinced that the Swaggarts were stepping up their campaign against him, too. He skipped the convention, canceling a speech he was supposed to give and missing the chance to be seen with Vice President George Bush, who was to address the 4,200 attendees.

Two days before the NRB convention began, Tammy Bakker checked into the Betty Ford Center in Rancho Mirage, California, near Palm Springs, to be treated for addiction to tranquilizers—Ativan and Valium were ones she was seen using most often. After one unhappy night, she checked out and became an outpatient (oddly, Jerry Lee had also checked out after a night or two, seven weeks earlier). But the PTL audience was told she was being treated for "exhaustion," and that she was at the Eisenhower Medical Center, which shared a campus with the Ford Center, instead of at Betty Ford.

The news of her drug problem stayed a secret for over a month, as PTL stonewalled its viewers, who clamored for news of her health, with chirpy tidbits about "checkups" and when she might be able to go shopping again. The Bakkers didn't reveal the nature of her treatment until March 6, and then they implied it was for over-the-counter allergy medicines.

Charlotte Observer reporter Charles Shepard was getting closer and closer to exposing PTL's payoff to Jessica Hahn. On January 18, Shepard flew to Los Angeles to meet John Stewart, an Orange County attorney-pastor who had drafted the complaint Hahn presented to Dortch. Stewart had sworn not to go on record by the terms of the trust that was created with the money, but he was willing to help set Shepard on the right path.

At the NRB convention, Stewart set others on the path, too. He conferred with two other ministers, one of whom was a California colleague, cult expert and radio host Walter Martin, the "Bible Answerman." The other was John Ankerberg, the Tennessee minister whose program PTL had axed in the fall of 1986 because, like Jimmy, Ankerberg had favored the book *The Seduction of Christianity.*

Stewart told his companions about the Jessica Hahn affair, feeling Ankerberg would be a good conduit to get the news into the Assemblies rumor mill and then up the food chain to Springfield via Jimmy and Frances Swaggart. Frances, described later to Shepard as ruthless, controlling, and fiercely protective of Jimmy, had shown with the Gorman affair that she was not afraid to get on the telephone when there was bad news. And Ankerberg and Jimmy were *simpaticos,* since PTL had dropped them both.

Ankerberg was shocked to hear about Hahn and the payoff, and that the *Observer* was chasing the story. As expected, he went straight to Jimmy. Of course, none of it was news to Jimmy; John Fletcher had told him the story five months ago and he had confronted Dortch with it a few weeks later. But it was a chance to check up on Dortch. He asked Ankerberg who his source was; if it was someone other than Fletcher, it was strong evidence that Dortch had lied to him back in September. The answer was: John Stewart.

Richard Dortch later wrote that PTL had been getting calls since before Christmas from concerned pastors and followers asking about a rumor that Bakker had had an affair. With the Bakkers absent from their program because of Tammy's secret drug treatment, the pressure for answers and information had become intense. At the convention, Dortch was braced by one of the Executive Presbyters in a hallway. Was it true? And was she paid? Dortch dissembled, misleading his colleague as he had done Jimmy the previous September—a decision he later regretted.

After returning to Baton Rouge from the convention, Frances called Jerald Ogg, Jr., who, as a child, had played with Donnie when Jimmy preached in Kansas City, into her office. Jerald Jr. had been hired as general counsel a few years before, but his main job was handling the press, since, in addition to his law degree, he had a bachelor's degree in journalism.

Since the church fathers didn't seem too eager to turn over the rocks at PTL and see what was under there, Frances wanted her press liaison to leak information to the *Observer.*

Frances explained to Ogg that Jimmy had already tried to confront Bakker Biblically, and not only would Bakker not meet with him, but the emissary he did send, Dortch, lied to cover Bakker's tracks. They weren't, she said, attacking PTL because it was a competitor, any more than they had come down on Gorman for that reason. They were simply interested in two things: that these preachers not be allowed to get away with sinning, and that their conduct not bring down the media and the government on the other television ministries.

Frances had another motive, too. The Gorman affair had characterized the Swaggarts as denominational pit bulls, and rumors flew that Jimmy was jealous of PTL if not covetous, and that he wanted Gorman's spot in the Assemblies. Frances wanted to operate behind the scenes this time. If the *Observer* exposed Bakker instead of the Swaggarts exposing him, the national presbyters would be forced to discipline him. The heat would land on the *Observer,* not Jimmy.

Frances had arranged plants at PTL, according to Dortch's later account. They and her other sources had reported that Tammy Bakker was not hospitalized for exhaustion as PTL viewers were being told, but rather was at the Betty Ford Center. Jerald Ogg Jr.'s first assignment was to feed this information to Charles Shepard, and to imbed a razor blade: a "rumor" that the

Observer already knew this, but couldn't print it because PTL had threatened to use some dirt it had found on one of the editors if the newspaper didn't back off. (Frances' sources had apparently heard that the *Observer* had declined to report on an in-house scandal because it involved a high-level employee's son, and that PTL was holding this over the editors' heads to keep the Hahn story at bay.)

On February 9, Ogg had his secretary call Shepard anonymously to test his receptivity. Shepard didn't fall for the editor-scandal gambit, but was eager to hear any information. After complaining to Shepard that the church hierarchy was closing its eyes to Bakker's sins, and mentioning the name Jessica Hahn, the caller said her boss would call Shepard back. Ogg did so in a couple of hours, using a pseudonym. Thus began a steady stream of information, gossip, and rumor from Frances to the *Charlotte Observer* that lasted two months—long enough to topple Jim Bakker.

Later, John Stewart would say that Jimmy and Frances did this because, as an ordained Assemblies of God minister, "it was Swaggart's duty to find out the truth and deal with it accordingly." Jimmy's later account of his involvement was far weaker: Ogg made a couple of calls to Shepard, he wrote, "in our effort to ascertain what was taking place" but Shepard "never revealed any information to Ogg." Of course, that was not the point; the point was whether Ogg revealed information to Shepard.

Astonishingly, Jimmy also claimed never to have read Shepherd's columns, saying that "someone told us" what he'd written. That gave the preposterous impression that he and Frances, who had set up a surveillance and intelligence network that fired back and forth many times a day among Baton Rouge, Charlotte, Springfield, and wherever she and Jimmy happened to be traveling, had no interest in the events unfolding around PTL.

Charles Shepard had been doing exactly what Frances wanted, trying to pin down someone who would go on the record about the payoff to Jessica Hahn. That was critical to his editors. Bakker's affair was just an age-old human weakness, but paying off Hahn with $265,000 of donors' money was an outrageous flouting of the law.

At the end of February, Shepard called Dortch with a list of questions that made it clear he knew too much about the Hahn affair to keep the lid on much longer. Dortch referred him to the Assemblies leadership in Springfield. But they claimed that no one had presented them with any written evidence of Bakker's misdeeds. Jim Bakker was a great man of God. Women made up these stories about preachers all the time. They were all sure everyone was dealing with everything completely ethically.

Frances and Jimmy had their co-pastor, Jim Rentz, pressing Springfield to do something about Bakker before Shepard's story broke and made them look gutless or corrupt for not dealing with him.

Just before the NRB convention, Tulsa televangelist Oral Roberts had made a pitch for money that hurt religious broadcasters and tainted George

Bush's upcoming presidential campaign, since Bush had so openly courted the Christian right. Roberts announced that if his followers didn't come up with $8 million by the last day of March, God would take his life.

Now, on March 6, Roberts made another gaffe. He appeared on PTL with Dortch and announced that God had told him Satan was barred from harming Bakker's ministry now, no matter what storms might rage.

In fact, just the opposite was true. Two days earlier, a former Dortch aide, who had crucial evidence of the Hahn payoff but had remained silent and loyal for 20 months waiting for PTL to clean up its act, made an agitated call to PTL board member Charles Cookman that "PTL is arrogant, proud, and a stench in the nostrils of God." In the next few days, the employee, Al Cress, would finally defect to the *Observer,* becoming a key figure in Bakker's undoing.

The second week in March, Jimmy was winding up a crusade tour of several Central American countries, all the while keeping in close touch with PTL developments via Baton Rouge. He became so concerned about the progress of Shepard's investigation that he called Springfield from Costa Rica, warning Assistant General Superintendent Everett Stenhouse that Shepard's story on Hahn was imminent. He was very much afraid the denomination would appear to be ignoring evidence against Bakker.

It was critical to the Assemblies that the *Observer* not break the story first. The last thing the church needed was the public's conclusion that it couldn't govern itself, and that the press was needed to police it. It was in everyone's interest for Bakker to be confronted.

Ankerberg wanted to form an interdenominational group of preachers to confront Bakker, putting together documentation so strong Bakker would not be able to refute it. He asked Jimmy to head the group, along with Jerry Falwell, and solicited other prominent ministers, including Pat Robertson and D. James Kennedy, to join in.

Many of the ministers pleaded other commitments, and by March 11, 1987 only Ankerberg, Jimmy, and Falwell remained. They wanted to at least give the impression that they had tried to confront Bakker Biblically, as called for in Matthew 18:15–17, and Stewart drafted a letter to Bakker to be signed by the three of them. It said they were aware of the Hahn matter and other activities and urgently requested a meeting "to seek a Biblical solution." In fact, Jimmy was ready, according to Stewart, to publicly support Bakker during the period of disgrace that would surely follow. Jimmy agreed to sign, but Falwell wanted to show it to his attorney first.

As the men were mulling over what to do if Bakker took them to court, Bakker appeared on videotape from California, where he was still in therapy with his wife. Warned by Dortch of the impending eruption, he laid the groundwork for damage control, speaking darkly of enemies that were out to destroy him. He threatened, with extraordinary hubris, that people who had tried to damage him in the past had seen "their whole lives disintegrated, their families have disintegrated." He was anointed by God, and you didn't mess with God's anointed, he stated.

He took swipes at Jimmy's pursuit of Gorman, and at Shepard: "I know of ministers . . . [who] have just become specialists in evil . . . They collect all the filth and all the material they can. Just like the reporters . . . trying to destroy the people of God."

Even as Bakker spoke, the Assemblies, under pressure from ex-PTL employees, Jimmy and Frances, the *Observer,* and other church leaders, was finally agreeing to open a formal investigation of him.

Jimmy had been reluctant to sign the letter to Bakker, telling Ankerberg he'd already done his Matthew 18 duty by inviting Bakker to Baton Rouge. Bakker had refused to come, sending Dortch instead, and Dortch had lied. But Ankerberg made a strong case, and Jimmy relented.

Then he talked it over further with Frances. Remembering what happened with Gorman, who tried to cover his tracks the minute he left Swaggart's presence, they could assume Bakker would do the same. He would use the letter to accuse Jimmy of coveting PTL for himself, or of wanting to destroy it out of jealousy, or wanting vengeance because PTL had kicked him and Ankerberg off the air the previous year. Bakker and Dortch would show the letter as proof that Jimmy was fueling the *Observer* story (which, of course, was largely true). Worse, they would probably use the letter to raise money.

The next day Jimmy decided not to sign. He dictated a blunt, clear-headed memo to Ankerberg saying why: Dortch and Bakker had lied all along and would continue to; they would distort the letter's purpose and use it in court if it ever went that far.

Then he left for a trip to Dallas. Ankerberg read Jimmy's memo and faxed it to Falwell.

Falwell had been trying to get information on his own about PTL, and had been stonewalled like Shepard. One of his staff suggested showing Dortch Jimmy's memo and seeing if that jarred anything loose.

Falwell's men tracked Dortch down on his boat in Florida and spoke to him on his cellular phone, asking if the Hahn rumor was true. Dortch blew the story off, complaining that Jimmy Swaggart was behind it, that Jimmy had a reputation for personal vendettas; Dortch hinted Jimmy was planning to steal PTL out from under Bakker. He had been after them for months, Dortch said. But he agreed to meet Falwell's representatives the next night at the Tampa airport.

Falwell's private jet was late, and it was after midnight when Dortch, an assistant, and two of Falwell's men went to a conference room in the airport's administration building.

They told Dortch that Jimmy Swaggart knew all about the Jessica Hahn affair. Dortch acted shocked, even though he had known for at least six months that Jimmy knew not only about Hahn, but about the homosexuality and other matters.

Then they showed him Jimmy's faxed memo. He read with an icy feeling what his old friend had written to Ankerberg: "Please believe me there is absolutely no chance of Bakker and Dortch stepping down for any type of rehabilitation. First, they will try to lie their way out of it . . . Then they will pull out of the Assemblies of God. Their last step will be to . . . elicit sympathy from the general public. If there are severe difficulties and problems, I will bear the brunt of it . . . you do not know these people as I know them . . ."

Caught in his charade of acting shocked that Jimmy knew about Hahn, and stunned at his old friend's blunt unveiling of him as a liar, Dortch broke and cried. He told them that the Hahn story was true, and said she had pressured and pressured for hush money.

According to Dortch, Falwell's men told him that Jimmy had enough people to file a class action suit against PTL and put it into receivership. They said the Swaggarts had a spy at PTL to keep them informed of what was transpiring.

That, said Dortch later, came as no surprise; a turncoat in Jimmy's own ministry had warned him that Frances Swaggart was sending a female employee to Heritage USA to "learn what she can about what's happening there." The source gave him details of her arrival and appearance. Dortch had her followed and had her telephone tapped. When she came to the services the first Sunday at Heritage USA, he tracked where she sat, and went to the control room before air time and had the director find her with one of the cameras. Then he gave instructions to cut to her at least 30 times during the sermon.

Jimmy and Frances always watched PTL. He figured it would send a message.

After Falwell's men left, Dortch called Bakker in Palm Springs and told him the jig was up. He told him about Swaggart's role. Jimmy's inflammatory fax, meant to be a personal reply to Ankerberg, was rapidly circulated among Bakker, his attorney, and others. It was worse than if Jimmy had just signed the "Matthew 18" letter.

Much happened during the next five days. Without revealing their names, Oral Roberts blasted Jimmy, Ankerberg and Falwell as the "unholy trio" for daring to pressure Bakker. Then Bakker forged an alliance with Falwell. He asked him to take over PTL, an astonishing move that would stun his followers. Falwell was a Baptist, doctrinally far from the Pentecostals, and very conservative.

But Falwell agreed. He flew to Palm Springs on Monday, March 16 to meet with the Bakkers and arrange it. He abruptly stopped returning Ankerberg's and Jimmy's calls.

Jimmy would later bitterly accuse Falwell of using the fax to spook Bakker so he, Falwell, could grab PTL. He wrote that he was extremely hurt when

Falwell joined the chorus accusing him of, in the lingo of the 1980s, a T. Boone Pickens-style "hostile takeover." He said he called Falwell over and over, bewildered, but his calls were refused; he was shunted to Falwell's gruff, brash attorney, Roy Grutman, who had now also agreed to represent PTL.

Bakker and Falwell left their meeting in Palm Springs with different ideas of what had been agreed on. Bakker, like Gorman, expected to simply go off the air for a couple of months while the Hahn affair blew over. He would blame his absence on Tammy's "health," and let Falwell answer the press. Falwell was expecting Bakker to submit to the Assemblies' two-year restoration period out of the pulpit.

But events favored neither scenario. Unknown to either of them, within days of their meeting, John Wesley Fletcher was flying by private plane to Springfield at the Assemblies' expense to spend 13 hours telling top officials about the years he'd spent at PTL as Bakker's companion.

On March 18, Bakker called his board in Charlotte and resigned over the telephone from his positions as President, CEO, General Manager, and board member of PTL. As planned, the PTL board resigned and voted in Falwell's crew.

Unaware of these developments, Jimmy was still working with Ankerberg and Stewart to evaluate the documentary evidence of the Hahn tryst. Comparing notes, the men discovered that Falwell had not been returning any of their calls. They planned a meeting without him, for Friday, March 20 at the Indian Wells condominium where Jimmy and Frances were vacationing near Palm Springs. Among the documents they were to review was a tape in which Jessica Hahn described what Bakker had done to her in December of 1980. John Stewart again got out his drafting paper, this time penning a public statement about how Jimmy, Falwell, and Ankerberg had at least tried to deal with Bakker Scripturally.

That statement would never be released.

On Thursday, March 19, just as Oral Roberts was about to ascend his 200-foot Prayer Tower in Tulsa to count down the last week of his showdown with donors over the $8 million God had told him to get or else He'd "take him home," Jim Bakker publicly resigned as host of his television show and as chairman of Heritage USA.

His speech was revealing: instead of confessing his weakness and apologizing for it, Bakker said, "I sorrowfully acknowledge that seven years ago, in an isolated incident, I was wickedly manipulated by treacherous former friends and then colleagues who victimized me with the aid of a female confederate."

Bakker also resigned from the Assemblies of God, as did Dortch. He announced that Falwell would be taking over, and suddenly Ankerberg and Jimmy understood why Falwell hadn't returned their calls.

Falwell's new seven-member board contained only three Pentecostals.

On March 20, the *Charlotte Observer* finally ran its PTL story. Stewart and Ankerberg joined Jimmy at his condo, and a crowd gathered—Paul Roper (John Stewart's ally in California in drafting Hahn's legal papers), Bill Treeby, Roper's and Ankerberg's wives, Frances, Walter Martin, and Donnie—to listen to Hahn's taped statement telling how Jim Bakker had forced her to have sex with him after Fletcher had given her drugged wine.

They discussed whether Falwell was drooling over PTL's satellite and $129 million in revenues, and why he had not told them what he was doing. They mulled over how to use their evidence to help with the Assemblies' investigation, and how to neutralize the effect of the scandal on other television ministries. They agreed that Roper and Ankerberg would take the tape and other evidence to Springfield on March 25, and say nothing to reporters in the meantime, referring them all to the Assemblies.

As the group met, Roy Grutman, Bakker's attorney, was ratcheting the tension to the breaking point, releasing a statement to the press that an unnamed evangelist—clearly Jimmy—was threatening to take over PTL: under a clip of Jim Bakker huffing across the set of one of his television shows like a snarling chihuahua, Jimmy's voiceover could be heard complaining publicly about him. Then Grutman spoke darkly of "dirtier laundry" in that evangelist's hamper than was in Jim Bakker's.

Over the weekend, Grutman called Treeby, who was back in Baton Rouge, and asked for a face-to-face confrontation with Jimmy. Treeby declined, offering instead to meet Falwell. Grutman then threatened to expose information about Jimmy that would make Bakker look good in comparison if Jimmy didn't let up on Bakker.

The next week, the Bakkers were on the cover of all the major national news magazines; they were interviewed on ABC's "Nightline," resulting in the largest ratings the show had ever had.

On March 23, Jim and Tammy made their last appearance on their show, portraying Bakker as a victim and ripping the *Observer*. All day, the "hostile takeover" story heated up. Robert Schuller publicly sided with Bakker, as, of course, did Oral Roberts. Schuller had disliked Jimmy since the early 1980s when Jimmy had approached Schuller's stations and offered them more money to air his show instead, driving up Schuller's air costs as the stations asked him to match Jimmy's offers. Other Pentecostals—Oral Roberts and Paul Crouch—had used similar tactics, but Schuller felt he had a good relationship with them. With Jimmy, he felt it was war.

But Pat Robertson, Bakker's old boss at CBN, said Bakker's resignation was a housecleaning.

The Bakkers alluded to Jimmy that morning, decrying his Satan-led "plot" to take over PTL (still without naming him). Bakker said, in fact, that he was resigning not because of the Jessica Hahn scandal, but to keep PTL from being taken over by this "rival evangelist." Charles Shepard called Jimmy in

California for a response, and Jimmy told him this was payback, for calling Dortch and Bakker liars in his memo to Ankerberg, and for exposing Marvin Gorman nine months ago.

Gorman himself had not been idle. On the same day, March 23, that the fallen Bakkers excoriated Jimmy on television, Gorman hurled a grenade from New Orleans: he was suing Jimmy, Frances, Treeby, Indest, and nine others involved in the July 1986 confrontation at Highland Road that had destroyed his ministry. He wanted $90 million.

"Anybody who'd ever eaten crawfish was named in Marvin Gorman's suit," said Jimmy's former researcher, Larry Thomas. He defended Jimmy's handling of Gorman. "Jimmy would have been satisfied just to keep Marvin Gorman out of the leadership, [but] Jimmy was asked, he replied, and then he had to go out and get documentation of it [Gorman's infidelities]. If you're gonna say these things, you gotta have something to back them up."

As if the evangelical community didn't have enough buffoonery, Oral Roberts that same Monday got a chunk of money—$1.3 million, several hundred thousand dollars over the $8 million on which his life hung—from a Florida dogtrack owner, Jerry Collins. The eccentric Collins commented that now Oral wouldn't have to commit hara-kiri, and opined that the preacher needed psychiatric help.

Not only did Roberts take the money from gambling interests, he tried to delay the news of Collins' rescue because it came a week before his deadline, and he'd lose the opportunity to bring in more money during that last week.

The evangelical community spent that busy Monday, March 23, trying to plug holes in the dike, the holes Jimmy had been trumpeting about for months—and some of which he'd helped drill.

His position was delicate; after his attacks on Bakker in the *Evangelist* and on the air, it was easy even for his allies and neutral ministers to believe in the "takeover" plot. In the evening, Ben Kinchlow, Pat Robertson's co-host on CBN's "700 Club," called Jimmy in Indian Wells and asked him to appear on the show to explain his side. Jimmy declined, afraid that no matter what he said, the media would cast it as some angle on a "takeover."

He reiterated his disinterest in acquiring PTL and its problems, and when Kinchlow asked him to speak with Bakker, Jimmy replied he'd be only too happy to. Kinchlow didn't want to give out Bakker's unlisted number, but promised to have him call Jimmy. Bakker never did, though Jimmy's phone rang off the hook otherwise with requests for interviews.

That night, PTL's attorney Grutman appeared on "Nightline," referring to Jimmy in veiled accusations and saying he had clear-cut evidence that a rival was trying to oust Bakker. Later that evening, he told Shepard that he just wanted Jimmy to "call off his dogs."

Late in the afternoon, Frances had returned Shepard's call. She and Jimmy had been resting in California since winding up Jimmy's tour of Central

America. He had returned exhausted and ill with a virus, and he had another crusade scheduled for the last week of March in Los Angeles.

It must have been heady wine for Frances, speaking to the person she had helped maneuver into bringing down the Bakkers via Jerald Ogg, Jr.—and it must have been even more exciting that he still didn't know she was behind it, though he had come to suspect that his anonymous informant was connected with the Swaggarts. Between the two of them, she and Shepard had every major news organization in America flurrying to Palm Springs, Springfield, and Charlotte. She giggled when she spoke to Shepard, saying the hostile takeover nonsense was "quite funny." Then she handed the phone to Jimmy.

Jimmy took Shepard through his objections to PTL's secularization and Hollywoodization of the Gospel, Bakker's thirst for sensation, his entertainment orientation, his failure to stick to Biblical principles, and the sordidness permeating both PTL's corporate culture and its finances. Now Bakker was trying to turn things around and make himself a victim so he could raise money off of his own failure. As to the rumors that he coveted PTL, Jimmy reiterated wearily that he certainly had no interest in taking on PTL's headaches.

Jimmy was, however, genuinely shocked and hurt that Falwell's attorney threatened to expose "dirty things" about him. He had felt a kinship with Falwell, both as head of the Moral Majority and because he had not compromised the Gospel, backed off of strong moral positions, or gone Nashville.

March 23 was a grueling day that ended with the Swaggarts watching Grutman vilify Jimmy on "Nightline."

The next morning, the gale blew stronger against Jimmy. He stood alone as Oral Roberts scolded him, *sotto voce,* for "sowing discord among the brethren, because somehow you think you're holier than thou." Others came out openly against him. Gorman's attorney, Tomy Frasier, held a press conference in New Orleans, accusing Jimmy of also trying to get Gorman's followers and their money. Grutman held a press conference in South Carolina, claiming to have clear evidence of a conspiracy by Jimmy Swaggart to get PTL's followers and their money. Jack Hayford, a prominent Los Angeles area pastor, said Jimmy was the kind of person to "topple anything that's unappealing to him." Robert Schuller had sided with Bakker before, and now other prominent churchmen, including Kenneth Copeland and Paul Crouch, weighed in for Bakker.

Only Ankerberg stood by Jimmy—and, of course, Stewart, Roper, and the others who'd tried to avoid a media mess with Bakker. Jimmy had wanted to abide by the vow he'd made with them to keep silent until the 25th, when they would discreetly turn their evidence over to the national Assemblies. But Tomy Frasier had made the lethal mistake of naming Frances in his press conference, accusing her of calling key denominational people last summer to pass on news of Gorman's adulterous affairs.

"There were strangers, even, who would say Frances was the driving force [behind Gorman's removal]," said Larry Thomas. "People have created a persona for Frances, she was the devil behind Jimmy, she's behind anything he does. . . . she was just a very, very strong individual . . . She knew what she wanted, she was very strong willed."

Threats against Frances were known to push Jimmy over the edge. Now he agreed to be interviewed. He talked to his old nemesis, WBRZ, and to a reporter from the *Baton Rouge Morning Advocate*. He also agreed to take time from preparing for his March 27 Los Angeles crusade to appear on CNN's "Larry King" program. He took Ben Kinchlow up on his offer to appear on Pat Robertson's "700 Club," and taped his appearance from Los Angeles.

He called the takeover rumors absurd. He called Bakker a cancer that needed to be excised from the body of Christ. (Later, Jimmy would protest that he had said this about PTL's philosophy, not Bakker, but the distinction hardly mattered.) Asked about Gorman's $90 million suit against him, he laughed. "The last place in the world [Gorman] wants to see is a court of law," he said. He responded to the Oral Roberts death-and-dogtrack fiasco by saying the denomination had sunk to a new low.

He said later that he had "squeezed the triggers on both barrels," and that he felt bad about it. But even if Frances' besmirched honor might have been the trigger, he was also angry on his own behalf. "My response was strong because I had been accused of grand theft before the whole world and it was a blatant lie," he said. "I was angry and indignant . . . I pulled no punches."

On Wednesday, March 25, John Ankerberg and a group of others went to Springfield as planned to give the Assemblies officials details of the Hahn settlement. Outside the headquarters, reporters swarmed, and back in California John Stewart, the attorney-pastor who had drafted Hahn's original complaint, was released from his confidentiality obligations and finally held a press conference.

Just before the Los Angeles crusade, Jerry Falwell finally returned Jimmy's calls. A day or so earlier, Falwell had suddenly turned on Bakker, saying that, if he tried to return to PTL, it would cripple the new board. On the phone, Jimmy wrote later, he asked Falwell if he, too, were accusing him of a hostile takeover. He said Falwell was evasive.

"Then," wrote Jimmy, "Frances came on the line. I had been somewhat mild in my probing, but Frances pulled the gloves off and read him the riot act."

After the reaming-out by Frances, Falwell told the press on March 27 that he no longer believed Jimmy had ever wanted PTL. Frances blandly told the *Washington Post* that she had merely called Falwell to see if he had heard anything about a disgruntled PTL employee saying Jimmy was trying to take over PTL.

That same day, the *Observer* broke more details about the money Jessica Hahn had received, further damaging Bakker's credibility. Soon the tide was turning for Jimmy. The Assemblies announced that there had been no Swaggart takeover plot.

JIMMY FOUND THAT he was adroit at handling the national media. They were respectful and appeared interested in cutting to the unvarnished truth. They liked his plainspokenness and earthy images. "I'm a target in a carnival," he told the *Washington Post* as he trumped Grutman by releasing to the newspaper his notorious memo to Ankerberg and the unsigned "Matthew 18" letter that he, Falwell, and Ankerberg had never gotten to send to Bakker.

Newsmen like Ted Koppel and Larry King treated Jimmy as an intelligent peer, not an incomprehensible grotesquerie. Accordingly, Jimmy answered straight, not retreating into Scripture or trying to come across as pious or otherworldly. Had the Bakker affair hurt televangelism? Not all of it, Jimmy answered, but "if it does hurt, it'll just have to hurt . . . [PTL] was a festering sore, and I think the *Charlotte Observer* has done the country a very valuable service."

Asked if he was maybe interested in PTL's satellite network, he said yes— because it was a powerful tool for the glory of God and he wanted to see it used in a good way. As far as why he'd been kicked off it, he answered, "It's his satellite, he had the right to do with it as he liked."

Asked why Bakker would accuse Jimmy of a takeover if he'd already given up his ministry, Jimmy replied that Bakker hadn't given it up. That was a sham, he said, he's planning a comeback, you watch.

Not for the first time, he saw that negative publicity raised money. His well-timed interviews just before his crusade at the Los Angeles Sports Arena packed the arena and brought out the media. He used the opportunity to preach especially colorfully, and he took a bold chance—he challenged Grutman to go ahead and reveal his dirty laundry "to the whole world." Even if Grutman could drag up some fallen woman from New Orleans, who would believe her under these circumstances?

By the first week in April—April being the seventy-third birthday of the Assemblies of God, which now had 2.3 million adherents in the U.S.—Jimmy was being portrayed in the press as the Assemblies' Holy Scourge, rebuking false doctrine, sorcery, and fads—all of which could be said to be hallmarks of PTL. Jimmy used his new stage to intensify his attacks on old targets: dancing, contemporary music, psychology, and feelgood theology. Before Jesus returned in the Great Tribulation, the church had to dissolve, and before that, the Gospel had to be spread to the whole world. Ministers who preached prosperity and counseling and positive thinking, he said, were tools of Satan.

That covered a lot of Assemblies of God preachers. He lodged charges of doctrinal deviation and slander against two more of his brethren—one of them another friend of Bakker—and spurred longtime rumors that he was going to split away from the Assemblies and start his own denomination.

Dortch gave a scathing account of another Swaggart confrontation during this period, with Falwell. Jimmy behaved in much the same way for Frances' benefit as he had in the meeting with Dortch, Cookman, Janway, Frances, Donnie, and Rentz back in September of 1986. In April, Jimmy and Frances attended a PTL board meeting in Nashville, where Jimmy poked his finger in board members' faces and aggressively demanded if first one and then another believed he had tried to take over PTL. He ended by demanding that Dortch be removed from PTL. This echoed other accounts of Jimmy's alpha-male behavior in Frances' presence.

Again the national organization came under criticism for failing to discipline its preachers, this time Jimmy. No smaller preacher, said one church source, would be allowed to get away with the excoriations Jimmy was lobbing right and left, but his ministry gave $10–12 million a year to the national organization for foreign missions. They hadn't disciplined Bakker, after all, and he gave less than $200,000.

Jimmy even agreed that a third of Assembly ministers were probably against him. But, drunk on power, he said he doubted his elders were strong enough to discipline him. "That sounds awful conceited, I guess, but I don't mean it that way. We respect those men very highly. . . . I will not usurp their position—even though I could." The flock, he said, was 90 per cent for him. "Most [Assembly of God] preachers cannot even get up in their own church and say anything against me. Their people won't stand for it."

In mid-April, WBRZ aired a special report on the ministry, reviving the Dwain Johnson sex scandal and alleging personal use of ministry money, printing kickbacks, and other aberrations. Still fighting, Dortch had unearthed Johnson, who couldn't say much because of the terms of his 1984 settlement with Jimmy, but who did show up at PTL around the time Jimmy appeared on "Larry King" again, sometime in April.

A caller to King's show, presumably a PTL plant, was supposed to embarrass Jimmy by asking if a member of his family had ever had an affair. But the caller blew it, asking if there had been an affair with a drummer in his band (Johnson was a guitarist). No, Jimmy answered quickly—no one in his family had ever had an affair with his drummer.

The *New Orleans Times-Picayune* followed WBRZ, dredging up old Jimmy Swaggart Ministry problems and providing details of the Johnson affair, the challenge to Zoe Vance's will, and a third court case involving a bizarre and horrible murder that resulted in a bequest to the ministry. Ida Lee Baugh, 70, was stabbed to death in December 1983 at her home near Waco, Texas. The murderer was a 19-year-old girl who had been hired to watch over the partially paralyzed woman.

Baugh's husband died of a heart attack five days after his wife's death, whereupon their son Larry Baugh discovered that both his parents' wills had been changed two weeks before the murder to leave most of their estate, estimated between $500,000 and $800,000, to the Jimmy Swaggart Ministries. Larry Baugh challenged the wills, claiming Jimmy's representatives not only pressured his parents to change them, but to hire the sick girl as well. She had been placed in the home by a family friend, Mario Scorzza, an employee of the Texas Rehabilitation Commission in Waco who had also helped the Baughs change their wills.

The suit left the outrageous impression that the ministry conspired with Scorzza to knock off the Baughs after getting them to change their wills. It was abandoned five days after filing, after it was discovered that Scorzza was a Catholic and had no connection with Jimmy. Six days after that, a contrite Larry Baugh, perhaps terrified at the liability he had invited with his suit, announced he was leaving even the paltry $25,000 he had inherited from his parents to the ministry as well.

By the end of April, Jim Bakker was thoroughly disillusioned with Falwell and wanted to return to PTL. John Stewart, John Ankerberg, and Paul Roper decided to tell more of what they knew to stop him. Ankerberg blasted Bakker on "Larry King" with rumors of wife-swapping at PTL, the diversion of PTL funds to private use, Tammy having to be physically restrained from running off with another man, Jim Bakker being serviced by prostitutes and keeping a stock of liquor at PTL, and Bakker being involved in homosexual practices numerous times.

Later, Ankerberg repeated the charges on "Nightline." Bakker denied them, but Falwell said Ankerberg was well respected and would be taken seriously. However, he noted, all electronic ministries were losing money over the scandals; his own had lost nearly $2 million the previous month.

When Falwell sided with Ankerberg, Richard Dortch resigned from PTL. Three days later, James Watt, PTL's trophy board member because of his position as Secretary of the Interior under President Reagan, also resigned, the last of the Bakker loyalists. These actions gave Jimmy great credibility.

A few days later, however, the *Baton Rouge State Times Sunday Advocate* dropped a weekly column by Jimmy which it had been running for the past 10 months. For the second time during that period, Jimmy had used copyrighted material without attribution. Jimmy apologized, saying he had been distracted by having to deal with the PTL scandal and that a secretary had sent an unedited column.

That same day, May 1, 1987, the other Baton Rouge newspaper, the *Morning Advocate,* did two uncomplimentary stories on ministry finances, infuriating Jimmy. After refusing to open his books since 1983, when he had cooperated with WBRZ and felt he'd gotten burned, he had granted reporters access to audited financial statements again because of the allegations of waste at PTL. Once again, he felt his attempt to cooperate with the hometown press had backfired.

That would be the last time Jimmy cooperated with the press about ministry finances—the last time, in fact, that he would cooperate with any writers. His inability to control the media had put him in a hopeless loop: he complained that the press always got everything wrong about him but refused to clear up the incorrect information because he'd have to talk to a member of the press.

Jimmy accused WBRZ of persecution in its April special report, saying John Camp had been overheard vowing to put him out of business whatever it took. Camp angrily challenged him to produce the informant; Jimmy declined. He seemed to be genuinely wounded by Camp, whom he'd once trusted and tried to befriend. Camp seemed to be blasting him when he didn't really need blasting, just because he was the only story in town and there was some discontent among his followers—not an unusual circumstance in an organization as big as Jimmy's. That Camp left WBRZ and moved on to CNN in 1989 seemed to validate Jimmy's sense that he was just being used to propel Camp's career.

AT THE END of May, an angry Jerry Falwell, increasingly disgusted with what he found at PTL, told the press what Jim and Tammy had demanded in return for resigning: a $300,000-a-year salary for Jim and $100,000 a year for Tammy—for life; a fully furnished PTL house; two cars; rights to book and record royalties; payment of all legal fees regarding any IRS actions; bodyguards, secretaries, and a maid; and free telephone calls for a year.

WBRZ was also in court with Jimmy, along with the Baton Rouge newspapers and the *New Orleans Times-Picayune*, over Marvin Gorman's $90 million defamation suit. They were opposing Jimmy's request to keep secret the names of women he and Frances had dug up who said they'd had relations with Gorman. On May 15, the judge denied Jimmy's request that pretrial motions be kept secret.

Because it concerned adultery and slander, the Gorman trial brought home the fact that, even though Jimmy himself might enjoy respect in the national media, the events that had brought him there were still largely seen by the leaders of those media as the affairs of hucksters who preyed on the hicks and ignoramuses from which they had sprung.

Though it was now the largest Pentecostal body in the world, the Assemblies was aware that the national media could turn against any evangelist in a flash, especially, it seemed, if it was suspected that the evangelical movement was pushing America to the political right.

By summer Jimmy reported donations were off by 10 percent. PTL's revenues fell from $96 million to $41 million. The revenues from Pat Robertson's

Christian Broadcast Network fell 32.5 per cent in seven months. Jerry Falwell said his income was down by $6 million. Broadcast ratings dropped for most of the televangelists.

Pat Robertson, who hoped to have a shot at the presidency, was making a determined effort to distance himself from the other televangelists, insisting that he was a "religious broadcaster, a businessman" as the media began producing a profile of the constituency that had formed Falwell's Moral Majority, helped elect Ronald Reagan, and might put Robertson in office. He was already in the process of suing for libel over an accusation that he had used family influence to escape military duty in Korea, and his presidential candidacy kept suffering as the PTL scandal produced deeper scrutiny of the evangelical phenomenon.

The profile of television preacher watchers, according to sociologist Jeffrey Hadden, was "disproportionately older . . . female, Southern, small town, lower socioeconomic level." Audiences were growing in the West and Midwest, partly because of the influx of Southerners to those places. It was suggested that the typical viewer was after a simple message, easy solutions, and authoritative postures that brought a sense of stability—not only to a socioeconomic group whose self-esteem had been devastated by the Civil War, but to a new generation that had grown up with cataclysmic social change, too much mobility, and uncertainty that it would prosper as much as the previous one.

The audiences were attracted to the upbeat music and dynamic ministers, echoing the showmanship that marked earlier evangelists: in the twenties, Billy Sunday broke chairs with his bare hands, pretending to wrestle with the devil, and lamented the existence of "hog-jowled, weasel-eyed, sponge-columned, mush-fisted, jelly-spined, four-flushing Christians"; 70 years later, a Brazilian evangelical slapped and kicked a statue of the Virgin Mary on live television, challenging it to get up and fight back, while he chided Catholics that "saints don't work."

By the end of June, Jimmy was again in court, this time to fight for the tax-exempt status of KJOJ, one of the ministry's six radio stations in Texas. The city, county, and school district where the station sat were demanding back property taxes of $157,000. After being accused of ignoring orders to produce financial data, Jimmy was forced by the court to disclose information about his contributions and sales of religious materials.

Someone had written the judge in February, accusing Jimmy of skimming $11 million in contributions and using them for his own personal expenses, a claim Jimmy stoutly denied, saying his income came from record sales. The court would not permit this letter to be released, but its contents were leaked to the press, and local broadcasters reported it on June 21. Some of the national media picked it up, and Jerald Ogg, Jr., spent the day asking for retractions, as the letter was merely the observation of someone who had read a 1984 ministry financial statement.

One of the national broadcasters that reported the skimming story was Paul Harvey. Afterward, he got a call from Frances. She set him straight, and put him on the phone with a ministry attorney. Two days later Harvey did an amended report, giving Jimmy a clean bill of health, but the ministry reported a $50,000-a-day drop in contributions due to the cumulative bad press from the spreading PTL scandal.

But even that claim was challenged by Stephen Winzenburg, the communications professor who had done exhaustive studies of televangelists' solicitation patterns for more than 15 years. Though Jimmy went so far as to tell his viewers that he had taken the brunt of the PTL scandal, Winzenburg told reporters, 1987 was actually his best financial year so far. The implication was that Jimmy had used the scandals to raise money.

Winzenburg soon received a call from Frances. "At first the sweet southern voice on the other end of the phone line attempted to be convincing and objective, quietly asking questions about my study and patiently listening while I explained academic analysis," he wrote when working up his notes of the call.

She objected to what Winzenburg had told the press. She KNEW they were losing money, she said. He asked her to check her figures and call him back.

She did, the next day, and, Winzenburg said, admitted he was right: the ministry would end 1987 eight percent ahead of 1986 in the U.S. and 30 percent ahead in Canada—confirming they were not losing money. But, he said, she tried to get him "to admit Jimmy was full of truth and that nothing he said was debatable." She challenged his analysis terms: Jimmy wasn't "preaching," he was "teaching." Singing wasn't "entertainment," it was "ministry." Jimmy didn't talk off the top of his head like Winzenburg characterized, she said; everything he said was well prepared.

She said Robert Schuller didn't preach the Gospel, and asked why Winzenburg's study had called him the most balanced televangelist. She asked for his figures on Billy Graham, who she insisted was Jimmy's "only real competition." She was convinced Winzenburg had underestimated the time Graham spent fundraising.

"When I called some of [Jimmy's] statements 'outrageous,' such as comparing the pope to Hitler or calling heaven a 'literal planet,' " Winzenburg said, Frances became angry. She tried one more time to get him to change his *USA Today* percentages of how much time Jimmy spent asking for money. When Winzenburg refused, she hung up. Shortly, *USA Today* called him to see if it was true that he had agreed to a retraction. Flabbergasted and angry, Winzenburg denied it. The reporter called Frances and confronted her.

"She called me again, this time super syrupy, saying there was a 'misunderstanding' . . . [and] to invite me to appear on Jimmy's daily show to defend myself in front of Swaggart and six of his hired 'experts.' " Winzenburg declined. Finally, Frances asked what denomination he was. Catholic, he replied. "There was a stony silence, and then, 'Ohhhh, now I understand.' She then said that she and Jimmy 'would have to come and have a talk with [me] sometime.' "

♦   ♦   ♦

The summer of 1987 was a roller coaster for Jimmy. It started high: Fourth Circuit Court of Appeal Judge Richard Ganucheau dismissed Marvin Gorman's suit, saying it was an internal church matter. Gorman, of course, would appeal.

But Winzenburg would see puzzling behaviors in Jimmy that he later realized were signs of distress. "All of a sudden, he started saying these negative, deprecating things about himself," Winzenburg noticed. "He seemed to be pointing a finger at himself." In July, he said, "I'm scared to death of money and scared to death of women. Those two things have caused more preachers' downfall than any other." Around the same time, he said that, for him, sexual straying was impossible. Frances "is with me all the time. She goes to every crusade we go to. And if she doesn't go, I have several people who go with me. I'm never alone. I'm never by myself." Frances, he said, was the only woman he'd ever kissed.

He may never have kissed another woman, but it wasn't true that Frances was with him all the time, or that he was never alone. As would soon be seen, Roy Grutman's threat to air Jimmy's "dirtier laundry" had legs.

That summer, Jimmy finally talked to Jim Bakker by telephone. Bakker claimed Falwell had tricked him, saying, just turn PTL over to him for a couple of weeks and he'd keep it safe from Swaggart, that Jimmy was trying to destroy him, too.

Jimmy immediately called Falwell to ask if the story was true. "Are you going to believe that liar, or are you going to believe me?" Falwell replied.

Jimmy knew Falwell was right, but for reasons of self-preservation that would present themselves shortly as he dealt with his own public travail, he eventually landed on Bakker's side. As he watched Falwell publicly recoil from the revelations of Bakker's excesses and expose PTL's financial records to the media, Jimmy ended up regretting having been so vitriolic about Bakker and PTL on national television, for he was trapped now in his own ever-escalating addiction. When Bakker was sentenced to a prison term for fraud and conspiracy, Jimmy said it was a travesty.

In the end, although the Baptist Falwell had taken the high road like the "good man" Jimmy aspired to be, Jimmy chose not to follow, returning instead to his own kind—the "dirty, smelly fishermen," as he noted, that Jesus chose to be his anointed.

In August, uncomfortable with his secret role in the Bakker affair and tired of the grueling work schedule that kept him from his wife and young children, Jerald Ogg, Jr., left the ministry.

◆   ◆   ◆

In 1986, Jimmy had tried to relieve the pressures of the ministry. He stopped answering the phone on Wednesdays and Saturdays, keeping those days entirely to himself. It meant more of a burden for Donnie and Frances, but, he told his audience several months later, he worked seven days a week, 18 hours a day, and he needed the time to himself for renewal and to be able to have the anointing he needed. He was in the habit of taking his car and parking it under a grove of trees in front of the house, reading in the car for 30 minutes, and then getting out, walking all the way around the fence surrounding the estate, and then getting back into the car and reading the Bible for 30 more minutes, then walking and praying again, and so on—for hours at a time.

Of course, sometimes he didn't stay in front of the house all day. Sometimes he drove down Airline Highway all the way to New Orleans. Witnesses later said most of his trips were during the day, when Frances and Donnie were at work.

He had noticed long ago that Marvin Gorman's old church on Airline Highway, the one Gorman had built in 1973 because his eight-year-old ministry was bursting at the seams, was on a part of the highway that soon turned into a trail of cheap motels on its way into New Orleans.

It was the old road between the capital city and its rival, the Big Easy. Once, these motels—the Sherwood, the Texas, the San Antonio, Toney's, the 42-room Travel Inn—had been ordinary resting places for travelers, vacationers, and businessmen. But Interstate 10 had forced some of them to reincarnate as pay-by-the hour bordellos, with adult movies and water beds, strung out in a de facto red-light district mingled with gritty tire warehouses and minor retail shops.

He drove down the street once a week, Debra Murphree said; once or twice a month if he was on the road doing crusades. He looked for her in particular. She said to him finally, you're Jimmy Swaggart, aren't you? No, he said, his name was Billy. She nodded, and said no more.

Blue eyeshadow complimented her black eyes and hair and pale skin. The little gap between her front teeth, and her slight Cajun-sounding accent, were attractive. Her voice was soft and feminine. People who knew her called her Debbie.

Randy Gorman met Debra Murphree about the same time Jimmy did, in the fall of 1986. For several years, he said later, rumors had floated around New Orleans that either Jimmy or his twin was fond of the women who came and went at the motels on Airline Highway. In 1982, a woman would later relate to reporters that she, a cook at the San Antonio Motel on Airline and a Jimmy Swaggart believer, saw him go into a room with two people who had arrived on a motorcycle—a man wearing a black leather jacket and a woman. She was shocked.

Another woman would later tell Larry King that, in 1983, her nephew, who worked in one of the motels, told her he had seen Jimmy there numerous times, but she didn't believe him. One day her nephew called her and told her to hurry up and come over, he'd spotted Jimmy going into a room with a man and a woman. She rushed over, and said she saw Jimmy emerge about 45 minutes after he'd gone in.

"There were rumors about Jimmy Swaggart in the early '80s, that he wasn't so clean himself," said Patrick Mahoney, a former Assemblies of God pastor who was connected to Bakker. "You could find episodes of people who were saying things like that back then. There are people around who know this, but of course Christians won't talk to you. This was all swept under the carpet, and I think God broke through and gave all of us in the leadership an opportunity to see what we were doing."

In 1987, two Airline Highway motel managers would report having seen him on the strip before.

Randy Gorman, 33, was Marvin's oldest son, an ordained Assemblies minister himself and a sheriff's deputy. In August and September 1986, he had watched his father attempt to defend himself before his superiors, and had seen Marvin utterly defeated and humiliated. "I never understood the way they discipline ministers, even when I was a little kid," he said.

At that same time, according to Hunter Lundy (Gorman's chief attorney) in his book *Let Us Prey*, rumors and jokes were circulating in the sheriff's department that a man closely resembling the 6'2", 220-pound Reverend Jimmy Swaggart had approached pimps in the area and was now seeing a woman at the Travel Inn. Randy started cruising the places along Airline Highway where Jimmy had reportedly been seen. As a reserve sheriff's deputy, he had a legitimate reason to be there.

Debra only saw Randy a few times in her room, Room 7. When she first met him, she was afraid he was an undercover policeman coming to arrest her.

But once he made it clear he wasn't, she started seeing him. She had dated a lot of cops, actually. Randy never offered his name and she didn't ask. Once, she realized she had seen him on the television news, but couldn't remember in what context. Later she would find out that it was the Gorman suit against Jimmy.

She had been telling people for months that she was dating Jimmy Swaggart, but no one seemed interested. One summer day, for no particular reason, she told Randy. He became extremely excited, and started visiting her once a week, calling every day. He asked her to get Jimmy's license number, but she refused. He gave her his beeper number. She threw it away.

All he really knew about her was her first name. He had her tailed. She saw him following her once and lost him, but another time, he followed her all the way home to her boyfriend's motel on Chef Menteur Highway. Every day he either called or dropped by the motel, to find out if she had seen Jimmy. Once she saw him parking between the Travel Inn and the motel next door, where he could see her room.

She never told Jimmy that "the cop" was asking about him. Another prostitute, Peggy Carriere, said she saw Jimmy in late March, around the time he had appeared on CNN's "Larry King" and given other national television interviews. He looked so very masculine and powerful on television; the sex and the "Holy Wars" were clearly invigorating him. Peggy spotted him pulling into the parking lot of the umber-painted Texas Motel, which charged $10 a day. He wore a T-shirt with a V-neck, a white sweatband around his forehead, and maroon jogging pants. She trotted over to his car, thinking he needed directions.

Hey, Jimmy Swaggart, she grinned, what do you think about this Bakker mess? He wasn't Jimmy Swaggart, he said. He came up with a tale—he was meeting another man here to help him adopt two little boys—that clanged so loudly against the empty, grimy parking lot and the rancid dumpster and the erection he was pushing down that it seemed a curtain had flicked aside for a glimpse of the family insanity. Peggy peered at him. Yeah, okay, she said as he drove off. You're here to adopt two little boys.

That was only days after he had challenged Roy Grutman, Bakker's attorney, on national television, to go ahead and reveal his dirty laundry "to the whole world." The challenge was suicidal, considering the number of disgruntled ex-Jimmy Swaggart Ministries employees roaming Baton Rouge, and considering the girls along Airline Highway who could testify to having seen him numerous times over the past six months, in his highly identifiable two-tone Continental, peering at the female figures walking along the street.

As the media incessantly pointed out later, it showed he wanted to be caught. That had to be true; Jimmy had spent a lifetime keeping things secret that he didn't want known, and he certainly knew how to do it. But it also showed how badly he needed *not* to be Jimmy Swaggart. The foul-smelling parking lot was the place he could be Billy, a guy with a need, and where sin could just be what it was—not demonic, not any big deal, just something to be taken care of.

A few days later, Peggy Carriere again saw a familiar car in back of the Texas Motel. She peeked inside: same plush seats, same telephone. Shortly Jimmy came downstairs, she said, wearing red jogging shorts, a V-neck shirt, white sweatband, and tennis shoes, and drove off. "That's Jimmy Swaggart," she told the pimp whose girl he had just given $20 for oral sex.

In a couple of weeks, Jimmy would allow himself to be photographed for a *Life* magazine spread on televangelists—out for a jog wearing the same type of V-neck shirt and running clothes he wore for carousing.

Peggy saw him again several months later, near a methadone clinic close to downtown New Orleans. He didn't remember her from the Texas Motel.

She approached the car and he discussed things they might do. He only offered her $10 and she was insulted; he was rich! She seldom did anything for less than $20.

She saw him another time, she said later, leaving the room of a girl named Susan. But mostly he was seeing a woman named Debbie, she told an investigator who began asking around in the late summer of 1987. She lived at Toney's Motel, one block from the Travel Inn, and she saw him down there, and at the Texas Motel down the street.

It was only during the last week of September and the first 17 days of October that an actual stakeout occurred. The curtain of Room 12, down the sidewalk and around the inside corner from Room 7 so that the two rooms nearly opposed each other, had a black drape over it and was open. Debra barely registered it, but later it would all come into focus.

◆　◆　◆

It was early in 1987 that Jimmy had the dream where he was inside a house desperately fighting a huge serpent with a sword, and after he killed it, a man in white led him outside to an even bigger one.

"I have to fight this thing, don't I?" he'd asked. The man nodded.

Later in the year, when Jimmy knew he was no longer going to be able to contain his battle inside his personal domain but was moving to the outside world, he had another dream, strangely touching: He was at a gathering with Frances. Several hundred people were there, in a big room with columns around the outside (columns were a motif in some of his most troubled dreams). He went over to the columns, away from the people, and God appeared, dressed in white. He asked if Jimmy wanted to see Satan. Jimmy said yes. God led him down the hall to a room and opened the door. Standing there, looking away and not seeing them, was a stunningly beautiful man. God told Jimmy not to go into the room. Jimmy asked, "So this is the one who has caused me so much trouble?" He started to sob as God answered, "Yes, this is the one."

October 17, 1987

On October 8, 1987, Jerry Falwell threw in the towel, resigning as head of PTL after a federal bankruptcy judge permitted four of the nine board seats to be taken by Bakker supporters, paving the way for Bakker's return to PTL. By this time, Falwell was sure Bakker was a thief. With such a narrow board majority, he said, there was no way to insure that Jim Bakker wouldn't pick more pockets. Calling PTL the "Watergate of evangelical Christianity" and Bakker "probably the greatest scab and cancer on the face of Christianity in two thousand years of church history," Falwell and his entire board stepped down after 29 weeks at the helm.

He was wrong, though; Jim Bakker would never return to PTL. He would go to prison.

Only two weeks before, Jessica Hahn had testified before a federal grand jury in Charlotte in connection with the PTL investigation; it was widely reported that she had just agreed to pose nude in *Playboy* for a rumored $1 million. It must have given Jimmy horrible anxiety—to think the same thing could happen to him, and soon. Even busy Frances sensed his tension. "During all of 1987," he said, "I was spending so much time in prayer that one day Frances approached me and said, 'We never have any time alone anymore. All you do is pray.'" Some of that prayer time, of course, was spent driving to New Orleans.

His anxiety would have been even worse if he had been aware that on September 3, Debra Murphree was arrested, right there at the Travel Inn, where they always met, on prostitution charges. She pled guilty and was given a six-month suspended sentence and fined $372.50.

If Jimmy had needed signs and symbols that he was flying far too close to the sun, he had them—the billboard across Airline from the Travel Inn, for example, that showed a huge open Bible and warned that "Unless a man is born again, he cannot see the kingdom of God!" The Travel Inn's telephone number, painted on the white board fence in front of the motel, ended in 666, the mark of Satan. The motel was less than a mile from Marvin's old church, four miles from his new one, and less than a mile the other direction from the Jefferson Parish Sheriff's substation. But it was as if these signs were beckoning him instead of scaring him off.

Debra later said he wanted her to get naked, to lie on the bed and pose, or to put on a dress with no underwear and ride around. He tried to get her to take her clothes off in the car. She refused.

It was always visual stimulation and masturbating, or oral sex; they never had intercourse, except once very briefly when she was on her hands and knees on the bed.

Sometimes he would return later in the day after he'd had her once. Sometimes he'd call and try to get her to get him off over the phone, promising to pay later. She said no.

He never laughed, never talked to her about personal things, except her schedule at the Travel Inn, because he had to go out of town a lot. He always said he was going to St. Louis. "You know, because he didn't want me to know." Once she asked if he was married, and he said yes.

Then he'd asked about her daughter, who was only nine. The child's photo was on her dresser. At first Debra thought his questions were just part of the sex, and she answered them. The times he asked about her daughter, he'd started out slowly: did she have breasts yet, or pubic hair? Another time he asked if Debra would ever let the girl watch her with a man? Surprised, Debra told him her daughter lived with her grandmother in Indiana, didn't even know what Debra did for a living. Another time he asked if Debra would consider bringing her daughter in and letting her watch them. But when he asked if she would ever let anyone screw her daughter and asked Debra to describe her genitalia, she put a stop to it. If he ever mentioned her daughter again, she said, she'd quit seeing him. He stopped talking about it.

Her regular rate was $30 or $40, but he never paid her more than $20. Of course, he never took up more than 15 or 20 minutes of her time. Whenever she happened to see him on television, all she thought was how cheap he was. But basically she shrugged. She understood—television preachers were no different from her: they did it for money.

♦   ♦   ♦

It was Saturday, October 17. Debra had not seen Jimmy for two or three weeks. She was in Room 7 at the Travel Inn at about two in the afternoon when she saw the beige Lincoln go slowly by. She went outside, dressed in white jeans, sandals, and a pink dotted blouse. She waved, and saw the big car hang a U-turn and come back. He pulled up and buzzed the window down. How were things, he asked. Not bad today, but a lot of cop activity lately, she answered. He pulled into a slot a few doors down and came back along the sidewalk. They went inside. He settled in the chair and put his $20 on the table.

As usual, he was dressed in his jogging clothes and sneakers. She had a bad feeling, though. She had been arrested in September and things hadn't been right since. She heard a car door slam, and peeked through the curtain. There, sprinting across the lot into Room 12, was her client, the cop.

Marvin Gorman was in the warehouse that was his new church, just a mile away, when the call came in: "He's here. Hurry up." Gorman hurriedly drove the short distance down Airline.

Debra saw a light blue car going back and forth on the highway. "It kept circling, looking at the hotel," she said later. She turned to Jimmy. I don't like this, she said, telling him somebody had just run into a room over there. He immediately heaved out of the chair, snatched up the twenty, and headed for the door, asking if she might meet him down the street at a fast-food place.

He hopped into his car and started backing out, but felt a flat tire. He pulled back in, this time in front of her door. She sat and watched as he jacked up the car, unscrewed the lug nuts, and took the tire off. In case he got stopped, she said, don't tell them anything you did. The blue car drifted back and forth as he got out the spare and put it on, tightening the nuts. He didn't know it yet, but he had it on backwards.

Suddenly she noticed the window of Room 12, which had had its black curtain hanging there for days, barely grazing her consciousness. Now she saw it behind the parted curtain: the camera lens. Jimmy backed out, but had to pull back in to flip the tire. He got out and started on the nuts again.

At that moment, she heard, "Jimmy!" as the blue car pulled into the lot. She slipped into her room and closed the door. This didn't concern her yet—unless Jimmy told on her. She peeked through a crack in the door. A man was walking over to Jimmy. Jimmy tried to shake hands, but the man wouldn't.

Even after the refused handshake, Jimmy had tried to tough it out, saying to the man who was suing him for $90 million, "Bud, what are you doing here?" as if they had run into each other at a hotel in Beijing.

They both got into the blue car and left.

JIMMY KEPT ASKING what Marvin Gorman wanted. "He mentioned jobs in his ministry for me and my family," Gorman said later. He offered to help Gorman get his ministry back. He offered to have Marvin on his television show—Gorman was not interested. How Jimmy thought Gorman would take on that humiliation is a mystery that shows either how out of touch he was or how fluid a world was the Pentecostal one, where forgiveness came and went so easily.

As they talked, Gorman said, Jimmy broke down and cried. He admitted seeing numerous prostitutes over the years, especially on the road, when he traveled. He confessed he'd had a problem for a long time—28 years, Gorman said later.

"If those women go to hell," he told Gorman, "I don't know what I'm gonna do."

Now, 15 months after the confrontation at Swaggart's home in July of 1986, it was Gorman's turn to bring up I Timothy 5:20, "rebuke before all." He had every justification, both Scriptural and worldly, for taking Jimmy's offense to Springfield, and exposing Jimmy just as Jimmy had done to him.

But Gorman believed—perhaps a bit self-servingly during his own travail—in restoration of fallen preachers, not condemnation, he said. He really didn't have any plan to run Jimmy into the ground; he wanted to get his name cleared and his ministry back. Despite the lawsuit—which, once filed, had to be fiercely fought—Gorman tried to convey to Jimmy that what he really wanted was for him to get his life straight, to get healing.

"How could you be living this kind of life," Gorman said to Jimmy, "and attack me? Your blasting days are over, man, that Bible is full of good things." It was what Jimmy's Nannie had realized at the crowded funeral of her daughter-in-law, Minnie Bell: "I shoulda been preachin' love."

"I'm sorry I've hurt you," Jimmy ended, "and I'm gonna make it right."

Gorman agreed to let Jimmy talk it over with Frances. At first, according to Hunter Lundy, Gorman was to follow Jimmy home to Baton Rouge to help him tell Frances. But outside of New Orleans, Jimmy pulled off the road. He walked back to Gorman's car; he'd had second thoughts—he'd tell Frances alone. He said he'd call Gorman tomorrow, and the two men parted. Best there be no witnesses to Frances' reaction.

Gorman left without mentioning that he might have photos. He didn't even know yet if they would turn out. He had caught Jimmy, but everything hinged on those pictures.

The next day, Sunday, October 18, 1987, Jimmy and Frances drove back down I-10, as Jimmy had done so many times before, alone and filled with need. This time he was headed not for the humble Travel Inn, but for the Sheraton Hotel in Kenner to meet Gorman.

They turned out onto Bluebonnet Road in bright sunshine and drove past the World Ministry Center, flanked by flags, past the Family Christian Academy, the gymnasium where the Bible College's award-winning basketball team practiced and played, the well-outfitted building where videotapes were edited, and the mail building where they were sent for distribution throughout the world.

They passed the college side of Bluebonnet—the Minnie Bell Swaggart Residence Hall and the D. Mark Buntain Hall, the H.B. Garlock Classroom and Faculty Building, the Maynard Ketcham Health Fitness Center, the A.N.

Trotter Student Life Center/College Administration building, and the new multi-story dorm going up next to the administration building.

The Jimmy Swaggart Ministries, forged over more than three decades from the dreams of two teenagers, was a triumph of faith, hard work, and determination. On the way to meet the defrocked preacher who now held a sword over it all, Jimmy would have to drive past the state highway signs directing tourists to the Jimmy Swaggart Ministries compound. It was like seeing your life passing before your eyes.

MARVIN GORMAN, waiting for Jimmy and Frances, had some needs. He had filed personal bankruptcy only a few weeks before, in September. Added to his Marvin Gorman Ministries, which had filed a few months earlier in January 1987 showing $2 million of debt, his bankruptcy tab totaled $3.5 million. It was easy to lay most of that trouble at Jimmy's door.

The Swaggarts met Gorman and his witness, attorney Marty Simone. Once again Jimmy wept, confessed, and asked forgiveness. He admitted again that he'd paid prostitutes many times to pose for him. He didn't try to evade as Bakker had.

Gorman asked that Jimmy withdraw his accusations of multiple Gorman indiscretions as opposed to the mild departures Gorman acknowledged, apologize publicly so Gorman could begin rebuilding his church, and get counseling. Jimmy promised to retract the charges he had been making against Gorman. He promised to tell church officials what he'd done. He promised to get counseling, and to publish a retraction in the *Evangelist*.

The confrontation would be strange to anyone unfamiliar with the kinds of contradictions the Pentecostal brotherhood permitted: two preachers looking each other in the eye, slipping into the disarming, emotional confessions they had both learned in church and had used to help so many of their followers lay their sins bare before God.

They were men who had bloodied each other and then said publicly that they loved each other, who had felt lust and done something about it and hated themselves, men who had felt the white-hot shame of being caught. They were men who had fought desperate spiritual and mental battles to separate themselves from the brotherhood of men right down the street, sitting over a weekend beer and editorializing juicily on the smells and sinews of passing women.

If Jimmy set an example of humility and contrition, Gorman equalled it by treating him the opposite of how Jimmy had treated him. Instead of immediately telephoning members of Jimmy's church and denominational leaders, cutting off his access to credit, and insisting on immediate and full exposure and resignation, Gorman asked for help to resurrect his ministry.

In return, he would keep quiet about the details of the Travel Inn and let Jimmy be the one to decide how to tell the church elders, how to pitch the matter in the *Evangelist,* what to tell his employees and his viewers. The arguments on his appeal of the defamation decision came up March 3. Jimmy could prepare for the financial fallout during the next weeks if the church elders pulled him from the pulpit, and line up support and substitute ministers during his rehabilitation. He could say he'd been in counseling for weeks or months by the time he had to fess up.

But Frances, even though upset about Jimmy being exposed, couldn't help playing hardball, according to Lundy. Would Gorman drop his lawsuit if Jimmy did all these things? Gorman refused to discuss the lawsuit; the meeting ended with Jimmy's promises of retraction.

It would have been natural for Gorman to immediately get on the telephone to influential friends in the national Assemblies who had a direct pipeline to non-Pentecostal bigwigs like Falwell and to the media, and make sure it was put immediately into the mill. But he didn't. Of course, he was very well aware from his own experience and Bakker's that the church leadership seemed to have little interest in disciplining a star. But his goal wasn't to hurt Swaggart so much as to build his own church back up.

Who in Springfield would believe that, not only had he caught Jimmy Swaggart red-handed, he had heard him confess to having done it many times, for many years? After all, Jimmy made a routine gift of between $10 and $12 million every year to the national Assemblies for foreign missions, and here was Gorman suing those deep pockets for years' worth—$90 million plus attorney fees.

But the photos, taken by his son Randy and son-in-law Garland Bilbo, had come back perfect. He wondered if Jimmy would ever have to learn about them, or if he would come through with his promises.

THE MONTH OF October seemed to mock Jimmy. The stock market had crashed early in the month, financially strapping many of his donors and causing a dip in giving. The ministry published *Straight Answers to Tough Questions,* penned by Jimmy; it warned extensively about how people got drawn into fornication. *Christian Wives,* a book about the spouses of prominent ministers that included a favorable profile of Frances, and a spread about him in *Current Biography* both came out.

Shortly after the sting at the Travel Inn, Debra fled town, surfacing in West Palm Beach, Florida.

Windy, cold November brought Pat Robertson's announcement that he would be a candidate for the Republican nomination for president, and Jerry Falwell's that he was abandoning politics, though it would be two years before he formally dissolved the Moral Majority. Gary Hart withdrew from the

Democratic presidential race after being caught and photographed with
Donna Rice.

At his Thanksgiving camp meeting, Jimmy said, "Demon powers, fallen
angels, work more in religion than they work anyplace else. I pray constantly:
'God don't let spirits get in this work. Don't let spirits get in Jimmy Swaggart.' " Arbitron ratings that month showed a healthy 2.1 million households
in the U.S. viewing his show weekly.

He plunged into a madhouse crusade schedule, holding huge services in
Liberia, the Ivory Coast, Panama City. He had returned from Brazil just before being caught by Gorman. The last day, a Sunday, a huge crowd had
poured into the brand new soccer stadium. About 15 minutes into the sermon, he heard dogs barking. The sound grew louder until it filled the auditorium. It took him a minute to realize that it was people barking. He was
overwhelmed by the presence of Satan. He commanded "every single demon
in this stadium to shut up!" There was silence.

When Jimmy told this bizarre story a year later, it wasn't to note how the
old "barking exercise" of the frontier camp meeting days had been resurrected by the voodoo cults of Brazil. It wasn't even to score the Catholics for
being open to things like stigmata, chanting, rituals, idols, and mystery in a
voodoo-active country, thus inviting demonic activities. It was to talk—
obliquely, of course—about his sexual addiction and muse that if he could
command all those demons to obey, you'd think he'd be able to get a grip on
the ones devouring him.

Gorman was patient through Jimmy's heavy November 1987 crusade
schedule. The Swaggarts had invited the Gormans to dinner and several social
outings during October and November, and held discussions about the progress of Jimmy's retraction. But the invitations dried up after that. All the
overtures were made by Gorman.

On December 9, the vanished Debra Murphree missed a court date on a
prostitution charge. A warrant was issued for her arrest. The next day, Jimmy
released information about his ministry that showed it to be squeaky clean
and sober. The evangelical community sorely needed a show of financial self-
policing after PTL, and Gorman watched as Jimmy burnished his image: the
ministry didn't provide him with a car, bonuses, or royalties; fewer than half
of his nine-member board were family members, and they couldn't vote on
his compensation package; full financial statements; a yearly CPA audit.

As 1987 drew to a close, Gorman waited and watched in vain for news or
hints of Jimmy's upcoming retraction on the air, in the *Evangelist,* or through
the religious grapevine. On August 20, Oral Roberts had publicly apologized
to Jimmy, saying he hadn't understood the Bakker situation. By year's end,
Gorman may have implored Roberts to intervene, for Roberts called Jimmy
and asked for a meeting. Jimmy was forced to comply, taking Frances along,
of course, but all the meeting produced was a notation in the February 1988

Evangelist that it "threw greater light on all questions involved" in their dispute, and the inevitable, "I love Oral Roberts . . ."

By Christmas, Gorman told his confidants that he was afraid Jimmy was going to try to "sweep it under the rug"—exactly what Jimmy had said Marvin was going to do about his own infidelities the year before. There were still rumors that Jimmy was planning to split off from the Assemblies of God and take some Assemblies and independent churches with him. Gorman had hoped that he wouldn't do that. It would make a retraction meaningless, and hurt the Assemblies. Marvin still had hopes of being restored to his old denomination.

◆ ◆ ◆

The consensus among those close to Jimmy is that the trickle of communication from him to Gorman ended abruptly because Frances nixed it. Think about it—who was going to believe Marvin Gorman, with that $90 million lawsuit coming up on appeal? And he'd probably lose the appeal; in the unlikely event they went to trial, how could confessing possibly help Jimmy's case? And who was going to take a tattooed whore's word over Jimmy Swaggart's? If Gorman was really going to expose him anyway, why confess? He could always confess if Gorman carried out his threat, but look at it: Debra Murphree had fled town. Gorman's suit had been dismissed.

As the first weeks of 1988 passed, Gorman seemed to confirm those assumptions, because he did nothing.

To Frances, whose instinct a year before had been to go for Gorman's throat, it must have been inconceivable that his silence might mean anything except that he had been bluffing. He didn't have the power to bring Jimmy down and he knew it. If he had, he would've done what she would do: close in for the kill immediately.

Jimmy had promised Gorman he'd get counseling. But he would come no closer than sponsoring a preacher rejuvenation conference in December, noting in the *Evangelist* that "The preacher today, even in Pentecostal and Charismatic circles, is in trouble. Scores are failing through immorality or just plain 'burnout.'" Four thousand ministers attended. But counseling was out of the question, especially after the diatribes against it he had printed in his magazine and his frequent preaching on its evils.

"Jimmy said [counseling] was of the devil, stay away from it, you're a child of God, you don't need that stuff," said his old friend Gerald Wilson.

Actually, Jimmy wrote later that he would have liked counseling, but his denomination made it impossible to ask for help.

"In this period of time [when the visits to Debra were becoming regular], I resolved in my mind countless times to go to particular individuals. Knowing the rules of the denomination I was in, however, I felt I would be totally destroyed if I did."

Many would nod, including Marvin Gorman, knowing the double-bind imposed by the Pentecostal church. You were supposed to get prominent enough to bring lots of souls to God, but then the higher you were, the more the brethren would be shocked, intimidated, unable to help if you had a moral failure or doubts—because *they* looked up to you just like the flock did.

"The trouble is," said Jack Wright, the attorney and minister who followed Jimmy's career for years, "there is no room for failure in the Holiness church [the precursor of the Pentecostal church]. In the Catholic religion, you go to confession. You admit you sinned, you get forgiven. But . . . in the Pentecostal church, you're either saved or you ain't. And one sin keeps you out . . . [Jimmy] fought battles with [pornography] and he fought them alone . . ."

"There were people in the denomination who would have destroyed him, who wanted to destroy him," confirmed his researcher and writer, Larry Thomas. "So if he'd gone under their discipline, whoever would have administered the rehab would have gotten him, too."

All that is what Jimmy would have liked people to think, said Gerald Wilson, but the truth was that good, confidential, healing Christian counseling was available to Jimmy when he needed it. Yes, there was a problem with going to the brethren—but only if you waited to do something about it until you were exposed. Wilson and others cited the counseling ministry of Richard Dobbins of Sarasota, Florida.

"If a person has a problem and goes to [someone like] Dobbins, it's private, just between you two and the Lord. But if you wait until you're exposed, you come under ecclesiastical rules, and the district deals with you," and of necessity your privacy is shot. "You can't walk into a district superintendent's office and tell him what you've been doing. Because he feels obligated to report it. But there WAS help available. But he was so hard against that stuff and [claimed] 'you can pray through and it's all gone in an instant.'"

Dobbins even offered to work with Jimmy, but he declined.

But Wilson acknowledged that Jimmy's stand against counseling had deep roots in the teachings of the Assemblies. "You just sucked it up and believed God," he admitted, "and if you die, well—you just didn't have enough faith. That's a terrible way to tell people to live, and it's an even more terrible way to die."

Despite the constant evidence in his own life to the contrary, Jimmy wrote that if a person will just sit and listen to the word of God enough, the problems can be solved. He really wanted to believe that. He felt that listening to people's problems all day corrupted counselors. In the same way Jerry sometimes hated his fans' worship and the weakness it showed, Jimmy had a revulsion for people's filth and flesh and degradation. He was compassionate, but people constantly wallowed and suffered in it when they went to counselors. He knew his own confrontations of sexual straying among his fellow ministers kept the subject of sex before him too much of the time. What must it be like for a counselor that specialized in such problems?

After it became clear that he was not going to find a defining experience on Airline Highway, that he was not going to be able to test himself and have an unambiguous victory, like Jacob wrestling with the angel, he just went there to get some vaguely unsavory business taken care of, like buying suppositories. Or taking out the garbage: it happens every week or two—something goes bad and has to be dealt with. He was getting used to that smell, and that was worrisome, but believing as he did that counseling led to even worse—wallowing in the smell, getting it all over you like a dog rolling in something dead—what else could he do but just deal with it as it came up?

Again, the consensus was broad among those close to Jimmy that Frances discouraged him from seeking counseling, even after he was caught. "Counseling is long-term and very painful, no fun at all," said a former teacher at the Jimmy Swaggart Bible college. "But solving the problem is ultimately less painful." So why would Frances discourage him? "I think it's simple pride, because how does it make her look, you know, that her husband went to prostitutes?"

Four or five advisers in Jimmy's inner circle, said Larry Thomas, advised him not to submit to the Assemblies' discipline after his sin came to their attention—including Frances, Donnie, and Jim Rentz.

In January 1988, Jimmy and Frances were at dinner with several top aides, according to Lawrence Wright's July 1988 *Rolling Stone* article about Jimmy. One of the men tossed Jimmy a candy bar containing bee pollen, saying it would increase his sex drive. Everyone laughed except Jimmy and Frances. Jimmy was silent, and then said he didn't need anything to speed him up, he needed the opposite.

Incredibly, he returned to Airline Highway that month, finding time in between a late-January Panamanian crusade and a February "add-on" in Nicaragua. Once again Peggy Carriere, walking down Tulane Avenue, saw him wearing jogging clothes and a white sweatband, driving a white Lincoln this time (Frances owned a white Lincoln at the time). He stopped and offered her $10 to play with herself while he masturbated. She laughed. "You don't remember me, do you? I talked to you before."

◆　◆　◆

The week of February 8, 1988 was once again time for the National Religious Broadcasters' convention; this year it was held in Washington, D.C.—an emblem of the Christian right's political power. Ronald and Nancy

Reagan attended the NRB meeting, and Pat Robertson had just come in second in the Iowa GOP precinct caucuses, where the mood was very pro-life and pro-family. The evangelical vote seemed extremely significant to the GOP as the movement entered the mainstream. Significantly, the evangelical publisher Word, Inc. of Waco, Texas would soon be bought by ABC. Zondervan, which had rights to the New International Version of the Bible, had already been bought by Rupert Murdoch's Harper & Row.

Gorman hadn't heard a peep out of Jimmy now for weeks. Around the time of the NRB convention, he had a note hand-delivered to Jimmy, warning him that the deadline was up. There was no reply. Jimmy was headed for Managua for the crusade that had been added on at the last minute through Jerald Ogg, Sr.'s connections in Panama.

Jimmy had made one anemic gesture. Sometime after Christmas, before the February 1988 issue of the *Evangelist* went to press, Jimmy penned a little note in his regular "From Me To You" column. He had, he wrote, recently met with Marvin Gorman. Apparently referring to one of the families' dinners after he was caught, he said it was a strictly personal meeting, "for the sole purpose of discussing our personal differences." They came to agreement on some areas; on others, he said, neither could find answers.

"I love Marvin Gorman," Jimmy wrote. "I am so pleased we were able to sit down and discuss our personal differences." Jimmy's note to his readers ended, "Wrongdoing must be repented of, put under the blood, and then forgotten." The implication was that he was going to be big enough to forget Gorman's sin now.

That was it. Clearly, this was all Marvin Gorman was going to get out of Jimmy.

◆   ◆   ◆

Upon arriving in Managua for his February 12–14 crusade, Jimmy was welcomed at the airport by government officials. He was received by President Daniel Ortega, taken to his villa, applauded by the Sandinistas. His warm reception was seen as a slap in the face of pro-Contra Cardinal Obando y Bravo. Forty thousand people, apparently getting the message that Jimmy was important to Nicaragua's powerful, came to hear him in the Plaza de la Revolución, where only revolutionaries—Ortega, Fidel Castro—had been permitted to speak before.

He flew home in triumph on Sunday night, the 14th, on the ministry plane.

While he was gone, Marvin Gorman had made up his mind.

Jimmy and Frances had badly underestimated him. Always comfortable with Assemblies insiders in a political way that Jimmy never had been (because Frances wasn't liked, according to sources in the Gorman camp; because he wasn't interested in denominational politics, according to those in Jimmy's), Gorman still had friends.

On Tuesday, February 16, 1988, he contacted a friend in the Assemblies who then contacted James Hamill, a member of the Assemblies' 13-man Executive Presbytery of which Gorman had once been a prominent member. Gorman flew to Memphis, where Hamill lived, with scores of photos.

Hamill called Raymond Carlson, the Assemblies' superintendent, in Springfield. Carlson called an emergency meeting of the presbyters and arranged for Hamill and Gorman to fly to Springfield the next day.

There were some 200 color photos; among them were numerous pictures of men coming and going from Room 7 of the Travel Inn—to establish that Room 7 was a prostitute's lair. Among them was Jimmy Swaggart, wearing light-colored pants and a sweatshirt and a red headband.

The next day, Thursday, February 18, an ashen Jimmy flew to Springfield in his Gulfstream jet, with Frances at his side. The denominational elders had been summoned from all over the country. By now, rumors were flying; Gorman was under siege by the media, and the fact that Jimmy stayed in the meeting nearly 10 hours confirmed that something big was afoot. By Friday evening, ABC News reported Jimmy's 10-hour meeting and details that seemingly could only have come from Gorman but were actually coming from the entire Assemblies rumor mill, as Gorman's attorneys had muzzled him: the years of Airline Highway rumors, the photos, the scene between Jimmy and Marvin at the Travel Inn, the date it happened, broken agreements afterwards.

Someone had certainly told Reverend Patrick Mahoney, the former Assemblies pastor who was now a Connecticut talk-show host and head of the Center for Christian Activism and an outspoken foe of abortion.

"A friend high in the AG came to me and shared the most incredible story, about Jimmy Swaggart's life and family problems and battle with Marvin Gorman, and the fact that Swaggart was involved in sexual immorality, particularly with prostitutes," said Mahoney. "He feared Swaggart would put a black eye on the AG, and to be honest, I didn't feel particularly compassionate for Jimmy Swaggart."

Mahoney called Jim Rentz and said, "Here's what I have: the motel, the thing about the lug nuts, the photos. I want to protect the church, but I also want to deal with this in an open and honest fashion." Rentz, he said, "passed the information on to Jimmy, but Jimmy never called me."

After the ABC News report on Friday, the floodgates opened. ABC's "Nightline" interviewed Cal Thomas, the Virginia-based syndicated columnist specializing in fundamentalist religion, who had clearly been contacted by Jimmy and Frances' damage control contingent. Thomas said his sources maintained there was only one encounter, and it did not involve a sex act, but rather "something pornographic." Thomas' sources said Jimmy would place himself under the Assemblies' discipline.

Jerald Ogg, Sr., Jimmy's longtime crusade director, had been overseas and was now at the airport in Oakland, getting ready to fly to Dallas to set up another crusade. He called his office from the airport, and found his secretary's voice strained.

"Something's happened. I think I better put you with your wife." Janett came on the line and told him the news. The shock, combined with jet lag, left him so disoriented he felt dizzy.

Reporters worked all night. The next day, Saturday, February 20, 1988, full details of the ABC story were carried in the *Baton Rouge Morning Advocate* and in newspapers all over the country. An evangelist friend of Jimmy's said that when he called Springfield to find out what was going on, "they were all in a prayer meeting with God." That was the kind of thing that caused the Assemblies trouble, its leaders' humanization of the Almighty, their readiness to see God like a CEO called away from his busy schedule to deal with the Jimmy Swaggart crisis. The subtext was, "All the big shots were in an emergency meeting. Even God was there."

JIMMY REPORTEDLY denied having intercourse but confessed to paying Debra to "perform pornographic acts." The Assemblies elders were trying to determine whether Jimmy had committed adultery or not. Gorman said he would have something to say about that soon, but arguments on his appeal of the dismissal of his $90 million suit were to be heard the following week, and he couldn't comment yet.

The Louisiana District, headed by Cecil Janway, Jimmy's old piano inspiration who had pressured Gorman at Jimmy's request, was investigating. Janway's office said the investigation might take as long as six months. Queried further, Janway hung up on reporters.

Jimmy was said to be cooperating fully. But he would make no comment to reporters. News accounts cited statistics on the wealthy ministry, including plans to enlarge the Family Worship Center to 10,000 seats. The average envelope addressed to the Jimmy Swaggart Ministries contained over $40. The ministry payroll was $11.5 million a year; some estimates were higher.

I Have Sinned

The encounter between "Billy" and Marvin Gorman had left Debra Murphree no doubt that Billy was Jimmy Swaggart, but beyond a brief reflection that he could have given her far more than $20 each time, she couldn't have cared less. She didn't concern herself with men's hypocrisies.

October 17, 1987 was the last time she saw him. Within a few weeks, she was again charged with prostitution—she was seeing up to ten men a day, six days a week—and it was hard for her to believe that the scene with "Billy" wasn't connected somehow. After all, her client in Room 12 was a cop. That was when she had fled to Florida.

It wasn't until she was watching television in West Palm Beach on February 21, 1988, that he even crossed her mind again. It was Sunday night, and there he was on national television news, crying.

"I do not plan in any way to whitewash my sin," he said, his face a tragic mask. "And I do not call it a mistake, a mendacity. I call it sin. I have no one but myself to blame. I do not lay the fault or the blame or the charge at anyone else but me. For no one is to blame but Jimmy Swaggart. I take the responsibility. I take the blame. I take the fault."

An eerie feeling came over Debra.

He's talking about *me,* she thought.

She remembered how he liked to drive around with her in the car; he asked her to wear a dress and no underwear, and position herself sideways in the seat with her dress pulled up over her hips and her legs open.

"God never gave a man a better helpmate and companion to stand beside him," Jimmy was saying. He wore a well-cut navy suit. His chameleon's eyes looked dull and small-pupiled, gone from blue-green to lifeless tan.

". . . as far as the Gospel has been taken through the ether waves," he said, "to the great cities of the world and covered this globe. It would never have been done were it not for her . . ."

He turned to Frances. "I have sinned against you," he hissed into the mike.

"I beg your forgiveness."

Frances kept a tissue in her hand when she was onstage, and dabbed at her eyes even when they were dry, which they usually were. Typically, her face was composed and neutral, but now her dark eyes looked reflective, as if she were seriously considering the request. Of course, she already had.

She was a vision, carefully coiffed and dressed for the occasion. For years, her outfits—dramatic, but never gaudy—had titillated followers across the country, and she didn't disappoint today. She wore a swirly peach-colored skirt and a matching oversized angora sweater with big, soft shoulder pads and white freeform shapes like amoebas, each one outlined with small silver beads ringed by tiny pearls. The shapes splashed over one shoulder and down one side of her body. She wore tiny gold loop earrings.

Jimmy had broken not only the matrimonial vow but some deeply personal, perhaps even unspoken one, made between two kids more than 30 years before. Minnie Bell had given Frances an assignment back in 1952, and she had carried it out with military discipline and iron will. When there was a setback, she said it was a trick of the devil. When he had doubt, it was of Satan. when he was weak, it was the work of demons. There was no place to go but where she pointed.

The demons in his groin, however, could not be prayed away, hallelujahed away, buried in work, or exorcised. They were simply something he had to deal with, and however Jimmy handled them was up to him, as long as he didn't violate that most important bargain: their privacy.

Now he'd done that.

He was looking at her, waiting for a response. She nodded, licking her lips. Yes, she assented. I forgive you.

Debra watched the screen as Jimmy turned toward his son and daughter-in-law, Donnie and Debbie. Debbie Swaggart watched, her face frozen in horror, as if she were watching "The Exorcist." She stared at her father-in-law, her thin lips parted, her black hair waving long around her face, framing fleshy cheekbones, black eyes, and carefully-plucked arched eyebrows. Next to her, Donnie mouthed three times to his father, "I love you."

The dark-haired Debbie on the screen was about Debra's age. They resembled each other, with their black hair, brown eyes, high cheekbones. They both had two sons and a daughter, about the same ages. One thing was surely different, though: thin, elegant Debbie Robertson Swaggart, once a ministry pianist, would not have tattoos. Debbie Murphree had two. She remembered one time when they were in the car and Jimmy tried to get her to strip naked in broad daylight. "Jump out in front of those people," he urged. He wanted to see the shock on their faces.

"And to the hundreds of millions," Jimmy was saying in a trembling voice, tears running down his good-looking face, "that . . . needed help [and] reached out to the minister of the Gospel, the beacon of light . . . I sinned against you. I beg you to forgive me."

Hundreds of millions. As she watched him, the enormity of her dealings with Jimmy Swaggart began to sink in. Not many days later, she began thinking about going to New Orleans to face the prostitution charges and look for an agent. The privacy rule for clients was void.

♦ ♦ ♦

The 7,500-seat Family Worship Center was overflowing on that first Sunday of Lent, February 21, 1988, with hundreds standing. The secretary-treasurer of the Louisiana Council of the Assemblies of God, Forrest Hall, read a prepared statement, saying Jimmy had made a detailed confession to his family and church elders and had shown true repentance and humility. He asked the congregation and all ministers not to gossip and advised Jimmy not to speak to the media.

Then Jimmy came up to the pulpit. He said his sin was done in secret like David's with Bathsheba. He said Ted Koppel, the national media, WBRZ, the other local news media, and even John Camp had dealt with him fairly.

He gave, without ever looking at a single note, a florid apology to the Assemblies of God, "which helped bring the Gospel to my beleaguered little town where my family was lost without Jesus," and to its pastors and evangelists, and its "missionaries on the front lines of darkness, holding back the tides of Hell."

Throughout his speech, members of the congregation interrupted him time and again with applause, standing ovations, and shouts of "We forgive you, Jimmy!" Donnie kept his face buried in his handkerchief much of the time, and Frances often placed her hand across her face, as he apologized to his church, his ministers, his Bible college, his fellow televangelists, his audience.

"It was," wrote communications professor Quentin Schultze, "fabulous television, more compelling than most made-for-TV films and more dramatic than any evening soap opera."

After Jimmy finished, he was mobbed by his family and supporters. Frances put her arms around his neck and they held tightly to each other, faces buried. They stood that way for a long time, and then slowly, like invalids, made their way backstage and down the back hallway to their exit.

In the parking lot in front of the building, the people milled around, dressed in their Sunday best, murmuring, talking to reporters. They sobbed, hugged each other, and wiped their eyes, struggling with the magnitude of the betrayal. Many were anxious to forgive and move on. Women hugged and kissed their Bibles.

Inside the Family Worship Center, many still knelt, lay on the floor crying, prayed for Brother Swaggart, and held their hands up to the sky. Gradually the sanctuary emptied, leaving only a few people, among them a black boy of twelve kneeling with his head and arms on a pew, sobbing. If such a great man of God as Jimmy Swaggart could sin badly enough to have to leave the pulpit, how could an ordinary, daily sinner hope to have victory?

◆   ◆   ◆

The reaction to Jimmy's confession filled the newspapers and editorial columns and letters to the editor for months. Bakker's response managed to inject self-righteousness into the words of Jesus. The only comment he wanted to make, he said, was "Ye who are without sin cast the first stone." Tammy, of course, cried.

Falwell was "saddened," and lamented the credibility crisis that had hit religion as well as Wall Street and presidential politics. Robertson was supportive, though he removed Jimmy's program from CBN.

Gorman's church in New Orleans was also packed as the congregation waited expectantly for him to mount the pulpit. But he only read a prepared statement: "My heart has been deeply saddened by the news of the past few days. We are praying for the Swaggart family . . . No one knows the pain they are encountering more than the Gorman family." He offered prayers for Jimmy.

The Assemblies begged readers of its magazine the *Pentecostal Evangel* to remember that even if the messenger was flawed, the message wasn't.

Four days after the confession, columnist Jimmy Breslin published a story in the *New York Daily News* about a hooker named "Precious" who claimed she had been with Jim Bakker several times. Three men from Baton Rouge asked her to swear out a deposition against Bakker, he wrote, and one of them—Jimmy Swaggart, she later said—asked her to have sex with him in the car.

Pat Robertson charged that such revelations were initiated by George Bush to try to tar him with the "immoral hypocrite televangelist" brush two weeks before the Republican primaries in South Dakota and Minnesota. An indignant Bush scoffed that Robertson was exploiting the bad news about televangelists to stay in the headlines himself.

WBRZ did another documentary, noting that any dent in the Jimmy Swaggart Ministries would have a devastating effect on the economy of Baton Rouge. The ministry had developed a yearly payroll estimated as high as $16 million. Jimmy was Baton Rouge's biggest generator of conventions, attracting thousands of visitors every year, over 90 percent from out of state. The ministry spent $32 million locally per year for daily operations.

Letters to major papers ranged from "Hey, let's give the guy a chance to repent" to disgust and ridicule. The ratio was about five to one against Jimmy. A typical writer scorned him as a "disgusting sobbing, whimpering excuse for a human being."

They said he was a phony, preying on poor, unsuspecting people. They said he only confessed because he was caught. They said it was great that the televangelists' hypocrisy had been exposed because it gutted the Christian right's bid for the White House. They asked why it was the sexual behavior that was the scandal and not the bilking of the innocent faithful.

The *Baltimore Sun*'s editorial chief, an Alabaman, said it was misleading to suggest that Jimmy was bilking widows; his followers' loyalty was "deeply rooted in the Southern experience . . . of poverty, isolation, poor diet, scanty education, and frightful vulnerability to the terrors of nature . . . [Jimmy's message] is basically an appeal to the Southern inferiority complex."

A *New York Times* writer said that Jimmy could come back; he compared Jimmy's clean confession to the extended soap opera of the Bakkers. Also, he pointed out, televangelism had many audiences. Jimmy's fall probably would not affect people like Robert Schuller and Jerry Falwell for long.

As the weeks passed and the press dug into Jimmy's background, it became more analytical, satirical, and critical. His past sermons were scoured for attacks on fornication and pornography. He couldn't win, said Larry Thomas. Whatever he did was seen as either preaching about it suspiciously often or being suspiciously silent about it.

"Jimmy didn't talk and preach about pornography that much, though he was involved in the boycott of Seven-Eleven [for selling *Penthouse*, *Playboy*, and other magazines]. It was only after the fall that people thought he preached a lot against pornography. But no matter what he was perceived to have done, it was used to explain his sin."

Jimmy's book *Straight Answers to Tough Questions*, released in October of 1987, was cited over and over for hypocrisy, projection, and sexual perversion. The 316-page book was filled with diatribes about lust and warned against movies, dancing, masturbation, swimming, and even aerobics. It said that being saved and getting the Holy Ghost gave people a special ability to fight sin. Pentecostals, for example, were more likely to quit smoking, he wrote.

Stephen Winzenburg, the Catholic communications professor who had been scolded by Frances in the summer of 1987, noted that Jimmy had begun preparing the flock for the bad news beginning in December 1987. He started putting himself down in sermons, calling himself a "pitiful, flawed preacher." He identified himself with Judas Iscariot, and said over and over that Christ was the only one who was perfect. He blamed the pervasiveness of pornography on the Supreme Court's wimpy definition of obscenity. Amazingly, he even told a story of a prostitute who had heard him through the wall separating their hotel rooms, "agonizing in prayer" at three a.m. and had knocked on his door and asked him to pray for her. He may have intended to evoke Christ's agony in Gethsemane before he was crucified, when the disciples failed to keep vigil but Mary Magdalene couldn't sleep, but it didn't work.

An example of gleeful malice in the press was a Nicholas Von Hoffman column full of good writing and bad will. "Jimmy is straight out of the molten, precognitive core of guilty fears, Sunday schools and the panic for grace and redemption." The part about the panic for redemption was astute, but von Hoffman couldn't resist describing Jimmy's congregation as twitching on the floor, yanking and jerking, eyeballs bulging and tongues lolling as they "take Jesus Christ for [their] personal, loving savior" in wall-eyed, unholy ecstasy.

He depicted Jimmy as a hypocritical, horny bully, made him out to be stupid and greedy, and concluded that there was more rejoicing in heaven over his fall than in the salvation of a hundred souls.

Ray Hale, Jerry's onetime manager who knew Pentecostal torquing first-hand said, "Jerry Lee and Jimmy Lee have this sex and guilt mentality. Like, it's okay to look at it, but it'd be a sin if I stuck it in there, you know? Jerry Lee has all these Pentecostal, backwards type things. Oral sex is a sin, but two women at a time is okay. You know that kind of double standard?"

◆ ◆ ◆

Sun Swaggart stepped up to defend his son on the one facet of the trouble he understood: "The whole world is on his shoulders, preaching to half a billion people every week. You're not knowing from one day to the next if you're going to have the money. And Satan is there to tell him during the night, 'You're not going to get it.'"

An interview with a stunned Mickey Gilley gave a glimpse into the pressures on Jimmy as he was growing up.

"The family always held Jimmy on a pedestal so high that this is a total shock to us . . . [he] built an empire that is far above anything Jerry Lee and I have done . . . Jimmy to us was like Jesus walking on the face of the earth again. We looked up to him and felt that he was above all of us." He supported Jimmy, saying he had done tremendous work, and was still a sincere man of God, and that it took a strong person to confess on television like that.

Back in Ferriday, David Beatty's brother Cecil was upset. "When I heard all this trouble, I went to Baton Rouge. I went in to talk, and Frances and Donnie tried to stop me. I pushed past them and went into Jimmy's office. He had some guy in there that he was meeting with. I said, 'I just wanna ask you one question, face to face. Is all this I've heard true? I'm askin' you face to face.' He asked the man to wait outside, and he closed the door. 'Cecil,' he said, 'I'm gonna tell you the truth. I got railroaded. I was framed.' 'This is YOU tellin' me this, right?' I asked him. And he said yes, that he was framed. I been knowin' him all his life, and I've never known him to run around."

Everyone inside the ministry, everyone close to the Swaggarts, people who had known them intimately for years, including Jerry, Mickey, the Andersons, David Beatty, all the other cousins, and even John Camp, were flabbergasted by the news that Jimmy had been caught with a prostitute. And though it seemed impossible, almost all of them felt that Frances knew nothing of Jimmy's secret life.

"I think she was *very* surprised," said her brother Bob Anderson. She had been focused so hard on building the ministry, keeping up with its rapid expansion, and "making Jimmy the biggest preacher in the world," as Anderson said, that she simply didn't see it.

She talked to her brother about it only once, and he found her very subdued. She said they'd been married 35 years, and she'd never suspected it. She said that even in unguarded moments, when she might have seen a clue, she saw none. For example, after they moved into the Highland Road house, they bought a television satellite. "Of course they blocked all the porno channels, but you could still see the ads for them. Of all the times she saw him clicking through the channels, she never, ever saw him even slow up on the porn ads."

She told Anderson, "I never heard even one curse word come from him" the whole time they were married.

Even if that sounds unlikely, Jimmy was still very, very experienced at hiding his misdeeds, and very smart, starting with his secret visits to Nannie. The extent of his teenage thefts was never found out, and his parents never suspected he was sneaking out at night with Jerry, nor did his cousins ever stop seeing him as "like Jesus walking on the face of the earth again." He had had the habit since youth, and was both disciplined about controlling his habit and practiced in finding ways to keep some time and space to himself that seemed entirely innocent.

Anderson heard Jimmy talking about the porn magazines after his confession. "He said an evil spirit [would] come all over him, and he was addicted to them since childhood." Sun, said Anderson, "was cruel, a hard man, he rode Jimmy hard. He was VERY, VERY jealous when Jimmy started making a name. He wouldn't come around."

As to Jimmy being careless enough to cruise in New Orleans at the height of his career, Anderson said, "You do things under pressure you wouldn't do any other time. Frances PUSHED him. I remember they did an album cover without Jimmy's picture on it, and Frances pitched a fit.

"I figure he just had a physical and mental breakdown. Jimmy changed [starting] in '84 and '85, because of the money and the power, and the huge pressure in the ministry. It was expansion, expansion, expansion. [And] he wanted everything NOW and he wanted it perfect."

Jimmy's cousin Gerald Lewis, who became an Assemblies minister, remembered being riveted by the Bakker scandal on television and feeling proud that Jimmy was standing so tall. He told people, "they'll never get anything on Jimmy Swaggart. I know him, I've known him all my life. They'll never get anything on HIM."

JIMMY'S OLD FRIEND from the early days, pastor Gerald Wilson, gave a calm assessment of the phenomenon that was Jimmy Swaggart.

"You know, humility is something that when you think you've got it, you just lost it. But I think a lot of my [colleagues] had a humble attitude, you know, 'I'm just a country hick that God touched, and I just want to be faithful.' [Pride] began to creep in when money became the primary goal. . . . They get single-minded, like, 'I've got to reach the whole world.' " But, Wilson said, that's not their job. "They forget that they aren't in charge, that someone was doing it before they came along."

What if it's the voice of God, telling you to cover the world with the Word? In the Book of Acts, he said, was a clue about what the voice of God probably really sounds like: "it seemed good to them." "That's about the best we can do. And in Malachi, where it says we GROPE after the Lord, as one feeling his way along the wall in the dark. This is more what we do, we muddle through, and at times we feel that this is what God wanted us to do."

It didn't say God told them, "Now Son, you need to get 20 more stations by the end of the year."

But of all the reactions to Jimmy's confession, it would be hard to find a more blunt and pragmatic assessment than that given by the reverend William Bibb, pastor of the First Assembly of God in Baton Rouge: "We're in a PR business, and when people lose confidence in us . . . they tend to keep their money."

◆   ◆   ◆

Denominational rules said that a minister who had committed adultery could enter a rehabilitation program, almost always two years, with no preaching the first year and a limited ministry the second. That was the standard the Louisiana district held Marvin Gorman to.

But with Jimmy, the equivocation started immediately. A Louisiana district official hinted at leniency right away, saying, "Justice can sometimes be best served with mercy" and noting that Jimmy had "shown true humility and repentance and had not tried to blame anyone else for his failure." Jimmy's lawyer, Bill Treeby, reiterated that staying out of the pulpit for a year was not a strict rule. He said it was unclear when Jimmy would resume his television ministry—unclear, it was hinted, whether the television ministry fell under the Assemblies' discipline at all; could they rerun tapes, for example? And what about existing crusade contracts?

Jimmy said he would step down for an indeterminate period, to be left "in the hands of the Lord." That was a gentle warning to his superiors in Springfield: don't forget the $12 million I gave last year. Let God do this.

He said his ministry would continue under the leadership of the Louisiana district council. That was where his power base was: his co-pastor, Jim Rentz, was a member of the council, as were three of his board members—council superintendent Cecil Janway, secretary-treasurer Forrest Hall, and presbyter F.C. Chamberlain. So was his cousin Gerald Lewis.

On February 22, the Monday after his confession, Jimmy, Frances, Donnie, and Debbie were ushered quickly through the back door of the Assemblies' plantation-style district headquarters in Alexandria after arriving with a police escort and dodging supporters and critics at the airports.

After interviewing Jimmy, the dozen or so Louisiana officials arrived at a five-point program. First, his rehabilitation was to last two years. Second, he couldn't preach in the U.S. for three months. Third, he could not be co-pastor of the Family Worship Center during rehabilitation. Fourth, he had to submit to weekly counseling and supervision with three Louisiana district presbyters. Fifth, he had to submit quarterly written reports on his progress to the district superintendent and monthly reports to the state presbytery.

The Louisiana men had worked into the evening hammering out the recommendations, to be passed on to the executives in Springfield. But the bottom line was really only a three-month slap on the wrist.

Jimmy's stalwart, Cecil Janway, announced the measures in a press conference as Jimmy's convoy, flanked by police, rolled out of district headquarters and headed for the airport. The announcement was just in time to be covered by ABC's "Nightline"; Janway again sternly warned Jimmy not to talk to the secular media, and refused all questions himself.

Springfield had earlier told the thronging media that Jimmy had admitted to sexual misconduct over a period of years, but said it would not reveal more; if Jimmy wanted to tell the press exactly what he'd done, it would be up to him to do so.

But listening to Jimmy during the ten-hour drama had been amazing and traumatic for the Executive Presbyters, and it was extremely tempting to talk to someone outside that room about it. It had been an ugly jolt, seeing the photos. They showed Jimmy and Debra standing by the motel room door together; Debra watching Jimmy change his tire; Jimmy's license plates; Jimmy in the car with Gorman. Debra with her little sneering Jerry Lee Lewis smile.

Reverend Glen Cole of Sacramento, one of the 13 Executive Presbyters who heard Jimmy's 10-hour confession in Springfield, lingered with the media, telling them, "He tried and tried and tried through prayer and fasting and everything he could do to lick it and it beat him." James Hamill, another Executive Presbyter, was more direct, saying Jimmy had admitted a fascination with pornography that dated back to his boyhood.

Jimmy knew they were repelled by him, a profound wound. Even if he got the help they demanded, he knew a glass wall had descended, cutting him off forever from the intimate company of the Good Men whose confidence and approval he had enjoyed for many years. He went into a kind of hysteria, said a source close to several of the presbyters.

They had separated Frances from him, and had glimpsed something of the interlocking dependency that had formed between two teenagers, poor and gifted and determined, more than 30 years ago.

"They sat in stunned silence as Jimmy went through the dog-and-pony show he had for them," said the source. "He was bawling, and Frances was standing outside the door, banging on the door, screaming, 'What are you doing to my husband?! What are you doing to my husband?!' "

Someone savvy about unconscious marital bargains might conclude that Jimmy was expected to deal with sex as best he could—as long as he delivered onstage. If sexual tension was a big part of that, then let there be sexual tension. If that tension had to come from wickedness—prostitutes or pornography or working out some issues over childhood sexual trauma, then let that happen—but keep up appearances. Tension, after all, was the constant companion of a sexual addict, from fear of being found out.

Indeed, Jimmy would write in puzzlement later about a three-month period when "There was absolutely no attack by the powers of darkness. At the same time, there was no anointing of the Holy Spirit. It was uncanny. It was as if Satan had left, but it was as if the Holy Spirit had left as well."

Perhaps Frances unwittingly knew from early on that Jimmy needed to prowl, to feel guilty and sick at heart and fearful for his soul, he needed an essential contact with evil, and needed it regularly, in order to get up and do what he did onstage at the pace he did it—a pace largely set by her, according to a great number of observers over the years.

Or perhaps it was as Larry Thomas said, "It wasn't because he had a cold, ruthless wife at home, and it wasn't demon oppression. He said, 'I have sinned.' He sinned, and that was the truth. He told the truth."

THE EVENING of February 27, 1988, Richard Dortch went on "Nightline" and non-answered every question in the evasive mode that, according to PTL biographer Charles Shepard, his exasperated staff had come to call "Dortching." Host Ted Koppel asked if favoritism was being shown by Jimmy's homeboys, and Dortch said the media shouldn't judge because it didn't have all the details. Koppel pointed out that Jimmy was under a virtual gag order from the Assemblies, so how could they get those details? Dortch replied, "I believe that those who have spiritual authority will know and do the right thing."

Koppel tried a couple more times and then gave up on Dortch. Ben Armstrong, head of the National Religious Broadcasters, cited the new ethics guidelines and told Koppel Jimmy could be stripped of his membership.

The five Louisiana recommendations went to Springfield. On Thursday, February 25, the national officials spent 11 hours with them, including four hours meeting with Jimmy that evening.

The next day, the Executive Presbytery booted the recommendations back to Louisiana for reconsideration. The Louisiana council was criticized for being too lenient and for announcing its decision to the media before sending it to Springfield. That violated Assemblies bylaws and was seen as an attempt to use popular opinion to bully the national council into accepting the recommendations. The Louisianans also attempted to stampede things by coming up with recommendations in a day, when they actually had six months from the time charges were filed to decide Jimmy's punishment.

The five-point Louisiana plan only made Jimmy stop preaching in his Family Worship Center. It did not necessarily deny him his television ministry. There were plenty of tapes to fill a three-month or even a year hiatus, and secular stations would be happy to run them as long as the checks arrived on time. Under the plan, he would be allowed to make some scheduled international appearances, and make day-to-day decisions to keep the ministry running. He could also counsel people.

The Assemblies' constitution and bylaws didn't say that the Louisiana district had to change its recommendation, just that it reconsider if asked. Amid accusations of favoritism, it was being pointedly asked. Twelve elders in Springfield would have the final say.

Springfield was taking 300 telephone calls an hour, many of them from members of the flock unhappy with Jimmy's three-month rap on the knuckles, and with three members of Jimmy's board sitting on the 19-member Louisiana council.

The state presbyters made few bones about wanting to go easy on their native son. Jimmy had come clean instead of trying to blame it on someone else—a swipe at Gorman and Bakker. Jimmy's cousin Gerald Lewis, a member of the Louisiana General Council, agreed. When some council members insisted Jimmy should not be treated differently from any other minister, Gerald replied, "Yes he should. He is different from any other Assemblies minister. He is special."

"Where do you find another Jimmy Swaggart?" said Jonathan Ziegler of Violet, Louisiana, one of the state presbyters. "We don't say he's God, but his ministry is a gift from God."

Even a PTL spokesman said Bakker had behaved a lot worse than Jimmy. If it had just been the Jessica Hahn matter, he said, Bakker would still be at PTL. There were no legal charges against Jimmy, no accusations of embezzlement; it was entirely a church matter. Perhaps the Louisiana council was being reasonable and the national one was being harsh to make up for its laxity with Bakker.

Sources close to Jimmy were now saying he'd only had the sex problem for four months.

It was almost exactly the same minimizing Marvin Gorman had done—except the witness was not a preacher's wife but a prostitute who was nowhere to be found.

Unfortunately for Jimmy, however, a New Orleans television station, WVUE, had tracked Debra down on February 24, in West Palm Beach. She gave an interview and then went back into hiding. Assemblies officials in Springfield had been looking for her to check Jimmy's story and asked to borrow WVUE's tape. They watched it: the woman in the photos was the same as the woman on the tape who was calling Jimmy a pervert. She said she had been meeting Jimmy at various places in New Orleans for about a year. As to his frequency, "I seen him drive down the street every week," she said.

She said she was the one who was photographed with Jimmy going into the motel room.

The grim presbyters watched as she told graphically what Jimmy wanted her to do: get naked, lie on the bed and pose, put on a dress with no underwear and ride around, and in the evening, take her clothes off and get out of the car and then get back in; this turned him on. Worst, she agitatedly told of his noticing the photograph of her three children—two young sons aged seven and eight and a daughter ten, whose ages and genders matched those of his own three grandchildren—and asking if the little girl might watch them sometime.

They also heard her say she performed pornographic acts but did not have sexual intercourse with him (it came out later that he had once crossed that line briefly). WVUE reported that Debra had already talked to the *National Enquirer,* who gave her a polygraph test that was so inconclusive the tabloid had decided not to use the interview.

Technically Jimmy might not have committed adultery, but the national officials had made up their minds. They gave the Louisiana elders until March 29–31, the next time the national body met, to respond to their request for reconsideration, sternly warning that the Assemblies had an "unbroken precedent" of insisting on a full year of no preaching.

The Louisianans didn't need until March 29. On March 2, they rejected the harsher recommendations of the national council, saying it hadn't taken into account the importance of Jimmy's ministry and how many souls would be lost.

Perhaps they were emboldened by the fact that Pat Robertson had made a special stop in Baton Rouge on February 27 and issued a supportive statement about Jimmy at the airport. This was partly to soften the blow that he was removing Jimmy from CBN the next day, and partly a sideways apology to George Bush for accusing Bush of engineering the Swaggart scandal. In any case, the state officials had stopped talking about the sincerity of Jimmy's confession and were stressing the pragmatics.

Two days after that, the national Assemblies rejected the milder sanctions, calling a special meeting of the 250-member Executive Presbytery of the General Council to meet on March 28 and serve as an appeals body.

Over the next month, as his fate was volleyed back and forth between Alexandria and Springfield, Jimmy sought solace in his congregation. He continued to visit the Family Worship Center on Wednesday and Sunday, not to preach—in his opinion, the clock was already running on his three-month suspension—but to chat. One night he told his followers he was fighting demons and that yesterday he had been visited by horrible ones—"the most debilitating powers of Hell that I have ever experienced in my life"—all of whom vanished without explanation after lunch.

"When your back's against the wall and your knees are buckling, this Gospel works!" They applauded. None of them, least of all Jimmy and Frances, seemed to notice that he was trying to will his ugly situation away—a strong signal that he was still in deep trouble.

There were 4,500 people—still a healthy crowd—at the Family Worship Center the Sunday after the confession. Jimmy made a brief appearance; there was some joking with the crowd; Jimmy said prayers and support had come from all denominations, including Catholics; people laughed.

Then Frances got up and said, "If you ladies want a good diet that will help you lose weight, I know one." She got a standing ovation. "This has been a million weeks rolled into one week," she said. "These days never ended and the nights never ended. But God's grace brought us through it. God specializes in things that seem impossible." Jimmy wiped away tears as she spoke.

Another strong signal that whatever counseling Jimmy might submit to was not going to work was his defiance. It had both his and Frances' signatures: first, he went back on the air on March 6, after only two weeks away from the pulpit. He didn't count it as violating the three-month probation because it was taped, not live, and because it was chatting, not preaching—he told his audience that he was eager to tell them what had really happened, and that he would when the time was right. As usual, he was pushing it to the edge, testing the definition of "probation" and "rehabilitation" and testing the patience even of his denominational elders in Louisiana, who had defied their own elders with the softer penalty.

The national Assemblies shrugged when asked whether Jimmy had violated his rehabilitation. As far as they were concerned, he hadn't even been disciplined yet. That would happen March 28.

The handwriting was on the wall. Jimmy was going to be disciplined with teeth. He'd probably leave his church.

◆   ◆   ◆

Jimmy and Frances got some standing O's at the Family Worship Center, but outside, the weather was getting nasty. The ministry had laid off 100 people and halted all new construction. Rumors flew (and were denied) about a relationship between Jimmy and popular ministry singer Janet Paschal, blond and gorgeous, who left abruptly after the confession. The *National Enquirer* ran a story: "Swaggart: He Threatens Divorce as Marriage Crumbles" saying Frances kept too tight a rein on Jimmy and quoting an unnamed family member saying, "She treated him like a little boy, and like a little boy he rebelled."

Jimmy was a sex addict, no question, said psychotherapists and clergy who specialized in counseling. There were 10 million of them in the U.S. Articles abounded about the 12-step program, the dynamics of addiction.

Oral Roberts surfaced again, saying he'd prayed for Jimmy and seen demons with long fingernails digging into his body, and that he'd exorcised them.

The NRB voted to drop him from its membership. He was constantly skewered by his own quoted words about Jim Bakker: "You cannot cover sin. It has to be exposed."

It was a beautiful, clear spring in Louisiana, but his family was staggering in pain as Jimmy was psychoanalyzed, ridiculed, and excoriated from news desks, comedy channels, and pulpits the world over. Worst was hearing himself despised by other ministers, whose approval he'd sought his whole life.

But Frances fought like a tiger. She and Donnie were doing fill-ins to air in place of the ministry's regular show, rotating their pleas for money. When it was her turn on one tape, Frances, wearing a striking red dress, hair fully blond, jewelry perfect, nails done, looked directly into the camera. Referring as always to Jimmy as "my husband," she read letters from people saying they had to have Jimmy's program, they couldn't live without it.

"I've heard him up walking the floor, crying and praying in the wee hours of the morning, praying for you, praying for your lost loved ones, you who are sick, you who are lonely . . . if there's a failure among the people that work around him, it's that we've depended on him too much." You hold the key, she told viewers, and then tightening the screws: "When you stand before God, He's going to hold you accountable for what you give to His work. . . . God doesn't just manufacture money out of wind . . . even you skeptics and you atheists . . . I'm asking you to help us in our time of need." She could not believe it was God's will, she said, for this ministry to cease. And indeed, if it had been God's will, He couldn't have convinced her.

Donnie, still a trooper, had not inherited his father's silky baritone, and his high-register keening and chin-trembling during the fill-in appeal quickly took on the allure of a root canal. He said things like he doubted his dad would live to 60, he was burning himself out, night and day, all to get the word of God out. "We're not perfect, we make mistakes, but Jesus Christ's mercy is sweeping them away," he pleaded as he asked for money to tide them over. "We don't ask you to feel sorry for us. We just ask you to help."

But another day at home, Frances, watching a television preacher flay Jimmy, finally gave in, and collapsed on the floor in sobs.

Jimmy felt outside his body, zombielike, as if it were happening to someone else, just as he had at nine, when he delivered the A-bomb prophecies. One day, alone at home as Frances and Donnie fought for the telecast, Jimmy felt a "terrible foreboding spirit." By 2 p.m., as he walked the perimeter of his estate, the attacks were so intense he had to brace himself on the fence. Hissing, spewing toxins formed themselves into sentences: "You have wrecked everything. You are nothing but a joke, a sideshow, a sneer all over the world, and that's all you will ever be."

Whose voice was this, nailing him to the cross? It was what he had feared his whole life, this derision and ridicule. The voice told him to do his family a favor: take some cash, get in the car, and leave. He fought the oppression for two hours before feeling the power of God wash over him. In the end, where would he go? Preaching was all he knew, and all he cared about. Frances and Donnie returned at 4:30 to find him praising God—a release that must have relieved them because it meant he hadn't chosen the alternative form of release this time.

♦　♦　♦

On Tuesday, March 29, 1988, the Executive Presbytery in Springfield gave its multi-million dollar decision: it would take away Jimmy's credentials for a year, not three months, and cease all distribution of his tapes in the U.S. and abroad. Moreover, his time out of the pulpit so far would not count against the year. He would have to undergo weekly counseling and file monthly reports. He could appeal, but the suspension was effective that day. If he didn't submit to the discipline, they would defrock him—huge donations and all.

Jimmy met with his ministry officials in midafternoon. Many, including an old friend and fellow traveling evangelist who often preached at Jimmy's church, Don Brankel, urged him to submit. The handful of advisers in his inner circle, including Rentz, Frances, and Donnie, advised him not to.

The next day, Treeby held a press conference. As usual, Jimmy was going to fight. He was looking forward to returning to the pulpit May 22.

Springfield had no comment. Leaders were praised for finally taking a stand on a big star. Even Mormon leaders called to congratulate the Assemblies (Jimmy later said this was because he was a threat, since so many Mormons had been saved by his telecast).

The Louisiana council was grim. They had tried to stand by their man, but now they voted to go along with the one-year suspension instead of their three-month one. And no credit for time served.

Jimmy mounted a multi-pronged attack against his elders, challenging Springfield's right to discipline local preachers, and lobbying presbyters to uphold local rules. No district council had ever resisted the Executive Presbytery before. Finally, he announced he'd go back on television May 22 in defiance of the ruling—"unless the rapture occurs first."

That meant he was leaving the Assemblies. Which meant the members of his church would have to vote to leave the church, too. The roster of Family Worship Center ministers would have to give up their credentials if they wanted to keep preaching there.

On Easter Sunday, April 3, Jimmy again appeared in the Amen Corner in violation of his vow. But by now it hardly mattered; the Assemblies were probably going to defrock him anyway. He sang counterpoint to the choir and bounced the big mike in his lap in unconscious burlesque of his sin. He fidgeted during Rentz' sermon, and then finally, after a hymn, leapt up and sprinted back and forth on the stage, yelling, "Satan says it's over! Jesus says, look at the blood!"

Then a teenaged boy stood up in the balcony and yelled out that Brother Swaggart was a liar and a hypocrite. Jimmy froze, did not turn or look up. It was as if the voice of his last real attempt at rebellion—his "running from God" as a teenager before he met Frances—had broken through to the present, angry at being denied out of existence for 37 years. Rentz asked the crowd to drown out the boy with "praise" and they did, as ushers rushed to drag him out.

A few moments later, Jimmy had recovered and he sang, again in unconscious burlesque, "I'll rise again. Ain't no power on earth can keep me down."

On Friday, April 8, Jimmy held a press conference in front of the ministry building flanked by 195 flags, one for each country where his message was heard. He resigned from the Assemblies of God, just two hours after it defrocked him. He said he had to do what God said, not what the Assemblies said. He apologized to officials for burdening them and promised to "never say a derogatory thing about the Assemblies of God"—a vow he would soon break.

The Oggs resigned from the ministry. Frances let her brother know she wanted the tan Lincoln sold—and not in Baton Rouge.

◆   ◆   ◆

Jimmy knew all along it wasn't going to work. When he had put on his best show in Springfield back on February 18, he had felt an old, familiar rift. It was an isolation entirely familiar to him, from being a scorned little Holy Roller kid, from living in a family with one crazy grandmother and one fanatical one, from being singled out and separated even within his own family, and from the long, long double life he'd lived.

His encounter in Springfield made it clear that he would never be able to get the relief addicts need most: trust and fellowship of other men. Twelve-step programs put addicts together in a healing context that is powerful because of the relief of being accepted even with the addiction. People can lay down their arms of secrecy and control and admit they are powerless—just as when they were children— but this time before helpers who know how to guide the addict. And indeed, risks like Jimmy took—going to New Orleans in the middle of the day when his face was all over the news because of the Bakker scandal—typically reveal a deep wish to be found out.

But Larry Thomas and Gerald Wilson were right: he'd waited too long to get help if he wanted to minimize or avoid discipline. And with Frances beating on the door, fearful about what might be coming out of him without her there to edit, the chances of his relinquishing secrecy and control were slim.

Indeed, Jimmy later denied saying he'd had a lifelong problem. "I just casually mentioned out loud, speaking more to myself than to any one else, 'I have fought this devil ever since I was a child,' " he wrote to his followers. "I was thinking of the tremendous spiritual conflict that had raged around me from the tender age of eight." The religious leaders, he said, misinterpreted that, "telling all and sundry that I had been plagued by some horrible demon of perversion, or lust . . . ever since I was a child."

Not credible, said Larry Thomas; Jimmy's problem hadn't developed over a couple of years. "To get to the motel stage it had to be longer than just three or four years." Exposure-wish notwithstanding, he was confident enough to do it right in the middle of the PTL stink, in which he was a central figure. He couldn't have gotten that confident overnight. He must have been getting away with it for a long time.

Back in the pulpit before his scheduled May 22 return for another unofficial chat with his congregation—to ask for $6 million to keep the broadcast on the air—he told them he'd often wished he was dead during this trouble. Losing $1.8 million a month, he had already sent a fundraising letter with an astounding claim that put him in competition with Jesus himself: "I have suffered humiliation and shame as possibly no human being on the face of the earth has ever suffered." Now he told his listeners that this was the "most crucial time of any ministry in the history of the world."

As for Debra Murphree, he gave his followers short shrift instead of the explanation he'd promised. He told them he didn't know how "it" had "happened," evoking the image of A.A. Allen, arrested for drunk driving, saying he'd been kidnapped and had awakened to find strangers pouring whiskey down his throat.

"I don't understand it myself. I have thought about it a lot. How could it happen? It is difficult to explain unless you have been in the arena I have been in." Psychologists and ministers all over the country shook their heads. Even if he could pull his ministry back together for awhile, he was clearly going to do something bad again.

In mid-April, Murphree had signed to tell her story and do a photo spread in *Penthouse,* whereupon her ex-husband sued to get custody of the children. The same month, the Fourth Circuit Court of Appeal in New Orleans agreed to revive Marvin Gorman's lawsuit against Jimmy.

At about this time, John Wesley Fletcher, Bakker's old cohort, filed bankruptcy, attempted suicide, and entered a mental hospital. While he was there, his wife left him.

◆　◆　◆

Jimmy liked the Drusilla Restaurant on Highway 12 in a Winn-Dixie shopping strip. The Drusilla, specializing in seafood, usually had people standing outside waiting, especially on Saturday night. Its motif was a bayou shack: faded barn-lumber, lanterns, rusty tin roof. Next door was the Drusilla Seafood Market, selling Hot Boiled Crawfish, fishing licenses, marine tackle, and boxes of Velveeta for bait.

Jimmy was coming out the door of the restaurant when lights suddenly flared and Geraldo Rivera stepped into his path. Furious, Jimmy told the tabloid television host he would not give him an interview.

But someone must have pointed out that Geraldo, whom Jimmy had called "Mr. Riviera," could give him a huge national forum, for Jimmy cooperated the next day.

"I'VE PREACHED to some of the largest crowds in the world, but I guess that I stand today with more fear and more trembling than I ever stood before in all my life."

It was Sunday, May 22, 1988, and once again Jimmy Swaggart stood in the pulpit at the Family Worship Center. There were about 5,000 visitors, close to the number he drew before his confession and defrocking; many, however, were strangers there out of curiosity.

But he was back. The Family Worship Center cameras were on him. He'd clawed his way to the top once, and he would do it again. He'd seen it many times in his youth, preachers who fell, and once they got back in the pulpit, people forgave them. Frances had fought so hard. How could he do less?

Outside on the grassy median dividing Bluebonnet Road, a swarm of photographers paced, forbidden to come onto ministry grounds. More than a dozen television cameras for stations and networks jostled for position, and reporters interviewed each other; the French and Italians, one international journalist said, were especially fascinated with televangelists, and the interest in Jimmy in Europe was very high.

Inside, Jimmy was in top form. Knowing there were reporters in the audience and that media analysts liked to make much of dreams, he fed them one: he was again fighting a giant serpent while God watched. Again he killed it, saw a bigger one, and asked God, "I have to fight this thing, don't I?" But this time God told him no. Jesus had already slain it.

He started yelling that he had suffered and come through, he had been burned and tempered. "CNN is going to be taking a picture! CBS and ABC and NBC! I want to serve notice on all the whole world, what's past is past! I'm not looking back!" The crowd leapt to its feet, cheering and sobbing.

A black woman had loudly interrupted his dream tale, erupting in tongues, and Jimmy had had her gently led out, after saying, "Sister, give me your utterance in just a few moments." Now she came back and finished her utterance, and someone interpreted, a trembling white woman who loosed a volley of admonitions about the life-giving water of the spirit that flows in abundance. Worshippers flooded down to the altar at the end to stick love offerings into Jimmy's pockets.

One of them stuffed in a whole envelope—a subpoena from Marvin Gorman's attorneys.

◆　　◆　　◆

The first week in June, the Debra Murphree *Penthouse* issue hit the stands and sold out immediately. Debra's interview was on sealed pages that couldn't be opened until after purchase. In New Orleans, the magazines sold at an average of four per minute. In Baton Rouge, twice the normal run was delivered, and it still wasn't enough; the issue outsold the record Vanessa Williams edition of September 1984. The unairbrushed black and white photos, showing a tattooed Debra with her fun-loving grin, sprawling in the poses she said were Jimmy's favorites in the ugly motel rooms where they met, lay on the pages like a gynecology text. *Newsweek*'s religion editor Ken Woodward called it "trashy journalism and trashy religion."

On a two-week, ten-city tour, she said Jimmy never talked to her about why she was a hooker or tried to get her to stop that kind of life, though some of her other clients did. He never paid her more than $20, and she seldom asked for more. As for the ugly black-and-white pictures, she said, "They don't bother me. That's how he saw me."

Once again Geraldo Rivera traveled to Baton Rouge to put a microphone in Jimmy's face. Once again polite words were exchanged, and then Geraldo did a show with Debra, two sex experts, and a former voyeur.

After the *Penthouse* article came out, Jimmy told his Wednesday night audience that he had asked God to take his life that day. Frances cried when he said it. The crowd, only 600 that night, was shocked. But, Jimmy said, he was healed now, no longer pursued by those devils.

"I do not deny that the wound was there. I do not deny that the hell was there. But I proclaim it to demons, and devils, and hell, and Satan, and angels, and you: IT IS HEALED BY THE POWER OF ALMIGHTY GOD!" His audience cheered wildly.

The ministry was in disarray as the Assemblies preachers who made the Family Worship Center their regular stop decided whether to keep preaching there. If they did, they would be disciplined, and if they persisted, they'd have to give up their credentials.

"All the people who had credentials in the AG had to choose between Jimmy and the AG" said Steve Badger, a biochemist and former teacher at the college. "The Swaggarts had what some of us said was a misplaced sense of loyalty. They wished the loyalty to them was stronger than to the AG."

Saddest for many in Jimmy's orbit was the fate of the Jimmy Swaggart Bible College. Badger, like most of the other professors, had come to Baton Rouge because Jimmy had assembled a powerful team at the Bible College.

"There were lots of people who felt like me," said Larry Thomas, "who felt we were really out in the forefront . . . it really was the West Point of Bible colleges. Now it's like there's a wall. Like nothing existed before 1988, like nothing good happened before 1988."

Graduates, he said, are now "ashamed to hang their degrees on the wall . . . For professors there, it's like three years is gone out of their lives; when they apply for jobs they don't want to say they taught there. Some of the younger ones who started out teaching there can't even say on their resumes they've taught at college level, because it was at JSBC. So the prospective employer asks, 'What about 1985–88? What were you doing? There's a big blank there.' They say, 'Well, I wasn't going to mention it, but I was at Jimmy Swaggart Bible College.' It's like his name is poison, you can't even say you got anything out of the experience."

One teacher took all his tapes and papers and books, anything that had anything to do with his years at the Swaggart ministry, and burned them. "That's indicative of how fanatical people can be on both sides. Jimmy has been demonized by these people," said Thomas.

Dr. Charles Greenaway, a highly respected minister and teacher, spent five years at the ministry. "Those were the best years of my life," he told Larry Thomas. "Don't get bitter. You and I helped turn out 500 of the best preachers in the world."

Jimmy asked Ray Trask, head of the Bible College, to stay, but he declined. Indeed, most of the 45 faculty members who quit said they did so to retain their Assemblies affiliation. Others quit because they resented the pressure to join Jimmy's long-rumored new rival group, the World Evangelism Fellowship, or because the ministry refused to honor the rest of their contracts or pay their full salaries.

Jimmy asked Janett Ogg to stay long enough to get a new publications staff in place for the *Evangelist* and all the books and pamphlets—Janett had manned a staff of about a dozen—and she stayed a few more weeks. Her husband and son Jeff, though, immediately left to start a rival church in Baton Rouge—a move greatly resented by Jimmy and Jim Rentz. The magazine was slashed from 64 pages to 16.

Stephen Winzenburg was baffled at how the Oggs, "wonderful, good, intelligent folks," could have been fooled by Jimmy for so long in the first place. But Ogg refused to criticize his old boss. "Those were wonderful years in Baton Rouge," he said.

The ministry faced $25 million in demand notes, outside of its long-term debt. Three networks—PTL and CBN, which had started running Jimmy's programming again, and the Black Entertainment Network—said they might drop him. Together they represented 68 million homes.

Jimmy's popularity dropped from the number-one-televangelist slot to number seven in a matter of months.

On September 23, the Louisiana Supreme Court turned down requests from Jimmy's attorneys to review Gorman's appeal; that resulted in an order to send the case to trial. Jimmy appealed to the U.S. Supreme Court.

In November the ministry sold its corporate jet for an undisclosed sum. A few weeks later, Jimmy had to give a deposition in the Gorman lawsuit. At about that time, he got a call from *Penthouse*. A reporter wanted to know what comment Jimmy might have on a story it was preparing for the February 1989 issue. In it, a blond stripper named Catherine Mary Kampen was going to claim she had performed sex acts for Jimmy in her home.

Treeby was furious. Gorman was behind this, he told the Baton Rouge papers. Jimmy had never laid eyes on this woman; she came out of nowhere just to capitalize on his misfortune. "Reverend Swaggart vehemently, totally, completely, and categorically denies that he is acquainted with and/or that he has ever seen or conversed with Catherine Kampen," said Jimmy's press release. If the article came out, Treeby said, "we're going to own *Penthouse*."

Those were the opening blasts in a bizarre battle that never definitively rang true or false. It left the impression that something had happened, but not what any of the parties said.

It started at the same time as the Debra Murphree story. An author of that piece for *Penthouse, Washington Post* reporter Art Harris, had heard of Cathy Kampen from Murphree. Kampen told Harris she met Jimmy at a New Orleans gas station in July of 1987, during the heat of the Bakker scandal. She was crying at a pay phone on Airline Highway; depressed already over personal problems, she had splattered gasoline all over her skimpy jean shorts and halter top just as her beeper went off for a job. Kampen worked for a singing telegram enterprise that sometimes used strippers to deliver messages.

She told Art Harris that Jimmy drove up and asked her what was wrong. She recognized him, she said, and he didn't deny it like he had with Debra Murphree. He acted like a preacher, comforting her and offering to call her in a few days to see if she was better, which the 37-year-old found flattering. He told her Jesus loved her.

He called a few days later, she said, and soon he came to her house to counsel her, sitting at one end of the sofa and admonishing her to stop the degrading work she was doing. She said he visited during the day every few weeks for about six months, listening to her troubles and flattering her by confiding some of his own emotional problems. He gradually made the intimacy sexual, she said, talking her into performing some of her erotic telegrams while he masturbated. She said he visited her every month almost until the time of his confession—about ten times in all. And he asked if her 13-year-old daughter could join them.

Parts of the *Penthouse* story sounded so comically corny that they seemed to belong in a lethally low-budget video. For example, Jimmy was depicted with his pants around his ankles asking her to use a dildo and saying, "You will be rewarded, I promise you. Jesus loves you"; and bending over a chair, bare-buttocked, while she wielded a flimsy toy whip, ordering her, "Beat me, bitch, beat me and hurt me."

Kampen's boss in the strip-o-gram company spoke up, saying Kampen had concocted the scheme during the Debra Murphree revelations to cash in on the notoriety, and that her claims were a "pornographic fairy tale." She said Kampen was vain and cunning, a woman who liked to show off her body and who believed in voodoo and crystals; she noted that "It was very interesting that many of the personality traits she assigns to [Swaggart] are actually hers . . ." Kampen, it was implied, had incorporated details of the Murphree story—the voyeurism, the jogging suit, the Lincoln, the child, and the watching of Jimmy's confession and thinking he was talking about her—into a saleable fantasy.

But there were some strange contradictions. Art Harris was a respected mainstream journalist, first for the *Washington Post* and then for CNN. His skills, judgment, and credibility were pristine. None of the tests he put Kampen's tale through as a professional journalist, he said, could knock it down.

And shreds of Kampen's story felt true: that he made no move toward her for the first couple of visits; that he gave her bear hugs that were affectionate, not sexual; that he counseled her to stop her line of work; that he told her his daddy was very mean to him when he was a child (and his mother too, according to a later account); that he told her in the beginning that he had to be careful about his counseling visits because if it got out that he was helping anyone, "then everybody gets in line." That last, in fact, was why he did almost no pastoral counseling.

Another item that rang true was that she felt jealous when she found out about Murphree. Kampen didn't seem subtle enough to have made that up.

There was one detail of Kampen's story that felt especially true but didn't appear in Harris' story: she said Jimmy frequently requested that she drive with him to the levee and, once there, get out naked and run to the front of the car. He would get in the driver's seat and "pretend like he was going to hit me, and then wanted to know what it felt like if somebody was . . . going to run over me." That was reminiscent of nothing if not Sun's hissed threat to Jimmy and other children who annoyed him: "I'm gonna get in my car and run you over."

But Jimmy never sued *Penthouse*. Whether it was because, as he wrote in the May 1989 *Evangelist*, he didn't want to spend donation money on a lawsuit whose outcome was stacked against him because of liberal First Amendment interpretations, or whether he didn't want to have to answer deposition questions that could legitimately delve into the Murphree affair, or whether he knew the Kampen story was true, he dropped it. He felt *Penthouse* had little to lose. It had the ability to spade up so much prurience in the course of a lawsuit that it could win no matter what: it could sell the new ugliness and pulverize Jimmy's reputation doing it (*Penthouse* had a policy of attacking religion in almost every issue, from its interview with former child evangelist Marjoe Gortner in 1973 through the cudgeling of Rancho Rajneesh, Sun Myung Moon, the Moral Majority, the Bakkers, John Wesley Fletcher, and others). It might even win the case.

By the end of 1988, in the general election, the religious right's gangbuster showing in the primaries had paled. Pat Robertson was defeated. Jerry Falwell withdrew from politics to concentrate on his Liberty University, formally dissolving the Moral Majority the next year. Jim Bakker and Richard Dortch were indicted on charges of mail fraud, wire fraud, conspiracy, and other articles; both eventually went to prison. And Jimmy attended to shoring up his plummeting ratings.

Still, the evangelical community remained united in its interests, and still a potent force with an intact, highly effective communications and institutional infrastructure. It simply began looking for new voices with more credibility.

◆   ◆   ◆

In 1989, Louisiana had the highest unemployment rate in the country: 11.8 per cent. A chunk of that was from the ministry's failure—which happened to come on the heels of a downturn in the oil industry. Jimmy had scheduled nine conventions in 1988 that were expected to bring $14 million into the city's economy. He cancelled conventions, laid off 600 of his 1,500 employees, and stopped all construction. Hotels and restaurants had come to use the *Evangelist*'s convention and camp meeting schedules as a virtual budgeting tool: their bookings and revenues were cut in half. Even the airport lamented the scandal, as it received $2 to $3 federal dollars per traveler.

Jimmy suffered another blow in February 1989: on the 21st, exactly one year after his confession, the U.S. Supreme Court rejected without comment his writ arguing that Gorman's lawsuit "unconstitutionally tangles Louisiana state courts in matters of church doctrine and discipline." Gorman was back in his hair; the case was on again. Trial would probably start in late 1989.

He wrote and spoke often about the unforgiving attitude of his fellow pastors, saying he felt the church was more guilty of flogging other people's sins than the *National Enquirer*, and that it did it to him without even knowing what he'd done. But that was a weak defense, because he refused to tell what he'd done—so the swipes from other pulpits continued.

The hostility from his denomination and other television ministers was the most difficult thing for Jimmy to deal with, said Larry Thomas. Battles with non-Christians were almost exhilarating, but it hurt him when it appeared the Assemblies had lodged an unofficial boycott, instructing its ministers not to preach in Baton Rouge. That wasn't true, said Assemblies spokeswoman Juleen Turnage. "The national Assemblies of God never sent a letter telling [local ministers] not to work with Mr. Swaggart. There was no organized effort by headquarters. When he refused rehabilitation, our local ministers stopped working with him."

The foreign missions, however, were directed not to work with him. "The Assemblies of God is there at the country's invitation," said Turnage. "Many of them have stricter moral codes than American churches or even the Assemblies. The media are owned by the government, and the governments moved to take Jimmy Swaggart off the air after his moral failure. The Assemblies had to work very hard to restore credibility."

"Ecclesiastical politics is maybe sometimes worse [than secular]. The infighting and backbiting are incredible," said Thomas. "He got into a fight with the AG, and the money and support dwindled . . . things didn't bounce back, the viewers didn't come back . . . [The boycott] focused attention on the fact that he'd never revealed what his sin actually was.

"Also, he began to rationalize. He began to say, 'I didn't want to do this, it was beyond my control.' He pleaded . . . money [and other] pressures, and so on, they combined to make him weak. Well, everyone has those pressures, everyone has money problems.

"Then he got into a period of denial, like it never happened. [He] tried to convince his followers that he didn't really sin because Satan forced him into it."

"A lot of the stuff that happened after [the defrocking] was uncharacteristic of Jim," said Gerald Wilson. "After that he started to denounce the ministry, he was very, very critical and hard."

Jimmy's friend Don Brankel, who was originally named in the Gorman lawsuit, tasted the denial; guest-preaching in Baton Rouge on the topic of sin, he found a note from Donnie slipped into his Bible during a break, saying that maybe he'd rather not preach at the Family Worship Center any more.

At the end of 1989, Jimmy wrote to his *Evangelist* subscribers of the "torrent of abuse" his family had suffered. They had been "caricatured, mocked, laughed at, lampooned, and made fun of from behind thousands of pulpits and in newspapers, periodicals, and magazines," he wrote.

He said he'd been holding a crusade in another city just days before, and a television preacher there read something derogatory about him from a local newspaper. It stunned and hurt him. Frances called the church, and when the preacher called him back, he told the man the story was a pack of lies. The minister apologized.

He had felt so helpless the past two years, he said, as "my name was slandered all across the US, Canada, and the world . . ." He said they were lies, lies, and that his heart and life were now as clean as the blood of Jesus Christ could make them. He said he had never been addicted to anything in his life. "There has never been anything in my life at any time that has been deviant or aberrant, whether it be psychological, spiritual, sexual, domestic, or physical," he wrote.

Forgetting about Debra, he said, "no one knows exactly what happened except Frances." He said that when he confessed in 1988, he thought he was doing the right thing, but he never dreamed that Christians would believe the rot in the filthy magazines, or that preachers would repeat them.

But he forgave them all. God called him to world evangelism, and millions had been brought to Christ, and the anointing was still with him, and—the ministry needed a year-end gift from YOU.

Comeback

"God put a man on this earth for one reason, and that's to chase a woman."

—Mickey Gilley, 1993

Gradually, despite setbacks, Jimmy began building his ministry back. The end of 1989 was tough; his crowds and revenues were down by three-quarters, he had started selling off radio stations, the Gorman suit was about to start, and once again Jimmy was at the U.S. Supreme Court with a church-state matter. He had challenged the right of California to charge tax on sales of religious materials. California, the justices were told in oral arguments in October, was the only state imposing this kind of tax.

Jimmy had some strange bedfellows in the suit, considering his past scoldings. They included the Hare Krishnas and Jehovahs Witnesses and the National Council of Churches, who called the levy "a forbidden tax on the exercise of religion." On California's side were the American Civil Liberties Union and the National Conference of State Legislatures.

Back in New Orleans, Gorman was trying to get evidence of the Murphree scandal into the court record, including a deposition from Cathy Kampen, but Judge Ganucheau ruled Jimmy's sexual indiscretions out of bounds.

Jimmy's attorneys asked for a protective order sealing the testimony of several of his witnesses. They'd all had affairs with Gorman, the attorneys said, and their privacy should be protected. The Capital City Press, the Times-Picayune Publishing Corporation, and Louisiana Television Broadcasting Company, all opposed the order, claiming it was an attempt to restrict media access to court proceedings.

Ganucheau ruled Jimmy couldn't keep the women's names secret.

BUT JIMMY WAS mending fences with some Assemblies preachers, including stars Benny Hinn and Paul Crouch, the latter a friend of Jim Bakker's whom Jimmy had tarred with innuendo in the past. "He needed a new base; he needed their mailing lists," said Larry Thomas. "It was a business decision. That's okay, . . . [but it] hurt those who had stood by him in the tough times."

Jimmy also said he'd been wrong to embrace *The Seduction of Christianity* so unquestioningly and that he'd been "too harsh." "He wouldn't take [author] Dave Hunt's calls any more," said Thomas.

Even the 1989 debut of "Great Balls of Fire," the film about Jerry's life made from a rich book penned by Myra with Atlanta writer Murray Silver, helped some. It provided a sense of perspective, a reminder of the great talent and determination in the family. Jerry's star was set into the sidewalk on Hollywood Boulevard. The closing of Gilley's Club that year, sorrowfully reported across the country after a feud between Mickey and his partner, Sherwood Cryer, added to the hint that dynastic talent such as this might carry with it a bit of license, and Jimmy might be cut a little slack.

Though January 1990 brought the first of a batch of lawsuits for collection of overdue bills and a unanimous U.S. Supreme Court ruling that states could collect sales tax on religious merchandise, Jimmy was getting money from the sale of his radio stations and advertising 178 retirement units in the middle of the ministry grounds, with tram service to the Family Worship Center and an elaborate seniors' program at the church.

In April, he was encouraged by the size of the crowd he drew in Fayetteville, North Carolina for a crusade. In the hotel Sunday morning, listening to Charles Kuralt, he heard a promo for a "Jim and Tammy Bakker movie" that was to air that night. He felt apprehensive, but he knew from long experience that very little publicity was 100 percent bad. The farther the real story receded into the past, the more resurrections of it could swell the crowds.

In May 1990, Arbitron showed viewership for his weekly television show at 359,000—much less than before but certainly nothing to be ashamed of; it was a solid base to build from. The Bible College still had over 400 students. The ministry grounds on Bluebonnet were busy, the parking lots full. The college bookstore, inside the A.N. Trotter Student Life building, was modern and brisk. The building had a trendy little restaurant bustling with wholesome, preppie-looking students. The college had applied for accreditation with the Southern Association of Colleges and Schools. Jimmy's ministry was a smaller but still important component of the Baton Rouge economy.

He continued to sell tours to Israel, and by 1990 was booking almost as many conventions as he had before the scandal. He was getting invitations to preach at other churches, and still preaching in auditoriums. Preachers were applying to his new organization, World Evangelism Fellowship; he claimed to have over 400 applications by spring of 1990, and wrote that "the world's largest Pentecostal fellowship," an Assemblies of God organization in Brazil, had joined as well. At a crusade in Tulsa, Oral Roberts and his wife attended one of the afternoon weekday services as a demonstration of forgiveness—forgiveness Jimmy had claimed was absent from his old denomination.

Geraldo Rivera dragged up Debra Murphree again in the fall of 1990, to appear on a show titled "Life After Sex Scandals." But Murphree didn't have much to say: she'd remarried, lived in Indiana, worked five days a week at a clothing factory. She owned a boa constrictor, the sort of snake that haunted Jimmy's dreams.

The Holy Wars faded into the past, with no new scandals to compete with the Persian Gulf war, the fall of the Soviet Union, and the surrender of Manuel Noriega, who had sat next to Jimmy at a crusade in Panama.

By November, Jimmy's Arbitron ratings had risen again. Frances' brother, Bob Anderson, moved out of his 4,300-square-foot house on the Swaggarts' estate in December; sale of some of the land would bring needed cash.

Early in 1991 Jimmy leased out the Minnie Bell Swaggart Hall to the Louisiana Department of Environmental Quality for $1.49 million a year. The ministry was also working on a deal to sell developers 68 acres for $11.2 million.

Late that spring, the Warsaw Pact dissolved, Communism crumbled, and the police beat Rodney King in Los Angeles. Sexual harassment hearings delayed the appointment of Clarence Thomas to the Supreme Court. Jimmy looked back, wondering how he and Frances "were able to stand . . . some very black days when Satan made some of his greatest efforts to completely destroy me."

There were blacker days ahead, despite the clearing sky over the ministry.

Unfinished Business

W hen Jimmy confessed on television and apologized to Donnie and Debbie, it was hard not to see the superficial resemblance of Debbie Swaggart to Debra Murphree. Out of all the women plying all the street corners near the methadone clinics and bus stations and cheap motel areas of New Orleans, Jimmy apparently sampled several—but selected one that had the same black hair, waving long around her face, the black eyes, fleshy cheekbones and thin lips and identically plucked brows, was close in age, had the same name and the same number, genders, and ages of children, as Debbie Swaggart.

Something had been tugging at him since his son's wife, carefully dressed, coiffed, scented, mascaraed, and manicured, mother of his two grandsons and his sharp-eyed granddaughter, had had that affair with Dwain Johnson, something heated, sad, and poignant.

The murderous rage Jimmy exhibited toward Johnson hinted at something more than just moral outrage. It was strikingly inappropriate: if someone were going to threaten Dwain Johnson's life, wouldn't that be Donnie's job? And yet Donnie was strangely underrepresented in accounts of the incident, including court pleadings.

It had happened in the early 1980s, with the sexual revolution going full bore. Women wore tight short shorts and thin ribbed undershirts with no bras that showed their nipples; Debra Winger did it in *Urban Cowboy,* shot at Gilley's. Debbie Swaggart didn't dress that way, but she and Johnson were young, financially secure, and free as Jimmy and Frances had never been free when they were young. What the couple had done was wrong, but more compelling was that they had been able to do it, right in God's house, and right under Jimmy's nose. Johnson had moved on to another church, his Christianity unquestioned.

Why had the Pentecostal ethos not curbed them? How was it that Jimmy was cut off from any legitimate passion other than that of the pulpit, from open fun and eroticism, and others were not? Even men of the cloth were loosening up; there were the rumors from PTL, the constant buzzing about Gorman.

"You got this hu-u-u-mongous organization that's bringing in 150 million dollars a year," David Beatty said, "and when you get home at night, you're pulling your hair out, because you have no outlet of sexual pleasure. Because your stupid WIFE is down there runnin' an organization that's 20 times bigger than you ever dreamed. So what do you do? What do you do?"

When Cathy Kampen, the housewife who said Jimmy visited her home a dozen times and asked her to beat him with a toy whip, gave her story to *Penthouse*, one detail wasn't included. It came out ten years later, in a book by Hunter Lundy, Gorman's attorney in the $90 million defamation suit against Jimmy, Frances, and others involved in Jimmy's ministry. In a sworn statement, Kampen said that Swaggart had shared his personal problems with her and that they included the fact that "his wife, Frances, didn't love him, that instead, she preferred women." He said one of his parishioners was her lover. He said she "had no interest in him sexually at all."

Whether that was just a line he fed to Kampen—or, indeed, whether Kampen's story is true at all—events and circumstances combined to entice Jimmy to act more like an ordinary man than his constituents or the media or his critics would have liked.

"I don't know very many men that don't like pornography," said Linda Gail Lewis, Jerry's sister. "You can almost see it on HBO now . . . when you've led a really sheltered life, then you see all kinds of wild things that you never have done with your wife, I can see how it would make a man want to go out on his wife. Especially when you have two kids that have only known each other."

A prostitute who was picked up by Jimmy asked lots of johns why they did it.

"The reasons are always the same, pretty much: either their wives won't give them what they want—usually a blow job, because women don't like to give blow jobs, or they don't have a woman." One man told her he had a beautiful wife who would do anything he wanted sexually, but he just got a thrill from paying a woman for sex. Others told her that cruising was the exciting part. And certain women, she said, especially wives of older men, only do sex one way. "The men see all these nasty movies with different positions, and they want to try it, but their wives won't hear of it."

But that wasn't all of it. As Jimmy and Frances fought for their lives, they made no response to the most damning and disturbing part of Debra Murphree's story: that Jimmy, seeing a photograph of her three children who lived in Indiana with her mother, had shown a sexual interest in her little girl, and pressed the subject until quiet Debra got angry.

"The addict who focuses on children usually has suffered some interruption in his or her own development while growing up," wrote Patrick Carnes, an authority on addiction and recovery. "There is a part of the addict which is not any older than the victim."

"Several people told me [Jimmy] was abused by a relative as a young child," said Patrick Mahoney, the Connecticut minister and talk show host who had called Rentz to try damage control before the news of Jimmy's entrapment at the Travel Inn had been publicized. He said he had information that Jimmy was eight or ten years old when this happened, that it was sexual abuse, that it happened more than once, and that it was supposedly a family member.

Pat Robertson told Larry King that he'd heard similar rumors of sexual abuse, but it sounded much milder: "some relative took [Jimmy] down to some bawdy house in New Orleans, and sort of a rite of passage [took place] that happens sometimes in some Southern cities, and this thing marred him psychologically . . ."

Prurient interest in children, Carnes wrote in *Out of the Shadows: Understanding Sexual Addiction,* does not necessarily involve an actual child; it could include images of children, or fantasies. But depending on the stage of the addiction, it can mean actually involving a child. Carnes noted that sexual abuse of children has a very long and secret history; it is, he said, a "major factor in the transmission of sexual compulsivity from one generation to the next."

Nine was the age at which several separations occurred in Jimmy's life. First, he was approaching puberty in a viscous Protestant subculture that saw the body as filth, something whose functions were suspect and vile, and whose lusts needed to be controlled with the mind. Both grandfathers were known carousers, and the grandmother that wasn't schizophrenic was something of a religious fanatic, beloved though she was.

Nine was also the age when he gave the "atomic bomb prophecies," a dizzying experience for a child, especially in a village where a new stop sign was front page news. Though some scoffed, the people who counted in Jimmy's world didn't. His parents were suddenly celebrities of a sort. When Sun remarked to Brother Culbreth that Jimmy's voice during the prophecies could be heard plainly over the noisy hubbub in the church, the pastor's explanation showed he was totally open to the possibility that Ferriday was the new Bethlehem. "Jesus," he assured Sun, "spoke to thousands of people at a time, and he never used a microphone or a loudspeaker."

For the next four or five years, Jimmy was not allowed to grow in the same media as his playmates did. Only in his teens, when unignorable amounts of testosterone blew into the picture, did nature begin to elbow aside the Pentecostal project that the boy had become, putting in motion a lifetime of compromise in which the work of the church was never quite able to eclipse the work of nature, and in which the virility and masculine poetry of the Lewis line was bled into the world just as proud and wild as with Jerry Lee, but in disguise, with its head bowed in prayer.

And much as he managed to penetrate the mainstream and achieve the respectability he craved, Jimmy also came from a background where some of the restraints on people are looser. Jerry saw little wrong in taking a 13-year-old cousin for a wife, nor had his father a 15-year-old, nor his grandfather a 14-year-old, nor Lee Calhoun a girl 28 years his junior, nor had anyone forbidden both of Jerry's sisters to marry at 12.

Key factors in a child's development, according to Patrick Carnes, may become part of his or her sexual addiction. These factors come to govern the addict's choices in adult life, and they are informed by a set of potent dynamics.

The most important dynamic, according to Carnes, is fear of abandonment, "a constant theme in all addictions." Being abandoned means being unwanted, and being unwanted means the child is fundamentally unworthy. The fear starts with a child perceiving himself as "bad." Carnes related the story of an addict whose problems started at 13, after his mother died; he was finally able to connect his exhibitionism as an adult with needing attention to fend off utter loneliness.

Jimmy's abandonment problems started much earlier; he related many times his terror that his parents had left him behind in the rapture. He told often how, awakened by fear during the night, he would tiptoe to their bedroom door and listen for sounds of life; apparently he was too scared of punishment to crawl into bed with his parents as many children would. Then, when he was only 12 or 13, his parents did leave him alone for days or weeks while they went on the evangelical trail. Of course, Jimmy didn't want to go along, but the fact that they chose God over staying home with him must have confirmed his unworthiness.

His fears of being cast aside surfaced in his sermons and writings. "A preacher of the gospel," warned Jimmy, "can fall into sin and lose his reward. He can even lose his soul. He will be laid aside and become—a *castaway*." It echoed the sad fears of his childhood, lying in bed like Mickey begging God not to send him to hell because he'd stolen a plastic comb or a piece of candy from the drug store. He must have been sucked toward sin ever more strongly at these times, for his writings returned again and again to the fear of falling into sin and being cast aside.

The need to have something he can depend on often leads a child to self-comfort—which, if it includes masturbation, becomes confused with pleasure. "Addiction is a relationship," according to Carnes, "a pathological relationship in which sexual obsession replaces people. And it can start very early . . . [it becomes] further complicated when the children are surrounded by negative rules, messages, and judgments about sex"—which the Pentecostal church saw to thoroughly in Ferriday.

Addicts almost always report having been sexually abused as children, Carnes said. And children are incredibly loyal, refusing to betray parents, uncles, family friends, siblings, cousins, or other relatives. Secrecy is absolutely the most necessary ingredient to the passing on of the practice to the next generation. As for Jimmy, the closest he came to addressing the question of childhood abuse was a statement saying, "Absolutely nothing ever happened to me as a child that was untoward or traumatic that would have caused me problems as an adult." He said over and over that he simply did not understand what "happened" between him and Debra Murphree and that the only conceivable explanation was Satan. Eventually he had to concede that secrecy played a role, but he never let go of Satan as the great instigator. The progress he did make happened only because of pressure from peers who had probably had some exposure to a 12-step program—the kind of therapy Jimmy spurned in favor of prodigious prayers for divine intervention.

"Immediately after the horror of 1988," he wrote, some of his brethren told him that he had to TELL one of them or Frances whenever he had a craving, "the moment Satan strikes." He was to be very specific, to say, "Satan is attacking me in this particular manner." He chose not to do that. Later, asked why, he explained that it was pride and shame: he kept thinking, "I will gain the victory and no one will have to know the battle I've been fighting." He also concluded that secrecy was probably Satan's greatest weapon. "I wanted so much to go to Frances, but I never did, because my reasoning was, 'What can she do?' " Instead, he wept, fasted, prayed—all the old tactics that had proven themselves stopgap at best.

There seemed to be a connection between pederasty and powerlessness, and the child-bride phenomenon that persisted in the family.

"Molestation, it was almost like a way of life," said Myra Lewis Williams, who kept her rape at age 12 by the man next door secret until she wrote *Great Balls of Fire*. "You wouldn't dare say anything. Mother and Daddy found out about it by reading the book." Her co-author, Murray Silver, had asked an innocent question one day: "Why would a 13-year-old girl get married?" Agitated, she paced, hesitated, and finally told him about the rape. "I was damaged goods," she explained. "Nobody else would want me."

Jerry treated Myra like he was a stern Pentecostal father. No haircuts, no movies, no makeup.

"He always liked me in a little pair of blue jeans and flats and a little top like I was going to school."

He made her say "ma'am" and "sir" to older people, including Mamie.

"He wanted me to be an extension of him, to be easily controlled and kept at home. He used to tell me I was stupid, I was ugly, nobody else would ever have me. So you get this image of yourself, they want to beat you into the ground so you will not leave."

The child-bride phenomenon and its cousin pederasty are almost bred in the bone in some areas of the South, seeming to arise from the very soil and landforms of the Mississippi delta. In frontier times, the physical boundaries of delta states like Louisiana—swamps, rivers, and waterways—kept populations isolated and gene pools concentrated. Added to this was the basic clan structure of the South, which was supported by a long and intimate association with power differentials. From its long participation in slavery to its humiliation after the Civil War, Southern culture developed eddies that revolved around issues of control, appearances, and power.

The obvious targets were women and children, and men who wanted to marry or have sex with young girls were acting out of a blurring of boundaries among the need to control, the desire to protect, and the breakdown of the outermost margins of incest taboos through scores of cousin marriages. The separations between love and exploitation break down.

It was about the time of the Dwain Johnson lawsuit that people reported first thinking they had spotted Jimmy on Airline Highway. There was something drugged and magnetic about New Orleans, where oil oozed into the offshore waters. There the dark, erotic side of the family's music and ecstatic worship lay close to the surface. There lay the dark church of sensuality and rhythm.

◆　　◆　　◆

Jimmy's ministry was coming back. There were still tremendous problems, but the crowds and money were stabilizing. He had said it many times himself: people were forgiving. All had fallen short of the glory of God, and they knew it. Little by little, they were inching back. Arbitron was still tracking him, which was a compliment. He had ratcheted up his viewership figures by sending his foreign missions director, Jim Woolsey, to get tapes into places like China and the ex-Soviet Union. Once he got the Gorman thing behind him, maybe it could all recede into the past and he could pretty much get back to where he had been before.

Inevitably, something else came creeping back, too. He had been so anxious to get off the hook through prayer and divine intervention, and had announced that that was exactly what had happened.

Then, "Satan came back again. In my spirit I panicked, 'Oh God, help me!' But we must never forget—Satan always returns . . . Satan came back and I found myself fighting in exactly the same manner as before. I doubled my prayer life and so forth. It was to be an endless treadmill."

Do Nothing

On June 25, 1991, John Camp made a courtesy call to Treeby. Camp, now with CNN, had called to warn Jimmy about the upcoming CNN broadcast airing some of the Debra Murphree snapshots taken by Gorman at the Travel Inn. The occasion was the beginning of the Gorman trial on July 8. Apparently CNN wanted to spend the week garnering an audience for that event, and it started running hourly promos for the June 27 airing of the photos.

Jimmy immediately called a meeting of his ministers to plan strategy, and called some of his former Assemblies colleagues who were still connected in Springfield and with whom he was still on good terms. He didn't want any Executive Presbyters reviving the old story. If he had any grace at all left with the Assemblies of God, this was the time to spend it.

Even as he made his calls, a CNN crew pulled up and started setting up cameras on the median dividing Bluebonnet Road.

He asked one of his attorneys how to block the broadcast; it might hurt his chances to get an impartial jury. There was no defense, the attorney said.

He and Frances got little sleep that night, agonizing over how to stop the bloodletting that would go on the next day. They awoke depressed.

Jimmy drove to McDonald's for his customary bacon biscuit, buying one for Frances as well. He returned to find her on the phone, but for once, her warrior instincts were no use. He went upstairs to the bedroom, and after an hour, he had decided what to do: nothing. No matter how many calls Frances made, or how fearlessly she faced her enemies, there were times when nothing could be done, and this was one of them. CNN had the photos. It was going to splatter them all over the U.S. and Canada and the scores of other countries around the world where it reached. It was running promos that moment. There was nothing to do.

Once he made this surrender, his depression lifted. In fact, he felt a sweet grace descend on him: "I sensed the love of God toward others . . . forgiveness toward others . . . compassion toward others . . ." It was a peace that stayed with him all day and informed his preaching at Wednesday night services that evening. He was sensational.

The next evening, the whole story ran like a half-healed wound torn back open—the Gorman suit, the interview footage of Debra describing what he'd asked her to do, and the photos: Debra leaning against him in the doorway, him in the car with Gorman, wearing the same t-shirt and sweatband in all the shots, Gorman telling the world that Jimmy had confessed to "chasing prostitutes for 28 years." And CNN's observation that Jimmy was making a comeback, that his show had risen back up to number six in the religious broadcast ratings.

Early Friday morning, on the way to McDonald's again, Jimmy saw a rainbow. He held a news conference at ten, still calm and peaceful. With Frances beside him, her usually trim figure looking a little heavy and haggard, he said, "I'm a fighter by nature, but the Lord has been changing Jimmy Swaggart's nature." He forgave everyone, he said, especially Marvin Gorman. When it was her turn at the bank of microphones, Frances spit fire, telling the assembled crowd of about 200 to leave the smut on the newsstand and give that money to the ministry. Cheers went up; singing began. Jimmy pleaded with the Assemblies to stop boycotting his crusades and threatening to yank credentials of its ministers who attended them. For crying out loud, it had been close to four years.

In some of CNN's photographs, Jimmy had a breezy, virile, completed look. Missing from his face was the emotional congestion of his craft; standing next to Debra, he looked clear and unshackled.

◆ ◆ ◆

Jury selection started July 8, 1991 in New Orleans Civil District Court. The defendants included Jimmy, Frances, Jimmy Swaggart Ministries Inc., Treeby, the Canal Street Assembly of God Inc. in New Orleans, and its pastor, Tom Miller—the preacher who had claimed to exorcise a demon who had Gorman's voice out of a deaf-mute woman. The trial was estimated to last six to 10 weeks.

Jury candidates were asked if they thought anyone in the room was without sin, if they believed in demons or would be prejudiced against anyone who did, and their feelings about exorcism, television evangelists, sin, and adultery. They were asked if they'd heard anything about Jimmy Swaggart and a prostitute. In the corridor outside the courtroom, Jimmy's supporters sang "Rock of Ages."

That night, CNN recapped the chronology of the suit; later, Larry King covered the story again, with a *Washington Post* reporter and a Louisiana minister.

Jury selection took a week. Twenty-four attorneys represented Jimmy and his co-defendants, Gorman, and various insurance companies.

Opening statements on July 16 were harsh. Jimmy was jealous, said Gorman's attorney, and brutalized Gorman, driving him into bankruptcy with claims that he'd had sex with 100 women, fathered illegitimate kids, and was possessed by the devil.

No, said Jimmy's attorneys, it was Gorman's insatiable sexual appetites that led him to prey on women and gave new meaning to the term "laying on of hands." With references to Jimmy's sex life forbidden, his attorneys went for Gorman's jugular, especially after Gorman's attorneys had made sure the subject of Jimmy and prostitutes came up during *voir dire*.

Nevertheless, it started rather badly for Jimmy. Testimony revealed that he'd written at least 13 letters about Gorman's infidelities; it made him look bad, taking so much time and trouble. And some that were sent to Assemblies churches nationwide were written after Gorman resigned.

Gorman's attorney, Hunter Lundy, tried to twist the knife further by aggressively questioning Jimmy on his first day on the stand, August 8.

"You don't believe Catholics are Christians, do you?" Lundy asked Jimmy, bringing a flock of attorneys to their feet in a chorus of objections. There were four Catholics on the jury.

Lundy's combativeness brought out the same in Jimmy. "Counsel," he said at one point, "you have looked the world over trying to find someone I have spoken to derogatorily about Marvin Gorman and I don't believe you have found anybody." Jimmy did acknowledge that he'd accused Gorman of 25 years worth of infidelities—a number that eerily approximated what he had told Gorman about his own addiction on October 17, 1987. "I believed that at that time, and I believe it now," Jimmy said defiantly. "I cannot give you a number, and if I did you'd probably be shocked," Jimmy said.

On August 12, Gorman took the stand and stayed there several days, often becoming emotional as he told of the humiliation he'd undergone.

Gorman's torture began on his second day, when Jimmy's attorney, Wayne Lee, made him describe how and where Lynda Savage had grabbed him and caressed him, and how he had lost his erection after penetrating her. Lee asked him so many questions about other women and his crotch—eliciting that another woman, Jane Talbot, had grabbed him there, too—that he pushed Judge Julian Bailes over the edge.

"Mr. Lee, I think you have beat this horse to death," the judge said.

Gorman had insisted he'd only had one interrupted session with Savage, but after he admitted the Talbot encounter, Lee produced a taped 1989 deposition where he had admitted to three months of kissing and petting Lynette Goux, the Swaggarts' family friend of a decade before. Goux could not be found to testify for her old friends. Gorman tried to explain that the petting was just affection—though at one time he had touched her breast. He protested that he'd confessed to her husband, whereupon Jimmy's attorney dryly made him admit that that confession came eight years later.

But some queer facts emerged about Goux. First, Hunter Lundy's investigations turned up that there was a close relationship between Goux and Gail McDaniel, the witness who said Gorman had coerced her into sex on his office floor when she was his 18-year-old babysitter. The sex was supposedly in return for Gorman's help in quieting rumors of McDaniel's lesbianism. The accusations of lesbianism, it turned out, came from none other than Lynette Goux's husband, Ronald, who was on Jimmy's board at the time. The girl McDaniel had allegedly approached was Ronald's young sister-in-law.

Second, Lynette at some point moved into Frances Swaggart's home (around the time she and Ronald were divorced; Ronald ended up testifying on behalf of Jimmy). Was she the parishioner that Jimmy allegedly told Cathy Kampen was Frances' lesbian lover?

Third, according to Lundy, Gail McDaniel went on to join a church in Shreveport whose pastor's wife was close friends with Frances and who was also named Frances. After Gail gave a deposition in favor of Jimmy, she was given a car—a 300ZX—by Frances Duron, the Shreveport pastor's wife.

To Lundy, the intimacy of these relationships smacked of possible collusion. Moreover, Lynette Goux managed to duck subpenas and never testified at trial or gave a deposition.

Gorman said his ministry had been thriving by 1986, having revenues of $4 million. His thwarted loan—described now as $20 million instead of the $16 million he'd originally cited—would have expanded his broadcast from Port Arthur, Texas, to Mobile, Alabama. His ministry salary and perks totaled $130,000, he was negotiating royalties for his books and tapes, and he had received job offers from other ministries. Now he was reduced to a $12,000 salary and $30,000 for housing from his new church, Metropolitan Christian Center.

But later testimony revealed that Gorman's ministry was in deep financial trouble long before his dalliances were made public. His ministry lost more than $266,000 in 1985, and $40,000 in the first five months of 1986, before he resigned. In fact, the ministry had financial trouble as early as 1980. He admitted his own church had refused his request to extend his $130,000 salary for a year. He also admitted that his ministry had had difficulty paying for its lease on Cox Cable in New Orleans.

Testimony ended September 5 with the sensational appearance of Gail McDaniel. She testified that he had spread false stories that she was a lesbian, and told her that the only way she could straighten out her life was to have sex with a man. Gorman did not dispute her testimony.

Marvin Gorman appeared to be in retreat.

◆   ◆   ◆

During August, even with the lawsuit on the newswires every day, Jimmy could feel the steady upward progress of his ministry. In July, Arbitron had reported another 40,000 or so viewers over the previous November. The crusades were smaller than in the glory days, but they were coming back. Success seemed within reach.

But "there was an ugly fly in the ointment. The power of darkness was starting to once again tear at me and I would not tell anyone. It became so acute I could almost tell what type of service we were going to have each night. If the Spirit of God were going to move in a powerful way, this thing would attack me ferociously. If there were no attack, the service would be, for the most part, somewhat mediocre."

Incredibly, Jimmy never realized that it was all coming from the same place, that he was channeling libido into performance the same as Jerry.

One August morning, Jimmy later wrote, he got up early to pray as usual, pacing in his circular driveway. Suddenly, for no apparent reason, he remembered with horrible clarity the nightmare he'd had back in 1954, pacing the blacktop near Aunt Reenie's house in Ferriday, of the evil bear-man he had disarmed with Jesus' name. He had the sense that something about that dream would soon revisit him.

"Had I known what Frances and I would have to undergo very shortly, I am not sure if I could have endured it . . . I believe the dream was fulfilled in October, 1991. I collapsed spiritually, physically, and almost every other way."

◆   ◆   ◆

On Tuesday, September 10, 1991, the Gorman case went to the jury, and the judge sequestered the panelists for the night. They were to consider damages for defamation, invasion of privacy, and emotional distress. The summation took more than eight hours, with both sides calling each other liars. Jimmy's attorneys had called four women to testify: Gail McDaniel and Lynda Savage, who both said they had had multiple sexual encounters with Gorman, and Cheryl McConnel and Jane Talbot, who said he kissed and fondled them during counseling sessions at his church. Lynette Goux was never located during the ten weeks of trial.

Jimmy and Frances were hopeful of a quick verdict in their favor. The next day, however, the jurors deliberated all day, asking at one point for an explanation of "defamation" and other instructions that Bailes had spent an hour explaining the day before. They asked to see the letters Jimmy wrote—a bad sign.

The third day, Thursday, September 12, dragged on, with no word. Jimmy began to hope for a hung jury.

No verdict was announced that day. Friday the thirteenth would be unlucky for someone.

At 10:30 the next morning, after a total of 26 hours of deliberation, the jurors filed into the packed courtroom.

They awarded Gorman $10 million.

Jimmy, bitterly disappointed, bit his tongue. "I have never said anything bad or untruthful about Marvin Gorman and I'm not going to start now."

Frances, along with exorcist Tom Miller and his church, Michael Indest's church, and the officials of the Assemblies of God who had been accused, was acquitted, but she was blunt as usual. "I'm just shocked," she said. "This is just totally ridiculous."

◆ ◆ ◆

Jimmy was sick the rest of September. In fact, he'd been sick off and on for almost a year—ever since the attacks of demon oppression had started coming back. His doctor diagnosed an old enemy: pneumonia.

It was called "walking pneumonia" because it was low-grade enough that it didn't flatten the patient, but virulent enough to cause trouble. In Rio Hondo, pneumonia had left Jimmy with the burdens of the only begotten son, and it almost derailed his brand-new ministry in 1958. Its onset was a bad omen.

Now, on October 1, 1991, he and Frances were preparing for a crusade in San Diego, and he couldn't get well.

In a small volume issued in 1992, he gave an account of the next few days.

Friday, October 4, the first day of the crusade, was tremendous. The crowd was electric. But on Saturday, October 5, Jimmy wrote, "This terrible thing was clawing at my mind . . . It was stronger than it had been in quite some time."

Frances went shopping with friends, leaving him in the hotel room. He was unable to read the Bible or get his mind on that evening's service, and he fell onto the bed. Frances returned to find him dizzy and sick. At 7 p.m., he struggled into his clothes. He made it to the auditorium with the help of Frances, singer John Starnes, and Bradley Stroud, his crusade director.

The crowd was large and excited, and despite his weakened condition, it was an encouraging emblem of returning success, of transcendence and forgiveness and another shot at the moon. This was happening in San Diego, Gorman lawsuit or none, Supreme Court tax decisions or none, drop in international ministry or none, denominational enemies or none.

It promised to happen in all the other sites on his crusade schedule—brutal as usual—over the coming weeks: San Jose in twelve days, Tampa ten days after that, Dallas November 15–17, the traditional Baton Rouge five-day Thanksgiving camp meeting starting November 27, Pasadena, California in January, Fresno a month later, and Tulsa a month after that.

He walked unsteadily onstage to face the crowd, as Jerry had done so many times for chemical reasons, and started singing with the band, "Blessed Assurance."

Deathly ill, he went on to give a fantastic performance. People poured to the altar, just as in the old days. He had the anointing.

Afterward, in the hotel room, he was nauseous.

Sunday, October 6 was his last performance. By three, nausea and clamminess had returned. And sure enough, he preached like crazy, an incredible, rousing success.

After the service, he and Frances immediately headed for the desert retreat of friends Clyde and Elizabeth Fuller in Indian Wells, California, relishing the prospect of a few days' rest. Jimmy planned to fend off oppression by praying an hour each morning, noon, and night.

He finally fell into bed at 1 a.m. Monday, utterly exhausted.

But he slept poorly, tossing, and awakened early. He went outside at daybreak, he said, to pray. But he couldn't, because of a "terrible oppression in my spirit." At noon, it was the same. It let up some by evening, but again he was unable to sleep most of the night.

On Tuesday, October 8, he was unable to stay with his scheduled hour of walking and praying. That night, in the crooning quiet of the desert, he didn't sleep at all.

Wednesday the Fullers were ready to take him to the doctor, but he demurred. That night, Frances had a nightmare she couldn't remember.

The next day, Thursday, October 10, was Jimmy's and Frances' 39th wedding anniversary. Jimmy still felt no better, but he pretended to. They went to dinner with a group that night, and he ordered flowers delivered to Frances at their table.

He reflected later that, had he known what he was going to do in just 12 hours, he would rather God had taken his life that anniversary night.

69

Under the Influence

On Friday morning, October 11, at 7:45, the first of 117 small earthquakes—called a "swarm" by geologists—rumbled near the San Andreas fault. The shaking went on all weekend and was distinctly felt in Indio, an old rail town a few miles east of Indian Wells off Interstate 10. Because of what would happen there in an hour, scientists dubbed the series of quakes the "Jimmy Swaggart swarm."

Indio was the last desert outpost before the eastbound traveler entered miles of desert. Palm orchards clustered at the west end of Highway 111 through town, with bleached-out signs advertising date shakes and tours of the Garden of Allah. A town of about 20,000, it was strikingly Biblical, this Judea of the Mojave, with dry mountains to the north and south, a hard, crisp blue sky overhead, and brown fruit bursting from the palms.

Jimmy knew how to find what he was looking for. He drove his friend's white Jaguar with Louisiana plates through the sleepy sunrise towns. Rancho Mirage, Palm Desert, Cathedral City. In Indio, he took Indio Boulevard, where the faded motels sat—the Safari, the Diamond, the Desert Star, the Motel Ruta.

Like Airline Highway, Indio Boulevard was the old business route through town, demoted by the freeway—the same one, in fact, that reached all the way to Baton Rouge—Interstate 10. Like Airline, it had a railroad track next to it. And girls drifting down the street.

One of them was Rosemary Garcia, 31, a thin woman with a hard, pretty face, a masculine, no-bullshit walk, and wiry, wavy black hair down her back. Up close, she had beautiful black eyes and long lashes, high cheekbones, a fragile mouth with sensitive lips, a couple of small tattoos, and a look that said nothing could ever please, displease, astonish, or delight her. She was very clean, but with bruises and hard lumps on her arms and hands; she had a heroin habit. Her fingernails were chewed to the quick, the cuticles missing. Small blue dots—gang tatoos—were on her hands.

Jimmy picked her out of three or four women in the parking lot at Clark's Cafe. She was standing near a phone booth.

It was a fluke; she almost never worked during the day. So many men wanted blow jobs, and she didn't like giving them in the daytime because it was too risky with the cops and too hot—120 in the summer—and they were usually not running the air conditioner because they were parked down some desert road. She loved working at night; the desert was beautiful when you could see all the stars. She started when the sun went down and quit at dawn.

This day, she had just had a fight with her "old lady" at the Desert Star Motel where they lived. She had recently taken a lesbian lover after having no luck at all with men over the years. She had just stalked out of the motel and headed for Clark's.

He pulled up while she was standing there, and asked if she wanted a ride.

"No," she said, "I'm working. Are you interested in a date?"

"Yes," he said, "Get in."

There were two or three pornographic magazines on the passenger seat, each one folded out to a certain page. He had to move them off the seat so she could sit down.

"Your place or mine?" she asked.

"Let's just drive for awhile."

He made a right onto Palm Avenue, behind the nest of ratty motels into a neighborhood of cheap stucco apartments and stumpy little houses painted in bleached pastels or sick-flesh pink. Evaporative coolers stuck out of the windows, and flatbed trucks slept in the yards where, later, groups of teenagers would be up to no good.

He was quiet, polite. He said several times that he was very nervous. She asked him where he was from. Rancho Mirage, he said—he had a house there. He wore a light-colored sweatband, a colorless old tee shirt with two little holes at the stomach, and brown pants. His tennis shoes were in the back seat with a brief case.

She picked up the magazines. One was open to a picture of two women together, another to a man and a woman, and one to a woman playing with herself—"the usual," she thought, "no kiddie porn or anything kinky."

She said, "Oh, you like these, huh? They don't do much for me. I've done all that, I guess it's not very interesting to look at."

She put the magazines down. What kind of thing was he interested in? she asked. He said he wanted her to start by playing with herself and letting him watch, and he would figure out what else he wanted her to do. He asked if there was a motel nearby that showed porno films.

They rolled up to the stop sign at Palm and Valencia. As soon as he turned left, he spotted a cop car parked down the street to the right. He started stuffing the magazines under his seat, which made him swerve into the oncoming lane on Valencia about the time he reached the stop sign at Biskra. He saw the cop pull out and swing in behind him, flashing.

"Get out of the car and walk," Jimmy told her urgently.

"No," she replied, "I'm under the influence. Anyway, they all know who I am. I'm not getting out of here, you're taking me home.

"Think about it," she said rapidly as the officer got out of his squad car, "they know who I am, they know what I do, and they know I'm under the influence because I'm always under the influence. If I get out, they're gonna think you're trying to date me. If I stay in, you can tell them you're just giving me a ride. There's no law against that."

He said, yeah, ok, you're right.

The cop asked Jimmy for his license and registration. His hand was shaking as he reached for the glove compartment. The cop, officer Burt, went back to his car. Then after a while he came up and asked Jimmy to step out. He took him to the front of the car and Rosemary couldn't hear what took place.

Suddenly squad cars arrived from all over. They swarmed around his car, trying to cite him for everything they could. In Indio, whenever anything happens that makes a cop call in, every other cop shows up.

Officer Garcia, no relation, asked her to step out of the car. He took her aside and asked if she knew who she was riding with. No, she said. He asked her to look again. She still didn't know.

"How about Jimmy Swaggart?" he asked.

She looked at Jimmy. "Well. Sure the fuck is," she answered.

They wrote Jimmy a citation for driving on the wrong side of the road, not wearing a seat belt, and not registering the 1989 Jaguar in California. He took the ticket and drove away, leaving Rosemary standing there surrounded by cops.

They took her to the station and recorded her statement and then let her go without charging her.

OFFICER BURT told her he had followed the car because it was a Jaguar. He had seen it turn onto Palm and said to himself, now what's a classy car like that doing on Indio Boulevard?

She told her old lady that she had been picked up by the cops with Jimmy Swaggart. Her old lady didn't believe her. None of her girlfriends even paid any attention to her attempts to relate it.

No one believed her until the camera crews showed up. Then business started to boom on Indio Boulevard.

Some girls even came up from Palm Springs to work Indio, and she learned from them that Jimmy had been cruising Palm Springs earlier that morning. The girls wouldn't go with him because of the Jaguar—men with enough money to have a Jaguar don't pick up street girls. So they thought he was either weird or a cop.

The Secret Room

J immy had to go back the way he'd come, along the ancient route of the Cahuilla Indians, whose oasis this once was and whose spirit still clung to the boulders perched above these white man's towns that had mushroomed after the war.

He had to drive back to Indian Wells, he had to get rid of the magazines, put on his tennis shoes. He had to go home and tell Frances they had part of one Saturday left before it all hit the fan and the cameras and jackals showed up to finish them off.

Frances was the one who had told a magazine reporter in 1986, "Whenever you have problems, you learn to overcome them, to solve them, to knock the door down or do whatever." But this time, the blow knocked her flat.

"Four years of horrible struggle had ended" that day, he wrote later. "I watched Frances dying by the moment before my eyes. I just sat there in a daze, a stupor. I didn't want to live."

There were arrangements to make, and that was a blessing. They had to get back to Baton Rouge ahead of the reporters. They had to call the ministry to warn Brother Rentz and the others. They had to pack, to call Donnie. Frances and Elizabeth and Clyde Fuller discussed when to fly back to Baton Rouge and how to keep Jimmy away from the press—he'd have to fly commercial since they no longer had the jet.

Jimmy scribbled a note, slipped out, and drove off in Clyde's car.

He drove more than 30 hours, most of it through barren, empty desert. First back through hateful Indio, the town that was in the wrong place at the wrong time, past Joshua Tree National Monument, through desert, past a place of beautiful tumbled boulders called Texas Canyon, at the border of Arizona. Into the blackness for hours, then sunrise on I-10, the occasional McDonald's and the comfort of a bacon biscuit and the vistas of New Mexico, with small towns like mystical Ferridays. And then El Paso, moving through the interface between First and Third Worlds where high-rises and irrigated landscaping rose on the left and what looked like broken crockery lay across the Colorado River on the right, and then he plunged into the Chihuahuan desert for hours and hours until he hit the Texas hill country, home of Lyndon Johnson, limestone escarpment, peach trees, lovely San Antonio—all the while looking for the right place to kill himself.

He would have, too, but it wouldn't help. He'd disgraced all the people who didn't abandon him after the Debra Murphree incident—his congregation, his staff, his friends, and the people who had sacrificed credibility and Assemblies credentials and other opportunities to stay with him because they believed he was anointed of God. Even burning in hell could never pay that debt.

It was so familiar, driving and driving, listening to the radio in the dark. Only this time, he was on the radio. By evening on Saturday, October 12, 1991, the story of Jimmy Swaggart being picked up with a prostitute was in all the papers, on all the wires. The only grace on him was that he was overshadowed by the U.S. Senate hearings on the confirmation of Supreme Court nominee Clarence Thomas, accused of sexual harassment.

When he hit the muggy air near Houston, his spirits lifted vaguely. The Coastal Bend, the smell of salt, water, fish, home. Around Houston, he remembered a little sliver of a tune, "Jesus' love has never failed me yet."

It was Sunday, October 13, when Jimmy's wheels crunched onto the drive of his estate. It was not yet dawn, and the frogs and nightbirds were trilling in the dark. Dirty, dazed, and exhausted, he collapsed against the steering wheel.

"We found him passed out at the gate," said Bob Anderson. "He had spilled some strawberry drink on his chest, and we thought it was blood." Frances had flown back with the Fullers earlier.

◆　◆　◆

Most people find the Bible, at least at first, obtuse; it's very hard to understand what's happening in the King James version. But here were these 16- and-17-year-old boys like Jimmy and his cousins, and Oral Roberts, and Richard Dortch, and Marvin Gorman, and other Pentecostal preachers who started out as teenagers, with no education, confidently quoting it, sure they understood.

And in reading the Bible over and over to master its forms and cadences, in order to get his passport to the power of the preacher man, something happened to Jimmy. It started to work on him. It wasn't just a tool to be used and then put down. It became part of him, got inside him. And the Bible's truth started to transform him.

But Jimmy had to draw the line when the Bible's truth threatened the formula of dogma, righteousness, sexual tension, and secrecy that made him so successful. His sinful urges had to be given their own room tacked onto the back of his house, with their own secret entrance; the understanding was they'd keep out of sight, no one in the house was ever to catch a glimpse of them. If they needed the things a groin demon has to have, they were to tap a secret signal to him while he was alone praying or writing a sermon.

The demons were under control for many years, and in those years God flowed through Jimmy. He gave people the truth they needed, that freed them inch by inch. He studied the word of God, he surrounded himself with people of the best caliber and the highest intentions. He informed himself about the linguistic roots of the Bible, to test the context of God's word, to expand it far beyond what his mentors in the muggy pines of Louisiana had taught, and to see what new glorious truth popped out in the wide plains of its Hebrew and Greek and Aramaic ancestry.

People came in droves, those who also had secret back rooms tacked onto their houses, and those whose demons were bold and unafraid to show themselves in the house—in divorces, alcohol-breath, ruined children, creditors, syphilis, needles. Jimmy showed them the opened gate and the sunny path winding toward the vanishing point.

But the secret tappings increased as the ministry grew and grew and Jimmy became filled with importance. The demons became unruly; they wanted to be seen. They had contributed much to Jimmy's style, his understanding of sin and failure and redemption. Frances heard muffled thumps from back there and ignored them. And surely one of the grandkids had chased a lizard into the bougainvillea thicket that covered the entire back of the house and seen the moldy extra wall, and registered that the house was a little bigger than it seemed from inside, before Frances or Jimmy came along and shooed them out of the back yard because it was dangerous, there were snakes back there.

Jimmy Swaggart was a man of power, and women were always after him, because in order to give them the release of tears and surrender, he had to get his congregation aroused. If he did his job, that arousal changed into spiritual ecstasy, for that was his task, to transform libido into worship. It takes a high degree of consciousness to direct that arousal while it is still undifferentiated. In order to do this, a preacher must be outside the realm of erotic vulnerability himself. "Inciting yet controlling [ecstasy]," says Garry Wills, "is the task of the lone preacher, whose own emotions are supposed to be inflammatory yet exemplary."

In Jimmy's church, there was little study of how to prepare, or what to do if the preacher's own state of arousal starts to take a sexual expression. Moreover, Pentecostals play with fire, channeling the arousal into touching, hugging, confessing, and laying on of hands.

Only the truly wise arouser knows how to use this power to direct this new life into something that is itself life-sustaining. Most entertainers work down in the lower levels of consciousness—desire, hunger, fear—where life simply gets devoured. The arousers who had the wisdom to use their power to actually feed their followers something besides the breaking down of aroused energy into attachment or sex or being good or giving money, to give them the highest transmogrification of this energy—higher consciousness—were people like Jesus and Mohammed. Marjoe Gortner and Jerry Lee Lewis and Jimmy Swaggart and countless other arousers are all gifted with the ability to draw up this energy, but their trajectories arc quickly and fall. And Jerry Lee may be right: he may be closer to hell, even the mildest definition of hell, than Jimmy is.

But Jimmy is actually a more tragic figure, because he saw the mutation of his arousal gift. First there was great sincerity and desire to do good, to transform. Then he addressed himself to fine-tuning the delivery of the message, seriously turning the communication into performance. He hit on a great formula, and success came in ever-increasing waves. But without Jimmy really realizing it, the sincerity he felt began to be corrupted, subtly, through a thousand tiny compromises and decisions. It got co-opted for the work of keeping the ministry alive and growing. Instead of being used for spreading the heartfelt word of God, the sincerity got frittered away in dealing with the bankers, media technicians, benefactors, construction supervisors, travel agents and staff members that it took to keep up a $150 million business. And it seemed natural for him to take on Bakker and Gorman. It didn't seem like competition. It seemed like leadership.

Before he knew it, Jimmy was deep into the territory of the con artist, putting more and more effort into believing what he was saying, to preserve the sincerity for which he had become highly respected, rather than in simply saying what he believed. And what he believed was becoming foggier and foggier as the demands of the ministry became greater.

To use his sincerity to get money and fancy cars was to abuse it. This tactic did make the ministry grow, and Jimmy got to drive a Lincoln; but Jimmy used his sincerity to rationalize that these worldly things were for God's work about a thousand times too many.

The outright license his church gave people to just attribute every whim to God pretty much drowned out his real, true spirituality. And that was a big job, because Jimmy was a sincere, spiritual person with the best of intentions, a person who wanted to do good in the world.

Jimmy Swaggart's preaching formula is to dredge up the misery and separation that his followers feel—a misery he knows firsthand—and then give them the illusion of a way out. Manipulative, his critics call it, exploitative, and it is, but what he does is not wrong because of that. We aren't divine—we are in a painful state of separation, and that is why we are mean, selfish, and foolish, and why we keep making the same mistakes over and over. Our spirits are distracted by desire like a dog by fleas, and every waking moment is taken up with our scratching. What Jimmy does is give humans one of many things they seek to get relief. His prayer meetings and shindigs are not bad for people. On the contrary, they are nourishing at their best and no worse than any other entertainment at their worst. Those who condemn Jimmy Swaggart because he is a hypocrite do not understand that his ministry came out of contradiction and is woven of it, that it came from flesh and depends on people's immersion in flesh, and that neither he nor anyone else is capable of raising it higher than its own terms.

For all the arousing and transforming that Jimmy did, he was never able to find even one way of carving legitimate sexual outlets for himself. If his church had an open, formal acknowledgement of the problem, some sort of institutional prayer about this responsibility, he might not have done what he did. But there was no such prayer in the Pentecostal church when Jimmy was being formed. The subject was not mentioned, because no Pentecostal would acknowledge the presence of a sexual element in the charismatic format. Jimmy, like other Pentecostal preachers who strayed sexually—from Aimee Semple MacPherson to Marvin Gorman and those who never got caught—have to just handle it somehow.

Eventually the ministry just got too big, its clamor so loud that no one heard the demons taking a sledge hammer to the sheet rock. They broke through into the house fully a year before anyone slowed down enough to see them. They were in full charge of Jimmy as he drove openly down Airline Highway in broad daylight at the height of his international visibility.

Epilogue

Thirty years ago, when Jimmy was building his little house on Tara and Trinity on faith, and Donnie got the Holy Ghost for the first time, you would have gotten few clues from television news that his constituency even existed. It dwelt below the radar screens of the country's media and publishing centers. But its ranks would swell to tens of millions.

Today, Jimmy's national television viewership is a fraction of its former self, but the televangelism scandals didn't really hurt the movement of which he was a part at all. Its members are a powerful force in the Republican party, and directed the agenda of the 1996 Republican National Convention. Their shadow looms large in Congress. More and more people describe themselves as born again. And the Christian right increasingly controls the dialogue about welfare reform, education, abortion.

The battle lines have become sharper over the years, from the heated sparring among groups like Americans United for Separation of Church and State, People for the American Way, the Moral Majority, and the Christian Coalition, to the proliferation of abortion clinics and of their bombings, from militant environmentalism to the militia movement. On freeways, car bumpers ornamented with a familiar Christian symbol—a fish outline with the word "Jesus" fitted inside—are challenged by cars carrying the same emblem, except the fish has feet and the word "Darwin" inside.

Tax-exempt entities can't engage in politics and they know it, but when Jimmy was threatened with revocation of his tax-exempt status for twice endorsing Pat Robertson for president, he fought it as if he did have the right, settling in 1992 for a heavy fine. That year, a New York church's status was revoked for placing a full-page ad in *USA Today* accusing presidential candidate Bill Clinton of supporting demand abortions, condom handouts at high schools, and homosexuality. Even though the ad was a brazen violation of IRS tax-exemption code, a legal fund founded by Pat Robertson fought the IRS ruling.

Poverty is no longer a cult in the Pentecostal church. The intense prayers for the Holy Spirit to visit the little church revivals, the congregation seized by tongues speech, the falling and jerking, are largely a thing of the past. The threats of rock and roll and Communism against which the church aligned itself are dissolved. The sacred music has been replaced, as Sun Swaggart has lamented, by Christian Rock and Roll. The sanctions against jewelry, makeup, and fancy hairdos are not observed in any churches except, as Larry Thomas noted, legalistic ones that house mostly old people.

By the early 1990s the Christian right knew who the typical religious television viewer was, according to Quentin Schultze. She was a female in her 60s. She had had no college. She lived in the Midwest, and spent her life in the conservative Protestant realm. She worried about declining morals in America, and counted on televangelists and Christian activists for her political perspectives on abortion, foreign and domestic policy, developments in the judicial system, militant separatism, and so on.

The Christian right made her feel connected to these matters, and fed her need to be used and instructed how to be a better person. When Jimmy, on the verge of single-handedly evangelizing several South American countries, exhorted, "El Salvador, you can have life! Brazil, you can have life! Soviet Union, you can have life! Mainland China, you can have life! Asia! Africa! Europe! North America! South America!"—she believed him.

When he bored quietly into the camera, saying, "You're sitting in a lonely hotel room and there are needle tracks up and down your arms . . . Maybe you sit there with a bottle of alcohol in your hands. Maybe you sit there watching me on television. You're hurting inside. Your life is a wreck. You've torn your family all to pieces. You have contemplated suicide. But through this TV screen, Jesus Christ is . . . telling you, 'I love you.'"—she wept and believed.

Petitions were sent her to sign; she had asked to contribute to specific causes; she felt her point of view was being represented.

By empowering people like Jimmy, she came, by 1997, to represent the most powerful single identifiable group in America. But when the liberal social agenda of the past four decades has been fully challenged, what will happen? If the new conservative regime—the typical religious TV viewer—finds children starving, what will its response be?

Worried liberals would probably answer "indifference." But those periods in the past when religion became powerful in America were not times of stinginess and pathological contraction. They did not result in right-wing extremism. Rather, once social conditions in America progressed to a point where religion was thoroughly aroused, the result has usually been progressive. Mainstream Protestantism, after all, fueled abolitionism, humane labor laws, and civil rights.

Quentin Schultze notes the changes in religious programs, citing "Day of Discovery," a top-10-rated religious show that alternates its hosts. "They have never asked for money on a single program," Schultze said. "That defies the logic of these people who assume you have to use hucksterism . . . to raise money."

◆   ◆   ◆

Several years after the Indio scandal, Wednesday was still prayer meeting night at the Family Worship Center. The ministry complex is now lit only perfunctorily, where before it had blazed, every building artfully lit. The service was in a small auditorium or converted classroom in the back of the parking lot. There were metal stacking chairs lined up in rows, a crowd of about 300.

There were four choir members. No stunning guest singers, no guest preachers. Instead of the horn section and organ and piano and harmonica and guitar players, there were four musicians: two guitars, drums, and piano. Donnie sat alone in the Amen Corner. Frances sat in the front row instead of on the tiny stage.

Jimmy was dead tired, but he preached beautifully anyway, passionate as always and full of heartfelt arguments. He made a reference to the ways God has of humbling us, and eyes turned toward Frances, who shifted in her chair and recrossed her nylon-clad legs. A look—fatigue or contempt—flicked across her face.

After the sermon, he sang with the little choir, one song. He gave an altar call, but no one spoke in tongues or got the Spirit. As soon as he finished, he sank, exhausted, into a chair in the Amen corner.

Driving near the Shady Acres Pentecostal Baptist Church, a cinderblock building painted blue, outside Baton Rouge, you see little kids out in the yard with their toys. You see washing on the line, little garden plots with ramshackle fences around them, beat-up stuffed chairs on the front porches. You see rusted appliances tossed out back, dogs running through the bar ditches. And you realize that, because of this uniquely American spiritual compost, all the people that Americans clutch and cling to as spiritual leaders are allowed to fail. Jimmy may be, as Jungian analyst Marion Woodman described, one of those people who feel that "life is a meaningless merry-go-round if they are not . . . living for a cause like Mother Theresa, or dying for a dream like Martin Luther King." Such people identify with an archetype, and "turn life into theater and themselves into actors on a stage, thus falling prey to demonic as well as angelic inflation . . . they confuse the sacred and profane worlds."

That inflation is what happened to both Jimmy and Jerry. But there's room for such failure in America. Jimmy staked out an extreme position and judged everyone from it and then fell himself. Whether he recovers is important to those who love and depend on him and Frances. But it hardly matters to the

Christian right, to the Shady Acres Pentecostal Baptist Church, or to the children who play in the bar ditches with the dogs. For:

> The great God that formed all things
> Both rewardeth the fool and rewardeth transgressors.
> — Proverbs 26:10

Acknowledgments and Sources

Jimmy and Frances Swaggart didn't want anyone to write a book about them, and influenced friends, immediate family, and colleagues not to talk. Some of this was understandable: a number of church people didn't want to dredge up the 1980s "Holy Wars" again. That dismaying chapter in electronic church history had hurt their images and incomes and they wanted it behind them for good. Others assumed the book was going to be exploitive and wanted no part of it. And there were those who told me that if they talked, they would be seen in the evangelical world as traitors and not be able to get jobs in other ministries. There were those who wanted to keep lines of communication open with the Swaggarts for their own reasons and knew they'd become instant enemies if their names appeared in a book as interview subjects.

But this has produced a vexation for the Swaggarts: they complain that the press always gets everything wrong, and so refuse interviews that might clear things up. They were invited numerous times to participate, to correct information they considerered wrong, and to have their side of every issue told in this book.

Because of the hurt and pain the Swaggart family has gone through, an unusual number of the people who did agree to be interviewed didn't want to be quoted, though they also wanted to express some of their own hurt. Nobody wanted to kick Jimmy while he was down; but if they refused to be interviewed, that meant they couldn't say anything good about him, either. Some who worked in the ministry had seen unfair treatment of the Swaggarts by writers, deliberate exaggeration of Jimmy's positions, and malevolent attacks on him for his bare-knuckled assaults on rock lyrics and pornography.

Others who cared for the Swaggarts but had been estranged from them had seen the couple so paranoid that it was hopeless for any writer to get their blessing. Mainly, I found my informants to be a group of people who try to do good in the world, who believe in being positive, and who don't want any more pain to come about. So much damage had been done to their belief system by stampeding, loutish reporters, they felt, that it took quite an act of faith to agree to talk.

Several informants declined to be named at all, and their privacy is respected, though the Swaggarts might be surprised that even perceived enemies were very respectful of Jimmy. So many other interviewees asked not to be quoted on certain matters that I decided not to state who the interviewees were for each chapter, as it would be possible to connect information to names. Suffice it that every chapter reflects interviews that contributed facts, insights, corroboration or denial of what others have said or written, ideas, anecdotes, or context.

This difficult book had many guardian angels.

Biographer Noel Riley Fitch is a wonderful author and unfailing friend who was my mentor from the University of Southern California and the catalyst for this book.

Professor John Riley and John Johnson read and commented on the unwieldy manuscript, acts of great generosity.

My agent, Julie Popkin, suggested the title. She is a lover of books and ideas who knows her craft and never gives up.

Similarly, I am lucky to have a real editor with a firm professional hand. Frank Oveis is focused on excellence. His guidance has made this book much better.

To supportive friends (and family members) too numerous to mention, especially Julia Jones and the Los Angeles "Get a Life" biographers' group, and my ever-patient colleagues at the Berger & Norton Law Firm, thanks.

I had many discussions with my husband, Gary Seaman, and my brother, Joseph Rowe, as well as friends and university colleagues, about religion, faith, music, psychology, culture, mysticism, spirituality, biology, genetics, and countless other topics. Those conversations are so thoroughly marbled into this book that it must be said to be theirs as well. Interestingly, the questions asked by my children about Jimmy Swaggart yielded some of the most fruitful discussions. In fact, my family hugged and urged me through this work with the kind of love that preachers preach about.

Longtime televangelism researcher Stephen Winzenburg generously provided clippings and videotapes from his collection, as did Ole Anthony of the Trinity Foundation in Dallas. Rev. Richard Lee of Pasadena, California and Spokane, Washington made his collection of books, clippings, and old *Evangelists* available to me for over a year and knew much insider information.

David Beatty's insights into the dynamics of church and family in postwar Ferriday were invaluable.

The late Larry Thomas spent many patient hours explaining the workings of the ministry at its height. Rev. Gerald Wilson did the same regarding traveling evangelism and Pentecostal beliefs. And Myra Lewis Williams extended help, hospitality, and savvy insights into the Lewis clan.

Special thanks are due Homer Williams, who fed me many articles and ideas; and Nell Arnold at the Vidalia Public Library, Kathleen Stephens at the *Concordia Sentinel* in Ferriday, the librarians at the Louisiana State Library in Baton Rouge, and Alice Traska at the Central Louisiana State Hospital in Pineville.

Last, this book would be poorer but for the generosity of Frankie and Marion Terrell of Ferriday. The Terrells graciously opened their home to me and made their photos, letters, memories, and memorabilia freely available. Frankie Lewis Terrell, Jerry Lee Lewis' sister, took time from busy family and work demands to show me locations, take me to cemeteries, introduce me to relatives and sources, and go over photos with me. But mostly the fact that the Terrells faithfully collected and stored thousands of items—religious tracts, revival posters, paintings, letters, vinyl records, photographs, diaries— over many years has made an important contribution to part of the cultural history of postwar America. Those items now reside at the Lewis House Museum in Ferriday, Louisiana.

The author thanks the following people:

Dan Alexander, Bob and Beverly Anderson, Steve Badger, Ari Bass, Cecil Beatty, Jo Ann Beatty, R.T. Bonnette, Sandy Brokaw, Clarence Brown, J.W. and Lois Brown, Stella Calhoun, John Camp, Norm Carlson, Dr. John Carroll, Hiram Copeland, Ruby Collins, Ed Cray, Jim Curtis, Una Daigre, Donald Dayton, Richard Dortch, Minnie Elerick, Mr. Ellis, Louise Forman, Carrie Lewis Gilley, Mickey Gilley, Myra Gilley, Sonny Boy Gilley, Prof. Pete Gregory, Gay Guercio, D.J. Haack, Jeffrey Hadden, Ray Hale, Skip Haley, Cecil Harrelson, Mary Jean Harrelson, Art Harris, Lois Hugghins, Rita Jackson, Jamie Jacobs, Julia Jones, Leola Kirkland, Richard Lee, Gerald Lewis, John Lewis, Linda Gail Lewis, Hunter Lundy, Mike Lupo, Rev. Pat Mahoney, Jerry Lee Lewis, Kenny Lovelace, Jerri Myers, Wave Nunnally, Rev. Jerald Ogg, Sr., James Petty, Bonnie Pittman, Rena Pitts, Ed Pratt, Frank Rickard, Prof. Cecil M. Robeck, Dr. Charles Saunders, Donna Saunders, Norma Shaw, Charles Shepard, Roger Shugg, Bobby Stephanow, Errol Stevens, Rocky Stone, W.L. and Dorothy Swaggart, Don Talakson, Juleen Turnage, Michael Ventura, Stephen Wallace, Arilla Wells, Rev. Gerald Wilson, Jack Wright, Lawrence Wright, librarians, archivistis, and reporters in Baton Rouge, Los Angeles, Austin, New Orleans, Vidalia, and Ferriday, Louisiana; various family members and residents of Louisiana, including Ferriday, Baton Rouge, Monroe, Tunica, Snake Ridge, and Black River and locales including Memphis, New Orleans, Atlanta, and Indio, California.

Archival Resources

Baton Rouge Morning Advocate archives, Baton Rouge, Louisiana
Clark's Auto-Truck Stop archive, Indio, California

Concordia Sentinel archives, Ferriday, Louisiana
Concordia Parish Library, Vidalia, Louisiana
Diocese of Baton Rouge
Doheny Library, University of Southern California
East Baton Rouge Parish Library, Baton Rouge, Louisiana
Family Worship Center bookstore, Baton Rouge, Louisiana
Letters, Carrie Lewis Gilley collection
Family Bible, courtesy of Sonny Boy and Myra Gilley
Gilley Family Archive and Genealogy, courtesy of Hiram Copeland
Glendale Public Library, Glendale, California
Heirlines Genealogical Research
Jerry Lee Lewis Fan Club Newsletters, 1960–1980
Richard Lee Archive
Lewis House Museum
Los Angeles, California Public Library
Louisiana State Library, Baton Rouge, Louisiana
Louisiana State Library, New Orleans, Louisiana
McAlister Library, Fuller Theological Seminary, Pasadena, California
Pasadena Public Library, Pasadena, California
Santa Monica Historical Society, Santa Monica, California
Santa Monica Public Library, Santa Monica, California
South Pasadena Public Library, South Pasadena, California
Trinity Foundation Archive
University of Southern California Visual Anthropology Archive
Myra Lewis Williams Family Archive
Stephen Winzenburg Archive
WBRZ-TV videotape archive, Baton Rouge
  a. "Prophet or Profit?" 1980
  b. "Give Me That Big Time Religion." 1983
  c. "Swaggart Response." 1984; Jimmy Swaggart Ministries produced this, and called it "Give Me That Old Time Religion"
  d. "The Holy Truth." 1987
  e. "The Evangelist." 1988
  f. "Fall From Grace." 1988
  g. Miscellaneous news clips and raw footage
  h. Debra Murphree raw interview footage, Jan 27, 1988
  i. Debra Murphree raw interview footage, undated, from WVUE-TV, New Orleans

Cemeteries:
  Calhoun Cemetery, Indian Mound area near Ferriday, Louisiana
  Hewitt Cemetery, Snake Ridge, Louisiana

Census Records:
  1. 1900 Census Population Schedules, Louisiana. Claiborne, Concordia, De Soto (part of) Parishes

2. 1900 Concordia Parish records
3. 1910 Census Population Schedules, Louisiana. Cameron, Concordia, Claiborne and De Soto Parishes
4. 1910 Census Records, Soundex
5. 1910 Parish records

Jimmy Swaggart Ministries videotapes:
    a. The Best of Jimmy Swaggart 1985
    b. Thanksgiving Camp Meeting 1987
    c. Camp Meeting 1987
    d. Fourth of July Camp Meeting 1989
    e. "Give Me That Old Time Religion"
    f. "A Study in the Word"
    g. Broadcast sermons:
        1. Late August or early Sept 1990
        2. 6/16/91
        3. 4/12/91
        4. 1/1/92
        5. 12/6/92
        6. 12/13/92
        7. 1/22/94
        8. 9/18/94
        9. 11/13/94

Notes

Jimmy Swaggart has penned numerous booklets and several books, sometimes in the same year. All are published by the Jimmy Swaggart Ministries. These books and booklets are noted by the year of publication followed by a keyword in the publication's title. For example, Swaggart 1991 (*Cup*) denotes one of Swaggart's two 1991 books, *The Cup Which My Father Hath Given Me*.

At the beginning of each chapter are set forth the publications that informed or provided insights, background, or context for that chapter, followed by specific citations.

Glossary of Abbreviations Used in the Notes

AJ/AC	*Atlanta Journal/Atlanta Constitution*
"Big Time Religion"	"Give Me That Big Time Religion" (documentary film)
BR Mag	*Baton Rouge* Magazine
BRE	*Baton Rouge Enterprise*
BRST	*Baton Rouge State Times*
BRMA	*Baton Rouge Morning Advocate*
CB	*Current Biography*
CNN	Cable News Network
CSM	*Christian Science Monitor*
FWC	Family Worship Center
GG	*Gris Gris* Magazine
GR	"Geraldo Rivera"
LAT	*Los Angeles Times*
MJ	*Mother Jones* Magazine
NOTP	*New Orleans Times-Picayune*
NSW	*Newsweek*
NYT	*New York Times*
People	*People* Magazine
PHSE	*Penthouse* Magazine
Reuters	Reuters Limited
RS	*Rolling Stone* Magazine
Time	*Time* Magazine
UPI	United Press International
WP	*Washington Post*

Chapter 1. Metairie, Louisiana, Fall 1987

Unpublished sources:
Interviews
Archives: WBRZ-TV; *Baton Rouge Morning Advocate*

Published Sources:
This chapter owes a debt for its descriptions of what happened inside Room 7 to WVUE-TV New Orleans's raw interview footage of Debra Murphree shot in 1988 and provided by WBRZ-TV, Baton Rouge; to Art Harris and Jason Berry's account in the July 1988 issue of *Penthouse*; and to Lawrence Wright's account in the July 14, 1988 issue of *Rolling Stone*. Other sources consulted for this chapter include:

    Charlotte Observer 2/25/88 and 2/26/88; *BRST* 5/24/88; *BRMA* 2/20/88; Schaffer and Todd; Swaggart 1991 (*Cup*); "Fall From Grace"; UPI 10/26/91; *BRMA* 3/26/87; *Time* 4/6/87; Shepard; Dortch; *Time* 3/7/88; *BRE* 7/3/80; "The Holy Truth"; *BRST* 4/16/87; *NSW* 1/9/94; *Texas Lawyer* 6/22/87; *RS* 7/14/88; *HC* 5/2/92; CNN broadcast 6/28/91; *NSW* 4/6/87.

PAGE

11   "Positively no refunds": photo, *PHSE* July 1988, p. 108.
12   "I don't like the way": *PHSE* July 1988, p. 142.
12   "the cops [are] bad": *PHSE* July 1988, p. 142.
12   "He never tried to hurt me": *PHSE* July 1988, p. 142.
15   "It's my business . . . to sleep": *CB* October 1987, p. 52.
15   "one of the most": *CB* October 1987, p. 51.
19   "I'm sick of filthy": *Dixie* 1/27/85, p. 11.
19   "old-fashioned, heartfelt, Holy Ghost": *Newsweek* 5/30/83.
19   "I can't handle it alone": "Big Time Religion."
21   "the most effective speaker": *CB* October 1987, p. 51.
21   "We never have any time": Swaggart 1991 (*Cup*), p. 16.
22   "What do you think": *PHSE* July 1988, p. 142.

Chapter 2. Rebuke before All

Unpublished sources:
Interviews

Published Sources:
BRMA 11/4/89; *RS* 7/14/88; Reuters 8/12/91; UPI 9/13/91; Reuters 7/16/91; UPI 7/16/91; *PHSE* July 1988; *BRMA* 2/20/88; UPI 7/8/91; *NYT* 2/22/88; *LAT* 5/22/88; *NOTP* 3/4/88; Lundy.

23   "Them that sin rebuke": I Timothy 20:5, *The Holy Bible*.
24   "I'm sorry I've hurt you": CNN broadcast 6/28/91.

Chapter 3. Frances

Unpublished sources:
Interviews
Archives: Lewis House Museum

Published Sources:
"Give Me That Big Time Religion"; Swaggart 1991 (*Cup*); UPI 7/16/91; *BR* Mag, September 1986; Nauer; *RS* 7/14/88; Swaggart 1996 (*Bible Commentary*) (photos).

26   "If I have to go . . . honest with you": Schaffer and Todd, p. 151.
26   "I personally think": Schaffer and Todd, p. 153.

Chapter 4. In the Beginning

Unpublished sources:
Interviews
Archives: Heirlines Genealogical Research; family Bible, Sonny Boy and Myra Gilley; Gilley Family archive and genealogy; Carrie Gilley archive; Williams archive; Lewis House Museum; Census Population Schedules of Concordia Parish, Louisiana; Hewitt Cemetery, Snake Ridge, Louisiana.

Published Sources:
Tosches; Burgess and McGee.

27   Old Man Lewis: Lee Lewis is supposed to have knocked a horse to the ground with his fist in a rage. He is said to have knifed a man to death on a country road when the man cursed him for spooking his mules. There are many tales of his drunken betrayals of wife and family.

But nothing is simple, and however tenacious is the legend of Lee Lewis as a violent and Godless wastrel, his children remembered him with forgiveness. His diary betrays a streak of tenderness and poetry. One page entitled, "A broken vow that was made 50 years ago" was written when he was 75: "I am glad," he wrote, "that I have had life, for many things here have afforded me the utmost pleasure. The love and laughter of little children, the smiles of true friends, and the sunlight and shadows that race across the hills and valleys.

"My wife is still with me. We have journeyed together 50 years. Many silver threads now shine among her golden tresses but she looks as fair and is as dear to me as she was the day I led her to the marriage altar. . . . Somewhere in the great unknown out in the still spaces of the great universe, I hope we shall find a resting place, the new Jerusalem, where Desdemona and I can walk the streets of that golden city hand in hand and meet our Pilot face to face."

This was written on New Year's Eve, 1929. However, a year later, Arilla asked for a divorce—not for the first time—and moved out of the house.

When Lee finally died of cancer in 1937, his sons showed little respect in handling his corpse. Nick Tosches' *Hellfire* says that his youngest son, Robert Jay, took his father's body out of the coffin, fitted it into Lee's favorite rocking chair on the front porch, placed the old man's pipe in his hand, tied a string to the leg of the chair, and, out of sight in the bushes, pulled it to start the chair rocking just as a carload of grieving relatives arrived. Another version, by an eyewitness, is milder: a nephew and son who were dressing the body called an in-law over on some pretext and then made the body jerk upwards out of the coffin to scare the in-law. In any case, Lee's sons revealed a telling lack of respect for their father.

Chapter 5. Cloven Tongues Like As of Fire

Unpublished sources:
Interviews; sermon notes
Archives: letters, Carrie Lewis Gilley; photos, Lewis House Museum; Gilley family archive

Published Sources:
Stagg, Hinson and Oates; Burgess and McGee; Wright 1990; Harrell 1985; Cantor; *Concordia Sentinel* 4/6/77.

29 The Fundamentals: Packard, p. 68.
30 "suddenly there came a sound": Acts 2:2–4: *The Holy Bible.*
30 "filled with words I": *Charisma & Christian Life*, January 1991, p. 83.
31 "I believe the whole": Blumhofer 1989, p. 85.
31 "those of his own color": Blumhofer 1989, p. 90.
31 "very untidy": Blumhofer 1989, p. 90.
31 "religious fakes and tramps": Blumhofer 1989, p. 90.
31 "New Sect of Fanatics": Blumhofer 1989, p. 99.
32 "negroisms": Blumhofer 1989, p. 99.
32 "decency and order . . . jerking fits": Blumhofer 1989, p. 108.

Chapter 6. Ferriday

Unpublished sources:
Interviews; sermon notes; photos, Lewis House Museum and *Concordia Sentinel* archive
Archives: Lewis House Museum; Census Population Schedules; Concordia Parish records; *Concordia Sentinel* archive; Heirlines Genealogical Research; Santa Monica Historical Society; Gilley archive; Sonny Boy and Myra Gilley family Bible.

Published Sources:
Concordia Sentinel 4/4/77; *The Evangelist* June 1985; *Louisiana Historical Quarterly*, January 1932; *Concordia Sentinel* 7/25/30; Swaggart 1984 (*River*).

33 But life abounded: The area's reputation for game attracted Teddy Roosevelt, who came in 1906 to hunt bear in adjacent Tensas Parish. With him was famed bounty hunter Ben Lilly, a local who had accompanied Roosevelt on safari in Africa. In need of a wagon and mule, Lilly confidently strode to an isolated cabin. Its inhabitant, an elderly black man, refused Lilly's request.
    Roosevelt stepped forward. "Do you know who you are talking to?" he asked. "You are talking to the President of the United States."
    "Boss, I don't care if you're Booker T. Washington," the old man answered. "You cain't get this wagon."
36 Neither of them could have cared less: Intermarriage was common in the South. Leroy and Arilla's 11 children—Ada and Elmo and Robert Jay, the twins John and Jane, little Mollie who got pressured into marrying the wrong man, Carrie whose young husband was murdered by a reported Swaggart relative at Snake Ridge and who, along with her sisters Irene, Eva, and Mabel, married Gilley brothers, and Leon Lewis, the brother who made good at farming in Arkansas—all of these 11 siblings were also each other's cousins, because they were

the products of a first-cousin marriage whose principals were themselves products of cousin unions. And by the time Sun and Minnie Bell were courting,
another generation of Gilleys was already eyeing its in-laws: Mickey's two older
brothers married Herron girls (the daughters of Minnie Bell's brother George);
and one of Mickey's brothers had also married a cousin of Theresa Herron's.

Chapter 7. Stars Are Born

Unpublished sources:
Interviews; sermon notes
Archives: photos, Lewis House Museum

Published Sources:
Tosches; Lewis 1982; Goldman; Williams.

39   "get her out of here": Swaggart 1984 (*River*), pp. 11–12.
39   It rained most of February: Cline, pp. 8, 14.
40   a tiny, quivering cry: Tyl, p. 77. Time of birth was 1:35 a.m.

Chapter 8. The Church That Darwin Built

Unpublished sources:
Interviews
Archives: Lewis House Museum

Published Sources:
Tosches; Burgess and McGee; Swaggart 1984 (*River*); Lewis 1982; Swaggart 1996,
(*Bible Commentary*) (photos); Dorough; Cantor; Packard; Schultze 1991; Wallechin-
sky and Wallace; Dundy; "Christianity, Cults, and Religions"; Johnson 1955.

41   "bellowing apocalyptic hymns": Packard, p. 71.
41   "propaganda stations": Schultze 1991, p. 31.

Chapter 9. A Goodbye, and a New Bargain

Unpublished sources:
Interviews
Archives: Lewis House Museum; Williams archive

Published Sources:
Tosches; Lewis 1982.

46   Theresa had once been a laughing: Many theories were advanced about Theresa
      Herron's fits: manic depression, inbreeding, and bad water (refineries, pulp
      mills, and carbon-black factories dumped untreated waste into Louisiana's riv-
      ers for generations; Ferriday's well water became foul during droughts and had
      to be boiled) were outsiders' hypotheses. The family's speculations ranged from
      early menopause to upset hormones from a change-of-life baby, her youngest
      child, Minnie Bell. Sun Swaggart claimed it was sunstroke, but others cited
      hereditary hormonal imbalance—and indeed, enough family members suffered
      from some sort of mental ailment that relatives called their syndrome "it."

"*It* was all through the family," said Frankie Terrell, Jerry Lee's sister. "Uncle Talley Forman [Theresa's brother] had it. Jerry Lee Jr. had it . . . but Jerry would never admit it." (Jerry Lee Lewis Jr. was disturbed for much of his life. According to Lewis biographer Nick Tosches, the boy told a member of his father's entourage during a London tour that he couldn't sleep, because a little boy and girl from Ferriday were living in his stomach, and they were troubled.)

Others said Theresa's trouble was triggered when she was disinherited and rejected by her parents, the Formans, and the entire Forman clan when she married broke, uneducated William Herron against their vehement wishes.

"They never spoke to her again," said a grandchild. "To this day, the Formans don't talk to us. They live on Black River and they're very well off. I've never met any of them."

Although her malady appeared to have some genetic components, Theresa's illness was compounded by her difficult life. Besides her extreme poverty and the estrangement from her family, she had suffered the deaths of three babies— Lily, Maud, and Johnny—and had buried them in unmarked graves because she and William couldn't afford headstones. When the Herrons' house at Winnsboro burned, destroying all their possessions, Theresa wept most bitterly over losing cherished photos of her dead children.

"[Papa Herron] ran wild, and left her in a dirt-floor shack," one of his granddaughters explains. "She had no medication, she was miserable. She cried, and retreated into another world. They said she was hostile and dangerous— well, she was pushed into a corner."

47   "Dear daddy, how are you": Lewis House Museum.
48   the one male who would not let Mamie down: this insight is from Lewis 1982.

Chapter 10. Another Goodbye

Unpublished sources:
Interviews; sermon notes

Published Sources:
Swaggart 1996 (*Bible Commentary*) (photos); Swaggart 1984 (*River*).

Chapter 11. Guilt

Unpublished sources:
Interviews; sermon notes

Published Sources:
Swaggart 1996 (*Bible Commentary*) (photos); Swaggart 1984 (*River*).

53   "It hurt my heart": notes from broadcast sermon 4/21/91.
53   "There was no other": Swaggart 1984 (*River*), p. 17.

Chapter 12. Belonging

Unpublished sources:
Interviews; sermon notes
Archives: Lewis House Museum

Published Sources:
Swaggart 1984 (*River*); Lewis 1982; "Christianity, Cults, and Religions"; Swaggart 1996 (*Bible Commentary*) (photos).

57   "had arrived to find everyone drunk": Dundy, p. 14.

Chapter 13. Softening

Published Sources:
Swaggart 1984 (*River*); *The Evangelist* June 1985; Swaggart 1996 (*Bible Commentary*) (photos).

Chapter 14. "Ninety-nine Cents out of Every Dollar"

Unpublished sources:
Interviews; sermon notes
Archives: Lewis House Museum

Published Sources:
Swaggart 1984 (*River*); Swaggart 1991 (*Cup*).

63   "If [Jimmy] challenged his father": RS 7/14/88, p. 104.
63   entangled with sexual desire: Jimmy has made a consistent association in his writings between his attacks of Satan, which led to his behavior with prostitutes, and depression.

Chapter 15. Texas Redux

Unpublished sources:
Interviews; sermon notes
Archives: Lewis House Museum

Published Sources:
Swaggart 1984 (*River*); *Academic American Encyclopedia.*

64   Once again, Sun, Minnie Bell, and Jimmy got into the family truck with a new baby: The story of the defense plant in Texas appears in Jimmy's autobiography, *To Cross a River*, and in his sermons and writings. Arilla Wells, Sun's sister, doesn't remember the family ever going to Texas for defense work, though. She said they all went to Alabama, including Ada and W.H., for a short time to work in a defense plant at a town called Sylacauga. Sun did carpentry work there. She remembers Minnie Bell being pregnant; Jeanette was not born yet. Sun Swaggart remembers a stint in Texas just after Jeanette was born, which matches Jimmy's version.

Chapter 16. The First Surrender

Unpublished sources:
Interviews; sermon notes

Published Sources:
Swaggart 1984 (*River*); *New York Times Magazine* 6/11/89; Williams.

Chapter 17. Taboo

Unpublished sources:
Interviews; sermon notes
Archives: photos, Lewis House Museum

Published Sources:
Swaggart 1984 (*River*); *Dallas Morning News* 8/25/86; Sims.

69   "She's gone crazy": Swaggart 1984 (*River*), p. 29.

Chapter 18. Revival

Unpublished sources:
Interviews; sermon notes
Archives: photos, Lewis House Museum

Published Sources:
Swaggart 1984 (*River*); *The Holy Bible*; "Marjoe"; "Holy Ghost People"; Tenney; Sims.

72   "I wanna feel God": after the style of "Marjoe" and "Holy Ghost People."
73   "These men are full": Acts 2:13: *The Holy Bible.*
73   "growing desperate": Swaggart 1984 (*River*), p. 33; sermon notes, late August or early September, 1990.
73   "I don't think the world": notes from visit to FWC.
74   "I prayed all the time": sermon notes, late August or early September, 1990.
74   "Believe BIG": sermon notes, late August or early September, 1990.

Chapter 19. The Theater of Salvation

Unpublished sources:
Interviews; sermon notes
Archives: photos, Lewis House Museum

Published Sources:
Swaggart 1984 (*River*).

76   "Do not go . . . My service": Swaggart 1991 (*Cup*), p. 53.
76   "as if a thousand pounds": Swaggart 1991 (*Cup*), p. 54.
76   "I didn't go . . . movies any more": Swaggart 1984 (*River*), p. 23.

Chapter 20. Defection

Unpublished sources:
Interviews; sermon notes
Archives: Lewis House Museum

Published Sources:
Swaggart 1984 (*River*).

80   "Step OUT": after the style of "Marjoe" and "Holy Ghost People."
81   cement him firmly to his own kind: That sense of being an outsider figures large in Jimmy's sermons; he and his visiting ministers frequently refer to the fact that everyone in the congregation is an insider, and an outsider in "The World." Jimmy frequently refers in church to the people who are out there doing the popular things, and how stupid his listeners all must seem for being in here

praising the Lord instead of watching the Super Bowl. "They'll just never understand our need to get the Holy Spirit," he tells his flock. "They just can't understand it." The church is also full of little insider gestures, such as the jig people break into showing that the spirit is really in them. This is always met with affectionate laughter and approval.

Chapter 21. The Blockbuster

Unpublished sources:
Interviews; sermon notes
Archives: Lewis House Museum

Published Sources:
Swaggart 1984 (*River*).

84   "standing outside my body": Swaggart 1984 (*River*), p. 44.
84   "a powerful bomb": Swaggart 1984 (*River*), p. 44.

Chapter 22. Rivals

Unpublished sources:
Interviews; sermon notes
Archives: Lewis House Museum

Published Sources:
The Evangelist August 1979; Lewis 1982; Tosches.

87   The nature of Jerry's relationship with his mother is found throughout Lewis 1982. After he was famous, Jerry was fully maneuvered into Elmo's role. One family member even made a Freudian slip: "Mamie worshipped the ground Jerry walked on. The only time they ever fought was over their kids." The relative was speaking of Jerry's little sisters. That she unconsciously saw the little girls as "*their* [Mamie's and Jerry's] kids" showed the extent to which Jerry had taken over the role of his father.
88   "kind of touchy": *LAT* Orange County Edition, 1/15/94.

Chapter 23. Last Chance

Unpublished sources:
Interviews; sermon notes

Published Sources:
Lewis 1982.

90   "I am become death": *MJ* July/August 1986, p. 37.
91   "Nobody thought the prophecies": Swaggart 1984 (*River*), p. 45.
94   "playing church . . . meant business!": sermon notes, late August or early September, 1990.
94   "terrible foreboding": Swaggart 1991 (*Cup*), p. 54.
94   "You will not do it": Swaggart 1991 (*Cup*), p. 55.

Chapter 24. Many Are Called

Unpublished sources:
Interviews; sermon notes
Archives: Lewis House Museum; Gilley family archive

Published Sources:
This chapter has drawn heavily on David Harrell's 1975 book *All Things Are Possible*
for history and insights regarding evangelism. Jimmy's and Jerry's early piano experi-
ences are related in Lewis 1982 and Swaggart 1984 (*River*). Other sources include
Malone; Tenney; Shepard; Tosches.

  96   "So the last shall": Matthew 20:16: *The Holy Bible.*
  97   "always use the talent": *RS* 7/14/88, p. 106.
  99   "son, I've called you" and "go into every land": Blumhofer 1989.
  99   "A generation grew up": Harrell 1975, p. 21.
 100   "God's reducing plan": Harrell 1975, p. 198.
 100   "spit up a bloody cancer": Harrell 1975, p. 87.
 100   "tired shoulders": Harrell 1975, p. 87.
 101   "more souls were begat": Dorough. This survives yet; a Baton Rouge reporter
       volunteered the results of an informal study in the 1980s that showed a business
       spike at local motels after Singles Night at the Jimmy Swaggart Ministries.
 102   "Could I ever forget": Harrell 1975, p. 31.

Chapter 25. Running from God

Unpublished sources:
Interviews
Archives: Lewis House Museum

Published Sources:
Swaggart 1984 (*River*); Lewis 1982; Balmer; Jung; *AJ/AC* 5/22/88; *Concordia Sentinel* 4/4/77; Carnes 1992.

 104   "running from the call": Swaggart 1984 (*River*), p. 41.
 104   "My goal was to become": Swaggart 1984 (*River*), p. 48.
 104   "going the wrong way": Swaggart 1984 (*River*), p. 50.
 105   "with the ironical result": Cash, p. 232.
 105   one of Jimmy's relatives: This was reportedly a place called Ma Dunn's near
       Under-the-Hill.
 106   to leave [Jimmy] behind: Later, in the aftermath of the Debra Murphree inci-
       dent, Jimmy would reportedly acknowledge to his superiors on the Assembly
       of God's national council that he had had an obsession with pornography since
       childhood. See also *RS* 7/14/88, p. 110 (Jimmy told his elders in Springfield that
       he had been a "slave of sexual perversion since the age of ten") and interviews
       with Patrick Mahoney and Pat Robertson in Chapter 67 of this book. In his
       1991 book *Satan Hath Desired You*, Jimmy denied that any such thing hap-
       pened in his childhood.
 107   went to one of those houses of ill repute: This information came from a source
       who was very close to all the cousins at that time. On the other hand, another

source almost as close to Jerry at the time stated that he was fairly sure Jerry and Jimmy were both virgins when they married (Jerry at 16, Jimmy at 17).

107   "I was afraid to ask": Swaggart 1984 (*River*), p. 46.

107   a self-feeding obsession with sex: Addiction to pornography almost always starts in childhood, is more likely to occur among children who feel unloved, and is about powerlessness, according to Patrick Carnes.

Chapter 26. The Anointing of Satan

Unpublished sources:
Interviews; sermon notes
Archives: Lewis House Museum

Published Sources:
Swaggart 1984 (*River*); Lewis 1982; *MJ* July/August 1986; Malone; Tosches.

109   "We'd go down there": Tosches, p. 58.

Chapter 27. Narrow the Path

Unpublished sources:
Interviews
Archives: Lewis House Museum

Published Sources:
Balmer; Tosches; Swaggart 1984 (*River*); Lewis 1982; Harrell 1985.

111   "Narrow is the way": Matthew 7:14: *The Holy Bible*.

Chapter 28. Girls

Unpublished sources:
Interviews

Published Sources:
Lewis 1982; *MJ* July/August 1986; Swaggart 1984 (*River*); Swaggart 1996 (*Bible Commentary*) (photos).

116   "She was 15": *RS* 7/14/88, p. 109.
118   "He had a touch . . . terrific lifestyle": Schaffer and Todd, p. 136.

Chapter 29. Into the Fire

Unpublished sources:
Interviews; sermon notes

Published Sources:
Harrell 1975; Harrell 1985; Swaggart 1984 (*River*); Blumhofer 1989.

120   "tent wars . . . 38,457 conversions": Harrell 1975, pp. 44–45.
120   "the souls that were saved": Harrell 1975, p. 104.
122   "If you'll let me keep": Swaggart 1984 (*River*), p. 66.

Chapter 30. Seize the Moment

Unpublished sources:
Interviews; sermon notes

Published Sources:
Packard; Harrell 1975; Swaggart 1984 (*River*); Schaffer and Todd; Lewis 1982.

123   "a life of perpetual": *LAT* 8/5/95.

Chapter 31. Back in the Fold

Unpublished sources:
Interviews; sermon notes
Archives: Lewis House Museum photos and tracts

Published Sources:
photos, Swaggart 1996 (*Bible Commentary*); Schaffer and Todd; *Baton Rouge* Magazine 9/89; *People* 3/7/88; Lewis 1982; Burgess and McGee.

126   "I knew it!": Swaggart 1984 (*River*), p. 68.
126   "What's wrong with you?": Swaggart 1984 (*River*), p. 69.
127   "derision and ridicule": Swaggart 1984 (*River*), p. 197. This suffering is widely
          voiced by Pentecostals of Jimmy's generation; Harrell 1985, p. 31 tells movingly
          of Oral Roberts' anguish.
128   "Judgment on America": Burgess and McGee p. 837.

Chapter 32. Out of Nothing

Unpublished sources:
Interviews
Archives: Lewis House Museum

Published Sources:
Swaggart 1984 (*River*); Lewis 1982; Swaggart 1991 (*Satan*); Malone; Goldman; Ventura.

130   "Before Elvis there was nothing": Goldman, p. 117.
130   Radio barn dances: Malone pp. 214, 72–73; Lewis House Museum. Ouachita
          Valley Jamboree: brochure, Lewis House Museum. Broadcast over local KNOE
          radio, the Ouachita Valley Jamboree was a corporation formed by local busi-
          nessmen to bring "good, clean" down-home entertainment to people of the
          area.
131   there was something hidden and dirty about the term "rock and roll": Michael
          Ventura's exploration of the spiritual, erotic, and psychological origins of this
          term in his essay "Hear That Long Snake Moan" in *Shadow Dancing in the
          U.S.A.* is without equal.
131   "I am come that": John 10:10: *The Holy Bible*.
133   slapped and punched: Jerry's family fights are well documented in Tosches and
          in Lewis 1982. An unpublished anecdote: when Jerry and Jane lived for a cou-
          ple of months in Stella's apartment above a little store near 4th and Louisiana,
          an argument broke out when Jerry announced one night he was going to

Natchez. He went downstairs and got into the car, and Jane ran down after him and threw a heavy glass milk bottle through the windshield.

Chapter 33. By the Grace of God and Women

Unpublished sources:
Interviews; sermon notes
Archives: Lewis House Museum

Published Sources:
Harrell 1975, text and photos; Bethards; Swaggart 1985, (*Biblical Solutions*); Horsfield; Packard; *Pentecostal Evangel*, 11/25/56 and 6/8/58; *Faith Digest*, April 1960; A.A. Allen tract undated, from the 1940s–50s; A.A. Allen tract 1944; Pilgrim Tract Society undated, from the 1940s; Swaggart 1984 (*River*).

134 "I was fiery . . . the small things": Swaggart 1984 (*River*), pp. 78–79.
135 "God won't forgive you": Swaggart 1984 (*River*), p. 79.
135 "In the name of Jesus!": Swaggart 1991 (*Satan*), p. 13.
135 Dream symbology: Bethards 113. The beast also echoed the sort of untrustworthy adult who would molest a child. A ten-year-old—Jimmy's age when he was rumored to have been molested, according to Patrick Mahoney—would have to be coerced into keeping silent—perhaps by someone who understood how to wield the concept of sin on a Pentecostal child.
136 slaughtering it in a surge of release: The suggestion that sexual release played a role in this is all through Jimmy's writings. Apart from the many observations that his jeremiads against pornography and fornication had the flavor of one who protested too much, he himself repeatedly relates performance pressure to "demon oppression" (see, e.g., Swaggart 1984 [*River*] p. 79, pressure to meet high standards accompanied by depression, weight loss, and sleeplessness [in addition to impending fatherhood and pressure from Ada and Minnie Bell to compete with famous evangelists]; Swaggart 1984 [*River*] pp. 172–73, pressure from performance schedule accompanied by fatigue, nerves, and sleeplessness; and Swaggart 1984 [*River*] pp. 78–81, 92–94, 98–100, 155–59, 166–68, 180–81; Swaggart 1991 [*Satan*], pp. 2, 12–14, 21, 23–25, 26–27, 33–36, 54, 68–69, 70–74, 79–82; and Swaggart 1991 [*Cup*] p. 54–55, 73–81, 186–88). In his 1991 book *Satan Hath Desired You*, he cites financial and performance pressure, ill health, physical exhaustion, nervousness, sleeplessness, and "demon oppression" as factors operating just before his encounter with Rosemary Garcia. We can assume that he has handled such pressures in the past the same way (after all, he was caught twice, reportedly sighted numerous times, and he did have pornography with him the second time; and he did reportedly admit to at least two sources in 1987 that he'd had a problem for many years, even though he denied that admission later. He does say that demon oppression has plagued him since childhood). It's reasonable to suspect that, whenever he has written in the past about poaching in a broth of exhaustion, depression, nerves, pressure, and so on, he might have handled such pressures in the same way at times.

He also writes about certain dreams, including the man-bear dream, in the context of the prostitute scandals and demon oppression.

He had this dream under the pressure of fatherhood and money, with his mother and grandmother insisting he would preach to thousands; he brought up the same dream years later to describe why he got into trouble with prostitutes. And in the earlier context he related it to "sinning again." Clearly, he's saying that the oppression, physical and emotional as well as spiritual, of 1953–54 is similar to what was happening to him in 1991. And he said he had sinned over and over and promised he would stop over and over, back in 1953–54. What else might that sin have been? As in his 1991 apologia, he didn't specify it. It's not likely to be gambling, or his temper, because he freely admitted to those in his 1984 autobiography. His own words and omissions practically say that it's pornography or prostitution, and of course his 1991 apologia for those is the context in which he remembers this dream. See Swaggart 1991 (*Satan*) 20.

The implication is that the reports of a lifelong problem with pornography are true.

136 "Three of the most": Swaggart 1985 (*Biblical Solutions*), p. 4.
136 "PUNY GOD": sermon notes, late August or early September, 1990.
136 "Whenever you have problems": Schaffer and Todd, p. 137.
136 "The Lord called Jimmy . . . escape that call": Schaffer and Todd, pp. 139–40; the story is also related in sermon notes, late August or early September, 1990 and sermon 1/19/92.
136 "I was sitting . . . of my eyes": Schaffer and Todd, p. 140; the story is also related in sermon notes, late August or early September, 1990.
136 "I'll remove you": Schaffer and Todd, p. 140.
138 "Over 300 hooks and pins": *Native Evangelism*, undated magazine, Lewis House Museum.
138 "For years I've lived": undated A.A. Allen tract from Lewis House Museum.

Chapter 34. Shakin'

Unpublished sources:
Interviews

Published Sources:
Grun; Herbers; Packard; *RS* 7/14/88; Lewis 1982; Lewis 1964; "High School Confidential."

141 "a new spiritual dimension": Swaggart 1984 (*River*), p. 85.

Chapter 35. Awakening

Published Sources:
Johnson 1955; Balmer; Schultze 1991; Dorough.

143 Its best-known proponent was Jonathan Edwards: Packard, pp. 52–53. Some of the country's best colleges were guided by evangelists; Edwards' evangelist grandson was president of Yale. Oberlin also had an evangelist president.
150 disseminated among everyone and owned by everyone: Interestingly, the popular form versus the rigid military form also speaks of private versus public institutionalization of ritual. The purpose of the Protestant Reformation was to

remove its adherents from the state structure of the organized, centralized church. The message of the preacher might still be linked to such a hierarchy, but the way the message is stated was highly privatized by the Reformation.

Chapter 36. Miraculous Healing

Unpublished sources:
Interviews; sermon notes
Archives: Lewis House Museum; Williams and Gilley archives

Published Sources:
Swaggart 1996 (*Bible Commentary*) (photos); *RS* 7/14/88; Swaggart 1984 (*River*); Schaffer and Todd; Swaggart 1986 (*God's Answer*); Lewis 1982; *Concordia Sentinel* 5/16/58; unidentified 1958 news articles from Williams archive.

153   "Have I not commanded": Joshua 1:9: *The Holy Bible.*
154   "Son, I'm gonna tell you": Swaggart 1984 (*River*), p. 7.
156   "Get Out, Lewis . . . Gang Out": 1958 clippings from Williams archive.
157   "Lord, tear this thing": Swaggart 1984 (*River*), p. 121.
157   "You can have . . . white car": Swaggart 1984 (*River*), pp. 121–22. How a 13-year-old girl who had only recently learned the truth about Santa Claus would know about tax deductions is a mystery, but the pressure on Jerry to do something for the Lord is very credible.
157   conned David out of that car: David added, "And he told me [on the flight back to Baton Rouge], 'I guess I'll have to tell you, David, I really took your car, but I figgered that if he was gonna start givin' cousins automobiles, I oughtta be the first in line.' "
158   You had to have spoken in tongues: Prof. Mel Robeck reported that in later years the Assemblies would try to overcome their lack of sophistication about psychological matters and the credibility problems caused by the ecstatic component of their practice. But the basic requirements in Jimmy's day were that you had a "calling" and that you had spoken in tongues.

Chapter 37. On the Road

Unpublished sources:
Interviews

Published Sources:
Swaggart 1984 (*Questions and Answers*), Vol. 3; Wallechinsky and Wallace; Harrell 1975.

161   "I wanted a genuine": Swaggart 1984 (*River*), p. 126.
162   "It was an exhausting . . . his peers": Harrell 1975, p. 6.
162   "It got very discouraging . . . another child": Schaffer and Todd, p. 142.

Chapter 38. The Color Line

Unpublished sources:
Interviews; sermon notes

Published Sources:
Dundy; Herbers; Lewis 1964; *MJ* July/August 1986; *Dallas Morning News* 8/25/86;
Harrell 1975.

164 "Get as rich and famous": *Dallas Morning News* 8/25/86.
164 "were a friendly buffer": *MJ* July/August 1986.

Chapter 39. Being Seen

Unpublished sources:
Interviews

Published Sources:
Lewis 1964; Balmer.

168 "decent Nigras": Lewis 1964, p. 76.
168 "[The Negro] has come to feel": Lewis 1964, p. 97.

Chapter 40. A String of Tragedies

Unpublished sources:
Interviews; sermon notes
Archives: Lewis House Museum

Published Sources:
Lewis 1982; Swaggart 1984 (*River*).

Chapter 41. Keeping the Faith

Unpublished sources:
Interviews; sermon notes
Archives: Lewis House Museum

Published Sources:
Packard; Horsfield; Armstrong; Lewis 1982; *The Evangelist* from Lewis House Museum; Swaggart 1984 (*Confession*); Swaggart 1981 (*Preacher*).

177 slapped her across the face: Though Jerry's violence toward his wives is widely reported, and certainly Jimmy's father believed in thrashing him, there are few documented incidents of Jimmy's temper crossing over into physical violence.
177 "buffet this sinful body": Romans 8:13: *The Holy Bible.*
178 "It was a hard life": Swaggart 1984 (*River*), p. 164.
180 The Protestant format: Garry Wills has noted how authority rests in the preacher, and Schultze 1991 has noted how evangelists' entertainments were remarkably similar in format to the traveling circuses that were their contemporaries and competitors in frontier America.
180 "Bro. Swaggart is a first": poster, Lewis House Museum.

Chapter 42. Just Do It!

Unpublished sources:
Interviews
Archives: Lewis House Museum

Published Sources:
Swaggart 1984 (*River*)

184 "But she kept on": Schaffer and Todd, p. 144.
184 "Just DO it": notes from sermon 6/16/91.
184 "seemed filled with power": Swaggart 1984 (*River*), p. 145.
185 "It seemed as if": Swaggart 1984 (*River*), p. 152.
185 "He made a phone call": notes from sermon 11/13/94.

Chapter 43. Demon Oppression

Unpublished sources:
Interviews; sermon notes

Published Sources:
The Evangelist, August 1979; Swaggart 1984 (*River*); Schaffer and Todd.

186 "demon oppression" and "nerves": Swaggart 1991 (*Satan*) pp. 70–73; Swaggart 1984 (*River*), pp. 172–73, respectively.
186 "You are being unfaithful": *The Evangelist* September 1986, p. 14.
187 "but once you get . . . I began crying": Swaggart 1984 (*River*), p. 159.
187 "The Lord's presence": Swaggart 1984 (*River*), pp. 167–68.
188 "I was sick . . . the failures": Swaggart 1984 (*Confession Principle*), p. 3.
189 "I would walk the floor": Swaggart 1984 (*River*), p. 173.
189 "I did, deep down": Swaggart 1984 (*Confession Principle*), p. 3.
189 "Suddenly I saw God": Swaggart 1984 (*Confession Principle*), p. 5.
189 "When you feel this": Swaggart 1984 (*River*), p. 174.

Chapter 44. A Good Man

Unpublished sources:
Interviews; sermon notes
Archives: Lewis House Museum

Published Sources:
Schaffer and Todd; Swaggart 1981 (*Divorce*); *National Examiner* 12/17/91; Swaggart 1984 (*River*); *The Evangelist* August 1979; Swaggart 1991 (*Cup*); Swaggart 1981 (*Preacher*).

Chapter 45. "What Hath God Wrought?"

Published Sources:
The author relied on Armstrong, Horsfield, and Schultze 1991 for historical perspectives on electronic preaching in this chapter. Other sources consulted for this chapter include Shepard; Packard; Schultze 1990; Harrell 1975.

195 "the Billy Sunday": Armstrong, p. 23.
195 "propaganda stations": Schultze 1991, p. 31.
196 "public interest, convenience": Horsfield, p. 4.
196 "to announce good news": Metzger and Coogan, p. 206.

198   "Dear Brother [Name]": Horsfield, p. 31.
199   "I've got some very": Horsfield, p. 32.

Chapter 46. Camp Meeting Hour

Unpublished sources:
Interviews

Published Sources:
Tosches; Lewis 1982; Swaggart 1984 (*River*).

200   "I want you to stop": Swaggart 1984 (*River*), p. 184.
200   "send a wave": Swaggart 1984 (*River*), p. 185.
201   "I sensed in my spirit": Schaffer and Todd, p. 145.
201   "In 1969, I knew": Fundraising letter 6/22/93.
202   "knock the door down": Schaffer and Todd, p. 137.
202   "share God's glory": Swaggart 1984 (*River*), p. 196.
203   "simple three-point plan": Swaggart 1984 (*River*), p. 200.
203   "I don't know where": Swaggart 1984 (*River*), p. 204.
204   "Fiscal carelessness will ruin": Swaggart 1981 (*Preacher*), p. 15.

Chapter 47. Voices

Unpublished sources:
Interviews
Archives: Lee archive

Published Sources:
Tosches; *The Evangelist* August 1979; Swaggart 1996 (*Bible Commentary*) (photos); Harrell 1975; *CB* October 1987; "Prophet or Profit?"; Burgess and McGee; Lewis 1982.

206   "Now about these record albums": Swaggart 1984 (*River*), p. 206.
206   "I think what happens": *People* 3/7/88.
207   only lost one other station: Jimmy doesn't say outright that he modified his message; he says he recognized this as an attack of Satan and prayed hard about it. But sources said he toned down the tongues, and within a few years, there was no hint of tongues, miracles, or magical healings. In the July 1986 *Evangelist*, pp. 17–19, he retells this story with a different ending: "I sought out the station owner who, believe it or not, was a Jewish brother. We . . . contacted our representatives, who, oddly enough, were Catholic. . . . The Jewish brother asked the question, 'Does the Pentecostal pay his bills?' When the answer was yes, Jimmy said, "the Jew told the Fundamentalist [station manager] to put the Pentecostal back on."

Chapter 48. "People Always Kill God"

Unpublished sources:
Interviews
Archives: Williams archive; Clark's archive

Published Sources:
Swaggart 1996 (*Bible Commentary*) (photos); unidentified internet JPEG; Joseph/Benton Harbor, MI *Herald-Palladium* 2/9/92; *Christian Century* 4/6/88; Swaggart 1981 (*Preacher*); Swaggart 1984 (*River*); Harrell 1975; *CB* October 1987; Shepard.

208   "the most spectacular": Harrell 1975, p. 214.
208   "determinedly honest and clean": Harrell 1975, p. 215.
208   "Preachers, painters, and prostitutes": Swaggart 1981 (*The Preacher*), p. 16.
209   "The old-fashioned whoop": Harrell 1975, p. 215.
209   "brought mass revivalism": Harrell 1975, p. 216.
209   "The only thing you": Harrell 1975, p. 216.
210   "Burdened by work, adored": Harrell 1975, p. 236.
210   "wept many tears": Swaggart 1981 (*The Preacher*), p. 9.
211   "nobody ever gives back": Swaggart 1981 (*The Preacher*), p. 23.
211   "They start to think": Swaggart 1984 (*River*), p. 232.
211   "Father, that boy can't": Swaggart 1984 (*River*) p. 238.
212   "millions on dope today": *Detroit Free Press* undated clipping from Williams archive.

Chapter 49. A Radio Station

Unpublished sources:
Interviews

Published Sources:
Diocese of Baton Rouge Demographic Analysis; *The Evangelist* July 1986; *The Evangelist* July 1985; Swaggart 1984 (*River*).

214   "No . . . Obviously I'm in": Swaggart 1984 (*River*), p. 223.
214   "There are some FCC": *The Evangelist* July 1985, p. 46.

Chapter 50. A Huge Burst out of a Shotgun

Unpublished sources:
Interviews
Archives: Gilley archive; Lewis House Museum; Trinity Foundation archive

Published Sources:
This chapter owes a debt to Tosches for the list of Jerry Lee Lewis' problems. Other sources include: *LAT* 9/4/91; UPI 9/11/91; Shepard; Hadden and Swann; *RS* 7/14/88; *GG* 9/18/85; Schaffer and Todd; *Houston Post* 1/28/90; *CB* 1976; 1974 press release, Gilley archive; *LAT* 4/1/89, *NYT* 9/27/90; Dortch; *NSW* 4/6/87; UPI 8/12/91 and 8/13/91; Reuters 7/16/91; Swaggart 1984 (*River*); Schultze 1991; Lundy.

217   "I can't do it": Swaggart 1984 (*River*), p. 216.
217   "like cursing me": Swaggart 1984 (*River*), p. 216.
218   "Radio is like a": Schaffer and Todd, p. 149.
218   "Just a bunch of tin": 1974 press release from Lewis House Museum.
218   "Hey now! Watch your . . . front door": *Chicago Tribune* 7/25/88.
221   "All at once she turned": Reuters 8/12/91.
221   "I was overcome": Reuters 8/12/91.

Chapter 51. "Don't Ever Let Me Get Like That"

Unpublished sources:
Interviews
Archives: Lewis House Museum, Williams archive

Published Sources:
This chapter owes a debt to Tosches for the information about Jerry Lee Lewis' legal and health problems. Other sources include: Swaggart 1984 (*River*); CB 1976 (clipping); *Houston Post* 6/27/76; Lewis 1982; *Memphis Flyer* 4/26/90; *Detroit Free Press* 10/2/83.

222   "I almost hate to answer": Tosches, p. 247.

Chapter 52. The Principality of the Powers of the Air

Unpublished sources:
Interviews
Archives: Lewis House Museum, Lee archive

Published Sources:
This chapter owes a debt to Tosches for the information on Jerry Lee Lewis' legal and personal problems. Other sources include: *LAT* 5/15/87; Internet Infidels; CB 1976 (clipping); *NYT* 9/27/90; *Time* 2/17/86; Armstrong; Horsfield; Schultze 1991; *Christian Science Monitor* 10/3/84; Shepard; Dortch; *Town Talk* 4/12/80; *The Evangelist* August 1979; BRE 7/3/80; "Gilley Gram" October 1978, from Lewis House Museum; Schaffer and Todd; *Christian Life* June 1979, cited in *The Evangelist* August 1979; *BR Mag* 9/86; O'Rourke; *NSW* 4/6/87; *BRMA* 12/28/82; *BRMA* 2/20/88; Swaggart 1984 (*River*).

224   "Wherein in time": Ephesians 2:2–3: *The Holy Bible*.
225   "It can't be too long": Packard, p. 74.
225   15,000 evangelical leaders: Schultze 1990, pp. 223–24. The poll was the *Times Mirror* poll two weeks before the election, which classified a group of people it surveyed as "moralists" and concluded 93% of them would vote for Bush.
227   "My mother saw through": Schaffer and Todd, p. 147.
229   "most of Louisiana is unaware": *Town Talk* 4/12/80.
229   "to thousands in the": *Christian Life* 6/79, cited in *The Evangelist* August 1979.
230   "packaged": *Town Talk* 4/12/80.
230   "pompadoured pretty-boys": *LAT* 2/22/88.

Chapter 53. The Mission of the Air

Unpublished sources:
Interviews
Archives: Lee archive

Published Sources:
Christian Life 6/79, cited in *The Evangelist* August 1979; Blumhofer 1989; *People* 9/15/80; *BRMA* 7/2/80; *Town Talk* 4/12/80; Swaggart 1984 (*River*); *The Evangelist* August 1979; *BRST* 10/6/80; Swaggart 1981 (*Preacher*); *The Evangelist*, July 1986;

NYT 9/27/90; *People* 3/15/81; *Jacksonville Times-Union* 1/30/81; *Norfolk Virginian-Pilot*, 6/29/89; *BRMA* 4/ 2/81; Horsfield; Shepard; "Big Time Religion"; *BRMA* 12/28/82; *NSW* 5/30/83; *BRMA* 6/26/84.

233 "Great announcements of mighty": *The Evangelist* September 1986, p. 22.
233 "The man closed the scenario": *The Evangelist*, September 1986, p. 13.
233 "The closer the light": Swaggart 1991 (*Cup*), p. 131.
234 "I wanna put out the": "Prophet or Profit?" 1980.
234 "healthy ego": *BRE* 7/3/80.
234 "a wealthy man": *BRE* 7/3/80.
234 "nothing but dusty old": *BRE* 7/3/80.
234 "vile, profligate, debased, filthy": *BRE* 7/3/80.
235 "We must have the": *BRE* 7/3/80.
235 "I been watching him": *BRMA* 7/2/80.
235 "all of a sudden": Schaffer and Todd, p. 149.
236 "Ronald Reagan will be shot": *BRMA* 4/2/81.
237 "systematic, sophisticated, and manipulative": *BRMA* 12/28/82.

Chapter 54. Guarding the Temple

Unpublished sources:
Interviews
Archives: Lee archive

Published Sources:
BRMA 6/14/83; *Town Talk* 4/12/80; Shepard; UPI 8/12/91; Reuters 8/6/91; *NOTP* 3/4/88; Dortch; UPI 7/16/91; UPI 8/13/91; Swaggart 1984 (*River*); *BRST* 4/16/87; *PHSE* July 1988; *BRMA* 1/22/82; *RS* 7/14/88; Swaggart 1982 (*Rebellion*); *People* 10/27/86; "I Am What I Am"; *Buffalo News*, 7/2/89; *Memphis Commercial Appeal* 8/13/80; Swaggart 1981 (*Preacher*); *The Holy Bible*; Lundy.

239 "We plan to become": *The Evangelist*, August 1979, p. 20.
240 "A woman can either": Schaffer and Todd, pp. 143–44.
240 "too many times the": Swaggart 1981 (*Preacher*), p. 27.
240 "preachers, sitting for hours": Swaggart 1981 (*Preacher*), p. 28.
241 "get her in bed": *NOTP* 3/4/88.
241 "I don't want this": UPI 8/12/91.
242 "tell that no good": Answer #21 to petition in *Jimmy Swaggart Evangelistic Association versus Janet Lynn Breland, wife of/and Dwain Johnson.*
242 "I want to tell you": Answer #27 to petition in *Jimmy Swaggart Evangelistic Association versus Janet Lynn Breland, wife of/and Dwain Johnson.*
243 "Whosoever among you": Lewis 1982, p. 364.
244 "Why Jimmy Swaggart! Son": "I Am What I Am."
244 "In the last few": Swaggart 1982 (*Victory*), p. 20.
245 "There is nothing like": *BRST* 5/6/83.
245 "biscuit and syrup kind": *CB* October 1987, p. 51.
245 "left-hand 'walks' . . . ear of Lazarus": *NSW* 5/30/83.
246 "screaming and crying out": Swaggart 1982 (*Rebellion*), p. 20.
246 "You've got to run": Swaggart 1982 (*Rebellion*), p. 22.

Chapter 55. Petra

Unpublished sources:
Interviews

Published Sources:
Grun; Swaggart 1982 (*Sodom*); Swaggart 1986, (*Christian Rock*); Metzger and Coogan; BRMA 12/28/82; Swaggart 1981 (*Preacher*).

248 "similar to Las Vegas": Swaggart 1982 (*Victory*), p. 9.
248 "one of those 'odd' ": Swaggart 1982 (*Victory*), p. 23.
248 "The rock star staggers": Swaggart 1982 (*Victory*), p. 23.
248 "strait is the gate": Matthew 7:14: *The Holy Bible.*
248 "One could sense": Swaggart 1982 (*Victory*), p. 22.
249 "wound to his maleness": Johnson 1974, p. 12.
249 "attacks the Christian with": Swaggart 1982 (*Victory*), p. 20.
250 "for he is the master of it": Swaggart 1982 (*Victory*), p. 26.

Chapter 56. Brimstone

Unpublished sources:
Interviews
Archives: WBRZ-TV archive; Lee archive

Published Sources:
Diocese of Baton Rouge Demographic Analysis; *Ministries Today* March/April 1991; Appel; *The Evangelist* March 1984; NSW 5/30/83; BRMA 9/26/84; BRMA 11/15/83; NSW 1/9/84; *The Evangelist* June 1985; Georgia Bulletin of the Catholic Archdiocese of Atlanta; *The Nation* 4/11/87; *Time* 3/16/87; GG 9/18/85; *Washington Journalism Review* May 1989; "Swaggart Response"; BRMA 6/14/83; BRMA 11/15/83; "Big Time Religion."

251 "Oh, there are plenty . . . double-barrelled shotgun!": Swaggart 1982 (*Sodom*), pp. 13–14.
251 "complete contradiction of the word": RS 7/14/88, p. 98.
251 "pitiful" for "[thinking] they": NSW 5/30/83.
252 "Catholics . . . believe that they": MJ July/August 1986, p. 45.
252 "Most Catholics are . . . Mardi Gras": MJ Jul/Aug 1986, p. 42.
252 "the people have . . . intellectual apathy": BRMA 6/4/83.
252 "sects . . . have taken advantage": *Time* 3/16/87.
253 "a very efficient, Spartan type": Dixie 1/27/85, p. 10.
253 "I went from . . . starving children": Dixie 1/27/85, p. 10.
255 "I always say": Schaffer and Todd, p. 148.
255 "Jimmy, I don't like this": "Big Time Religion."
256 "that bunch down there . . . sucking eggs": BRMA 5/28/83.
256 "This ministry is totally": NSW 5/30/83.
257 "I hate alcohol": Schaffer and Todd, p. 138.
258 "No, John, . . . it was": *Washington Journalism Review* May 1989, p. 21.
258 "king of the TV evangelists": NSW 5/30/83.
259 "The pervasive net": Schultze 1991, p. 242.
259 "try to pick apart": BRMA 6/9/83.

259   "None of the things": *NSW* 1/9/84.
259   "does not accept Jesus": *NSW* 1/9/84.
259   "It was a distortion": *The Evangelist* March 1984, p. 37.
260   "Mother Teresa is going": *NSW* 1/9/84.
260   "Catholics, Jews, and some Protestants": *Dixie* 1/27/85, p. 8.
260   "to suggest that the": *NSW* 1/9/84.
260   "I admire what Mother Teresa": *The Evangelist* March 1984, p. 37.
260   "because of their rejection": *Dixie* 1/27/85, p. 8.
260   "the Jewish people started . . . eternally lost": *The Evangelist* April 1985, p. 14.
261   "The tree that bears": *The Evangelist* March 1984, p. 37.
261   "you had the media": Swaggart 1991 (*Cup*).

Chapter 57. A Son of the Reformation

Unpublished sources:
Interviews
Archives: Lee archive

Published Sources:
Shepard; Packard; Harrell 1975; Schultze 1990; *The Evangelist* March 1985; *The Evangelist* July 1985; *RS* 7/14/88; Lundy.

262   "policy adviser": *BRMA* 9/26/84.
262   "Jimmy got a laugh" However, Jimmy would later write that in about 1983, he was "called to Washington" to meet with Reagan's Cabinet about a crisis concerning two jailed preachers (*The Evangelist* March 1993).
262   "show as much courage": *Catholic Twin Circle* 4/14/85.
262   "An apology is definitely": *BRMA* 9/26/84.
263   "been to various meetings": *BRMA* 9/26/84.
263   "Communist insurgency . . . evil empire": *The Evangelist* March 1985, p. 10.
264   "pig-ignorant . . . telling the truth": *Commonweal* 12/26/86.
264   "rendered the commission": *The Evangelist* November 1984, p. 26.
265   "They tried to portray": *The Evangelist* June 1985, p. 21.
265   "presume to read or possess": *The Evangelist* May 1985, p. 33.
265   "the bright thoughts": *BRMA* 2/16/85.
265   "preach what I tell you": *Dixie* 1/27/85, p. 7.
265   "If you don't like": *Dixie* 1/27/85, p. 7.
265   "Swaggart, more than": *GG* 9/18/85, p. 24.
266   "economists might forget": *GG* 9/18/85 p. 23.

Chapter 58. "I Don't Want This Thing to Come Back and Haunt Me"

Unpublished sources:
Interviews

Published Sources:
Shepard; *PHSE* January 1989; *BRMA* 4/14/88; *NOTP* 3/4/88; UPI 7/16/91; *PHSE* September 1989; Dortch; Reuters 8/14/91; Swaggart 1991 (*Cup*); *Charlotte Observer* 3/26/87; *Time* 2/17/86; Stewart; Reuters 8/12/91; Reuters 8/6/91; *BRMA* 3/2/88; Lundy.

267 "take care": *PHSE* January 1989 p. 194.
270 fathered an illegitimate child: this rumor, like the Carlos Marcello and "Satan's messenger" rumors, was false.
270 "Jimmy, I don't want this thing": UPI 8/12/91.
270 "I realized I either had": Reuters 8/6/91.

Chapter 59. The Highland Road

Unpublished sources:
Interviews
Archives: WBRZ archive

Published Sources:
BRMA 12/28/82; historical marker, Catfish Town, Baton Rouge; UPI 12/14/91; *RS* 7/14/88; Schaffer and Todd; GG 9/18/85; *Dixie* 1/27/85; WBRZ-TV unpublished video archives on Jimmy Swaggart; "The Evangelist"; *The Evangelist*, June 1985.

273 "I don't want any walls . . . all I want": Schaffer and Todd, p. 151.
274 "It only has two . . . something I'm not": *MJ* July/August 1986, p. 44.
274 "We have no investments": *Dixie* 1/27/85, p. 8.
274 "Crazies": *Dixie* 1/27/85, p. 8.
274 "we're like public property": *MJ* July/August 1986, p. 44.

Chapter 60. Gorman and Bakker

Unpublished sources:
Interviews

Published Sources:
This chapter owes a debt to Charles Shepard's detailed accounts of affairs at PTL in the *Charlotte Observer* and *Forgiven*. Other sources include *USNWR* 4/11/88; *GR* 6/10/88; *GR* 11/19/90; *LAT* 3/25/87; *BRST* 1/30/89; *BRST* 5/24/88; "The Holy Truth"; *Time* 2/17/86. *RS* 7/14/88; *NOTP* 3/4/88; Reuters 8/12/91; *BRMA* 3/2/88; Reuters 8/12/91; *BRMA* 5/16/87; *BRST* 3/30/88; UPI 8/12/91; *BRMA* 2/22/88; UPI 9/13/91; *BRMA* 11/4/89; *BRST* 11/10/89; *BRMA* 2/20/88; Reuters 8/6/91; *PHSE* July 1988; Dortch; *Time* 4/6/87; Swaggart 1991 (*Cup*).

275 "a TV and VCR": Shepard, p. 491.
276 "I didn't know who else": UPI 7/16/91.
276 "and at that very time": *NOTP* 3/4/88.
277 "had not repented": *BRMA* 3/2/88.
277 "Them that sin": I Timothy 20:5: *The Holy Bible*.
277 "You're going to have": *NOTP* 3/4/88.
278 "If they still want": *NOTP* 3/4/88.
278 "numerous adulterous and illicit": *BRMA* 3/2/88.
278 "millions are deceived": *LAT* 2/22/88.
278 "I don't know how much": Shepard, p. 424.
279 "We drive our preachers": Shepard, p. 424.
279 "report feelings of shame": *Pentecostal Evangel* 4/24/88, p. 6.
280 "If he gets Gorman": *Charlotte Observer* 3/26/88.
280 "You know, it's a strange": *The Evangelist* September 1986, p. 45.

281   "I want it clearly understood": *BRMA* 3/2/88.
281   "unscriptural lascivious conduct": *BRMA* 3/2/88.
282   "Foolishly, Jim Bakker": Dortch, p. 144.
282   "was an unsavory situation": Swaggart 1991 (*Cup*), p. 312.
282   "safe haven": *PHSE* January 1989, p. 194.
283   "Your superintendent": Dortch, p. 146.
283   "Jimmy Swaggart, you are": Dortch, p. 146.
283   "You be quiet": Dortch, p. 147.
283   "crossed his desk": Shepard, p. 428.
285   "if a preacher of the Gospel is caught": *The Evangelist* December 1986, p. 46.

Chapter 61. Do Not Fail

Unpublished sources:
Interviews
Archives: Winzenburg archive; WBRZ-TV archive, Lee archive

Published Sources:
Schultze 1991; *RS* 7/14/88; *NOTP* 8/18/88; *GR* 6/10/88; *GR* 11/19/90; *PHSE* July 1988; *BRST* 1/30/89; *BRST* 5/24/88; *The Evangelist*, December 1986; *The Evangelist*, October 1987; *The Evangelist*, February 1988; *Dallas Morning News* 8/25/86; *BRMA* 2/20/88.

286   "God has ... given me": *GG* 9/18/85, p. 25.
286   "God spoke to my heart": Winzenburg archive; harvest cite was taken off the air by Winzenburg.
287   "D-day or Delay": Schultze 1991, pp. 58, 60.
287   "every man in our own tongue": Acts 2:1–4: *The Holy Bible*.
287   "a prostitution-related offense": *BRMA* 2/25/88.
288   "Do you want a date?": *PHSE* July 1988, p. 123.
288   "No ... I can prove it": *GR* 6/10/88, p. 4.
288   "All I want ... Let me see what I've got": *PHSE* July 1988, p. 123. She later told Geraldo Rivera that Jimmy let her out of the car and came back in an hour with $20 (*GR* 6/10/88, p. 4).
289   "put the telecast on ... you to say!": *RS* 7/14/88, p. 98.
289   "charnal [sic] house of the damned": *GG* 9/18/85, p. 24.

Chapter 62. Francesville

Unpublished sources:
Interviews
Archives: Lee archive

Published Sources:
Swaggart 1984 (*River*); fundraising letter 6/22/93; *BR Mag* September 1986; *RS* 7/14/88; *Dixie* 1/27/85; *MJ* July/August 1986; *CB* October 1987; *The Evangelist* July 1985.

291   "the perfect marketing mix": *GG* 9/18/85, p. 23.
291   "I have heard Jimmy": Schaffer and Todd, p. 154.
292   "I'm not a weakling": Schaffer and Todd, p. 137.

294 "just praising the Lord": *BR* Mag September 1986, p. 46.
297 "He'd notice": *BR* Mag September 1986, p. 72.
297 "I wouldn't change my life": *BR* Mag September 1986, p. 72.
298 "I guess this will go": *People* 10/27/86, p. 122.
300 "The overall temperature . . . on one leg": *Dixie* 1/27/85, p. 9.

Chapter 63. The "Hostile Takeover"

Unpublished sources:
Interviews; notes from news reports; sermon notes
Archives: Trinity Foundation archive; Lee archive; Winzenburg archive; WBRZ-TV archive

Published Sources:
CB October 1987; *AJ/AC* 3/20/88; UPI 7/18/91; *Houston Chronicle* 5/2/92; *BRMA* 5/4/87; *LAT* 5/22/88; *NOTP* 9/24/88; *BRST* 3/17/88; *The Evangelist* September 1986; Trinity Foundation Fact Sheet; printed materials from the Trinity Foundation; Schaffer and Todd; *Greater Baton Rouge Business Report*, January 1989; UPI 7/16/91; UPI 8/12/91; . Reuters 8/12/91; UPI 9/12/91; *BRMA* 3/2/88; Reuters 9/13/91; Reuters 7/16/91; UPI 9/13/91; Dortch; *NSW* 4/6/87; *WP* 6/28/89; Shepard; Stewart; Nauer; *PHSE* January 1989; *BRMA* 3/25/87; *LAT* 3/25/87; *NSW* 4/6/87; *Time* 4/6/87; unlabeled video clip from Trinity Foundation archive; "The Holy Truth"; Penner; *Charlotte Observer* 3/24/87; *LAT* 3/12/87; *WP* 3/27/87; *LAT* 2/22/88; *WP* 4/8/87; *PHSE* July 1988; *BRST* 4/16/87; *BRST* 1/14/84; *BRST* 1/19/84; *BRMA* 1/26/84; *BRST* 5/1/87; *BRMA* 5/4/87; *BRMA* 6/22/87; *LAT* 3/16/91; *BRMA* 5/16/87; *LAT* 5/15/87; *AJ/AC* 3/20/88; *Time* 2/15/88; *USNWR* 6/6/87; Winzenburg notes 6/22/87; *The Evangelist* September 1987; *AJ/AC* 2/24/88; *BRMA* 2/20/88; *BRST* 3/17/88; undated video clip from Winzenburg archive of Larry King's interview of Art Harris; Debra Murphree raw interview footage, January 1988, WBRZ archive; *GR* 6/10/88; *BRST* 5/24/88; *BRMA* 2/25/88; *RS* 7/14/88; *Life* June 1987; Lundy.

301 "fanatics, extremists, and ideologues": *The Evangelist* September 1986, p. 41.
301 "a vacuum of leadership": *The Evangelist* September 1986, p. 41.
302 "a hundredfold": Reprint of Trinity Foundation testimony before Ways and Means Subcommittee, 1986.
302 "like a huge stanchion . . . fight this thing": Swaggart 1991 (*Cup*), pp. 75–76.
306 "It was Swaggart's duty": Stewart, p. 69.
306 "in our effort to ascertain": Swaggart 1991 (*Cup*), p. 317.
306 "someone told us": Swaggart 1991 (*Cup*), p. 318.
307 "PTL is arrogant, proud": Shepard, p. 484.
307 "to seek a biblical solution": *Charlotte Observer* 3/26/87.
308 "their whole lives disintegrated": Shepard, p. 493.
308 "I know of ministers": Shepard, p. 494.
309 "Please believe": Dortch, pp. 140–41.
309 "learn what she can": Dortch, p. 142.
309 "unholy trio": Stewart, p. 104.
310 "hostile takeover": Swaggart 1991 (*Cup*), p. 328. Grutman had had past flirtations with both sides of the televangelist world: he had defended *Penthouse* in a suit filed by Falwell; Falwell had then hired him to sue *Hustler* in 1988.
310 "take him home": *USNWR* 4/6/87.

310   "I sorrowfully acknowledge": Bakker, p. 55.
311   "dirtier laundry": Stewart, p. 103.
311   "rival evangelist": *Time* 4/6/87.
312   "call off his dogs": *LAT* 3/25/87.
313   "quite funny": Shepard, p. 523.
313   "dirty things": Stewart, p. 105.
313   "sowing discord among": *LAT* 3/25/87.
313   "topple anything that's unappealing": *LAT* 3/25/87.
314   "The last place in the world": *Time* 4/6/87.
314   "squeezed the triggers . . . pulled no punches": Swaggart 1991 (*Cup*), p. 329.
314   "Then, Frances came on": Swaggart 1991 (*Cup*), p. 330.
315   "I'm a target": *WP* 3/26/87.
315   "if it does hurt": *BRMA* 3/25/87.
315   "It's his satellite: *BRMA* 3/25/87.
316   "That sounds awful conceited . . . won't stand for it": *WP* 4/8/87.
319   "religious broadcaster, a business man": *US News and World Report* 4/6/87.
319   "disproportionately older . . . female": *US News and World Report* 4/6/87.
319   "hog-jowled . . . Christians": Packard, p. 101.
319   "saints don't work": *Chicago Tribune* 12/31/95.
320   "At first the sweet . . . talk with [me] sometime": notes, Winzenburg archive.
321   "All of a sudden": Untitled news clipping from Winzenburg archive, dated 3/5/88; Winzenburg notes.
321   "I'm scared to death": *LAT* 3/5/88.
321   "is with me all the time": *Time* 3/7/88.
321   "Are you going to believe": Swaggart 1991 (*Cup*), p. 331.
321   "dirty, smelly fishermen": notes from sermon, date unavailable.
324   "to the whole world": *Time* 4/6/87.
324   "That's Jimmy Swaggart": *RS* 7/14/88, p. 151.
325   "I have to fight": Swaggart 1991 (*Cup*), pp. 73–76.
325   "So this is the one": Swaggart 1991 (*Cup*), pp. 30–31.

Chapter 64. October 17, 1987

Unpublished sources:
Interviews
Archives: Lewis House Museum; Lee archive

Published Sources:
"Fall From Grace"; *AJ/AC* 5/22/88; *The Evangelist* May 1987; *The Evangelist* November 1987; Shepard; *BRST* 3/17/88; *NOTP* 8/18/88; *Charlotte Observer* 8/18/88; *RS*, 7/14/88; *PHSE* July 1988; *BRST* 5/24/88; WBRZ archive raw video footage; *GR* 6/10/88; CNN broadcast 6/28/91; *BRMA* 2/20/88; UPI 6/28/91; Reuters 9/13/91; *LAT* 5/22/88; *WP* 2/22/88; *The Evangelist* February 1988; *AJ/AC* 2/24/88; *The Charlotte Observer* 2/26/88 and 3/26/88; *LAT* 3/5/88; Schultze 1991; *LAT* 3/16/91; *Christianity Today* 12/11/87; *Charlotte Observer* 8/22/87; *Time* 2/15/88; Balmer; *The Nation* 3/19/88; NOTP 2/20/88; *LAT* 2/20/88; Lundy.

326   "Watergate of evangelical Christianity": *Time* 3/7/88.
326   "probably the greatest scab": Shepard, p. 548.
326   "During all of 1987": Swaggart 1991 (*Cup*), p. 16.

327 "You know, because he": *BRMA* 2/25/88.
328 "He's here": CNN 6/28/91.
328 "It kept circling": *GR* 6/10/88.
328 "Bud, what are you doing": CNN 6/28/91.
328 "He mentioned jobs": *NYT* 2/28/88; *Charlotte Observer* 3/26/88.
329 "If those women go to hell": CNN 6/28/91.
329 "How could you": CNN 6/28/91.
329 "I'm sorry I've hurt you": CNN 6/28/91.
332 "Demon powers, fallen angels": *RS* 7/14/88, p. 152.
332 "every single demon": Swaggart 1991 (*Cup*), p. 301
333 "threw greater light": *The Evangelist* February 1988, p. 57.
333 "sweep it under the rug": *PHSE* July 1988, p. 106.
333 "The preacher today": *The Evangelist* September 1987.
333 "In this period of time": Swaggart 1991 (*Satan*), p. 25.
335 "You don't remember me": *RS* 7/14/88, p. 152.
336 "for the sole purpose": *The Evangelist* February 1988, p. 57.
337 "something pornographic": *BRMA* 2/20/88.
338 "they were all in": *BRMA* 2/20/88.
338 "perform pornographic acts": *Charlotte Observer* 2/25/88.

Chapter 65. I Have Sinned

Unpublished sources:
Interviews
Archives: WBRZ-TV archive; Lee archive; Winzenburg archive

Published Sources:
"Fall From Grace"; Packard; *BRMA* 2/22/88; *NOTP* 2/22/88; *Charlotte Observer* 8/18/88; *BRMA* 4/14/88; *BRMA* 6/7/88; *LAT* 3/14/88; *NYT* 2/22/88; *BRST* 3/18/94; *Chicago Tribune* 4/22/88; *Time* 3/7/88; *RS* 7/14/88; *AJ/AC* 2/24/88; *Pentecostal Evangel*, 4/17/88; *Charlotte Observer* 3/4/88; *NYT* 2/28/88; *LAT* 3/5/88; *People* 3/7/88; *BRMA* 2/23/88; *NOTP* 2/23/88; *PHSE* July 1988; CNN broadcast 6/28/91; *NSW* 2/29/88; *BRMA* 2/25/88; *BRMA* 2/27/88; *NOTP* 2/24/88; *NSW* 3/7/88; *GR* 11/19/90; *The Evangelist* June 1989; *BRMA* 3/2/88; *NYT* 3/4/88; *NYT* 3/7/88; *BRST* 3/30/88; *BRMA* 3/30/88; Swaggart 1991 (*Cup*); *BRST* 3/29/88; *BRST* 4/9/88; *Time* 4/18/88; *BRST* 3/18/94; *Charlotte Observer* 4/14/88; *LAT* 4/4/88; *Charlotte Observer* 4/4/88; *LAT* 3/16/91; Reuters 10/15/91; Carnes 1992; *NOTP* 9/24/88; *PHSE* January 1989; *BRMA* 5/23/88; *BRMA* 5/24/88; *Charlotte Observer* 5/23/88; *NOTP* 6/7/88; *BRMA* 6/16/88; *Greater Baton Rouge Business Report*, January 1989; *LAT* 3/16/91; *The Evangelist* September/October 1990; *AJ/AC* 10/30/88; *AJ/AC* 6/13/88; *LAT* 5/22/88; *Baton Rouge Sunday Advocate* 2/19/89; *BRST* 1/30/89; Dortch; Schultze 1990; *AJ/AC* 6/24/89; *The Evangelist* May 1989; *The Evangelist* July 1989; *The Evangelist* October 1989; *BRST* 1/26/84; Lundy.

339 "I do not plan": video clip, Winzenburg archive.
339 "God never gave a man": video clip, Winzenburg archive.
339 "as far as the Gospel has": video clip, Winzenburg archive.
339 "I have sinned against you": video clip, Winzenburg archive.
340 "I love you": video clip, Winzenburg archive.
340 "And to the hundreds": video clip, Winzenburg archive.

341   "which helped bring": *BRMA* 2/22/88.
341   "We forgive you, Jimmy!": *NOTP* 2/22/88; *LAT* 2/22/88.
341   "It was fabulous television": Schultze 1991, p. 39.
342   "Ye who are without sin": *LAT* 2/22/88.
342   "My heart has been": *BRMA* 2/22/88.
342   "disgusting, sobbing whimpering": *LAT* 2/27/88.
343   "deeply rooted in the Southern": *NYT* 2/25/88.
343   "pitiful, flawed preacher": *LAT* 3/5/88.
343   "agonizing in prayer": Winzenburg notes, p. 95.
344   "Jimmy is straight out": *The Nation* 3/5/88.
344   "The whole world": *NYT* 2/28/88.
344   "The family always held Jimmy": *NYT* 2/28/88.
346   "We're in a PR business": "Nightline" 2/22/88.
346   "Justice can sometimes . . . for his failure": *LAT* 2/22/88.
347   "in the hands of the Lord": *LAT* 2/22/88.
347   "He tried and tried": *NOTP* 2/23/88.
347   fascination with pornography: *BRST* 3/17/88; *RS* 7/14/88, p. 110; *BRMA* 2/23/88; *LAT* 3/5/88; *The Nation* 3/5/88; UPI 7/9/91.
348   "There was absolutely no attack": Swaggart 1991 (*Satan*), p. 68.
348   "Dortching": Shepard, p. 458.
348   "I believe that those": "Nightline" 2/27/88.
349   "Where do you find . . . gift from God" : *NOTP* 2/24/88.
350   "I seen him drive": *BRMA* 2/25/88.
350   "unbroken precedent": *BRST* 2/29/88.
351   "most debilitating powers . . . this Gospel works!": *NYT* 3/4/88.
351   "If you ladies . . . rolled into one week": *BRST* 2/29/88.
351   "These days never ended": *BRST* 2/29/88.
352   "Swaggart: He Threatens . . . he rebelled": Undated clipping, Lewis House Museum.
352   Jimmy was a sex addict: *AJ/AC* 5/22/88.
352   "You cannot cover sin": *Time* 2/29/88.
352   "I've heard him walking": Winzenburg archive videotape.
353   "We're not perfect": Winzenburg archive videotape.
353   "a terrible foreboding spirit": Swaggart 1991 (*Cup*), p. 5.
353   "You have wrecked everything": Swaggart 1991 (*Cup*), pp. 5–6.
353   release that also must have relieved Frances: Swaggart 1991 (*Cup*), p. 10.
354   "unless the rapture occurs first": *BRST* 4/9/88.
354   "Satan says it's over!": *RS* 7/14/88, p. 103.
354   "I'll rise again": *RS* 7/14/88, p. 103.
354   "never to say a derogatory": BRMA 4/9/88.
355   "I just casually mentioned": Swaggart 1991 (*Cup*), pp. 56–57. It was widely reported that he admitted this, but Turnage said the Assemblies of God doesn't reveal the nature of a minister's failure.
355   wished he was dead: *BRST* 5/2/88.
355   "I have suffered": *BRMA* 4/6/88; *Time* 4/11/88.
355   "most crucial time of": *BRST* 5/2/88.
356   "I don't understand it": *BRST* 5/2/88.
356   "Mr. Riviera": *GR* 5/25/88.

356 "I've preached to some": *RS* 7/14/88, p. 152.
357 "I have to fight": *RS* 7/14/88, p. 152.
357 "CNN is going to be": *RS* 7/14/88, p. 152.
357 "Sister, give me": *RS* 7/14/88, p. 152.
357 "trashy journalism and trashy": unlabeled video clip from Winzenburg archive.
357 "They don't bother me": *BRST* 6/16/88.
358 "I do not deny": *BRST* 5/26/88.
359 "Reverend Swaggart vehemently": February 1989 video clip, Trinity Foundation archive.
360 "You will be rewarded": *PHSE* February 1989, p. 61
360 "Beat me, bitch": *PHSE* February 1989, p. 60.
360 "pornographic fairy tale": *BRMA* 2/7/89.
360 "It was very interesting": *BRMA* 2/7/89.
360 "then everybody gets in line": *PHSE* February 1989, p. 42.
361 "pretend like he was going": Lundy, p. 151.
362 "unconstitutionally tangles Louisiana": *BRMA* 2/22/89.
363 "torrent of abuse": 12/5/89 fundraising letter, Lee archive.
363 "my name was slandered . . . domestic, or physical": 12/5/89 fundraising letter, Lee archive.
363 "no one knows exactly": 12/5/89 fundraising letter, Lee archive.

Chapter 66. Comeback

Unpublished sources:
Interviews
Archives: Lewis House Museum; Lee archive; Winzenburg archive

Published Sources:
Dallas Morning News 8/25/86 and 2/2/92; *Baton Rouge Sunday Advocate* 2/19/89; *LAT* 3/16/91; *BRST* 11/10/89; *BRMA* 11/4/89; *BRMA* 11/4/89; *UPI* 7/7/91; *LAT* 4/1/89; *AJ/AC* 6/29/89; *The Evangelist* October 1989; *UPI* 10/19/91; *The Evangelist* March 1990; *The Evangelist* June 1990; *GR* 11/19/90; *UPI* 12/14/91; *BRST* 1/17/90.

364 "a forbidden tax": *BRST* 1/17/90.
365 "Jim and Tammy Bakker movie": Swaggart 1991 (*Cup*), p. 310.
365 "the world's largest Pentecostal": *The Evangelist* April 1990.
366 "were able to stand": Swaggart 1991 (*Cup*), pp. x–xi.

Chapter 67. Unfinished Business

Unpublished sources:
Interviews
Archives: Lewis House Museum; Trinity Foundation archive

Published Sources:
"Urban Cowboy"; Swaggart 1984 (*River*); Swaggart 1991 (*Cup*); *Philadelphia Inquirer* 2/24/88; *GR* 5/22/88; *RS* 7/14/88; Lundy.

368 "his wife, Frances, didn't love": Lundy, p. 145.
368 "had no interest in him": Lundy, p. 148.
368 damning and disturbing: *PHSE* July 1988.

368 "The addict who focuses on children": Carnes 1992, p. 45.
369 "some relative took [Jimmy] down to some bawdy house": unlabeled video clip, Trinity Foundation archive.
369 "major factor in the transmission": Carnes 1992, p. 46.
369 "Jesus spoke to": *MJ* July/August 1986, p. 38.
370 "a constant theme in all addictions" Carnes 1992, p. 68.
370 awakened by fear: *RS* 7/14/88, p. 106.
370 "A preacher of the gospel": Swaggart 1981 (*The Preacher*), p. 5.
370 "Addiction is a relationship": Carnes 1992, p. 72
371 "Absolutely nothing untoward": Swaggart 1991 (*Satan*), p. 24.
371 "Immediately after the horror . . . particular manner": Swaggart 1991 (*Satan*), p. 60.
371 "I will gain the victory": Swaggart 1991 (*Satan*), p. 62.
371 "I wanted so much": Swaggart 1991 (*Satan*), p. 63.
372 about the time of the Johnson suit video clip of Larry King Live from Winzenburg archive: video clip from Winzenburg archive.
372 "Satan came back again": Swaggart 1991 (*Satan*), pp. 26–27.

Chapter 68. Do Nothing

Unpublished sources:
Interviews; notes from broadcasts; sermon notes
Archives: Winzenburg archive

Published Sources:
Reuters 8/13/91; UPI 6/28/91; Swaggart 1991 (*Cup*); undated video clip of "Entertainment Tonight" segment, Winzenburg archive; UPI 7/7/91; UPI 7/8/91; UPI 7/15/91; UPI 7/9/91; UPI 8/6/91; UPI 9/11/91; Reuters 9/10/91; UPI 9/10/91; Reuters 8/12/91; Reuters 8/14/91; *People* 11/4/91; Reuters 9/7/91; Reuters 9/10/91; *The Evangelist* September/October 1991; *LAT* 10/13/91; Lundy.

373 "I sensed the love of God": Swaggart 1991 (*Cup*), p. 46.
374 "chasing prostitutes for 28 years": CNN 6/27/91 broadcast; UPI 6/28/91.
374 "I'm a fighter": CNN 6/28/91 broadcast.
375 "laying on of hands": UPI 7/16/91.
375 "You don't believe": UPI 8/6/91.
375 "Counsel, you have looked": UPI 8/06/91.
375 "I believed that at the time": Reuters 8/6/91.
375 "Mr. Lee, I think you have": UPI 8/13/91.
376 salary and perks: Gorman said his perks included cars and gasoline for himself and his wife, $29,000 for housing from his church, $16,000 in health insurance, $40,000 in gifts and honoraria for weddings, funerals, and speaking engagements, and $10,000 as an official of the Assemblies in Springfield.
377 "there was an ugly fly": Swaggart 1991 (*Satan*), p. 68.
377 "Had I known": Swaggart 1991 (*Satan*), p. 16.
378 $10 million: UPI 9/13/91; *Houston Chronicle* 5/2/92; Indest had already made arrangements for a private settlement with Gorman. Jimmy, the ministry, and Michael Indest had maliciously defamed Gorman with reckless disregard for the truth. The same three plus Treeby had conspired against him, costing them

$600,000, and they had caused him emotional distress worth $400,000. The remaining $9 million was awarded to Gorman's ministry.

378   "I have never said": Reuters 9/13/91.
378   "I'm just shocked": UPI 9/13/91.
378   "walking pneumonia": Swaggart 1991 (*Satan*), p. 1.
378   "This terrible thing was": Swaggart 1991 (*Satan*), p. 71.
379   "Blessed Assurance": Swaggart 1991 (*Satan*), p. 71.
379   "terrible oppression in my spirit": Swaggart 1991 (*Satan*), p. 73.

Chapter 69. Under the Influence

Unpublished sources:
Interviews

Published Sources:

380   "Jimmy Swaggart swarm": *LAT* 10/18/91.
381   motel nearby that showed porno films: *LAT* 10/13/91.
382   he took the ticket: three weeks later, Jimmy paid the fines by mail. *LAT* 11/6/91.

Chapter 70. The Secret Room

Unpublished sources:
Interviews

Published Sources:
LAT 2/27/88; *LAT* 10/12/91.

383   "Whenever you have problems,": Schaffer and Todd, p. 137.
383   "Four years of horrible struggle": Swaggart 1991 (*Satan*), p. 74.
384   "Jesus' love has never": Swaggart 1991 (*Satan*), p. 75.
385   "Inciting yet controlling": *New York Review of Books* 12/21/89.

Epilogue

Unpublished sources:
Interviews; sermon notes; notes from broadcasts

Published Sources:
Americans United for Separation of Church and State, 1996 download; Schultze 1991; *Houston Post* 5/2/94; *The Holy Bible*; *LAT* 1/15/94.

389   "El Salvador, you can have life!": *Commonweal* 5/8/87.
389   "You're sitting in a lonely hotel room": *Commonweal* 5/8/87.
389   "They have never asked": *LAT* 11/20/93.
390   "life is a meaningless . . . profane worlds": Woodman, p. 20.

Bibliography

A. A. Allen tract undated, from the 1940s-50s, Lewis House Museum.

A. A. Allen tract 1944, Lewis House Museum.

Academic American Encyclopedia. Princeton: Arete Publishing Company, 1980.

Alexander, Bobby C. *Televangelism Reconsidered: Ritual in the Search for Human Community.* Atlanta: Scholars Press, 1994.

Appel, Willa. *Cults in America.* New York: Holt, Rinehart, and Winston, 1983.

Armstrong, Ben. *The Electric Church.* Nashville: Thomas Nelson Publishers, 1979.

Bakker, Jim. *I Was Wrong.* Nashville: Thomas Nelson Publishers, 1996.

Balmer, Randall. *Mine Eyes Have Seen the Glory,* New York: Oxford University Press, 1989.

Bethards, Betty. *The Dream Book.* Petaluma, CA: Inner Light Foundation, 1983.

Bobo, James R. *Statistical Abstract of Louisiana,* Division of Business and Economic Research, Louisiana State University, New Orleans, 1965.

Blumhofer, Edith. *The Assemblies of God,* Vols. I and II. Springfield: Gospel Publishing House 1989.

Burgess, Stanley M., Gary B. McGee, editors, and Patrick H. Alexander, associate editor. *Dictionary of Pentecostal and Charismatic Movements.* Grand Rapids: Zondervan, 1988.

Cantor, Norman F. *The Age of Protest,* New York: Hawthorn Books, 1969.

Carnes, Patrick. *Contrary to Love,* Minneapolis: CompCare Publishers, 1989.

———. *Out of the Shadows,* Minneapolis: CompCare Publishers, 1992.

Cash, W.J. *The Mind of the South.* New York: A. A. Knopf, 1941.

"Christianity, Cults, and Religions." Chart. Torrance, CA: Rose Publishing, 1994.

"Churches, the IRS and Political Activity," internet download, copyright Americans United for Separation of Church and State, 1996.

Cline, I. M. "Climatological Data, Louisiana Section." [n.p.] Vol. XL, No. 9, 1935, p. 8 and p. 14.

Coffin, Tristram P., and Hennig Cohen, *Folklore in America.* Garden City, NY: Doubleday, 1966.

Dayton, Donald W. *Discovering an Evangelical Heritage*. New York: Harper & Row, 1976.

Dorough, C. Dwight. *The Bible Belt Mystique*. Philadelphia: Westminster Press, 1974.

Dortch, Richard. *Integrity, How I Lost It and My Journey Back*. Green Forest, AK: New Leaf Press, 1991.

Dundy, Elaine. *Ferriday, Louisiana: Portrait of a Remarkable American Town*. New York: Donald I. Fine, 1991.

Goldman, Albert. *Elvis*. New York: McGraw-Hill, 1981.

Goodman, Felicitas D. *Speaking in Tongues*. Chicago: University of Chicago Press, 1972.

Grun, Bernard. *Timetables of History*, Third Revised Edition. New York: Simon and Schuster, 1991.

Hadden, Jeffrey K., and Charles E. Swann. *Prime Time Preachers: The Rising Power of Televangelism*. Reading, MA: Addison-Wesley Publishing Co., 1981.

Harrell, David Edwin, Jr. *All Things Are Possible*. Bloomington and London: University of Indiana Press, 1975.

———. *Oral Roberts: An American Life*. Bloomington: University of Indiana Press, 1985.

Herbers, John. *The Lost Priority*. New York: Funk and Wagnalls 1970.

"High School Confidential." Film. Republic Pictures, 1958.

The Holy Bible. London: The British and Foreign Bible Society, Oxford University Press, 1954.

"Holy Ghost People." Film. McGraw-Hill Films (date unavailable). University of Southern California Visual Anthropology Archive.

Horsfield, Peter G. *Religious Television*. New York: Longman, 1984.

"I Am What I Am." Film. Hallway Productions, 1987.

Lawsuit Petition and Answer: *Jimmy Swaggart Ministries v. Board of Equalization*, 493 U.S. 378, 384–85 (1990).

Lawsuit Petition and Answer: *Jimmy Swaggart Evangelistic Association versus Janet Lynn Breland, wife of/and Dwain Johnson* (1982).

Johnson, Charles. *The Frontier Camp Meeting*. Dallas: Southern Methodist University Press, 1955.

Johnson, Robert A. *He: Understanding Masculine Psychology*. New York: Harper and Row, 1974.

Jung, Carl. *Man and His Symbols*. Garden City, New York: Doubleday 1964.

Lewis, Anthony, and the *New York Times*. *Portrait of a Decade*. New York: Random House, 1964.

Lewis, Myra, with Murray Silver. *Great Balls of Fire: The Uncensored Story of Jerry Lee Lewis*. New York: Quill 1982.

Lundy, Hunter. *Let Us Prey*. Columbus, Mississippi: Genesis Press, 1999.

Malone, Bill C. *Country Music, U.S.A.* Austin and London: University of Texas Press, 1968.

"Marjoe." Film. Mouser Productions, Inc., 1972.

Metzger, Bruce M., and Michael D. Coogan, editors. *The Oxford Companion to the Bible*. New York: Oxford University Press, 1993.

Nauer, Barbara. *Jimmy Swaggart—Dead Man Rising*, Baton Rouge: Glory Arts 1998.

O'Rourke, P. J. *Holidays in Hell*, New York: Vintage Books 1989.

Packard, William. *Evangelism in America*. New York: Paragon House, 1988.

Penner, James. *Goliath, the Life of Robert Schuller*. Anaheim, CA: New Hope Publishing Co., 1992.

"Powerhouse for God." Film. National Endowment for the Humanities, 1985. University of Southern California Visual Anthropology Archive.

Rhodes, Shari. *Hollywood, Gilley's and the Urban Cowboys*. Dallas: Sydney Publishing, 1980.

Schaffer, James, and Colleen Todd. *Christian Wives*. New York: Doubleday, 1987.

Schultze, Quentin, editor. *American Evangelicals and the Mass Media*. Grand Rapids: Academic Books/ Zondervan, 1990.

———. *Televangelism and American Culture: The Business of Popular Religion*. Grand Rapids: Baker Book House, 1991.

Shepard, Charles. *Forgiven*. New York: Atlantic Monthly Press, 1989.

Sims, Patsy. *Can Somebody Shout Amen! Inside the Tents and Tabernacles of American Revivalists*. Bowling Green: University of Kentucky Press, 1996.

Stagg, Frank, E. Glenn Hinson, and Wayne E. Oates. *Glossolalia: Tongue Speaking in Biblical, Historical, and Psychological Perspective*. Nashville: Abingdon Press, 1967.

Stewart, John. *Holy War*. Enid, Oklahoma: Fireside Publishing and Communications, 1987.

Swaggart, Jimmy. *Biblical Solutions to Marital Problems*. Baton Rouge: Jimmy Swaggart Ministries, 1985.

———. *Christian Rock and Roll*. Baton Rouge: Jimmy Swaggart Ministries, 1986.

———. *The Confession Principle and the Course of Nature*. Baton Rouge: Jimmy Swaggart Ministries, 1984.

———. *The Cup Which My Father Hath Given Me*. Baton Rouge: Jimmy Swaggart Ministries, 1991.

———. *Divorce and Subsequent Remarriage*. Baton Rouge: Jimmy Swaggart Ministries, 1981.

———. *God's Answer to Fear, Depression, and Discouragement*. Baton Rouge: Jimmy Swaggart Ministries, 1986, 1978.

———. *Homosexuality: Its Cause and Its Cure*. Baton Rouge: Jimmy Swaggart Ministries, 1982.

———. *Jimmy Swaggart Bible Commentary, Luke*, Vol. Nine. Baton Rouge: World Evangelism Press, 1996.

———. *Music: The New Pornography*. Baton Rouge: Jimmy Swaggart Ministries, 1984.

———. *The Preacher*. Baton Rouge: Jimmy Swaggart Ministries, 1981.

———. *Questions and Answers*, Vol. 3. Baton Rouge: Jimmy Swaggart Ministries, 1983.

————. *Rape of a Nation*. Baton Rouge: Jimmy Swaggart Ministries, 1985.

————. *Rebellion, Retribution, and Redemption*. Baton Rouge: Jimmy Swaggart Ministries, 1982.

————. *Satan Hath Desired You*. Baton Rouge: Jimmy Swaggart Ministries, 1991.

————. *Sodom and Gomorrah*. Baton Rouge: Jimmy Swaggart Ministries, 1982.

————. *That* Thing. Baton Rouge: Jimmy Swaggart Ministries, 1985.

————. and Robert Paul Lamb. *To Cross a River*. Baton Rouge: Jimmy Swaggart Ministries, 1984.

————. *The Unpardonable Sin*. Baton Rouge: Jimmy Swaggart Ministries, 1983.

————. *Victory over the Flesh*. Baton Rouge: Jimmy Swaggart Ministries, 1982.

Tenney, T. F. *The Flame Still Burns*. Tioga, LA: Focused Light, 1989.

Tosches, Nick. *Hellfire: The Jerry Lee Lewis Story*. New York: Dell 1982.

Tyl, Noel. *Sexuality in the Horoscope*. St. Paul: Llewellyn Publications 1994.

Ventura, Michael. *Shadow Dancing in the USA*. Los Angeles: Jeremy P. Tarcher,1985.

Wallechinsky, David, and Irving Wallace, editors. *The People's Almanac*, Garden City, New York: Doubleday and Co., 1975.

Williams, T. Harry. *Huey Long*. New York: Alfred A. Knopf, 1969.

Woodman, Marion. *The Pregnant Virgin*. Toronto: Inner City Books, 1985.

Wright, John W., editor. *The Universal Almanac 1990*. Kansas City and New York: Andrews and McMeel, 1989.

Index